D1282551

Presidential Transitions

Presidential Transitions

From Politics to Practice

John P. Burke

LYNNE
RIENNER
PUBLISHERS

BOULDER
LONDON

Published in the United States of America in 2000 by
Lynne Rienner Publishers, Inc.
1800 30th Street, Boulder, Colorado 80301
www.rienner.com

and in the United Kingdom by
Lynne Rienner Publishers, Inc.
3 Henrietta Street, Covent Garden, London WC2E 8LU

Library of Congress Cataloging-in-Publication Data
Burke, John P., 1953–
    Presidential transitions : from politics to practice / John P. Burke.
        p.   cm.
    Includes bibliographical references and index.
    ISBN 1-55587-916-0 (alk. paper)
    1. Presidents—United States—Transition periods. I. Title.
JK516.B79   2000
352.23—dc21   00-036610

British Cataloguing in Publication Data
A Cataloguing in Publication record for this book
is available from the British Library.

Printed and bound in the United States of America

⊗ The paper used in this publication meets the requirements
of the American National Standard for Permanence of
Paper for Printed Library Materials Z39.48-1984.

5 4 3 2 1

For Fred I. Greenstein,
scholar, teacher, mentor, friend

Contents

Acknowledgments

I would first like to thank Fred I. Greenstein, Harry N. Hirsch, Martha Joynt Kumar, Robert Kaufman, Phillip Cooper, and James Pfiffner for their able assistance in reading this manuscript and offering suggestions and criticisms that helped make it a better work. I would also like to thank my colleague Joshua Forrest for suggesting Lynne Rienner Publishers to me; it was excellent advice.

I am particularly indebted to those who participated in these presidential transitions and administrations and took the time and effort to be interviewed for this project and otherwise provided assistance and encouragement: David Q. Bates, Ralph Bledsoe, John Block, Danny J. Boggs, Herbert Brownell, Andrew Card Jr., Robert Carleson, James Cicconi, Al From, William Galston, Mark Gearan, John Hart, Frank Hodsoll, Elaine Kamarck, John McClaughry, Alonzo McDonald, Edwin Meese, J. Bonnie Newman, James Pinkerton, Roger Porter, Bruce Reed, Richard Schweiker, Leslie Thornton, Chase Untermeyer, Harrison Wellford, Anne Wexler, and Richard Wirthlin. I owe special thanks to James A. Baker III for granting me access to his papers at Rice University, as well as to Alonzo McDonald and Richard Wirthlin for providing me with a variety of useful materials from their personal collections.

As always, the archivists of the presidential library system, in this case the Carter, Reagan, and Bush Libraries, were patient with my requests and queries and helpful in leading me to collections and materials that pertained to this research. I would also like to thank Kenneth W. Thompson, former director of the Miller Center of Public Affairs at the University of Virginia, for permitting me to visit the Miller Center and providing me access to the materials there; in addition, the numerous interviews of former administration officials conducted during his tenure as director have been an invaluable resource not only to myself and this project but to countless scholars seeking a better understanding of the American presidency. Finally, I would like to thank three friends, R. Stafford Johnson and Jim and Ruth Pacy, for providing me with encouragement and moral support as I have labored on.

This study was conducted with support from the University Committee on Research and Scholarship and the Faculty Research Support Fund of the Dean's Office, College of Arts and Sciences, University of Vermont. I am grateful for their assistance.

—John P. Burke
Burlington, Vermont

Introduction

The idea for this project began with an article in the *Sunday Los Angeles Times Magazine* on August 1, 1993. Entitled "Educating Bill" and written by two veteran White House correspondents, Jack Nelson and Robert J. Donovan, it detailed the travails of Clinton's first six months in office. In the piece, Nelson and Donovan quote a senior White House aide who acknowledged that during the transition little systematic study had been undertaken of the organization and operations of the White House staff. Although several Clinton transition teams laboriously examined many agencies and departments, no team had been crafted to look at the White House. It was, in the words of the senior aide, "an insane decision. We knew more about FEMA [the Federal Emergency Management Agency] and the Tuna Commission than we did about the White House. We arrived not knowing what was here, had never worked together, had never worked in these positions."[1]

It was a startling admission. Clinton's activities during the transition period were widely reported, particularly his cabinet selection process and his economic "summit" (an event that was carried live on C-SPAN). By most accounts, it seemed to be a very active, well-publicized transition. It was headed by two well-known political "insiders," Warren Christopher and Vernon Jordan. Signals were clearly being sent about an activist presidency-to-be, one committed to a "New Democrat" political agenda and with "putting people first."

Yet Clinton had not, in fact, devoted much attention to the White House staff or, more broadly, to what the decisionmaking processes of his presidency would look like. After further research and interviews with some of the participants, I was to discover the situation was more

1

complex, though still perplexing: analysis of the White House staff had been undertaken in the preelection period and a task force on White House planning had been proposed, but in the days following the election the idea had been dropped. The preelection planning reports were given to Clinton, but they apparently had little impact. Furthermore, it was not until December 12 that Clinton announced the appointment of his chief of staff, and the next layer of White House staff positions, the "assistant to the president" level, would not be set until six days before inauguration on January 20; other staff members would learn of their positions only a day or two before that. Clinton's delay violated conventional wisdom and the advice of Clinton's own preelection transition planners that he settle on these matters early during the transition period so that he could "hit the ground running" come inauguration day.

By the time the *L. A. Times Magazine* article ran in August 1993, a spate of stories had appeared suggesting that, if anything, Clinton had hit the ground stumbling with respect to the White House staff and the other components of his decisionmaking processes. Major shake-ups in his White House staff took place in May and June; minor ones were to continue through the summer. His domestic policy agenda had been deflected by the gays-in-the-military controversy and a series of bungled nominations. Health-care reform and other major domestic initiatives were taking longer to develop than had been anticipated. Foreign policy problems loomed larger than had been expected in November, particularly with Iraq, North Korea, Haiti, Somalia, and, most intractable of all, Bosnia, and no easy solutions were in sight. The president's economic program became bogged down in Congress, and the administration appeared to have made a number of strategic and tactical mistakes in its lobbying and negotiating efforts. As well, the Clinton presidency was becoming enmeshed in unprecedented scandals, questionable decisions, and embarrassing revelations: Nannygate, the misuse of confidential FBI personnel investigations of Bush administration officials, the assault on the Branch Davidian compound in Waco, the firing of the White House travel office, the death of Vince Foster and the removal of materials from his office, and the $200 haircut aboard Air Force One at the Los Angeles airport. In September, Whitewater—a story about a failed investment scheme that had been reported more than a year before but had faded from attention—loomed again. But now it had achieved a much larger scale with the investigation of the bankrupt Madison-Guaranty Savings and Loan, which had been owned by Jim and Susan McDougal, Whitewater partners and friends of Bill and Hillary Clinton. It would eventually lead to the appointment of a special prosecutor and an ever-expanding investigation of allegations, culminating in the impeachment of the president by the House of Representatives and his trial before the U.S. Senate, the first elected president to face such a fate.

Not all of Clinton's difficulties during the first six or seven months of his presidency can be attributed to what he and his associates did—or, perhaps more correctly, failed to do—during the transition. But it did seem the case then—and I think it still is true—that the Clinton presidency was not well equipped to handle the challenges it faced and that at least part of its difficulties stemmed from a failure to marshal, during the transition period, some of the resources it would need to perform effectively. Those organizational and management difficulties, in turn, continued once Clinton was in office. Some would be corrected in the June 1993 shake-up of his staff, some with the appointment of Leon Panetta as chief of staff in 1994, but still others persisted through the final years of his presidency.

And as I would learn while I researched this book and looked more closely at the Carter, Reagan, and Bush transitions, Clinton's problems were not unique among any of the presidents elected after Watergate. Reading through the media accounts of Carter's first year in office revealed a presidency in which White House staffing was particularly singled out for criticism, as was his conception of cabinet government. So, too, for Reagan (less so for the cabinet, but instead for an overreliance on staff) and for Bush (for a staff lacking ideological commitment and for an inability to convert vague rhetoric about and attempts to be portrayed as the "education president," the "environment president," and the "thousand points of light president," into a coherent political agenda).

My sense that transitions matter has been reinforced by conversations and interviews with a number of participants in the Carter, Reagan, Bush, and Clinton transitions and presidencies. Many stressed that the some seventy-five days (give or take, depending on the date the first Tuesday of November happens to fall) of the transition period are "chaotic," "pressure-filled," and "unbelievable" times. Yet almost all agreed that they were critically important to the new administration. Interestingly, several participants, often reflecting on different transitions of different presidents, cited common problems: errors made during the preelection period, too much attention to the appointment of cabinet members compared to the White House staff, conflicts between various "camps" during the transition process that carried over once the administration was in office, problems in communication and the division of labor between Washington-based operations and the president-elect's home base in Pacific Palisades, or Little Rock, or Plains, or wherever it may be.

Transitions are also important given conventional wisdom and expectations about the new administration's first "one hundred days." For better or worse, Franklin Roosevelt's benchmark is one that still persists. This holds true both for those outside the White House expecting palpable signals about the new administration's energy, commitment, skill, and direction, as well as those inside the White House actively taking steps or otherwise bracing for the inevitable first milestone measure of its success or failure. At a minimum, the transition's seventy-five or so days predating this period can be a crucial window of opportunity for effectively lengthening this time frame and getting the new administration up and running by inauguration day rather than February or March—perhaps even later—as the clock ticks away. Especially with respect to the president's policy agenda, while presidents benefit from a "cycle of increasing effectiveness," as Paul Light has noted, they also are hindered by a "cycle of decreasing influence."[2] An administration's transition, therefore, is crucial in taking advantage of the political capital that usually accrues in its early days.

Modern presidents and their successors face an added difficulty stemming from adoption of the Twentieth Amendment in 1933 (Dwight Eisenhower, elected in 1952, was the first newly elected, nonincumbent president subject to its provisions), which moved inauguration day from March to January 20. Before that, the transition period was, at least comparably, more relaxed. Following his election in 1928, for example, Herbert Hoover embarked on a two-month goodwill tour of Latin America, returned home for two weeks, then promptly went on a Florida fishing trip until February 19, only two weeks before his inauguration.

Hoover's successor in 1932, Franklin Roosevelt, may have been more active during the transition period, but both Hoover and FDR shared at least one common experience: they did not have much in the way of a White House staff to worry about. Staff resources at the time were markedly slim—a mere handful of aides compared to the five to six hundred positions in today's White House Office alone. Nor did the Executive Office of the President (EOP) yet exist: that would not come until 1939, following the Brownlow Committee's report. There was no real "institutional presidency" to speak of. The Bureau of the Budget (today's Office of Management and Budget, or OMB) was lodged in the Treasury Department. There was no National Security Council (NSC), no NSC adviser and staff, no Council of Economic Advisers (CEA), no science advisers, no formally structured domestic policy operation, no National Economic Council, no U.S. trade representative, no chief of staff, no congressional lobbying unit, no political affairs office, no liaison units with interests groups, women, and minorities, no intergovernmental affairs operation, no White House offices dealing with consumer affairs or environmental issues, no staff units dealing with cabinet matters, no drug czars. There were a couple of speech-writers, a press secretary, a handful of general advisers, and a small personal staff, but there were no large-scale communications operation, no media advisers, and no scheduling and advance office. All of that would come later.[3]

The Approach and Argument of This Book

Presidential transitions have not been ignored by scholars, but in this study I approach them from a particular perspective.[4] The central thesis of this book is that *it is decisions that matter, and transitions, in turn, are critically important because they are a time when the processes leading to policy decisions first begin to take shape and are organized.* Thus, I propose to look not only at transitions but also at the early administrations that followed. I do so through a special lens, if you will: the organization and management of decisionmaking processes and their effects on policy outcomes. I will first focus on how these choices about organization and management began to develop during the transition, and second I attempt to trace the impact of these choices on the decision processes and policy outcomes of the new administration.

In so doing, I hope not only to answer the question of whether transitions matter but also to determine how and why certain actions (or, in some cases, inactions) affected a central activity of the presidency, that is, the process of making policy decisions.

Analyzing transitions in this way is useful for other reasons. First, through the use of interviews, archival material, and other sources, I hope to present in more depth the genesis of the four presidencies beginning with Carter and running through Clinton.[5] I think this is important because we need a rich account of what went on in these transitions in order to understand and explain their impact on subsequent decisionmaking.

Second, simply put, the devil is sometimes in the details, and so too are some of the important lessons. To take one example, it might suffice to simply assert that Ronald Reagan proved adept in selecting

Jim Baker as his chief of staff and go on from there. Yet closer examination of how Baker became chief of staff—a story that involves several people among Reagan's inner circle—is revealing about the intramural politicking that can go on as well as Reagan's own role as a decisionmaker. The agreement that Edwin Meese and Baker worked out in November 1980 about their respective jobs, moreover, would create spheres of responsibilities that would have later repercussions. The Baker case is also an interesting contrast to events in the Carter and Clinton transitions. Whereas Reagan's lieutenants were able to amicably overcome disappointments and differences, conflict and tension were allowed to fester in the Carter and Clinton camps. And in Carter's case, one of those squabbles—between Jack Watson and Stu Eizenstat—would have subsequent implications for Carter's ability to make his cabinet a more central part of his decisionmaking process.

This project thus differs from the approach of James Pfiffner, who offers a more general treatment that focuses on a "strategic approach" and encompasses more extensive analysis of personnel and control of the bureaucracy than is directly germane to this study.[6] It also differs from the way Charles O. Jones has framed the issue of moving from campaigning to governing. For Jones, the core chapters in *Passages to the Presidency* move from the prepresidential and campaign experiences of the presidents-elect, to the "campaign psychology," then to the "governing" issues raised in the transition, and, finally, to relations with the press during the transition. For Jones, moreover, the underlying theme is not the one I shall focus on (although some of it is discussed in his chapter "Preparing to Govern"), but rather a change in presidential politics that now blurs the distinction between campaigning and governing; although the "passage" still exists, "within that generic transition is a shift from campaigning for election to campaigning for policy."[7] Both of these works have a lot to tell us about "becoming president," yet I would argue that we need to dig deeper and learn more about how the organization and management of decisionmaking develops. If the Clinton presidency offers any lessons (aside from an obvious skill in "campaigning for policy"), it is the importance of these organizational and management issues. Even in a presidential campaign that was attentive to issues, it faced the difficulty of translating campaign promises into public policy (its ability to later sell them notwithstanding). The Clinton presidency did not hit the ground running; it stumbled out of the blocks in worse shape than any modern presidency. Even Jimmy Carter looks accomplished by comparison—no small feat.

Second, this study speaks to important strands of scholarship about the presidency, which I take up in Chapter 9. There is a variation and richness in opportunities for choice and the outcomes of choice in the four presidencies we consider, which offers an interesting test of rational-actor models of the presidency, with associated assumptions about the predictive power of actor rationality, the impact of institutions as constraints on choice (the so-called new institutionalism), and an emphasis on presidential centralization of power and bureaucratic control. In fact, transitions are especially important in this regard because they offer the first opportunity for "principals" to assert control in an environment where their degrees of freedom are greatest. Do we find presidents-elect crafting organizations with their strategic needs consciously in mind? Or do other motivations enter? How much centralization and control does in fact occur? How do institutions constrain when they are, in some measure, the result rather than the predicate of choices made during the transition?

With respect to scholarship on the institutional presidency by myself and others, one issue is how the large-scale staffs that have developed as part of the modern presidency can themselves become a force with which presidents must contend. At the very least, today's large staff system offers common challenges to presidents, particularly in managing resources for effective presidential performance. Although such institutional constraints may arguably be operative once an administration is under way, how do they figure—if it all—at the start of a presidency? How does an early recognition of opportunities and constraints affect what transpires later?

A Cautionary Note

I want to clarify at the outset: I am not claiming that transitions are the only things that matter in understanding the evolution and developments of new presidencies. The logical fallacy of "post hoc, ergo propter hoc" should remind one to be careful in attributing causality to antecedent factors. The transition sets the stage to some extent, but the dialogue and the plot are continually evolving. Early mistakes can be corrected, omissions rectified (by the same token, strengths can devolve into weaknesses and advantages can be squandered). It should also be noted that the transition itself does not cleanly begin the day after the first Tuesday in November. Indeed, well before election day, each of the four presidents I discuss took steps as a candidate for a possible transition to the presidency.

Yet historical causality is complex, with a range of factors involved. Some are synchronous to events, whereas others develop over time. Important causal forces can also exist on a number of levels: the impact of individual decisionmakers (itself a multilayered, complex factor), the effects of the organizational environment in which they operate, and the broader political environment in which they are situated.

To return to Clinton's case, it can be argued that a range of these factors can be profitably brought to bear—I will point to some of them in Chapters 7 and 8—in understanding the early phases of his presidency. There is the decisionmaking style of the president himself, both as it confronts a new set of responsibilities and as it developed over time in his prepresidential experience. There are the effects of the differing political and policy views of those around him, a factor that Bob Woodward has emphasized in his reconstruction of Clinton's economic deliberations in his book *The Agenda.* With respect to the broader environment, the media's propensity to engage in investigative journalism and to report unflattering stories seems to have heightened in 1993 compared to 1989, 1981, and 1977; one might also point to the effects of congressional behavior, particularly in the wake of twelve years of Republican control of the White House. Several Clinton associates whom I interviewed also cited the difficulty of getting the Democratic Party to accept Clinton's New Democrat political agenda, an allegiance that may have been unsettled at times even in Clinton's own mind.

Bearing this in mind, I look at four presidencies—Carter, Reagan, Bush, and Clinton—through the lens of decision processes, organization, and management, with particular attention to their development during the transition period and the days and months that followed. This is important, because each presidency was affected in varying ways and degree by their transitions, and many of these administrations' members viewed their respective transition as consequential for what followed.

Furthermore, we need to know *how* each transition had impact on the presidency that followed. And here it is important to recognize that transitions can do so in different ways for each of these administrations. There is no Rosetta Stone that offers up simple propositions to explain the respective strengths and weaknesses of presidents, their transitions, or their subsequent administrations. Here we have four very different presidents in terms of their styles as decisionmakers; we have four transitions that, while facing some common tasks, often did things differently; and we have four very different ways in which components of a decisionmaking process—the White House staff, cabinet, and other advisers—were organized and managed. While there are some institutional constraints on what presidents can do in this regard and some institutional forces at work, there is also great fluidity and a considerable degree of freedom. That is why transitions are important and deserve in-depth study in and of themselves.

I begin with the Jimmy Carter presidency. I do so not because earlier transitions are uninteresting or inconsequential but because Carter's efforts in 1976 were more ambitious than what preceded; in their scope they have largely been followed by his successors. The most noticeable difference is that Carter and those that followed began their transition planning well before election day. This is in marked contrast to Eisenhower's effort in 1952, where little in the way of pre-election planning occurred.[8] In John Kennedy's case, he turned to two sources: Washington lawyer Clark Clifford and Columbia political science professor Richard Neustadt. Clifford would later claim much credit for the 1960 transition, but he produced only one memorandum on transition matters, which was delivered to Kennedy the day after the election. Neustadt would produce a series of thoughtful memos for Kennedy, but almost all of the postelection transition was handled informally by Kennedy and his closest aides. In 1968, Richard Nixon very reluctantly established a personnel operation before the election, but its work proved virtually useless. Martin Anderson, one of the members of Nixon's transition staff, later recalled that after the election eight boxes of material the group had produced were opened up. But rather than finding useful information, Anderson was "shocked. . . . We could hardly believe what we were seeing. Most of the people were already in their jobs, or were Democrats or Independents."[9]

Still another difference is the matter of federal funding. Neither Eisenhower nor Kennedy had federal funds available to finance their preinaugural activities. Nixon would be the first incoming president to receive federal funds for that purpose. But even here Nixon got short shrift: Lyndon Johnson divided the funds so that he got $375,000 to finance his departure from office, with an equal amount going to Nixon. In 1976, Carter would have $2 million available to finance the transition.

The Carter presidency is a useful starting point for two other reasons, one internal to the presidency, the other external. Internally, as Lynn Ragsdale and John Theis observe, it is only by the late 1970s that the presidency becomes institutionalized, attaining (in their measure of institutionalization) high degrees of autonomy, complexity, adaptability, and coherence.[10] Presidents from Carter through Clinton have thus operated within a White House that differs to some extent from that of their predecessors.

With respect to the external political environment, the Carter presidency is a useful starting point because it was the first administration to take office in a political context that had changed in important ways. The political parties had markedly declined by 1976, making them less a resource for assistance but also less of a constraint in personnel and appointments.[11] Carter was the first newly elected president nominated by his party under the new rules that had been put in place by the McGovern-Fraser reforms, and this—plus his own status as a political "outsider"—further attenuated his links to the Washington establishment as well as the Democratic Party organization. Carter also faced a more assertive Congress in the post-Watergate period, though traditional centers of power had been weakened. In short, Carter and his successors would face added challenges in taking office and achieving a successful presidency.

Plan of the Book and a Framework for Analysis

The book's eight main chapters cover the presidencies from Carter through Clinton. Each presidency will be divided into two chapters: The first is a reconstruction of relevant aspects of each transition roughly up to inauguration day; the second takes the analysis through the early days and months of the presidencies. Finally, in Chapter 9, I offer some general thoughts and analysis.

The eight core chapters will structure the relevant material for easier study. In the preinaugural chapters (i.e., the first chapter on each president), I look at five tasks that bear on our understanding of how each transition began to organize, staff, and structure a decisionmaking process for the presidency that followed:

Recognizing the Task at Hand: The Preelection Effort

Presidential candidates begin the process of planning for their presidency well before the November election. But how they do so can vary. What is the scope of efforts assigned planners in this period? What is the size and expertise of the staff assigned to this task? How does transition planning relate to the ongoing campaign? To what extent do the candidate and key advisers provide direction and oversight to these efforts?

Organizing a Transition: The Postelection Effort

Following the election, the transition begins in earnest. The transition must now be organized: transition leaders picked, personnel matters attended to, contacts with the outgoing administration established. At what point do these efforts begin to take shape? How are they organized? What impact did preelection planning have on this stage of the transition? How is the campaign staff and the preelection transition group integrated, if at all? In particular, do any decisions or actions here suggest effects—positive or negative—for the upcoming presidency?

Filling the Cabinet

For most presidents, picking the cabinet is the most visible part of the transition process. How they undertake that task is important. What does this process begin to reveal about the administration's decision-making? What signals, for example, are sent to constituency groups? What do the choices reveal about the president-elect's own expectations for his cabinet? Is there any consideration of how the cabinet and its members might figure in the decisionmaking processes of the new administration? Also important is the process of making subcabinet appointments. Is consideration given to how these might figure in the administration's policymaking? Does the transition control these appointments, or are they the province of individual cabinet officers?

Crafting a Policy Agenda

For each of the four presidencies we will look at, the transition provided an occasion to begin to develop a policy agenda. But what they did and how they did it varied enormously. Were policy teams established? If so, how were they organized? Were efforts made to prioritize an agenda? Were any policy proposals developed during the transition itself? Were any efforts made to build bridges to Congress and others who would soon affect how policy proposals get translated into legislative reality? And what did these various policy efforts portend for the policy agenda of the administration once in office?

Shaping the White House Staff

Decisions about the organization and staffing of the White House are particularly crucial matters for the transition, not the least of which is the fact that bodies need to be placed in the White House after noon on

January 20. At what point does the transition team begin the search for personnel? How is the staff organized and how are decision processes formed? How, in particular, are key roles, such as chief of staff or NSC adviser, defined? How do prospective staff members "get up to speed" in learning about and understanding their responsibilities?

Following each chapter on transition, another chapter examines the early decisionmaking and policy outcomes of each presidency. These "president in office" chapters begin with a set of questions—hypotheses, if you will—about the possible effects of the transition on the staffing, management, and organization of decisionmaking.

These chapters are in turn divided into four sections:

Decisionmaking Processes

How are channels of information and advice coming to the president organized and structured? In particular, how does the White House staff operate? Does the cabinet have a role in the policy process and, if so, how is that structured? How is the chief of staff's role defined? How are any developing problems managed or otherwise handled? To what extent can these components of decisionmaking be linked to developments during the transition, in the sense of prior decisions having direct effect or in the ways decisions not made and tasks left undone come back to haunt the administration once in office?

The President as Manager and Decisionmaker

While presidents are, in some sense, the recipients of information and advice in their capacity as decisionmakers, they are also participants in that process; the way presidents interact with their staffs, cabinets, and other components of the decisionmaking process is important in its own right. What do these patterns look like, and what consequences do they bear? Presidents can also serve as the managers of the decisionmaking process. How and to what extent are they concerned not just with information and advice but also how this process operates? Again, what linkages can be established between their roles as decisionmakers and managers and their earlier transitions?

Policy Outcomes

The issue here is the effect of what transpired before as to the administration's policy proposals. Can we see, in particular, any effects of the decisions and actions of the transition on policy decisions and actions once an administration is under way? How and to what extent did the administration begin to prioritize its policy agenda? What were its relations with Congress, and how did they develop?

Foreign Policy Decision Processes and Outcomes

For purposes of clearer explication, I have decided to separate out foreign policy and national security issues. Because they are important in their own right, I will cover, albeit more briefly, developments in these areas. The aim here will be the same as in the earlier discussions. What did the decision processes look like, how did they relate to policy outcomes, and what relationships are present linking them to events in the transition?

Finally, in Chapter 9, I draw on some of the lessons and implications that are presented here, both as to transitions and their relationships to the presidencies that follow them. In so doing, we will gain some additional insights on these presidencies, helping us to better understand the general challenge that president-elects face—and will continue to face—in planning for their term in office and, once there, in meeting the demands and expectations for effective governance through their decisionmaking.

Notes

1. Jack Nelson and Robert J. Donovan, "Educating Bill," *Los Angeles Times Magazine,* August 1, 1993.
2. Light, *The President's Agenda,* pp. 36–37.
3. For further discussion of the development of the presidential staff resources, see Burke, *The Institutional Presidency,* and Hart, *The Presidential Branch.*
4. Lauren Henry's 1960 study of the four interparty transfers of power from Taft-Wilson to Truman-Eisenhower (Henry, *Presidential Transitions*) offers an important and comprehensive account of transitions earlier in this century. In the 1980s, works by Carl Brauer (*Presidential Transitions*), Stephen Hess (*Organizing the Presidency*), James Pfiffner (*The Strategic Presidency*), and a collection of articles and essays prepared under the auspices of the Center for the Study of the Presidency and edited by James P. Pfiffner and R. Gordon Hoxie (Pfiffner and Hoxie, eds., *The Presidency in Transition*) expanded analysis through the Carter and Reagan years. During the 1980s, work on presidential transitions was also significantly enhanced by the reports, oral histories, and task forces commissioned by the Miller Center of Public Affairs at

the University of Virginia, especially the volume *Presidential Transitions and Foreign Affairs* by Frederick C. Mosher, W. David Clinton, and Daniel G. Lang and a valuable series of "intimate portraits" edited by Kenneth W. Thompson. More recently, the second edition of Pfiffner's work plus Charles O. Jones's *Passages to the Presidency,* Thomas J. Weko's analysis of personnel operations in *The Politicizing Presidency,* and Shirley Anne Warshaw's *The Domestic Presidency* and *Powersharing,* most notably, have brought analysis through the Bush and Clinton years. Our understanding of presidential transitions and the early days of recent administrations has also been continuously refreshed and enhanced by the appearance of memoirs written by officials who have participated in transitions and served in subsequent administrations during this period.

5. The presidential library system administered by the National Archives has also been an important and continuing source of documentary evidence relevant to scholarly investigation of this and related projects. But I would also caution that many relevant materials remain to be processed and opened. In particular, under the terms of the Presidential Records Act of 1978, preinaugural materials for the Reagan administration (the first affected by the act) and the Bush administration, while deposited at their respective libraries, are subject to a deed of gift that has yet to be finalized by the two former presidents. Thus, although financed by public monies, documents produced during the transition period are not subject to the same federal regulations as postinaugural materials. Some transition materials, however, can sometimes be located in other collections that are accessible. A second problem that can handicap research is that both the Reagan and Bush libraries are processing materials only following Freedom of Information Act requests, rather than systematically opening file series, papers, and collections, as is the practice at other presidential libraries. This does allow researchers to request access to materials of particular interest, but it involves a lengthy process—often up to a year—and piecemeal processing and availability of some collections. Third, the Presidential Records Act contains provisions, particularly those that seek to protect the confidentiality of deliberative and advisory processes, that can block access to portions of even processed documents for a period of twelve years following the end of a presidential administration. Thus, some materials at the Reagan library will only become fully available in 2001, at the Bush library in 2005, and, presumably, at the Clinton library in 2013.

6. Pfiffner, *The Strategic Presidency.*

7. Jones, *Passages to the Presidency,* p. 3. Jones also only focuses on interparty transfers of the office and does not discuss the Bush transition in 1988.

8. In 1952, there were only two cases of any even modest preelection efforts. A group of New York supporters (the "Commodore group") commissioned the McKinsey management consultants to conduct a study of jobs subject to presidential appointment. During the transition, Eisenhower and his advisers were also provided an independent study of presidential transitions undertaken at Temple University. In Eisenhower's own case, while undoubtedly drawing on his considerable prepresidential organizational experiences,

there was little systematic examination of the task that might confront him before election, save for some thought on his part that he wanted a White House chief of staff. Henry, *Presidential Transitions,* pp. 491, 644; Brownell with Burke *Advising Ike,* pp. 131–141.

9. Anderson, *Revolution,* p. 191.

10. Ragsdale and Theis, "The Institutionalization of the American Presidency," pp. 1314–1315.

11. For further discussion, see Weko, *The Politicizing Presidency,* pp. 13–44.

1

Jimmy Carter:
An Organized Effort?

Recognizing the Task at Hand: Preelection Efforts

Jimmy Carter's preparation for the presidency marks a watershed in the ways presidents have assumed office. It began early, it was the most ambitious in the scope of its undertakings of any transition up to that point, and it was highly organized in its attention to personnel, policy, and staffing matters. Although Carter's successors in office would sometimes do less, sometimes more, and often with different emphases, the Carter transition set out the basic formula each would follow. It is difficult, if not impossible, to imagine a future president-elect turning back to the transitions undertaken by Carter's predecessors. Yet Carter's experience also reveals powerful lessons about what even ambitious transitions can and cannot accomplish. Although admirable in its intent, in a number of ways it proved deeply flawed in its details and execution; it affected, in turn, his presidency.

The most noticeable change was that Carter began early. Kennedy had turned to Clark Clifford for advice following the Democratic National Convention in 1960, and Nixon reluctantly commissioned a personnel operation in the fall of 1968; in contrast the Carter effort began even before the primary season was over.

Carter's initial steps were taken in the spring of 1976, following a key victory in the Pennsylvania primary over his last serious contender for the nomination, Senator Henry Jackson of Washington. Jack Watson, who had worked in Carter's 1970 gubernatorial campaign and had been active in Carter's reorganization efforts as governor, took the initiative. Watson was then a thirty-seven-year-old attorney in the law firm of Carter's friend and political confidante, Charles Kirbo, and was serving as Georgia finance chairman for the Carter campaign.

Watson first talked over the matter of a possible Carter presidency with Kirbo and Jule Sugarman, the chief administrative officer of Atlanta. The upshot was that Watson decided to prepare a memorandum to the candidate outlining the need to begin planning for a transition to the presidency.[1] In Watson's view, Carter's status as a political outsider with little previous Washington experience especially suggested the desirability of such an effort.

Carter was apparently impressed with the work that Watson had done and, on June 10, the two met to discuss it. Carter told Watson that he wanted him to undertake the work he had outlined. According to Carter friend and adviser Peter Bourne, Watson was taken aback by the assignment and had envisioned a Washington insider like John Gardner, former secretary of the Department of Health, Education, and Welfare (HEW), as the sort of person who might be enlisted. "I was more of an outsider than Jimmy Carter and fourteen years younger. I was utterly not the right person to do this," Watson would later recall.[2] But Carter was persistent and stressed to Watson that his familiarity with him, his stands on the issues, and his approach to government were more valuable than any expertise a Washington insider might bring. It was not the last time Carter would make such a calculation.

Watson accepted the job. But Carter had one major instruction: Watson was to undertake his work independently of campaign operations.[3] Both recognized that Watson should proceed quietly and with a low profile, lest publicity suggest overconfidence of a victory that was in sight but not yet achieved and lest the campaign staff become distracted from the more immediate election task at hand.[4]

Following the Democratic convention, Watson began to put together a staff. Although operating on a meager budget of $150,000, Watson assembled a core group with extensive governmental and policy-related experience. The foreign policy team was codirected by Anthony Lake, a former member of Henry Kissinger's NSC staff. Senator Philip Hart of Michigan offered the services of his chief legislative assistant, Harrison Wellford, who was assigned to oversee White House staffing and government reorganization. It would be the first of a number of subsequent transition planning efforts that Wellford would participate in on behalf of successful and unsuccessful Democratic candidates: Mondale in 1984, Dukakis in 1988, and Clinton in 1992. All but one of those enlisted were in their thirties. And in stark contrast to the campaign, few were from Georgia and most had some kind of "inside the Beltway" Washington experience.[5]

Their tasks involved not just planning the mechanics for a new presidency—including the initial development of a list of possible appointees—but also developing the issues and legislative agenda that would mark the first months of the Carter administration. They were housed separately in an office with an unlisted address, several miles away from the headquarters of the campaign staff, particularly its issues operations. The latter was headed by Stuart E. Eizenstat, who had been Carter's point man in the drafting of the 1976 Democratic Party platform and issues director in Carter's 1970 gubernatorial race.[6]

By late August, Watson had established a time chart, based in part on a study by the Arthur Anderson management firm. The chart began with September 1976 and ended in mid-February 1977, and it set out priorities and deadlines in six areas: (1) policy options, divided into ten to fifteen high-priority items, second-priority items, and remaining items; (2) budget and economic forecasts; (3) a "talent inventory pool" (TIP), divided into a "critical list," a "200 list," and "TIP printouts"; (4) strategic advice on government reorganization; (5) development of agency and department briefing books; and (6) ethics policy. Points along the time line were marked by "policy planning action," "review by Jimmy Carter," "agency recommendations," and "final decision."[7]

Over the next two months, Watson met with a number of former administration officials, academic experts, and Washington insiders. Among those whose advice he sought were Clark Clifford, Ted Sorensen, Bill Moyers, and Joe Califano from the Kennedy and Johnson administrations, and Harvard's Richard Neustadt and the Brookings Institution's Stephen Hess. Watson also met with Fred Malek, Richard Nixon's personnel director.[8] On budgetary matters, Watson and Bowman Cutter, one of his budget team members, consulted with Arnold Packer and Nancy Teeters of the Senate and House budget committees, spent a day in Washington during August being briefed by members of the Senate Budget Committee, and contacted members of the Brookings Institution, which had recently published *Setting National Priorities,* a volume on the shape of the federal budget over the next ten years.[9]

But Watson was not operating invisibly, Carter's initial directive notwithstanding. The names of the staff he hired were reported in the media, and he gave several interviews to the press during this period about the wide-ranging activities his transition group was undertaking. In one October interview, he speculated openly about what the organization of a Carter White House might look like and confided that personnel operations were under way, although no effort had been made to contact likely candidates for positions.[10]

Conflict Begins to Develop

Watson's preelection effort generated a management issue that was to crop up repeatedly during the transition and posttransition periods of Carter's presidency: conflict and competition among various parts of the Carter camp.

Watson's efforts had not gone unnoticed by his campaign colleagues across town. Tension began to emerge between the campaign staff, headed by Hamilton Jordan, and Watson's group. Stu Eizenstat would later recall that the existence of Watson's operation "aggravated Hamilton to no end." He "had put two and a half years into running the campaign only to find that decisions were . . . being made by someone who had not participated at all."[11] The fact that Carter had personally directed Watson to undertake transition planning was apparently of no concern to Watson's critics. According to Eizenstat,

> I have a faint recollection that there was a leak or two from [the transition team] about what Carter was going to do when elected and it was embarrassing because it was more specific than some of the things, and different from some of the things, we had said in the campaign. It was a sort of fifth wheel in the sense that it was out there but none of us in the campaign had any control over it. It was doing its own thing without any central direction and without any relationship to what was happening in the campaign. And this was later to make the transition a very strained and difficult transition.[12]

Although Watson had instructed his staff to establish better communications with Eizenstat and Jordan, there was not much actual interchange between the two groups. "I frankly don't think [we met] more than twice, once when I found out about the existence of it I talked to Jack, went to his office and got some idea of what was happening," Eizenstat would later observe.

> We had a little bit of interchange between our staff and theirs, but we were so preoccupied with getting things done that there wasn't very much more than that. I think that what I asked Jack to do is to share with us papers they were putting out and that we would share with them campaign papers that we were putting out, and that in fact did occur the last month or so of the campaign.[13]

Even though they were busy with the campaign, Jordan and his aides were especially wary of what Watson was doing.[14] Jim Gammill, Jordan's twenty-two-year-old assistant, was assigned to act as liaison to

Watson's operations, but he would have his work cut out for him. According to one member of Watson's staff, they tried to keep their work from Gammill because "we didn't want it to get back to the campaign."[15]

Some of Jordan's other assistants also expressed their displeasure with Watson's operation. Rick Hutcheson, Jordan's twenty-four-year-old deputy campaign director (who would later become staff secretary in the White House), composed a six-page memo that, among other points, was concerned that Carter's campaign pledges would "go out the window" with a "new crew of policy experts" coming in.[16]

Landon Butler, another Jordan deputy, worried that Watson's effort would be "conventional and overly cautious." In his view, "Any group of reasonably bright graduate students, working with a six-figure budget and with access to the big names of the Sixties, could produce a comparable work product." Butler felt that the transition "baton" should not have been passed to a separate organization: "Watson should be working for Hamilton Jordan the same way that Jim Gammill works for Hamilton Jordan." And also, "Jack appears willing to play to the prejudices of the political community in order to advance his position."[17]

Jordan's supposedly busy staff had evidently not been that preoccupied with the campaign to register their anxieties about Watson and his operation. Ironically, the very concern that Carter and Watson had discussed back in June—that campaign workers not get distracted, which had led Carter to set up Watson's efforts on a separate track—now came back to haunt them as suspicions and infighting began to develop. Reports even began to spill into the media of the developing rivalries between the Jordan and Watson camps. According to one account in late October, there was a "festering antipathy . . . between those who had been with Carter since the beginning of his quest for the presidency and Watson's transition policy planning group. Suspicion grew that since the transition group was dealing with appointments, its members would have an inside track in obtaining them for themselves." "The relationship was further chilled," the report noted, "by the notion that the transition members operated independently, were late-comers to the Carter campaign and were elitists . . . Washington establishment types."[18]

Watson's notion that Carter, as a political outsider, needed a head start on a possible transition and that he needed to reach out to those with expertise and experience was arguably correct. But it did not anticipate the reaction from Carter's more insular inner circle. No warning bells sounded as conflict with the campaign staff developed, nor was a concerted effort made to still the developing controversy by either Watson, Jordan, or, most important, Carter. The fact that Watson operated apart from the campaign allowed him to act with a great deal of independence; there was little supervision of his activities, little external direction by Carter or others. The absence of such oversight and management of a preelection effort that itself was so attentive to organizational and staffing issues so early on would prove to have significant consequences once it became a transition in fact.

Organizing a Transition: The Postelection Effort

Although Carter had been up in the polls by as much as twenty points over President Gerald Ford, election night was a cliff-hanger. Yet even as the returns came in and Carter's initial lead narrowed, Kirbo sought to press his case for his law partner, Jack Watson. According to Peter Bourne's account, Kirbo thought Watson should be Carter's chief of staff, even though everyone in the Carter inner circle—including Watson—knew that Carter especially regarded a chief of staff as one of the hallmarks of Nixon's "imperial presidency" that he found repugnant. "I can guarantee, Charlie, there will be a role for Jack in the White House," Bourne quotes Carter as saying, "but I don't want to talk about it anymore."[19]

During his first few days as president-elect, Carter made few decisions about his presidency. He did ask his top aides what jobs they would envision in the new administration, but he made no firm commitments, save that Jody Powell would remain as his press secretary. He was also forced to confront the mounting conflict between Watson and Jordan. How he did so would be revealing.

The Struggle for Control Continues

On November 3, the day after the election, Watson sent Carter a raft of materials on transition matters. These included a forty-eight-page memo on White House organization and staffing, a sixty-page document on cabinet matters, an eighty-page document on the budget, a briefing book of several hundred pages on foreign policy issues, fifty option papers on domestic policy proposals, a study on how Carter might begin to reorganize the federal government, and a thick notebook containing organizational information and appointment opportunities for each of the cabinet departments. Topping all of this off was a twenty-six-page memo, entitled "Transition Overview," in which Watson outlined the main tasks Carter would face during the transition, the duties of a proposed "transition coordinator," and a proposed budget.[20] Again it was a milestone; none of Carter's predecessors had received so much, so soon.

But it also brought to a head Watson's conflicts with Jordan. Jordan was reportedly incensed to discover that in Watson's proposed budget only one staff position had been allocated to him. According to one account, "Jordan exploded, accusing Watson of trying to undercut him."[21] On November 4, the two met with Carter in Plains. "It was all quite polite," said one person close to the campaign. "There was no blood spilled, but they were clearly maneuvering for position."[22] According to another report, "Carter, irritated at the squabbling, interrupted with some words of reproof for Watson and a brusque command for both men: 'Let's stop the meeting and when you all get together, we'll talk about this some more.'"[23]

Carter himself was apparently displeased with some of Watson's work. On election day, he proudly told reporters that Watson had prepared a "working list" of some seventy-five names from which he would begin to make top-level appointments. Yet Watson's TIP operation had not yet winnowed their thousands of names into such a manageable group as Carter seemed to have assumed. John Connally, Nixon's treasury secretary and a prominent Ford supporter, was one of the persons whose name appeared on the TIP inventory.[24]

Yet Carter largely stood aside, hoping that any difficulties between his two associates would work themselves out in due course. Carter was, however, concerned about the prudent use of transition funds. Watson recalls Carter telling him:

> Jack, I want this to be a tightly managed, tightly budgeted, efficient transition between November 5th and January 20th. I want to use what monies we need to prepare ourselves to the fullest extent possible in that ten-week period, but I also want to turn back a portion of that two million dollars which has been allocated to us.[25]

It would take several more meetings for Watson and Jordan to work out their respective roles in the transition. On November 10, Jordan and Watson again met with Carter. Following the meeting, Jody Powell told reporters that each would be working in separate, specifically defined areas: Jordan in White House staffing and Watson in all other matters, although neither would be given formal titles.[26] It was a division of labor that would be adjusted again in a few days to Jordan's advantage.

On November 12, following yet another meeting with Carter, Jordan and Watson held a joint press conference. Jordan announced that he would now be spending the bulk of his time in Washington with the transition team and that "some differences of opinion were resolved." Carter still resisted, however, choosing between his two top aides. As Jordan put it, "I don't expect to be working for Jack and I don't expect him to be working for me." But Jordan had clearly and successfully reasserted a measure of personal control. Watson, for his part, conceded that "I needed help; I needed Hamilton and others brought in." But Carter still had made "no final decision" on transition matters, the press accounts noted, and an announcement would be forthcoming in a few days.[27]

On November 15 that very announcement came, during Carter's second press conference since the election, and it gave Jordan primary responsibility for presidential appointments, "in effect stripping Watson of some of his power."[28] But Carter told reporters that he planned to be personally involved in selecting the top seventy-five officials. Carter also announced his first appointment: Jody Powell would be White House press secretary (a position, according to Powell, that Carter had offered him on election night).[29]

The whole episode proved costly. In the interim between election day and November 15, valuable time had been lost. According to one transition staff member, during that period "basically nothing was happening."[30] Furthermore, tensions between Watson and Jordan still lingered. On November 16, Watson was reported to have delivered a "condescending introduction of Jordan at a transition staff meeting in Washington," where he described Jordan's duties as helping with inaugural plans, debriefing state campaign leaders, and only incidentally mentioning that he would be in charge of personnel for the new administration.[31] Jordan, for his part, criticized Watson's transition memoranda in writing to Carter, especially their insensitivity to politics, and Jordan provided Carter his own lengthy memo on White House staffing and personnel. The fact that Carter was reviewing Jordan's memo made its way into press reports.[32] Jordan also publicly joked with reporters that he had proposed that Watson be appointed a regional director of the Department of Housing and Urban Development (HUD) "in Alaska."[33]

In subsequent press reports, Watson was depicted as personally wounded by the episode, and he reportedly had even been advised by one associate to return to his law practice in Atlanta. Watson's failure to be made OMB director (Carter was apparently ready to do so following the election but changed his mind) was taken by transition staff members as a sign of his waning influence in the Carter inner circle, and "many young people on the team hired by Watson now fear that they bet on the wrong horse."

Most noticeably, the Watson-Jordan squabble was now being linked to problems with Carter's management style. "It's troubling that an organization man like Jimmy Carter can't set a clear line of command," one staff member was quoted as saying. According to one account, "Some who have watched the confrontation unfold believe it reflects badly on Carter's managerial skills." Jody Powell, appearing with Watson before the press, put a more positive spin on the episode, attributing it to a "degree of creative tension," not unlike the managerial practices of FDR or Admiral Hyman Rickover.[34]

A Transition Finally Organized

A few days later, the new transition team finally assembled in vacant office space on the fifth floor of the HEW building. A number of members of the campaign staff, those working on issues for Stu Eizenstat, and others were folded into Watson's operation. Watson remained in charge as coordinator of the transition office, with his personal staff expanded to include members from the campaign.[35] As to Watson's duties, one top aide reported that "he fits wherever he wants to fit. This is a collegial operation, it isn't General Motors, and the lines of command are a little blurred."[36]

Separate units were created to deal with congressional liaison (a staff of nine headed by Frank Moore), press operations (also a staff of nine, headed by Jody Powell), and staffs dealing with Walter Mondale's and Rosalynn Carter's respective transitions. Most notably, Hamilton Jordan and a number of high-level campaign staff members were given responsibility for "political coordination."[37] Their chief responsibilities were in the area of finding talent for the new administration, with particular responsibility for cabinet appointments. Almost all members of Jordan's staff would also end up with important White House positions.

Watson's earlier talent inventory program was now headed by Matthew Coffey, former president of the Association of Public Radio Stations and a former member of the personnel unit in the Johnson White House.[38] Stu Eizenstat, who had headed the campaign issues staff, was placed in charge of policy analysis and agency liaison, including coordination of the issue clusters that had been created in Watson's earlier transition effort.

The number of issue clusters was expanded, and staff from the campaign as well as other policy experts, especially from congressional staffs, joined Watson's group. Several members of Watson's initial staff continued as leaders of particular clusters.[39] Other clusters had new leaders.[40] All told, 215 persons were on the transition payroll, with an additional seventy-nine serving in other capacities.[41]

In its basic organization, the 1976 transition would resemble that which its successors would utilize. But there were some important differences, which would reveal themselves again once Carter was in office. Just as Carter resisted appointing a chief of staff once he was in office, he avoided delegating authority to one person during the transition. Watson was transition "coordinator," but some areas remained outside his jurisdiction, Jordan's efforts and those of Jody Powell most notably.

Lines of responsibility blurred. The demarcation between Jordan's personnel operation and Coffey's, for example, was not clear, although at least one report indicated that Coffey reported to Watson through Jordan.[42] Jordan's group also overlapped into other areas. On one organizational chart of the transition staff, "Hamilton's lead person" is indicated at the top, followed underneath by the cluster leader on Eizenstat's issue staff (which would have indicated that issues as well as personnel were under Jordan's control).[43] Other personnel groups, as we shall see, would also be created as the transition proceeded. Although Watson had melded new members into his operation, Jordan's group retained its exclusivity. Its homogeneity was a recipe for continued conflict. A transition organization had been created, but there were problems in design and, especially, management.

Filling the Cabinet

Management of the transition did not occupy much of Carter's attention. His principal preoccupation was in picking his cabinet. Given Carter's hopes to decentralize power away from the White House staff and give his cabinet members both greater authority and an enhanced role in his own deliberations—goals he had spoken about in the campaign—it is not surprising that Carter took great pains and was personally involved in their selection. But it was not until just before Thanksgiving that Carter began his work in earnest, when he met with Hamilton Jordan and Walter Mondale to begin to discuss possible candidates (Charles Kirbo and Rosalynn Carter would also be part of the core group as the selection process proceeded). The fact that Mondale was a participant (as he was to be throughout, either in many personal visits or by telephone) was both a sign of a new, more active role for the vice president that Carter and his running mate had agreed to craft, as well as an indicator that cabinet selections would be informed by a consummate Washington insider. Carter's choices were solid and competent, and many had prior experience in past Democratic administrations. But they far from met his goal of a cabinet of "new faces," nor did they all clearly share his political vision and agenda. "Cabinet government" would become even more difficult to achieve as a result.

In making his selections, Carter proceeded deliberately and slowly, and he personally interviewed or telephoned a number of potential candidates, as he had done over the summer in selecting Mondale. As well, in the last week of November, the transition staff had finished preparing their briefing books on each department, and the various personnel groups forwarded to Carter's home in Plains the lists of potential nominees, biographical information, and confidential evaluations.[44]

On December 3, Carter announced his first two choices: Cyrus Vance as secretary of state and Bert Lance as director of OMB. Lance was a bit of a surprise to outside observers, but not to Carter. He had been a political supporter of Carter since 1966 during Carter's first bid for the governorship, had worked his way up from a small town bank to the presidency of the National Bank of Georgia, had served as his transportation commissioner, and had been Carter's handpicked candidate to succeed him as governor (he came in third in the Democratic primary). Although Watson's name had been floated early in November, there is little evidence that Carter seriously considered anyone else for OMB besides Lance after Watson's light dimmed. Lance was a trusted associate and a friend; his lack of experience in federal budgetary matters or in the other management functions of the office mattered little to Carter.

Like Lance, Vance also had little competition. He had the advantage of having known Carter beforehand, but unlike Lance he brought extensive political and diplomatic experience to the position. In addition, he was a low-key figure, certainly no Henry Kissinger, and his nomination was well supported by the foreign policy community. In announcing their appointments, Carter particularly stressed that each was a "good manager." Carter also emphasized at the press conference that he intended to have "good representation" of women and members of minority groups, as well as good geographical distribution and a balance between those who served in Washington and those who had not.

It was not until December 14, eleven days later, that Carter announced his next round: Congressman Brock Adams of Washington State as secretary of transportation, and W. Michael Blumenthal as secretary of the treasury. Blumenthal, a childhood refugee from Nazi Germany, held a Ph.D. in economics from Princeton, had served as a U.S. trade negotiator in the 1960s, and was head of Bendix Corporation. Two days later, Carter announced the names of three more persons who, like Lance, would have cabinet rank. The first was Congressman Andrew Young of Georgia, an African American and civil rights activist who would become UN ambassador. The second was Charles Schultze, who was tapped to chair the Council of Economic Advisers (Schultze was also considered for the Treasury slot, as was Bert Lance). Schultze had served as Lyndon Johnson's budget director and was then a fellow at the Brookings Institution. The third person named was the most important: Zbigniew Brzezinski as NSC adviser. Brzezinski, a professor at Columbia, had been Carter's chief campaign adviser on foreign policy.

Throughout these weeks, Carter's selection process was a matter of public scrutiny, not unlike the "cattle call" of potential candidates that had been paraded through Plains during Carter's summertime selection of a running mate. Not surprisingly, as time wore on, various groups and constituencies began to press Carter to make good on his pledge for a more diverse cabinet; it was to be the first—but not the last—time a president-elect faced such concerted pressure. In response, Carter listed a number of women and minority-group members whose availability to serve had been sounded out but who, for a variety of reasons, had declined. Among those he named were Mayors Tom Bradley (Los Angeles) and Coleman Young (Detroit), Judge Reynaldo Garza of Texas, Franklin Thomas of the Bedford-Stuyvesant Development Corporation, Vernon Jordan of the Urban League, and Jane Cahill Pfeiffer of IBM. Privately, Carter told Jordan that he wanted two blacks and two women in his cabinet.[45]

Carter felt pressure of a more traditional sort in selecting a labor secretary. Here, George Meany of the AFL-CIO wanted one of Gerald Ford's labor secretaries, John Dunlap, to return, but Dunlap was unpopular with consumer groups and the Congressional Black Caucus. Carter eventually decided on Ray Marshall, a University of Texas labor economist. The choice was acceptable to labor, but just barely. Divisions also complicated his choice for defense secretary. Conservatives supported James Schlesinger, who had been fired by President Ford, but liberals thought him too hawkish and preferred Paul Warnke. In the end, Carter settled on a compromise choice, Harold Brown, who had been secretary of the Air Force under Lyndon Johnson and was then the president of Cal Tech. But Carter had a consolation prize for Schlesinger: he would be designated a White House assistant in charge of energy issues with the proviso that he would become secretary of that department once it was elevated to cabinet status as Carter had proposed. All three choices came late: Marshall and Brown on December 21, Schlesinger on December 23.

For the Interior Department, the traditional province of a Western politician, Carter made an easy choice, on December 18—Governor Cecil Andrus of Idaho—and one that had the strong support of environmental groups. Two days later, on December 20, Carter announced that Juanita Kreps, an economist and vice president of Duke University, would head Commerce, while Congressman Bob Bergland of Minnesota would be given Agriculture. Like the choice of Andrus, Bergland's nomination had the strong support of the department's constituent groups; as well, he came strongly recommended by Walter Mondale.

Carter's third announcement of December 20 would prove more controversial: that of Griffin Bell as attorney general. A few days later, a *New York Times* article intimated that the search for an attorney general had been a charade and that Carter had settled on Bell from the start, "perhaps even before the Nov. 2 election."[46] But it is not clear that Bell, who had been a federal appeals court judge, was Carter's first or even early choice. Another distinguished Southern jurist with a more impressive civil rights record, Judge Frank Johnson, had been contacted by Carter but apparently declined. Barbara Jordan's name was floated, but Carter thought she lacked experience for the post (there was also talk of offering her the UN position that went to Young).[47] In his memoirs, Bell himself notes that he was sent to Texas by Kirbo and Carter to check on the credentials of Texas's attorney general for the position; while there Bell solicited the views of a former colleague on the U.S. Fifth Circuit Court of Appeals, Judge Reynaldo Garza, and, according to Bell, Carter began to explore the possibility of the latter's interest in the position (Garza declined).[48]

But Bell, after leaving the bench, had been Kirbo's law partner at Atlanta's prestigious King and Spalding firm and that was no small connection, especially given that Kirbo took a leading role in advising Carter on choosing an attorney general. Bell's nomination would prove controversial, especially because of his membership in private clubs that had no black members as well as some concerns over his court opinions, but he would eventually be confirmed by a vote of 75–21.

The next day, perhaps as a counterweight to Bell's nomination, Carter announced the appointment of Patricia Roberts Harris, an African American woman, to head HUD. Harris was well known in Democratic Party circles and had served as ambassador to Luxembourg and dean of Howard University's law school. Finding a HUD secretary, especially one who might fit Carter's diversity goals, was no easy task. Before Harris was picked, Carter had sounded out Mayors Bradley and Coleman for the post, as well as Franklin Thomas.

Finally, on December 23, Carter finished his cabinet announcements. In addition to announcing Schlesinger's position as White House energy czar, Carter presented two final nominations. Both of them would prove controversial, one in the long run, the other in the short run. The former was Joe Califano, who was picked to head HEW. Califano had been Vance's assistant at the Defense Department under Kennedy, and he had served in Lyndon Johnson's White House as a domestic policy adviser. Both a consummate bureaucratic politician and a policy expert, Califano would soon find himself at odds with the Georgians in Carter's White House.

The short-termer was Theodore Sorensen, JFK's chief aide and wordsmith, whom Carter picked to head the Central Intelligence Agency (CIA). Sorensen's nomination quickly catalyzed opposition (among the concerns voiced were that he was too liberal and too eager in wanting to reform the CIA, with which he had no experience, and that he had been a conscientious objector and had used classified documents in writing his biography of JFK). Following lukewarm support from Carter (Carter offered his support but warned that Sorensen did not have the votes to win approval), he asked that his name be withdrawn on January 17, three days before the inauguration. It was an ill-considered choice from the beginning.[49]

A "Bureaucratic Disaster"

The process undertaken for appointing subcabinet and other political appointees offers an especially revealing glimpse into some of the internal problems of the Carter transition, which, in turn, would have some effect on his presidency. Carter's failures in this regard are often cited as a textbook example of how a president-elect can begin to lose control over his administration. They were also lessons on "what not to do" that subsequent presidential transitions would be quite aware of.

Carter and Jordan: mixed signals. One set of problems stemmed directly from Carter and Jordan. Although both at some level realized the need to retain some measure of control over subcabinet positions, their own efforts proved self-defeating; the signals sent to cabinet members were decidedly mixed. Carter had sent each cabinet member a two-page memo emphasizing that he would personally approve all deputy and assistant secretary appointments, an estimated eighty-eight positions in the eleven departments existing at the time, while Jordan publicly described the process as one of "mutual veto." But Jordan also went on record as saying that Carter, in the final analysis, "is going to let these people put together their own teams but he wants them to consider the people we are suggesting." Jordan added that the system would be "tilted in favor" of the cabinet members and Carter would not impose his choices.[50]

In a memorandum of January 11, 1977, to his secretaries-designate, Carter told them that all names should be forwarded to Jordan and that "he [Jordan] will advise you promptly as to whether the nominees have my approval." Carter also instructed that "you not make commitments to individuals or public announcements concerning appointments until your recommendations have been reviewed for conformance to my overall policies." But the way Carter worded his instructions—"your recommendations"—may have given the signal that cabinet members had a freer hand than Carter might have intended and suggested something much less than a mutual veto.[51]

That signal was repeated again shortly after the inauguration in a memo Carter sent to his cabinet officers. In it, he once again instructed them to forward all names to Jordan. But as with his earlier effort, he indicated that the choices essentially were theirs to make: "Hamilton will present them to me and in most instances there will be no problems with our final approval."[52]

Organizational confusion. The second set of problems was internal to the transition's personnel operation. Although Jordan seemed to have won the day in his battle with Watson by gaining control over personnel, in the weeks after it was still unclear who was really in charge of the appointments process. Landon Butler advised Jordan to meet with his personnel officers assigned to the transition and "underscore the point that they are working for you not Jack."[53] Jordan's deputies also pushed him to place Tim Kraft in charge of a new personnel group explicitly charged with making sure campaign staff got jobs. Kraft's operation, dubbed the Personnel Advisory Group (PAG), would in effect serve as a back channel for campaign staffers and others seeking employment as well as a way for Jordan to monitor the TIP process.[54]

In early December, Rick Hutcheson sent two memos to Jordan concerning his fears and frustrations with Watson's operation. In a memo of December 6, he noted that "TIP is just treading water" and was not organized to provide recommendations on subcabinet personnel. Hutcheson then recommend that we "ought to *complete* the taking over of the TIP operation."[55] On December 10, Hutcheson covered similar ground, now noting that the "present confusion between TIP and the so-called lead people on your staff" remains unresolved and was contributing to the lack of organization in appointing subcabinet personnel. In closing, Hutcheson told Jordan, "Your present absence from the office is probably the right thing for you to do, considering what you are working on, but it leaves things extremely disorganized." Hutcheson, ever helpful, then volunteered to "try and start handling some of the stuff that flows in to you."[56]

As a result of the various tensions among Carter's associates, the appointment process underwent considerable evolution during the transition. But the end result, according to one aide, was a "bureaucratic disaster":

> There are at least five TIP projects. First, there was Watson's but that was replaced by Hamilton Jordan's, with Matt Coffey and Dick Fleming in charge. TIP III is headed by Landon Butler, Anne Wexler, and Joe Duffy: they gather and supply information on names that go up to Carter. TIP IV is conducted by Tim Kraft: he directed the campaign field operations and now makes sure that people who worked for Carter out in the field receive consideration for administration jobs. Finally there is TIP V led by J. Paul Austin (the Atlanta-based Coca-Cola Co. executive) who scouts corporate executives for Carter.[57]

The Carter Cabinet and Presidential Decisionmaking

Carter's rhetoric about cabinet government, his distrust of the White House staff as it had evolved in recent administrations, and his own attention to picking his prospective cabinet might have suggested further effort on his part on ways of making the cabinet work, particularly its integration and coordination with the White House staff. Yet there is little evidence that Carter undertook—or even understood the need for—this kind of analysis.

In fact, some of the materials presented to him during the transition explicitly raised the issue of how the cabinet might factor into his policymaking. In Watson's forty-eight-page November 3 memo, he outlined a more cabinet-oriented model of policy development. The White House staff would identify problems and create ad hoc task forces, but "the task force would be chaired by the cabinet member from the lead agency on the issue, and its members and staff would be selected from other interested agencies, Congress and experts in private life. Your program aide or his deputy would have a watching brief on the task force but would not direct it."

Harrison Wellford's work on executive-branch reorganization also raised cabinet-related matters. In one report on December 1, Wellford proposed that the White House staff "must serve as workshops where cabinet heads make decisions under the guidance of the president, or, if unable to decide, propose options for the presidents." But in a second report on December 23, Wellford warned of the dangers of relying too heavily on the cabinet: each member "to varying degrees must satisfy a 'constituency' comprised of his own department, Congress and its relevant committees, interest groups, etc." Nor would cabinet meetings solve the problem: "the cabinet is generally thought to be too large to function as a deliberating body."[58] Wellford then proposed either an informal system of cabinet-based task forces or a more formal system of cabinet councils as a solution.

But neither this proposal, the more general issue of how to incorporate the cabinet into his decisionmaking, or, also important, some of the dangers of relying on the cabinet caught Carter's attention. In fact, had the date of Wellford's report been changed to four years later, the council system he outlined matched very closely the system that Ronald Reagan and his advisers would devise. But for Jimmy Carter in 1976, it was the full cabinet or nothing. A more organized way of making cabinet government work fell by the wayside.

Crafting a Policy Agenda

The tremendous effort to produce policy proposals for the upcoming administration is another feature of the Carter transition that distinguishes it from transitions that preceded. It is not that prior presidents had failed to recognize this task—they had—but it is that Carter did so much. During the preelection period, Watson had recognized early on that developing policy proposals was a central part of his task and not something to be left to Eizenstat's shop in the campaign operation across town. Watson's August time chart, moreover, had noted the need to identify ten to fifteen high-priority policy items, second-level items, and remaining policy issues. Points along the time line were marked by "policy planning action," "review by Jimmy Carter," "agency recommendations," and "final decision." Had this recognition of the need to prioritize—to winnow down policy proposals—been followed, the early months of the Carter presidency might have looked a bit different.

Yet proposed policy initiatives grew, and a recognition of the political realities requiring some setting of priorities faded. By October, the list had expanded to twenty issues that would now form the basis of Carter's legislative agenda, including such major items as national health insurance, energy policy, job creation, government reorganization, and welfare reform. In fact, Watson stated at the time, "One of the tests of our ultimate work product will be whether or not either in the transitional period itself or the first six months of the administration, every piece of work we did is used up."[59] On November 3, Watson delivered to Carter fifty option papers on domestic policy and a briefing book of several hundred pages on foreign policy issues. It was a laundry list in the making.

The postelection transition would also complicate Carter's efforts with Congress. First, it served as the incubator of several proposals that would prove particularly controversial. Carter's policy planners, for example, uncovered sixty federally subsidized water projects of questionable worth. They were just the kind of pork-barrel politics to which Carter had always been averse, and which he now decided to eliminate. Another proposal, a $50 rebate to each taxpayer, had been devised by soon-to-be chair of the CEA, Charles Schultze, and it would be the centerpiece of Carter's economic stimulus package. Still another was Carter's decision to pursue both a comprehensive plan for dealing with energy issues and to ask new energy czar James Schlesinger to do so secretly. All three would generate controversy with Congress.

Second, Carter's delay in naming his cabinet took its toll. Transition staff working on policy issues found it increasingly difficult, according to one member, "to write option papers for God knows who." "We can't really go ahead much further until we know who the cabinet secretary is going to be," reported another. "We thought [Carter] might make some decisions that would help us proceed, but he has been preoccupied with picking his cabinet."[60]

Finally, efforts of the transition staff varied by department, depending on the competence of those involved. According to the *Washington*

Post, "Interviews with numerous participants in this process in three departments—Commerce, Agriculture, and Labor—suggest that it is uneven. . . . Those working on the transition for the president-elect are not birds of a single feather. Some are old hands in this city's bureaucratic maze. . . . Others are neophytes who may not know their CETA from their ERDA."[61]

Building Bridges?

Carter's relationships with Congress were clouded by his own distrust of the Washington establishment and a failure to establish cordial relationships with congressional power brokers during the transition. And he often complicated the situation with his own personnel choices.

Shortly after arriving in Washington to begin transition operations, Watson became aware of the general dissatisfaction with Frank Moore's role as Carter's liaison with Congress during the campaign. An article on Moore's difficulties in mobilizing congressional Democrats to support the ticket had even appeared in the *Washington Post,* replete with critical comments about Moore, most notably his failure to often return phone calls from members of Congress and stories about his heavy-handedness in dealing with the Georgia legislature.[62] Watson, recognizing the need to build bridges to Congress, called Carter and requested that someone with Washington experience and stature be appointed as soon as possible to head up congressional liaison. But Carter was adamant about keeping Moore, whose lobbying experience had been confined to the Georgia legislature: "Frank Moore is my man," Carter curtly informed Watson. "He'll be there Monday morning and I want you to have an office ready for him."[63] Not only did Moore head the operation during the transition, Carter picked him to lead the White House's congressional relations staff.

Hamilton Jordan, whom Carter had relied on for political advice and personnel matters, did not fare much better. Congressman Tip O'Neill of Massachusetts, the new Speaker of the House, was infuriated to discover that the seats he had purchased for an inaugural gala at the Kennedy Center were located in the last row of the second balcony. The next day, O'Neill called Hamilton Jordan to complain; Jordan offered a refund, to which O'Neill replied, "Don't be a wise guy. I'll ream your ass before I'm through."[64] O'Neill's relationship with Jordan, Carter's key political operative, would never prove smooth.

Before and during the transition a number of factors had thus come to bear that would make policy efforts more difficult. The transition effort, surely, had assiduously developed a range of policy proposals, but the Carter team members had not used the time as an opportunity to craft a more limited, politically feasible agenda. Moreover, they had not been successful in smoothing the way with Congress. If anything, congressional relations had worsened as the Carter team moved into place.

How political calculations and analysis, more generally, would figure into Carter's policy decisions would prove to be a problem not only for the transition but into his presidency. Jordan's mandate to serve as "political coordinator" and to oversee the personnel process was one approach taken during the transition. But as we shall see, it was a role he was not fully prepared to take or, for that matter, much enjoyed. Moreover, the integration of policy and politics had not figured much in Watson's lengthy briefs. In his November 3 memo, there is mention of inclusiveness—reaching out to Congress and others—but little attention to the place of political analysis and calculation in making sound policy choices. In his discussion of political relations (one paragraph in length), Watson focused exclusively on liaison with the Democratic National Committee (DNC) and preparing for the 1978 midterm elections.

But Carter had at least recognized one political danger sign in his dealings with Congress during the transition period: he quickly pulled Sorensen's nomination to head the CIA as soon as it became clear he was running into opposition. As we shall see, it was not a lesson that some of his successors would necessarily learn; both Bush and Clinton would stick with some of their nominees far too long and at significant political cost.

Shaping the White House Staff

Carter's approach to how his presidency would be organized was particularly manifest in the appointment of a White House staff. There was an initial flurry of attention, then a period of little activity, followed by the reappearance of conflict, and then a reliance on his aides' ability to work things out among themselves. Carter would on occasion show his propensity to submerge himself in detail, but it took the form of ad hoc dialogues with particular aides and little in the way of follow-up or more general attention to how he wanted his White House staff to function and his decisionmaking processes to be organized. Carter held strong views about the size and hierarchy of the Nixon presidency, but beyond that there was little in the way of a game plan for a Carter presidency. And with Jordan's lack of familiarity with White House matters and Watson's diminished stature, there were not any major players with knowledge, experience, and clout to fill the breach.

Shortly after the election it looked as if Carter would move quickly to firm up his White House staff. On Thursday, November 4, he convened a meeting of his top aides—Jordan, Watson, Robert Lipshutz, Powell, and Eizenstat—and asked them about what positions they would like to have in the new administration. That same day, the *Washington Post* quoted Watson as saying that "the first priority will be to determine the organizational framework of the Carter White House."[65] However, Carter would not settle on how his staff would be organized and who would occupy key positions until one week before the inauguration.

Carter was not bereft of policy advice on staff. He had received Watson's memos the day after the election, and others in his inner circle, such as Eizenstat and Jordan and Stephen Hess of the Brookings Institution, offered their own memos on White House organization and operations. Carter also asked Greg Schneiders, his personal aide, to solicit comments from the Carter inner circle on several proposals for reorganizing the White House staff and the EOP.[66]

Carter's comments on some of these memos provide an interesting window into his own thinking and indicate that at least some of them engaged his own thoughts and reflections (Watson's memos, however, elicited few comments).[67] Carter's copy of one of Harrison Wellford's memos on reorganization has two pages of notes attached, on Blair House stationery, and they clearly indicate some awareness of the complexity of White House staffing on Carter's part, as well as an awareness of some of the problems that had beset his predecessors. Many are in the form of questions:

"OMB vs Pres. vs Cabinet vs Congress" "Need for Domestic Council?" "OMB lead reorg effort?" "Assess ZBB [zero-based budgeting]" "Multiyear budget?" "Degree contact OMB staff/my staff" "WH staff size-structure"

Several also pertain to the question of foreign policy decisionmaking, which had not been raised in the memo:

"Improve NSC" "How to mesh State/DOD" "Role of NSec Adviser: Kis [Kissinger] vs Scocft [Scowcroft]" "President's role" "How centralized should DOD be? Organization (structure)? 2 Deputies?" "Role of joint chiefs—Qual. of advising" "Role of Dir. Cent Intel" "How has Def. [Intelligence Agency]—Sec/JChiefs [organized] in

handling Nat Intel Est" "Functions Mil Asst. Wh. H—rank?" "When
must/will decisions be made on: new tank, ICBM-MX, arms sales, B-
1, CMs" "Budget—Services vs. Sec vs OMB Issues in Dispute"[68]

Eizenstat was especially prolific in circulating his thoughts on
White House matters, no doubt motivated by the possibility that he
would lead its domestic policy operations.[69] In one memo, he went
through a unit-by-unit review of the EOP. He supported continuation of
the Council on Wage and Price Stability (to which Carter wrote
"agree") and the Office of Science Adviser (Carter: "if smaller, OK").
Abolition of the Office of U.S. Trade Representative would "entail
enormous political risks with little political gain (Carter: "agree"), as
would elimination of the Council on Environmental Quality (Carter:
"OK"). Eizenstat supported the proposed elimination of the Office of
Telecommunications Policy (Carter: "agree"),[70] the Council on International Economic Policy (Carter: "agree"), the Office of Federal Procurement Policy (Carter: "agree"), the Energy Resources Council
(Carter: "OK, if Schlesinger agrees"), the Federal Property Council
(Carter: "agree"), and the Foreign Intelligence Advisory Board (Carter:
"OK"). Carter did take issue with one of Eizenstat's proposals, a rov-
ing "domestic ambassador" who would serve as the president's representative to a variety of groups and organizations; Carter thought the
idea "silly."

Carter's apparent agreement with the bulk of these recommendations on the EOP are also interesting in their own right since they pre-
date Harrison Wellford's reorganization report of December 23, which
had been specifically charged with their analysis. It is also clear that
Carter carefully read Eizenstat's memo: in addition to his marginal
notes, Carter also circled grammatical and usage errors, such as "pre-
requisite" for "perquisite" (twice, in fact).[71]

Also notable is whether Carter thought his comments on the memo
were an intellectual exercise, or, more troubling, whether it constituted
a decision on his part or perhaps even an instruction about how he
wanted his staff structured and that he somehow thought Eizenstat, his
issues person, would carry out. If the latter, it indicates a profound lack
of understanding of how his own transition was operating or how his
decisions might be effectively implemented. There is also little evidence that these memos and their variety of proposals for White House
organization led to some concerted effort to think about organizational
matters on Carter's part or to translate them into structures and
processes that would take effect once he assumed office.

The Transition's Problems Continue

In fact, a lack of direction and closure would once again lead to tensions in the Carter inner circle, this time between Eizenstat and Watson over what the domestic policy process would look like and their respective roles in it. And again, while brought in to mediate, Carter's response was essentially to let them work out their own differences.

By early December, the press was again reporting renewed friction in the Carter transition effort. According to the *New York Times,* "the Carter people are finding it more difficult to exercise power than to keep it—harder to keep peace among themselves."[72] On December 13, the *New York Times* reported that Carter had seemed "intense" and "severe" in meeting with his top staff at Blair House in Washington. One aide especially attributed Carter's behavior, which had "psyched out some of the staff and made them stiff in his presence," to a new rift that had developed, this time between Watson and Eizenstat, who "have evidently been left with the impression that they are in competition for certain White House responsibilities."[73]

On December 23, Eizenstat brought the issue to Carter's attention in a memo entitled "Prospective Problem." Although the memo covered a number of matters on Eizenstat's "prospective position" as domestic policy adviser (an appointment that still had not been settled), at the end Eizenstat alerted Carter to an article in the *Atlanta Constitution* that very day. The piece indicated that someone else (i.e., Watson) would be convening meetings and a cabinet-level task force to deal with welfare reform. Eizenstat told Carter that this responsibility should belong solely to the domestic adviser.[74]

Eizenstat would later recall that there "continued to be substantial confusion about the responsibilities of Jack and myself." In part, this stemmed from the Carter meeting with top aides in early November during which he asked them to describe the position they wished to hold in the Carter White House. Although Eizenstat did not see Watson's description, "I think Jack's description was probably not far different from mine." Carter, however, "simply didn't see or refused to recognize, because I think it was pointed out to him, the overlap." Finally, Carter "at last saw" that there was a similarity "in what we could do and that only one person could do it." "He asked Jack and I to try to work the thing out."[75]

In part, their disagreement stemmed from differences in style and personality, but it was sparked by common ambition. As Patrick Anderson notes, while both were able lawyers, "Jack was the golden boy, and Stu—thin, homely, perpetually worried Stu—was the class grind. A certain rivalry was implicit in their roles, for only one of them could be the top White House domestic adviser, and it was assumed that was the role they both coveted."[76] But part of their disagreement stemmed from substantive differences over how domestic policy should be formulated. While there was general agreement that Nixon's Domestic Council apparatus needed to be replaced, there were differences as to what should replace it. Watson favored more ad hoc task forces in which his presumed job of coordinating the cabinet would give him a central role, whereas Eizenstat favored a more permanent, White House–based domestic policy staff. They also had different views about their responsibilities. Watson apparently thought that long-range planning was part of his responsibilities in dealing with the cabinet, with Eizenstat's domestic staff handling only short-term problems, whereas Eizenstat regarded all domestic policymaking within his bailiwick, with Watson restricted to coordinating only the implementation of policy once decided.

Jimmy Carter spent Christmas Eve day once again straightening out the rivalries among his top assistants. Eizenstat had thought the matter settled (and to his satisfaction) following his meeting with Carter. But it would take several more weeks, more meetings, and further memos before the matter was fully resolved.[77] As with the earlier Jordan-Watson episode, some of the intramural politicking found its way into the press. As earlier, Carter's own comments did not help the situation. On December 26, the *New York Times* reported that "discussions" in Plains and in Washington had been taking place concerning top staff positions. The report particularly noted that Watson's responsibilities would concern the cabinet and further that Carter himself had "said this week . . . that Mr. Watson would plan and manage 'cluster' sessions of cabinet members," a job that might involve a more active role in the policy process than Eizenstat had envisioned or that Carter had indicated in his talk with Eizenstat.[78]

The fact that Carter ultimately sided with Eizenstat would also affect his hopes for the cabinet. First, Watson's more ad hoc, task-force approach offered a better venue for bringing departments and agencies more centrally into the policy process, whereas Eizenstat's approach represented a more traditional White House staff–based model. Carter apparently did not realize that more was at stake here than two close aides squabbling over jobs. Second, some confusion over responsibility for policy development would persist into the new administration. During the first six months, departmental "clusters" had a direct role in policy development in some areas, but there was a lack of integration and coordination with the work of Eizenstat's domestic policy staff. A June 1977 report by the president's reorganization project especially cited two separate memo processes, one run by Watson, the other by the White House. Integration of their recommendations, the report noted, "often occurs late in the process," and "White House staffing papers may be developed without benefit or full knowledge of departmental positions or vice versa."[79]

A White House Staff Finally Takes Shape

By the end of December 1976, the cabinet selection process was complete, and now more attention was focused on the White House staff itself. Carter's own sense of the kind of staff he wanted and the general theme he had articulated in the campaign (i.e., avoiding a Nixonian "imperial presidency") provided general guidance. As reported for some months and as Carter himself had indicated, a smaller staff was envisioned; there would be no chief of staff, and a more informal collegial decisionmaking process would be created, with eight or nine top aides who would report directly to the president. Somehow all of this would be linked to Carter's goal of enhancing the role of the cabinet as the central body for policy deliberation, with the staff in a more subservient role. Yet despite all the memoranda back and forth, the transition studies, and the reorganization analyses, decisions about the White House staff were surprisingly ad hoc. In some sense, Carter might have skipped all of it.

Although Carter's thoughts and prior comments as to staffing had defined some broad parameters, specific duties and authority were largely worked out informally among top aides. As late as the end of December, one aide remarked that "we don't know yet how the White House will be structured." For his part, Carter, the aide noted, "doesn't know what's going on here. He doesn't like to get involved in staff conflicts; we have even heard that he doesn't read any papers but the *Atlanta Constitution* and doesn't realize what's happening in Washington."[80] According to Frank Moore, Carter had "largely a residual attitude from the Nixon years. He didn't want a strong White House staff. Other than that, he looked at it primarily in terms of numbers. How many people does Stu get to have, how many people does Hamilton have to have? Getting an extra staff member out of him was tough."[81]

By late December, reports began to leak out concerning the jobs Carter's top aides would be assigned.[82] On December 30, 1976, the

New York Times reported in a page-one article that Barbara Blum, Watson's deputy and the director of transition operations, had disclosed to two dozen reporters at a breakfast meeting that seven key posts had been decided upon and would be announced by Carter at an afternoon press conference. These positions included Jack Watson as secretary to the cabinet, Jordan in charge of "White House personnel and something to do with the Democratic National committee," Eizenstat assigned policy analysis and legislation, Frank Moore to head congressional liaison, Lipshutz as White House counsel, and Greg Schneiders as appointments secretary. However, Blum's announcement, according to the report, was "premature and possibly, though not necessarily, inaccurate." (With the exception of Schneiders's position, Blum's account was eventually borne out.)[83]

Blum's announcement set off what the *New York Times* termed a "minor to-do" within the Carter inner circle. Jody Powell told reporters, "There are some things that she does not know." But Powell himself had already told reporters that White House staff organization had been discussed by Carter and some of his aides at a meeting at St. Simons Island, Georgia, the day before; other Carter aides acknowledged that a press conference had indeed been tentatively scheduled. Powell did not disclose why the conference was not held, nor did he indicate "whether Mr. Carter was encountering new difficulties in organizing the White House staff." Powell did state that an announcement would likely come within two weeks.[84]

Meanwhile, on Sunday, January 2, a group of Carter's top aides met to firm up White House organization. They now dubbed themselves "Members of the White House Management Committee," with Lipshutz as their nominal head. Attending the meeting were Lipshutz, Jordan, Watson, Eizenstat, Moore, Powell, Hugh Carter (the president-elect's cousin, who would be placed in charge of White House administration), Dick Moe, Frank Moore, Jim Gammill, and Richard Harden. Fifteen "responsibility centers" were identified to be headed by the counsel to the president, press secretary, eight assistants to the presidents, the First Lady's assistant, and four special assistants. The next day, Harden prepared a memo to the group outlining what had been discussed, as well as staff allocations (which took account of Carter's call for cuts) for each White House unit. Harden also included floor plans of the West Wing, with the names of most of the principals already penciled on the choicer office locations.[85]

At a press conference in Plains on January 14, 1977, less than one week before the presidential inauguration, Powell unveiled Carter's choices for top staff positions. The assignments generally reflected press speculation and other reports that had surfaced the preceding three weeks, as well as the work earlier in the month of the new White House Management Committee. Jordan would hold the simple title of "assistant to the president," with Eizenstat as assistant for domestic affairs and policy, Watson as assistant for both intergovernmental relations and cabinet secretary, Frank Moore as assistant for congressional liaison, Robert Lipshutz as counsel to the president, and Rochester, New York, Vice Mayor Midge Costanza as assistant for public liaison. Of the top seven presidential assistants (Powell's appointment had been announced in November), all were Georgians and close Carter associates, with the exception of Costanza. In addition, five other aides holding the lower rank of special assistant to the president were announced: Tim Kraft for appointments, Jim King for personnel, Peter Bourne for mental health and drug abuse, Joseph Aragon as ombudsman, and Martha "Bunny" Mitchell for special projects.

Powell also announced that the senior aides would hold daily staff meetings to be presided over by Lipshutz, who at age fifty-five was described by Powell as the "senior statesman" of the group. Powell insisted that none of the seven senior aides would hold the position of chief of staff and that Jordan would provide political advice and perform other administrative duties. Powell used the familiar spokes-and-wheel metaphor to explain the arrangement. According to one "well-informed source," the *New York Times* reported, "Hamilton will be the main guy"; the same newspaper took note that Jordan would occupy the corner office in the West Wing that had been used by H. R. Haldeman in the Nixon years and Sherman Adams under Eisenhower. The *New York Times* also observed that the "great tension" between Eizenstat and Watson had been apparently worked out and that Carter himself had remarked in a conversation on January 12 that he had "left the staff alone to evolve among themselves their hierarchy and working relationships."[86]

At a luncheon that day with reporters, Watson told them that Richard Moe, Mondale's chief of staff, would join the daily staff meeting. He indicated that Hamilton Jordan's role would be to "facilitate politically what we do substantively." Confirming the division of labor he had worked out with Eizenstat, Watson also said that Eizenstat would be responsible for policy issues before they were enacted, while he would be responsible once they were adopted. The White House staff, Watson emphasized, would not exercise any "command role" over cabinet departments. According to the *Washington Post*, "Beyond

the names and titles that were announced today, the manner in which the
Carter White House will function remained largely unknown and is likely
to evolve over the first several months of the new administration."[87]

* * *

As noted at the outset, Carter's transition to the presidency was more
ambitious in scope than any to date. Not only did it begin so early and
enlist the work of so many; it encompassed an elaborate personnel operation, numerous teams to look into departments and agencies, staffs
to develop policy options, groups to deal with the press and Congress,
and an effort directed at executive-branch and White House reorganization. Numerous studies, papers, and memoranda were produced by
many of its participants, particularly relating to how the Carter presidency would be organized and function. No prior administration could
match the wealth of material available to this incoming president.

Yet despite its size, structure, and effort, the 1976 transition was
something of a lost opportunity. With regard to its political agenda, although policy proposals were produced, little effort was given to prioritizing them or reckoning their political feasibility. Relations with
Congress appeared to have deteriorated over time; they certainly did
not get better.

Especially with respect to its planned decisionmaking and policy
processes, transition planning was largely a bust. Staff matters remained unresolved until January, and despite all of the studies and
memos, the details were largely left to Carter's aides to work out
among themselves. Carter's wish not to have a chief of staff and his
predilection of having eight or so aides report directly to him was followed, but there was little sustained consideration to how this arrangement might work out in practice come January 20. At best, the efforts
of the so-called White House Management Team to informally demar-
cate their respective duties would have to suffice.

So, too, with the hope for "cabinet government." A cabinet was
picked, but no further steps were taken to factor it into the administration's policymaking processes despite a number of proposals made by
Watson, Wellford, and others. This would prove an especially egregious
omission. Carter's expectation that the cabinet would serve in a policymaking role, with the White House staff in a coordinating capacity, was
a marked change from cabinet-staff roles in recent presidencies and no
easy matter to achieve. The fact that little attention was paid during the
transition to crafting a new relationship would doom the experiment
from the start.

Most noticeable within a transition effort that sought to be organized and prepared for the tasks ahead, it was an operation that itself lacked proper management. Almost from the start conflicts developed, and they continued to fester. Once Watson lost out, no one was clearly in charge, responsibilities became unclear, participants fought over turf, and matters were not brought to closure.

Much of this can be traced to the principal himself—Jimmy Carter. At times he could clearly be engaged in the matters before him, devoting great time and attention to their details. As we saw, on some memos his handwritten margin notes could be insightful. Yet he seemed to lack the skill or willingness to move from thought to deed. He was irritated at times at having to resolve the various squabbles that, predictably, emerged among his associates, preferring instead to have them work things out themselves. He was often the source (although not alone) of mixed messages, particularly in the matter of how much control cabinet officers would have in picking their subcabinet. He was the one, ultimately, who refused to choose among his aides and vest one of them with the kind of authority needed to make the transition work. Even from the start, he was the one who decided that Watson should run his initial transition effort, even though Watson had no prior experience for the job and even though his selection might generate tension with the campaign staff. For Carter, it was Watson's loyalty and commitment to him that mattered most, which became a repeated pattern as the top levels of the White House staff came to be populated almost exclusively by Georgians who had served Carter in the past.

Carter's impact here strongly illustrates the role of the principal actor over what transpires in the way he assumes office. That is an important lesson of this transition. Transitions are themselves matters of organization, management, and choice, and the president-elect obviously is in a position of great influence on these matters.

But that is not to say that the 1976 transition is therefore inconsequential and all that counts here is Jimmy Carter. The consequences of his personnel and organizational choices came to be influential in their own right. The actions of the Jack Watsons, Hamilton Jordans, and Stu Eizenstats, for example, are also important in understanding the Carter transition and its effects. Indeed, Carter's own managerial proclivities might have made them more consequential than would have been the case under a different president-elect. Carter would also come to feel the effects of other decisions made during the transition, as well as some that failed to be made: a hoped-for collegial staff, but with little attention to how it might come to pass; a White House management committee that had not yet done much management; a willingness to dispense with a chief of staff, but with little attention to how some of the work of that position, particularly staff coordination, might be parceled out.

As for this transition, it may have been a missed opportunity that did not reach the goals envisioned for it. But did it, either by commission or omission, still have significant effect on the presidency that would soon follow?

Notes

1. Dated May 11, the memo bore the title, "Preparing for the Presidency: Some Thoughts on Organizational and Action Requirements, June 1, 1976 to January 20, 1977," Bourne, *Jimmy Carter*, p. 358.

2. Bourne, *Jimmy Carter*, p. 358.

3. The fact that Watson operated independently of the campaign staff would be a decision that would have serious implications throughout the transition process and even thereafter. One possible explanation is that Carter might have sought to skirt campaign-funding laws that prohibited the campaign from soliciting private donations once federal funds were accepted following his nomination. In fact, Morris Dees, the campaign's general counsel, appeared before the Federal Elections Commission (FEC) on July 7, 1976, requesting that Carter be permitted to raise private funds for the transition effort since its purpose was not to further his election but plan for an orderly transition of power. Watson was operating independently of the campaign, which would have further bolstered the logic of Dees's request. But on July 21, the six FEC commissioners on a straight party vote denied Carter's request; Watson's effort would have to be budgeted out of limited campaign funds. The FEC action also had another consequence: it made public Watson's operation, which was subsequently deluged with job requests and résumés. See Warren Weaver, "Carter Asks Funds to Study Transition," *New York Times,* July 8, 1976; see also Adams and Kavanagh-Baran, *Promise and Performance,* pp. 15–16.

4. Watson, Miller Center Oral History, p. 1, Carter Presidential Library, Atlanta, GA (hereafter cited as CL).

5. Richard Fleming, head of the Atlanta civic group Central Atlanta Progress, was initially given the job of serving as the team's chief talent scout, with Jule Sugarman serving as Watson's deputy. Others enlisted were Lawrence Bailey (an assistant director of the U.S. Conference of Mayors) and Joe Levin (director of the Southern Poverty Law Center), with responsibilities in the area of community and human-resource development, while Curtis Hessler, a Los Angeles lawyer and former Rhodes scholar, and John Harmon, a lawyer from North Carolina, were assigned business, labor, and regulatory issues. Matt Schaffer, a Georgian and former Rhodes scholar, was assigned foreign policy along with Lake. Joe Browder, executive director of an environmental lobbying group in Washington, was placed in charge of natural-resource issues, and

Bowman Cutter, assistant to the president of the *Washington Post,* was assigned economic issues, budgetary matters, and the OMB. Among the group—save for Watson and Sugarman—only Schaffer was from Georgia. See Richard Corrigan and Joel Havemann, "The Issues Teams: The People Who Prepare Jimmy Carter for the Presidency," *National Journal,* August 21, 1976, pp. 1166–1172. Bruce Kirschenbaum, director of New York City's Washington office, was later hired to assist Cutter with budget issues, as was Chester Davenport, who was assigned transportation and housing, and Katie Beardsley, who was given the task of assisting Wellford on government reorganization. In the area of environmental policy, David Freeman, Jim Rathlesberger, and Kathy Fletcher were brought on board. And to assist in personnel matters, Bob Etchison, Tom Reston, and Jeffalyn Johnson were hired.

6. Eizenstat was one of the few Georgians in the Carter camp who had wider political experience: he had served in the Johnson White House and as research director for the 1968 Humphrey campaign. A third group, smaller than Eizenstat's, was located in Washington. Headed by Joseph Duffy, a 1970 Connecticut senate candidate and then executive director of the American Association of University Professors (AAUP), it administered the Atlanta task forces under Eizenstat, notifying them when issue papers were needed and making sure that deadlines were met.

7. On August 24, Watson presented this plan to his top coordinators and circulated a seventeen-point memorandum that outlined the coordinators' responsibilities in preparing briefing books for the departments and agencies they were assigned. This task included not just the preparation of information about their respective units; it also specified a list of key positions and their current incumbents, budgets for the last three years, organizational charts, staffing patterns, lists of expiring legislation, lists of congressional committees with agency jurisdiction and a list of congressional staff assigned to the agency, copies of Carter's speeches and statements relevant to the agency, all relevant option papers prepared by the transition group, lists of critical problems facing the agency, lists of administrative problems and possible management consultants to remedy them, a description of the process for filling non–civil service positions, lists of senior people who might be considered for retention or promotion, and a TIP printout of persons who should be considered for appointment to available positions. A target date of November 8, six days after the election, was set for completion of the briefing books, and each team coordinator was expected to be ready to serve as liaison between outgoing and incoming officials. Memorandum from Jack Watson to Coordinators, August 24, 1976. "Briefing Packages for Department and Agency Heads," Staff Secretary Files—Hutcheson, Box 249, CL.

8. Bourne, *Jimmy Carter,* p. 358; and Adams and Kavanagh-Baran, *Promise and Performance,* pp. 13–14.

9. Joel Havemann, "Carter Team Aiming to Put His Budget in Place Immediately," *National Journal,* October 9, 1976, p. 1422.

10. Dom Bonafede, "Carter Staff Is Getting Itchy to Make the Move to Washington," *National Journal,* October 30, 1976, pp. 1543–1546.

11. Eizenstat, Miller Center Oral History, p. 15, CL.

12. Eizenstat, Miller Center Oral History, p. 14, CL.

13. Eizenstat, Miller Center Oral History, p. 14, CL.

14. Jim Gammill had attended the August 24 meeting of Watson and his top staff, as the campaign's representative. In a memorandum that same day to Jordan, Gammill noted that "Jack has reacted to what he has sensed to be the new mood over here, and urged his staff to develop closer relations with the campaign. He will set up a meeting this week between his staff and Stu's staff, and also requested after the meeting that we resume weekly meetings over here with him." Gammill also alerted the campaign staff to the impending discussion of White House staffing to be held with Carter: "There is a Plains [Georgia] briefing next week about government reorganization, which I think to them right now means White House staff structure. I encourage some campaign staff participation." Memorandum from Jim Gammill to Hamilton Jordan, August 24, 1976, Staff Secretary Files—Hutcheson, Box 249, CL.

15. Shogan, *Promises to Keep,* p. 78.

16. Hutcheson stressed the need to hire campaign workers to serve on the postelection transition staff and then in the White House. And he helpfully listed the names of those whom he presumed would fill major staff positions, all of whom, with the exception of Watson, held positions on the Carter campaign staff. Hutcheson also noted that Carter's options needed to be guarded so that Watson's policy groups did not work everything out beforehand and present "JC with fait accomplis or unnecessary tough choices." Memorandum from Rick [Hutcheson] to Hamilton [Jordan], September 30, 1976, "Some Political Aspects of the Transition," Staff Secretary Files—Hutcheson, Box 249, CL.

17. In Butler's view, Jordan was a far better choice to lead the effort: "Events proved that we were right. . . . Ham's plan will again be crucial." Memorandum from Landon [Butler] to Jim Gammill, "Idle Thoughts on Transition, 10/11," Chief of Staff Files—Butler, Box 84, CL.

18. Bonafede, "Carter Staff Is Getting Itchy to Make the Move to Washington," *National Journal,* October 30, 1976, p. 1545.

19. Bourne, *Jimmy Carter,* p. 359.

20. Memorandum from Jack Watson to Jimmy Carter, "The Executive Office of the President," November 3, 1976, Staff Secretary—Handwriting Files, Box 3, CL; "Transition Documents Ready for Your Review," November 3, 1976, Plains Files, Box 41, CL; "Transition Overview," November 3, 1976, Chief of Staff Files—Butler, Box 84, CL. The content of Watson's work was promptly reported in the next day's *New York Times;* see Hedrick Smith, "Georgian Is Urged to Appoint 100 to Prepare Washington Takeover," *New York Times,* November 4, 1976.

21. Kaufman, *The Presidency of James Earl Carter,* p. 25. It is also likely that Jordan was upset with the job description of the "transition coordinator," a position Watson was likely to hold. Moreover, in the "Executive Office of the President" memo, Watson advised Carter that "for your protection, no one person should have an exclusive assignment as 'job dispenser.'" This passage is one of the few underlined by Watson in his memo, and the job to which it

refs would become the other of Hamilton Jordan's chief duties in the transition and the first months of the new administration. Memorandum from Jack Watson to Jimmy Carter, "The Executive Office of the President," November 3, 1976, Staff Secretary—Handwriting Files, Box 3, CL.

22. James T. Wooten, "Carter Aide Chosen to Guide Transition," *New York Times,* November 11, 1976.

23. Peter Goldman and Eleanor Clift, "Carter: Taking Charge," *Newsweek,* November 22, 1976.

24. Shogan, *Promises to Keep,* pp. 75, 79–80.

25. Watson, Miller Center Oral History, p. 2, CL. Watson did at least meet this expectation of Carter, and $350,000 was returned to the government. Unlike the 1963 Presidential Transition Act, the 1976 legislation did not leave it to the discretion of the outgoing president to determine how the fund would be divided (Johnson had split the $900,000 in funds evenly in 1968, with Nixon receiving $375,000 and the vice president–elect $75,000, with Johnson and Humphrey likewise getting $375,000 and $75,000 respectively). In 1976, the total fund was increased from $900,000 to $3 million, with $2 million made available to the incoming administration, while only $1 million was available for the outgoing administration. Carter would use some $1.7 million, while Ford spent some $687,000. Draft report, "Transition of the President and the President-Elect," Meese Files, OA 5097, pp. 9–10, Reagan Library.

26. James Wooten, "Carter Aide Chosen to Guide Transition," *New York Times,* November 11, 1976.

27. Edward Walsh, "Carter Plans Thorough, Open Selection Process," *Washington Post,* November 13, 1976.

28. Kaufman, *The Presidency of James Earl Carter,* p. 25. Also see Edward Walsh, "Carter Sees No Jobless Dip," *Washington Post,* November 16, 1976.

29. Powell, *The Other Side of the Story,* p. 28.

30. Shogan, *Promises to Keep,* p. 81.

31. Rowland Evans and Robert Novak, "Hamilton Jordan Rolls Along," *Washington Post,* December 1, 1976.

32. Edward Walsh, "Carter Reviewing Memo on Selecting Top Aides," *Washington Post,* November 10, 1976.

33. Hedrick Smith, "Strains in Carter Transition," *New York Times,* December 10, 1976.

34. Robert Kaiser, "Clash Shakes Carter Transition Team," *Washington Post,* December 8, 1976.

35. They included Barbara Blum, a deputy director of the campaign staff who now served as director of transition operations; Walter Kallaur, deputy administrator of the campaign who was assigned duties as transition administrator; and psychiatrist and mental-health adviser Peter G. Bourne, who handled "special projects." Lawrence Bailey, who had been working in the area of human resources on Watson's preelection staff, was tapped as Watson's new deputy, replacing Jule Sugarman.

36. Matt Coffey quoted in Joel Havemann, "Carter Is Taking Pains in Picking His Plums," *National Journal,* November 20, 1976, p. 1650.

37. Jordan's staff included such Carter veterans as Landon Butler, political director of the campaign; Jim Gammill, the campaign's convention coordinator; Rick Hutcheson, the delegate-selection coordinator; Tim Kraft, the campaign's field director; Mark Siegal, executive director of the Democratic National Committee; Phil Wise, who had served as Southern regional coordinator during the campaign; Anne Wexler, associate publisher of *Rolling Stone* magazine; and Benjamin Brown, a Georgia state senator and deputy campaign director.

38. Richard Fleming, who had been Watson's initial talent coordinator, was tapped as Coffey's deputy.

39. Most notably Harrison Wellford on government reorganization, Bowman Cutter on budget analysis, Anthony Lake in State/Defense/Intelligence, Joseph Levin on Justice/EEOC, and Chester Davenport on HUD/DOT. Jule Sugarman, who had been Watson's deputy, now served as consultant to Wellford's government reorganization cluster. Eizenstat was assisted by two Watson staff members, Curtis Hessler and Bruce Kirschenbaum (who both held titles as "senior policy adviser," immediately below Eizenstat).

40. Interior/Energy (Katherine Schirmer, a member of Senator Philip Hart's staff), Agriculture (Lynn Daft), HEW (June Christmas, a New York City mental-health commissioner), Treasury/Labor/Commerce (Jerry Jasinowski, an economist with the Joint Economic Committee).

41. Attachment II, "Carter/Mondale Transition Planning Group, Transition Budget—Public Funds," not dated, Chief of Staff Files—Butler, Box 84, CL. Another document indicates that 310 persons were employed on the transition from November 3, 1976, through January 20, 1976: see Attachment I, Memorandum from W. Kallaur to H. Jordan, R. Lipshutz, and J. Watson, "Weekly Report—Administration/Finance," January 18, 1977, Chief of Staff Files—Butler, Box 84, CL.

42. See Joel Havemann, "Carter Is Taking Pains in Picking His Plums," *National Journal,* November 20, 1976, p. 1650.

43. Untitled and undated organizational chart of the transition staff in Chief of Staff Files—Butler, Box 84, CL. "Hamilton's lead persons" are interesting in their own right: they included not only members of Jordan's staff but also others in the Carter-Mondale inner circle (including Robert Lipshutz for Justice and Richard Moe for Treasury) and Carter and Mondale themselves for State and Defense. Box 84 also contains the original draft (the first document has the names penned in) of the persons assigned to recruitment for key staff and cabinet positions. In the original list, Carter has direct responsibility for State, Defense, NSC, and CIA. In the next list, these are also shared with Mondale.

44. Although Watson had encouraged him to spend two or three days a week in Washington, D.C., the fact that Carter chose to remain in Plains was consequential: it was a long journey from Atlanta, much less Washington, D.C., where most of his transition staff was located. Eisenhower and Nixon, by contrast, operated their transitions out of New York City, while Kennedy divided his time between Georgetown and Palm Beach.

45. Shogan, *Promises to Keep,* p. 87.

46. David Rosenbaum, "Bell Reported Carter's Choice from the Start," *New York Times,* December 24, 1976.

47. Shogan, *Promises to Keep,* p. 87.

48. Bell and Ostrow, *Taking Care of the Law,* p. 68.

49. During the 1980 transition, there were reports that CIA Director Stansfield Turner had been angling to remain in his job. Carter and staff director Al McDonald discussed the rumors and Carter noted that George "Bush was almost on his knees 4 years ago for me to keep him" on as director of the CIA. Al McDonald, handwritten notes of meetings with President Carter, November 17, 1980, Al McDonald Donated Papers, Box 15, CL.

50. Hedrick Smith, "Aides Say Carter May Leave Some Top Positions Vacant," *New York Times,* December 29, 1976.

51. Memorandum from Carter to Secretaries-Designate, January 11, 1977, Staff Offices/Staff Secretary—Handwriting Files, Box 1, CL.

52. Memorandum from Hamilton Jordan to Jack Watson and Frank Moore, Jordan Files, Box 51, CL. The document is undated, but "1/25" is written at the top.

53. Memorandum from Landon Butler to Hamilton Jordan, November 16, 1976, Chief of Staff Files—Butler, Box 84, CL.

54. Memorandum from Tim Kraft to Hamilton Jordan, November 22, 1976, "Placement/Personnel," Chief of Staff Files—Butler, Box 84, CL.

55. Hutcheson also offered his advice on which TIP members were doing a good job and which should be eased out. See Memorandum from Rick Hutcheson to Hamilton Jordan, December 6, 1976, Staff Secretary Files—Hutcheson, Box 249, CL; emphasis added.

56. Hutcheson proposed the remedy that one person from Jordan's staff should act as liaison with the secretaries-designate and that "Coffey should understand that he works to assist these lead persons, not to entrepreneur on his own with the Secretary-designate." Memorandum from Rick Hutcheson to Hamilton Jordan, December 10, 1976, Staff Secretary Files—Hutcheson, Box 249, CL.

57. Dom Bonafede, "The Carter White House—the Shape Is There, but No Specifics," *National Journal,* December 25, 1976, p. 1801.

58. Memorandum from Harrison Wellford to the President-elect, "Executive Office of the President—Transition Agenda," December 1, 1976, Jordan Files, Box 10; Memorandum from Harrison Wellford to Hamilton Jordan, "White House Study Project Report No. 2, Analysis of the Current Executive Office of the President," December 23, 1976, Staff Secretary Files, Box 264, CL.

59. Dom Bonafede, "Carter Staff Is Getting Itchy to Make the Move to Washington," *National Journal,* October 30, 1976, p. 1547.

60. Hedrick Smith, "Strains in Carter Transition," *New York Times,* December 10, 1976.

61. Walter Pincus and Robert Kaiser, "Transition: A Busy Bunch of Grapes," *Washington Post,* December 5, 1976.

62. Mary Russell, "Hill Democrats Unhappy with Carter's Emissary," *Washington Post,* November 5, 1976.

63. Bourne, *Jimmy Carter,* p. 361.

64. O'Neill, *Man of the House,* p. 372.

65. Jules Witcover, "Blueprint for Transition Going to Carter," *Washington Post,* November 4, 1977.

66. The fact that Carter would ask Schneiders, his personal aide during the campaign, to undertake such a task is itself interesting since Schneiders had no prior White House or organizational expertise, save for the management of a Washington, D.C., bar.

67. In the body of the November 3 memo "The Executive Office of the President," two handwritten comments appear, one where Carter corrects the spelling of "premises," another where Carter underlined the list of departments involved in a decentralized national security structure. At the top of the document, two other notes appear: "Meeting on overview (composition)," and "Expedite TIP," a reference to the talent inventory pool. The memo also has a cover memo from Maxie Wells, Carter's secretary in Plains, to Jack Watson, dated December 18, 1976: "Jack: I wasn't sure you had gotten feedback from JC on this memo, even though it is so old (I just got it back from him today; guess he's been studying it). . . . I've filed memo down here." Memorandum from Jack Watson to Jimmy Carter, "The Executive Office of the President," November 3, 1976, Staff Secretary—Handwriting Files, Box 3, CL.

68. Memorandum from Harrison Wellford to Hamilton Jordan, "White House Study Project Report No. 2, Analysis of the Current Executive Office of the President," December 23, 1976, Staff Secretary Files, Box 264, CL.

69. Eizenstat had expressed an interest in the position at the November 4 meeting and then formalized that in a memo several days later; see Memorandum from Stu Eizenstat to Carter, November 8, 1976, "Possible Positions in Administration," Eizenstat Files—Staff Offices/DPS, Box 119, CL.

70. By December 23, Eizenstat had apparently reconsidered his position, noting the need for a small White House office that would assist the president in transmitting messages to the public, assisting in "television matters" such as fireside chats, and arranging televised "educational sessions." He thought Barry Jagoda would be an appropriate person for this job. It is interesting to note that copies of the memo were sent to Jody Powell, Jordan, Schneiders, and Bert Lance, but not to Watson or any other members of the reorganization staff. Memorandum from Stu Eizenstat to Carter, "Public Affairs Office," December 23, 1976, Staff Secretary—Handwriting Files, Box 3, CL.

71. Memorandum from Stu Eizenstat to Greg Schneiders, December 12, 1976, "Thoughts on Your Memo on the Organization of White House Staff and Executive Office of the President," Staff Secretary—Handwriting Files, Box 3, CL.

72. Hedrick Smith, "Strains in Carter Transition," *New York Times,* December 10, 1976.

73. Hedrick Smith, "Carter's Aides Fear Tight Security Might Cost Him Touch with Public," *New York Times,* December 13, 1976.

74. Memorandum from Stu Eizenstat to Carter, "Prospective Problem," December 23, 1976, Eizenstat Files—Staff Offices/DPS Files, Box 199, CL.

75. Eizenstat, Miller Center Oral History, p. 18, CL.

76. Anderson, *Electing Jimmy Carter*, p. 76.

77. Following their Christmas Eve talk, Eizenstat prepared a memo for his files (an interesting action itself) in which he summarized their discussion. In his "file memo," Eizenstat noted that he had stressed to Carter the importance of not separating long- and short-term policy development. Eizenstat then wrote, "In discussing the division of work between Jack Watson and myself, he [Carter] made the following points: (1) I would be responsible for the evolution and development of all policy, including the calling of inter-agency task forces to develop such policy; (2) Mr. Watson would be responsible for the implementation of such policy *after* it had passed. . . . He would also speak at conventions; (3) I used several specific examples including development of welfare reform program, and he made it clear that would be my responsibility. . . . He made it very clear that policy development and legislative drafting of policy would be entirely my responsibility." Memorandum from Stu Eizenstat to File, "Conversation with Governor Carter at 2:24 P.M. on Friday, December 24, 1976," same date, Eizenstat Files—Staff Offices/DPS, Box 119, CL. On December 26, 1976, Eizenstat forwarded a memo to Jack Watson in order to "follow-up our conversation of the other day with a brief memorandum describing my understanding of the assignments Governor Carter would like us to take." As he had with Carter, Eizenstat again stressed his role as the president's chief policy adviser (in contrast to Watson's responsibilities to oversee implementation), his direction of both short- and long-term planning, and his responsibility for calling meetings and otherwise serving as the president's chief coordinator for policy development. Memorandum from Stu Eizenstat to Jack Watson, December 26, 1976, Eizenstat Files—Staff Offices/DPS Files, Box 119, CL. On December 27, Eizenstat forwarded to Carter yet another memorandum in which he again outlined and "present[ed] for your approval" a specific description of his responsibilities. Memorandum from Stu Eizenstat to Carter, December 27, 1976, "Job Description," Eizenstat Files—Staff Offices/DPS Files, Box 119, CL. On January 3, 1977, Eizenstat prepared still one more memo for Carter, in which he outlined his proposed functions for the domestic policy staff as well as preparing a plan for its reduction in size. Memorandum from Stu Eizenstat to Carter, "Organization and Size of Domestic Policy Staff," January 3, 1977, Eizenstat Files—Staff Offices/DPS, Box 199, CL.

78. James Wooten, "Carter Set to Draft Economic Package in Talk This Week," *New York Times*, December 26, 1976.

79. President's Reorganization Project, Recommendation Memo No. EOP-1, June 29, 1977, Jordan Files, Box 37, CL.

80. Bonafede, "The Carter White House—the Shape Is There, but No Specifics," *National Journal*, December 25, 1976, p. 1799.

81. Moore, Miller Center Oral History, p. 20, CL.

82. See, for example, James Wooten, "Carter Set to Draft Economic Package in Talk This Week," *New York Times*, December 26, 1976. In that article,

Wooten's "sources" list the prospective appointments of Jordan, Watson, Eizenstat, and Schneiders.

83. Schneiders's appointment may have been the cause of the delay. Before joining the campaign, Schneiders had owned a Washington, D.C., tavern that had failed, and there were debts that remained to be paid. His FBI background check also apparently revealed that he had been receiving unemployment insurance at the time he was starting a restaurant-consulting business, which may have been a technical violation of the law. Schneiders was subsequently cleared on the financial matters and received a lower-level appointment. Patrick Anderson, *Electing Jimmy Carter,* p. 148, and Dom Bonafede, "Carter White House Staff Is Heavy on Functions, Light on Frills," *National Journal,* February 12, 1977, p. 235.

84. Hedrick Smith, "Carter Jobs 'Filled' but Only for a Day," *New York Times,* December 30, 1976.

85. Memorandum from Richard Harden to Robert Lipshutz, Members of the White House Management Committee, "White House Office," January 3, 1977, Richard Harden Files, Box 15, CL.

86. Charles Mohr, "Carter to Announce Staff Today; Jordan to Stay as Principal Aide," *New York Times,* January 14, 1977.

87. Edward Walsh, "Carter Names 12 Key Staff Aides," *Washington Post,* January 15, 1977; see also James Wooten, "Free Access by Staff to Carter Is Planned," *New York Times,* January 15, 1977.

2

Carter in Office

Although the Carter transition may not have lived up to its ambitious promise, both what it did and what it failed to do may have left an important legacy for the Carter presidency. At the beginning of each "in office" chapter (i.e., this one, as well as Chapters 4, 6, and 8), I will review the transition's likely effects on the early days of the new presidency; these are hypotheses, in effect, for testing how and why transitions might matter.

In terms of the basic decisionmaking processes of his administration, Carter placed great faith in using the cabinet as a source of policy information and advice. He invested much personal effort in its selection. Yet as we saw in Chapter 1, during the transition steps were not taken to facilitate the goal of cabinet government or to organize it to work in practice. The fact that Carter would have a talented cabinet was likely, but it was less likely to meet Carter's expectations as a deliberative body or as an important source of policy advice.

With respect to the White House staff, Carter had broadly envisioned it as serving a coordinating rather than a policymaking role. Yet throughout the transition, much of its organization and structure remained undefined, with details left to participants to work out. The so-called White House Management Committee had been formed in the last weeks of the transition, but little in the way of managerial decisions had been made. For both the staff and the management committee, the early days of the Carter presidency would either be a time to do what was not done in the transition or, more likely, a period of disorganization and disarray. Coordination of the policy and decision processes was especially likely to be problematic. Hamilton Jordan was widely touted in the press as Carter's "principal aide" and a likely candidate to provide staff leadership and direction in the absence of a chief of staff. Or, as during the transition, would staff coordination prove more elusive?

As for Carter, the transition indicated that he loomed large over the planning of his presidency. He saw himself as front and center, did not think he needed someone to hold and control the organizational reins for him, and at times was willing to immerse himself in detail. But the transition also indicated potential fault lines: an absence of a recognition that more was needed to translate his own preferences and instructions into reality; an unwillingness to clearly establish lines of authority and define responsibilities; and a belief that staffing issues and problems are best left to be worked out by staff members themselves. Did some of those problems during the transition reappear during the early days of his presidency? Or did Carter's own considerable intellect, hard work and determination, and conception of his political agenda enable him to overcome them and, further, yield the decisions that would make for a successful early presidency?

With respect to policy, much work had clearly been undertaken both before and after the election. Yet as we saw in Chapter 1, little effort was made to prioritize the president's agenda. Would that now take place, or would the legacy of the transition yield a presidential laundry list of proposals? Furthermore, with regard to Congress, relations got off to a rocky start during the transition. Could they now be repaired? More generally, the absence of an organized decision process did not bode well for policy decisions that would yield successful policy outcomes. In particular, during the transition three policy decisions were set in motion that could prove potentially troublesome: Schlesinger's "secret" energy proposal, the cancellation of water projects, and the $50 tax rebate.

Decisionmaking Processes

The Carter White House Staff

On the surface, Carter's senior staff resembled the collegial, spoke-and-wheel model that had been widely discussed during the transition and in press reports. The White House Management Committee had devised, albeit late in the game, a setup with Carter in the center, surrounded by a ring of eight assistants, each of whom had somewhat different but often not clearly defined responsibilities. In addition, a third level of "special assistants" had been created, most of whom were assigned functional tasks, such as staff secretary, personnel, and administrative management.[1]

An organizational chart was drawn up on January 25, 1977, just after the inauguration, but it only briefly listed each person's job description, demarcated no lines of clear authority, and often contained overlapping descriptions of duties. (Hamilton Jordan, for example, was listed as in charge of "staff coordination" and "political/general.")[2] It seemed to match Carter's organizational preferences, but there is little evidence that the problems of a collegial system had been considered, such as the pressure it puts on a president's time, the particular need it creates to handle interpersonal dynamics, or some of the pathologies that can develop in a small-group setting. It also seems that the arrangement had not been devised as a *deliberative* collegial body in the mold of Kennedy's ExCom, in which the group collectively would have a place in Carter's decisionmaking.

There was a kind of unfinished quality to the staff system as the administration began, and much of its workings and details would evolve over time. As he had done earlier when the dispute between the campaign staff and the transition group erupted, and later between Watson and Eizenstat over their respective roles, Carter preferred to stand aloof and let his associates work out their own responsibilities and disputes.

Another major problem stemming from the transition was Carter's near exclusive appointment (with the exception of Midge Costanza) of his Georgia associates to positions in his inner circle. Although appointments of staff members with broader experience would occur at other places in the Carter White House, the Georgians prevailed at the top. As David Rubenstein, who served as Eizenstat's deputy for domestic policy, would later observe, it was one of several "mistakes that really hurt. . . . He picked a very, very weak White House staff in my view. . . . It had a lack of real Washington experience. . . . I think it would have been some value having more seasoned people. If we'd had Anne Wexler and Lloyd Cutler early on I think it might have made a difference."[3]

For Carter, however, the value of loyalty trumped Washington experience and did so quite consciously and deliberately: "I saw the need . . . for an immediate core of people around me that had been tested in the crucible of election and gubernatorial experience, who knew each other's strengths and weaknesses and had learned to accommodate them, who were compatible with each other and who were loyal to me." Loyalty, in particular, was of some concern to Carter in making staff appointments. Although he deleted it from his memoirs, he later confided that "there was a problem in my mind about loyalty": "A portion of what I wrote that wasn't included in the end was about some experiences during the campaign when we would bring people into our bosom that we trusted [but who later] betrayed us, who came there as spies or who were just incompatible. . . . We didn't want that to happen in the White House."[4]

Initial press reports were not encouraging. On February 22, the *Washington Post* reported that "there is a general perception that the Carter operation is still in disarray. It is a perception that grows out of a trail of unreturned phone calls and broken appointments, of still unfilled high administration jobs, of the sound of harassed presidential aides rushing from one meeting to another." The same newspaper reported one leftover gift from the Ford administration: at his farewell party, Chief of Staff Richard Cheney was given a bicycle wheel with broken spokes and a bent frame. Mounted on a plaque, its inscription read, "The spokes of the wheel: a rare form of artistry conceived by Donald Rumsfeld and modified by Richard Cheney." Cheney left the gift behind in his old office, now to be occupied by Hamilton Jordan. On it, Cheney added his own note: "Ham: beware the spokes of the wheel."[5] It was an astute warning.

A Senior Staff at Work

The lack of coordination that had plagued the transition continued into the presidency itself. One source of early disarray was the inability of the senior staff to develop mechanisms to coordinate their own work. For recent presidents, the morning meeting of his senior staff—usually held at 7:30 or 8:00 A.M. depending on the administration—is a critical venue in this regard. It is an important occasion for collecting timely information about pending policy issues, fighting political fires, alerting members to media reports, planning strategy, making last-minute adjustments to the president's daily schedule, eliciting the concerns of staff members, and otherwise bringing the key members of the president's team together for advice, analysis, and discussion. Although it is only one part of the White House's role in the deliberative process, it is crucial in its impact on day-to-day operations.

Yet for the Carter White House, the senior staff meetings exemplified its organizational difficulties and did not operate as the White House Management Committee envisioned during the transition. On

January 14, press secretary Jody Powell had announced that Robert Lipshutz, the president's legal counsel, would chair the senior staff meeting. Lipshutz was the senior member—in age, that is, but not so much in stature or influence. Perhaps it was thought that Lipshutz's reputation as thoughtful, less combative, and less interested in protecting bureaucratic turf made him a good choice for the job. Perhaps the thinking was that Lipshutz's legal skills might serve them well or that he could best fill the role as neutral broker of the group. Or perhaps he was the senior member who carried the least baggage in the aftermath of the transition and was thus more acceptable than Watson, Eizenstat, or Jordan. Whatever the reason, Lipshutz emerged as the choice.

Yet Lipshutz approached the task tentatively, and the senior staff continued the pattern during the transition of not being able to function effectively as a group. At 4:00 P.M. on the afternoon of inauguration day, Carter's senior staff convened their first meeting, but minutes passed and nothing happened. Finally Lipshutz spoke up: "I guess because I'm the oldest one here, I'll call this meeting to order." According to one account of that first meeting, as Lipshutz "moved to the head of the table, there was an awkward silence because Lipshutz was really a secondary player. Others ignored him." Frank Moore turned to Hamilton Jordan and asked, "Ham, what do we do now?" "People laughed nervously. There was no order. No one giving instructions. No one taking notes. Moore's question got no answer." "Should we meet every day?" someone asked. "We'll meet when there's something to meet about," Jordan replied. The discussion turned to Congress, with several members falling into "congenial reveries about Georgia legislators. The meeting dribbled on. After a while people left, without coming to any decisions or conclusions."[6] It was not a propitious beginning.

At the staff meeting the next day, sixteen members attended, and Lipshutz announced that the daily staff meeting would include only the eight senior staff members, with a full staff meeting of a more inclusive group to be held once a week. But he did invite anyone with a specific item for discussion to attend regardless of the day. Jody Powell immediately requested that his deputy, Rex Granum, be permitted to attend all meetings. Mary Hoyt, of the first lady's staff, asked that she be included in any meeting involving Rosalynn Carter. Among the items discussed were an announcement by Jody Powell concerning Carter's executive order granting amnesty to draft evaders, a reminder by Lipshutz to make sure personnel forms were being processed, a request by Powell that he be informed of all staff contacts with press, and a presentation by Tim Kraft on appointments with the president, including

President Carter's instruction that staff members not "pop in" but be scheduled "in the normal way." No management issues were discussed; no ways of operating for the group were raised.

Until mid-May, senior staff meetings were held every morning, with at least one meeting per week of the larger staff group and one meeting per week, usually on Monday, with the president. Although Lipshutz had hoped that the meetings of the senior staff would include only eight staff members, attendance in almost all cases was greater, averaging eleven or twelve. When the larger group convened once a week, the number of attendees crept up to twenty. The personalities who attended would also vary. Lipshutz, Powell, Watson, Eizenstat, Hutcheson, Costanza, and Dick Moe of the vice president's staff were usually there, but some, such as Frank Moore and Brzezinski, only periodically showed up. Others attended even more infrequently, depending on the item up for discussion.

The brief records of these meetings kept by Rick Hutcheson, the staff secretary, suggest that the meetings served to inform the senior staff of what was going on in the administration rather than serving as a collegial forum for advice, debate, and deliberation. When the president was in attendance, the meetings often served as occasions for him to give instructions to his top aides. Sometimes matters were quite trivial: Hugh Carter announcing that the new White House correspondence manual was ready for distribution (January 24) and discussing parking and perks (January 29); Greg Schneiders noting that the mail-room staff had been instructed to pull letters for "special attention" from those writers who seemed to know the president personally (February 2); Eizenstat "reemphasizing" that $1 million could be saved by using postcards to respond to public inquiries rather than letters (February 3); Lipshutz notifying all present that a special "presidential edition" of Carter's book *Why Not the Best?* could be purchased for $3.20; Hugh Carter reporting on typewriters, with Midge Costanza suggesting that new models replace old ones and Eizenstat noting that a different model of dictaphone might be used (February 15); Hugh Carter serving notice that parking places were in the process of being reassigned (February 14); Jody Powell asking for larger iced-tea glasses and Tim Kraft noting that the new White House barber was nonunion (February 22); Hugh Carter reporting that "we will be able to trade in old IBMs [typewriters] for new self-correcting models"; Hugh Carter noting that the use of the White House pool and tennis courts was restricted to the First Family unless the president agreed otherwise (February 25). Later in the year, on September 26, President Carter complained about rats in his private study; he found them "distracting."[7]

Starting in mid-May, the staff began to meet every other day rather than daily. If these meetings were intended to provide an opportunity for senior members to come together in a collegial, deliberative structure—and they might have provided a key occasion for such—they did not fulfill that role. That failure was particularly important in the Carter White House, since the daily meeting was, in fact, the White House Management Committee in practice, and thus never emerged as the ongoing, collective body that could provide organization, coordination, and direction to the White House staff.

Hamilton Jordan's Role

Jordan's role as a member of the senior staff is particularly enlightening as to the early days of the Carter presidency and its connection to the transition. Had Jordan emerged as first among equals in the Carter inner circle, he might have provided the leadership and coordination that was lacking. At the same time, his close relationship to Carter and the fate of those who crossed him during the transition—most notably Watson—made it difficult for another to emerge in his place.

Jordan's situation was compounded, moreover, by the multiple, ill-defined tasks assigned to him: personnel, "political" adviser, and, on the January 25 organizational chart, "staff coordinator." His duties in the personnel area, however, overwhelmed him, while his political role was not much in evidence and staff coordination simply failed to materialize. Jordan did not even regularly attend the morning senior staff meetings (he was usually replaced by his deputy, Landon Butler). Among the first thirty staff meetings, from January 21 to February 28, Jordan attended nine. Jordan did not attend senior staff meetings on a regular basis until the end of January 1978, when Carter appointed him "staff coordinator."[8]

As for the meetings he did attend, Jordan was not a central participant. The records list Jordan as speaking at only three of nine meetings he attended through the end of February 1977. All of his comments were on personnel and appointment matters, with none on broader political matters. Jordan also began to skip other meetings where his presence and his political mandate might have dictated otherwise. At the start of the administration, for example, Jordan attended the daily morning meeting that Carter held with Frank Moore, but after a few months he stopped going: "I made the decision that it was Frank's time."[9]

For his part, Jordan felt that his plate was full enough with personnel matters during those early months of the new administration: "The first thing I did for the first three or four months, the most debilitating and terrible thing, was staffing the government. . . . Just to keep that away from the President, I spent an enormous amount of time the first three or four months going around and around with cabinet secretaries and trying to weigh political considerations in terms of who was going to be the assistant secretaries and so forth."[10]

In Richard Moe's view, however, Jordan and his staff were ill-suited for dealing with appointments: "Jordan hated dealing with personnel. Hated it. Tried for years to get rid of it. . . . But we paid a price for that. Because there's no more important thing a president does than the key appointments he makes." Yet "we had a bunch of campaign kids . . . running our personnel operation. I mean it's just incredible."[11]

Both Carter's and Jordan's difficulties were complicated by their choices for who would oversee White House personnel operations. The head of the office was Jim King, whose previous job was head of marketing and community affairs for the Boston-area transit authority. He was assisted by Jim Gammill, Jordan's young campaign aide, who had taken a seminar from King while a student at Harvard.

Carter would state, several years after his presidency, that had Hamilton Jordan been willing to be designated chief of staff in January 1977, "I would have had no objection to that." Jordan, in Carter's view, was the only senior adviser who could have taken on that job: "No other person . . . could have taken his place." Jordan "was a natural leader among the staff members."[12]

Yet initially—and for a full year—Jordan did not want the responsibility of staff coordinator, much less the much-feared title of chief of staff. Jordan, for his part, was concerned that he lacked the staff to serve Carter in a larger capacity (not an insurmountable problem) and did not feel he had authority to do so (a more difficult hurdle). As Jordan would later recount, "I had the perception of being a guy who could do all of these things but no real mandate from the President or my colleagues. . . . It was hard for me to focus in a sustained way on things."[13] Carter, moreover, contributed to the problem, publicly stating that Vice President Mondale would be his "senior staff person" or his "chief staff person."[14]

Compartmentalization in a Supposedly Collegial System

Carter's staff was vexed by an unexpected difficulty for such a fluid, collegial arrangement: a marked tendency among the staff (and Carter) to view responsibilities as confined to separate spheres of authority, often without clear guidance as to what that authority entailed. Yet absent much attention during the transition to how a collegial arrangement might work in practice, it is perhaps not surprising that staff members fell into particularized niches. And here we see another layer of problems originating in the transition and stemming from the vagueness in how staff members would coordinate their efforts and operate together.

A sense of "compartmentalization" is manifest, in varying ways, in a number of the oral histories of members of the Carter White House. According to Watson, "We started off with too many people having too much distributed authority for separate responsibilities. We regarded ourselves, and President Carter regarded each of us, too categorically," each operating in a separate area.[15] According to Bruce Kirschenbaum, one of Watson's deputies, Carter "trusted Jack with certain things, and he trusted Frank. He didn't trust any one person with the ball of wax."[16]

This compartmentalization had a number of consequences that affected decisionmaking and, as a result, policy outcomes. First, it created odd, if not artificial, boundaries. For Jack Watson, his compartmentalized niche involved the "execution of policy." Yet as Watson came to realize (even during the transition), it was difficult if not impossible to separate the "formulation" of policy—Eizenstat's job as assistant for domestic policy—from his own role in intergovernmental affairs and as cabinet secretary in its "execution":

> For about the first two and a half years that integration was virtually impossible. I frequently made a nuisance of myself, and thereby got myself in trouble with some of my colleagues in areas which counted a great deal because I wouldn't honor the complete separation of the categories. I would insist on crashing the party, so to speak, even though it violated the institutional arrangements. I did it very carefully, and never any more frequently than I thought was necessary. I was swimming against an established pattern.[17]

Second, compartmentalization affected the integration of policy analysis and politics. Peter Bourne recalls that the "political people" (i.e., Jordan, Powell, and Moore) saw themselves as opposed to the "policy people" (Eizenstat and Watson). As a result, "policy recommendations were forwarded independently to Carter and without assessment of their political implications, and political advice was given by people who often had little grasp of the issues involved."[18]

Third, valuable input could be lost. Kirschenbaum would later recall that we had a young lady on our staff who was very close to the majority leader and other members of Congress, yet the CL staff [congressional liaison] did not like her presence. Instead of learning how to use her resources to our advantage, a friction developed. Her contacts could have been used tremendously to our advantage. It was crazy, but that was the way people were categorized. We had an inter-government or cabinet secretary role, not a congressional relations role.[19]

Fourth, compartmentalization could affect the ability of the senior staff to communicate with each other or otherwise weigh in on policy matters. Kirschenbaum recalls that "it was hard for me to pipe-up at the last minute when a decision memo was going to the president and to comment on something of Stu's when I didn't have the time to research it, think it out, and put together the kind of memo on which I would want Jack to put his name."[20] In Peter Bourne's opinion, compartmentalization led to "little or no lateral communication. Phone calls from one 'spoke' to another were often deliberately never returned." In fact, in Bourne's view, compartmentalization generated organizational pathology—"destructive competition and undercutting through leaks to the press that served Carter poorly."[21]

Finally, compartmentalization contributed to the overload on Carter. Absent a chief of staff or a collegial mechanism of coordination, in Jack Watson's view there were "tracks that went separately all the way up to the top."[22] "Except through Carter," in Peter Bourne's view, "coordination was minimal."

Cabinet Government to the Rescue?

The difficulties with the White House staff might have been remedied, at least in part, by Carter's intent to rely more heavily on his cabinet. During the campaign and the transition, Carter repeatedly voiced the hope that his cabinet would serve as a major channel for information and advice in his policy deliberations, if not as the locus for policy development and formulation. Reliance on the cabinet also fit with Carter's own fears about a too-powerful White House staff and his sense that his departments and agencies possessed better knowledge and expertise on policy matters. According to Eizenstat, Carter "felt it important to talk about cabinet government, the importance of the cabinet relative to the White House staff and anything that could be done to denigrate the importance of the White House staff was something that fit in with this overall theme."[23]

At one level, Carter was right in attempting to redress the cabinet's atrophy during the Nixon years: presidents need to reach out beyond the confines of their own staffs, and agencies and departments can make a positive contribution to the development of policy. But at another level, how Carter undertook the process of reinvigorating the role of departments and agencies in his administration's decisionmaking was deeply flawed, leading to much confusion in the first year of his administration as to the policymaking roles the departments and the White House staff were supposed to play.

Part of the problem was that a definition of "cabinet government" was not clarified during the transition. Did it mean departments would be delegated much policymaking authority? At times, Carter's comments to Stu Eizenstat, his in-house domestic adviser, that he was taking on too much and should rely more on the departments suggest this was what Carter had in mind. Through the summer of 1977, moreover, cabinet "clusters" were often created to develop some policy proposals. Did this mean that the cabinet would collectively serve as a deliberative body? Carter's frequent meetings with the cabinet during the first year suggest that this, too, was something he wanted. How would the cabinet and the White House staff interact in formulating policy? Here Carter had little to contribute, save for telling his aides to make sure the departments were doing their share of the work.

If Carter hoped to delegate a good measure of policymaking to agencies and departments while avoiding the parochialism and turf battles that had plagued his predecessors, he made the task more difficult during the transition by granting cabinet-designates great leeway in determining who would be appointed to subcabinet positions. According to Richard Moe, Carter "gave away the government":

> Every secretary and particularly the forceful ones like Califano felt they had complete carte blanche and did. . . . And this initial failure to get a handle on those people in key policy making decisions I think had a lot to do with the lack of responsiveness through the government that later had a crippling effect. . . . The primary loyalty was to the cabinet secretary and not to the President. . . . Califano and Blumenthal and others were perceived as being totally unresponsive and in fact going out of their way to show the White House staff that they didn't have to deal with them.[24]

With regard to cabinet members themselves, Carter had better relations with them personally than did most of his predecessors since Eisenhower. Yet cabinet meetings quickly proved unproductive and never developed into the collegial, deliberative body Carter had perhaps envisioned. Brzezinski recalls that

> they were just awful . . . two hours of wasted time [on Monday mornings]. I started bringing the Monday morning new issues of *Time, Newsweek,* and *U.S. News and World Report* to cabinet meetings. . . . So I always had these magazines on my knees . . . and I read three magazines in these two hours because it was a waste of time. After a while we had cabinet meetings every two weeks, and then after a while I think we had them on the average maybe once a month or so.[25]

Attorney General Griffin Bell recalls that "the discussions were too disjointed, given the range of cabinet positions, to produce any coherent themes." In Bell's view, "It was adult show-and-tell. . . . Carter became entangled in trivial, technical minutiae that occupied too much of his time and attention."[26] The tip-off for Bell that they were a waste of time was when Jordan and Powell began not to attend.

Policymaking also suffered. Cabinet clusters were created to address several policy issues during the first six months of the new administration, but the White House and Eizenstat in particular lacked the ability to set their agendas or coordinate their work. As Shirley Anne Warshaw notes, "Neither Watson's nor Eizenstat's office attempted to guide or control the proposals developed within the cabinet clusters."[27]

In Eizenstat's view, the agencies and departments had a role to play in formulating the administration's policies, but Carter's emphasis on cabinet government and the tendency of some cabinet members to take the lead in particular areas weakened the ability of the White House staff to coordinate the process and provide timely, balanced policy advice to the president. Cabinet government led some to believe they could ignore the White House staff and deal directly with the president: "The greatest disability under which I labored in the early months of the administration was the President's repeated emphasis on cabinet government which gave a signal to the cabinet officers that this meant that the White House staff was less important and that they could go directly to him on things and that they could coordinate their own efforts."

When this happened, according to Eizenstat, policy initiatives generally floundered. For example, early in the administration Pat Harris, secretary of HUD, was asked by Carter to develop a major urban policy initiative. "She chaired an inner agency group of principles and after six fruitless months of trying to get the agencies together [she] finally came to me and said look you've got to take this thing over. I can't get the other agencies to listen to us in terms of deadlines and so forth."[28]

In the case of welfare reform, according to Eizenstat,

> Carter ended up getting a decision memorandum on welfare which was some sixty single spaced type written pages, utterly incomprehensible, in which the Department of Labor and the Department of HEW could not even agree on the language to be used in various sections because each felt that the other agency was not accurately stating its arguments on certain options. That's what the White House staff is there for. It's a non-turf interested, presidentially oriented, neutral arbiter, and when it's not allowed to serve that function, which it was not allowed to do because of some of the signals that were sent up by cabinet government, then you get a policy muddle. And I think it became increasingly clear that you couldn't continue and largely toward the end of the first year it didn't.[29]

Reliance on cabinet departments for policy initiatives and the absence of a clear plan about how the White House staff would monitor and coordinate their efforts also affected Carter's relations with Congress. In Richard Moe's view, "During the transition one of the biggest mistakes made was the failure to settle on the President's early policy priorities." Carter had a "willingness to allow cabinet secretaries to come forward with their own initiatives and to get presidential approval on them and send them up to the Hill. And so the White House became a funnel for all these different things, very few of which were stopped or altered or slowed down. But all of which went up and overloaded the circuits in the Hill." "We sent up too much legislation, we did not accurately tell [Congress] what was most important or what was least important. As a result, I think we got off to a bad start with the Congress, and most of those programs floundered."[30]

For Bert Lance, there was great irony in how the cabinet members failed to help Carter in his dealings with Congress. Unlike Carter's staff, most members of the cabinet were Washington insiders or had some prior experience there: "Cyrus Vance, Joe Califano, Brock Adams, James Schlesinger, Mike Blumenthal, Andy Young and Zbigniew Brzezinski. All of these men could have helped Jimmy on Capitol Hill. But some of them developed agendas and constituencies of their own."[31]

Better coordination of the White House staff system and a more realistic assessment of what cabinet members could contribute to the policymaking process might have remedied some of the problems besetting the Carter administration. But the transition had failed to resolve how the White House and the cabinet were to be brought together in a coherent, organized, and effective decisionmaking process. Coordination proved particularly elusive; according to Richard Moe, the way Carter "had set up the White House structure, he was the only one in a position to be an enforcer."[32]

Carter as Manager and Decisionmaker

Absent a game plan for the cabinet and a clearer understanding of how the staff would be organized and operate, Carter was confronted with a decision process that was heavily dependent on presidential direction. But that dependence did not serve Carter well. It forced him at times to be too deeply involved in some matters. But at other times, it required attention, management, and leadership that he either did not or could not provide.

The result cut against the grain of Carter's own conception of how he related to staff. Carter felt that he could and did delegate responsibilities to others; as he would later recall, "Once I've got or get confidence in somebody else, I don't mind loading them up with as much as I think they can bear and then I forget about it." "When I delegate authority, I don't look over somebody's shoulder."[33] Yet as other members of the administration recognized early on, Carter's "own inclination [was] to make decisions that other presidents or other administrators might choose to delegate. . . . That's why the system ran into trouble later on."[34] Another problem—one that revealed itself in the transition—was that Carter was often averse to the managerial tasks that came with such a president-dependent system. While immersing himself in policy details, he did not have the skill or will to manage the organization processes from which they issued, nor had he vested power in another to do it for him. Furthermore, while the transition placed added pressure on Carter as a decisionmaker and manager, there is little evidence that it prepared him *personally* for the challenges ahead.

Carter as De Facto Chief of Staff

Why Carter reacted against appointing a chief of staff, and in effect acted as his own chief of staff, is subject to numerous conjectures. For some, it was an overreaction to Watergate, or an example of his misplaced faith in his own talents.[35] For others, it was the lack of talent around him, Hamilton Jordan in particular, who could be entrusted with the job. Jack Watson would later recall that Carter's closeness to his chief aide, plus Jordan's own lack of managerial ability, made the situation difficult to change once it proved unworkable: "[One reason] for Carter's wanting everything to feed into him was Hamilton. . . . He has talents that are extraordinary but he was not a man of talents or inclinations suited to be chief of staff. . . . In many respects, he and Jody were in the closest personal relationship to the president. That also served as an obstacle to the designation of someone other than Hamilton to do that particular role. It took us three years to get there."[36]

But Bruce Kirschenbaum, Watson's deputy, saw Carter and the system that had been created as the indirect culprit: "Some were urging Hamilton for at least a year to be a vigorous chief of staff. He didn't want to do it, we were told through the grapevine, because he felt that the president wouldn't back him up at all times. He was not going to take on cabinet officers if they went around him and he got reversed all the time. This was the perception of most of the junior staff people."[37]

Regardless of the reason, in Watson's view Carter's failure to respond to the need for a chief of staff was a critical error during the transition and the early days of the administration: "Somebody's got to be in charge; *unquestionably, unmistakably* in charge. . . . We had stubbed our toes in countless ways, at countless points along the path because of a lack of having someone below the President in charge of *overall* coordination of things."

The absence of someone in charge, in turn, was a critical source of many of the problems with the Carter staff system that were noted earlier. One result, in Watson's opinion, was that it contributed to discord among Carter's senior aides: "Because there was no clear delegated authority, from the president, to any one person to bring about a merger and integration, we often wasted energy and time deciding who would do what and who would play the lead role. This struggle was undesirable, and enervating to everyone involved."[38]

A second result, with Carter alone pulling the strings, was a lack of coordination among and between staff members that affected the policy process. As David Rubenstein, Eizenstat's deputy, would later point out,

Everybody sort of reported to the President loosely . . . and each person handled their own agenda with the President. Early every day Zbig would go in and see the President separately, no one else. Frank Moore would go in maybe with one of the staff people, nobody else. Jody would go in separately. Hamilton would go in separately and occasionally Stuart would go in separately. It took us about two years to realize that maybe if we had one meeting with everybody there Carter

wouldn't have to repeat himself and it might lead to greater coordination. Not having a chief of staff early on left the White House staff,
in my view, very unstructured. . . . I think it got us off to a very bad
footing.[39]

A Penchant for Detail

The absence of a chief of staff affected Carter as well as his staff, and
he quickly became enmeshed in monitoring the details of the policy
process. Thus, while he preferred to let staff work out broad duties, he
micromanaged their day-to-day activities, an odd combination.

Carter's interaction with Stu Eizenstat is particularly interesting on
this point. Starting on March 1, 1977, Eizenstat began to send the president weekly progress reports on the various projects he and his staff
were working on; Eizenstat noted that "I will mention only those major
projects, many of which you have asked us to pursue."[40]

In the first report, Eizenstat listed nineteen projects. Carter
checked off each one, writing at the bottom: "Stu—this is a heavy load
for you. Be sure to let agencies do as much of this work as possible. J."

By April, these reports, which by now included over forty projects,
were broken down into topic areas—agriculture, human resources, energy
and natural resources, housing and urban affairs. Week by week, they are
indicative not only of the growth of Eizenstat's duties and the burgeon-
ing Carter domestic agenda; they also are revealing in the way Carter possibly used them to prioritize his agenda (checking some but not other
items), make further suggestions, and pass instructions to Eizenstat.

For example, on May 5, 1977, in an item dealing with comprehensive reform of the federal criminal code, Eizenstat informed Carter:
"The justice department was involved in working out a compromise between Senators Kennedy and McClellan to which the Administration is
substantially committed, de facto. The bill was introduced May 2. To
my knowledge, it was neither cleared by OMB or you, yet it appears to
have the Administration's blessing. I was not involved at any point." To
which Carter replied, "Nor I." Carter then added: "Stu: I need to understand, influence, re vote, impoundment, etc. to the bitter end. J."

On May 20, in an item dealing with sugar price supports, Eizenstat
noted that the "USDA [Department of Agriculture] is preparing administrative regulations for the new producer payment program. There has been
considerable pressure from the Louisiana Congressional delegation to
make program applicable to '76 stocks but we have resisted." Carter underlined "applicable to '76 stocks" and wrote an emphatic "No!" in the
margin. In the same memo, Eizenstat noted an effort to save $1 billion

by eliminating duplication of radio navigation systems. In the margin Carter replied: "One page summary to me."

On June 17 sugar appears again. Eizenstat indicates that processors were protesting the administration's proposed policy; Carter underlined "protesting" and in the margin wrote "good." On other items, Carter made brief comments:

> Combining DEA and FBI for drug enforcement—"good";
> Consulting Joe Pechman of Brookings and other experts—"How about consumer group experts?"
> National health insurance advisory committees meetings in Los Angeles and San Francisco—"Why all over the country?"
> Preventative care fluoridation—"Georgia passed a good law."
> Vote on a strip mine bill—"Tell Cecil [Andrus] I'll help if necessary."
> Lobby reform—"Be short."
> OSHA reform, Lance–Ray Marshall task force to be operating soon. Expect public announcement in two weeks—"Let me approve."

By June 23, the weekly report was eight pages in length and covered some sixty-three items. At the top, Carter wrote: "Stu: checked items most important to me." Twenty were checked: undocumented aliens, equal employment reorganization, Law Enforcement Assistance Administration (LEAA) reorganization, grand jury reform, world hunger, cost containment, Alaskan natural gas, water projects, Clinch River breeder reactor, budget, regulatory reform, Occupational Safety and Health Administration reform, lobbying reform, federal filmmaking, tax reform, *Adams v. California,* Veterans Administration, minimum wage, farm bill, and world nutrition.

Not only was Carter concerned with the nitty-gritty of his policy agenda; he frequently acted as editor in chief of his presidency, often correcting grammatical and spelling errors on the memos sent to him. On one occasion, he sent his staff a handwritten memo on a grammatical point: "There is a persistent error which continues to cause problems for Susan [his personal secretary] and *me* (not Susan and I) in correspondence and memos coming to the Oval Office. Please read the attached pages. JC."[41] Carter then included a page from *The Secretary's Handbook* dealing with proper use of personal pronouns.

A Tendency to Dominate

Carter's propensity to work from written memos rather than in face-to-face contexts compounded his difficulties, for its effectiveness was premised on a system to provide information and advice that was often lacking in the Carter White House. Early in Carter's presidency, David Rubenstein recalls, "I had the sense that he felt he could make the decision based on the paper. He could sit down, read these thirty-page memos and send them back, check off what he wanted, and that would be the policy process. If he had a couple of questions, he'd ask Stuart for some more information."[42] Later on, Carter began to understand that some of the nuances of policy could only be brought forth in meetings; as Rubenstein notes, "He had a sense he really needed to have more than just the paper."

Yet Carter's interaction with others when meetings were held was sometimes wanting. Many in the Carter administration noted a tendency for Carter to show off his knowledge and intelligence rather than listen to others.[43] Even a close confidant like Bert Lance sensed the problem: "There's something about sitting there [in the Cabinet Room] and he gives you the impression that he knows more about it than you do, then the chances are pretty good you aren't going to say anything." Lance even brought the problem to Carter's attention, telling Carter, "You don't have to prove you're smarter than anybody in that room any more. . . . You're not being well served by having all this great talent and knowledge and ability sitting around that table, that you intimidate into not telling you what they really think. . . . Don't intimidate them any longer. Let them express themselves."[44]

Even Hamilton Jordan had difficulty getting through: "I'd orally present objections and concerns whenever I felt them, but I also learned when Carter was governor that if I went into the governor's office to see him and had five arguments against something, I wouldn't get beyond point one before he'd be arguing back with me."[45]

But Carter's propensity to show off was not his only problem in such settings; many would leave a meeting without a clear sense of where he ultimately stood. Madeleine Albright, who served on the NSC staff and acted as its congressional liaison, later recalled that when Carter "met with a group he never really told them what he wanted. We all finally learned the trick, that when the President said, 'I understand,' that really meant he disagreed with the person."[46]

A Problem of Loyalty and Discipline

Perhaps the greatest difficulty Carter faced was not in decisionmaking per se but in managing the processes that led up to those decisions. Some of the problem can be attributed to Carter's own makeup and interpersonal style, but some of his difficulties here were again compounded by the absence of a chief of staff or an ability to delegate such tasks to others.

Carter was not without his strong points. "One of the interesting things about Carter," according to Bert Carp, another of Eizenstat's deputies,

> is that he really was both intellectually pure and very loyal to the people around him. A member of the senior staff could lose an argument in front of Carter and not be weakened in terms of the next argument. That helped to take a lot of this heat out. . . . Nobody would think that when you came back . . . you'd be in some inferior position on the next issue. That's a very important part of his management style.[47]

Carter also was not shy about making his concerns felt to staff either in written memos or in meetings he attended. Hutcheson's notes of the senior staff meetings, for example, contain a number of complaints that Carter brought to their attention. On a number of occasions he spoke about the excessive paperwork he was getting, the poor quality of staff work, missed deadlines, too many press leaks, and reports of infighting; on one occasion, he asked that "people not go through his IN box."

Yet while airing these issues, there was little in the way of substantive follow-through.[48] Many of Carter's assistants felt that while supportive, he exercised little discipline over his staff. According to Richard Moe, Carter "assumed that everybody would be a team player," but he "found it very difficult to be critical of those people working for him. Sometimes he would do it but it was very difficult personally for him to come to terms with this or to dress somebody down, let alone fire him. And as a result there was nobody really fired with the exception of Midge Costanza in the first two and a half years of the administration."[49]

Brzezinski's recollections are similar: "He didn't use people well at times, and certainly didn't know how to discipline them. . . . I managed to ease out four or five people and each time it was a battle to get it done."[50]

Moreover, Carter was not willing to listen to complaints coming from his staff or about his staff. Patrick Anderson, who served on the speechwriting staff during the campaign and the transition, recalls that Carter was somewhat averse, if not defensive, to criticism coming from the staff. Anderson had prepared a memo to Carter during the transition in which he cautioned against hiring "retreads" from Senator Edward

Kennedy's staff. He sent the memo to Carter via Greg Schneiders, Carter's personal aide. But Schneiders promptly returned the memo with a note: "Pat. I strongly recommend not giving this to Jimmy. I will, of course, if you want me to. I've experienced his reactions to staff criticisms on a few occasions and it is not pleasant. Jody [Powell] concurs. I suggest you talk to him."[51]

Yet perhaps there was a deeper current at work: Were Carter's problems of staff management related to his sense that, in the end, staff was not all that important? David Rubenstein, an Eizenstat deputy, felt that while Carter may have had a good relationship with his close aides, it did not always extend to second and third levels in the Carter White House. Indeed, it was his view that "on the subject of staff, Carter did not like staff. That was something drummed into me by people like Frank Moore, Hamilton and Jody."

In part his prepresidential career was formative, according to Rubenstein: "As governor he had a very tiny staff and he did so many things himself. He was so much into the details of things that he didn't understand what staff did." In part, the campaign contributed: "Carter basically thought that he and Rosalynn won the election by doing it themselves." In part, his inability to manage staff may have come from his own personality, both in distrusting others and in emphasizing his own skills and abilities: "I think he had a fairly distrustful attitude towards staff in general. I think subconsciously . . . he didn't want to have to acknowledge it in other people's presence or maybe to himself that there were other people who were actually doing all this work. He hated to think of how many staff people were involved . . . because he liked to think you didn't need that many people."[52]

Although Rubenstein's comments are telling about the effects of Carter's prepresidential experience—his confidence in his own skills as a decisionmaker and a tendency to downplay, perhaps even disregard, the role of staff—they also point to problems in his transition. Given a president-elect whose chief political experience was serving a term as Georgia's governor, the transition did little to prepare him for the role staff can play in the decision processes of a large institutional presidency and the workings of a broader political context with which he was little familiar. In some ways for Carter personally, there was no "transition" to the presidency from his prior experience as governor of Georgia. The transition, moreover, had done little to meld a decision process that could compensate for this weakness; indeed, one emerged that required more active participation on Carter's part, both in placing a management burden on him that he was not prepared to accept and in making him the focal point of policy analysis and political judgment that would overburden him.

Policy Outcomes

Carter's staff system, his use of the cabinet, and his own proclivities as a decisionmaker would come together in a series of policy decisions that got the administration off to a rocky start. Carter's difficulties in-house, moreover, were compounded by his difficulties in his relationships with Congress.

Problems with Congress

In sheer numbers, Carter was in an enviable position: sixty-one Democrats in the Senate and 291 in the House. Yet Carter took office during a period when Congress, in the aftermath of Watergate, was reasserting its powers. And Carter himself had won the Democratic nomination by running against Washington and the traditional liberal ideology of his own party. Few party leaders had supported him early on and few Democratic members of Congress (only 14 percent) had even been delegates at the party convention that had nominated him.

Carter's difficulties with Congress, however, are attributable not only to the political environment in which he operated but also to consequences of his own making. Carter's staff was a particular source of annoyance. As we saw, Speaker Tip O'Neill's problems with Hamilton Jordan stemmed from the transition, and they were to continue. "As far as Jordan was concerned," O'Neill observes in his memoirs, "a House Speaker was something you bought on sale at Radio Shack." O'Neill never forgave Jordan for the slight over the inaugural event tickets (he took to calling him "Hannibal Jerkin"). And O'Neill was particularly critical about Jordan's absence at political strategy meetings: "To this day, I can't understand why the closest man to Jimmy Carter, the key staff guy at the White House, didn't even join us at the White House breakfast meetings where we discussed upcoming legislation with the President."[53]

As for Frank Moore, the White House's chief legislative lobbyist, "he didn't know beans about Congress," in the Speaker's view. Indeed, O'Neill had a raft of complaints about how he was treated by the Carter White House and felt that many "came to Washington with a chip on their shoulder and never changed." In fact, "When it came to helping out my district, I actually received more cooperation from Reagan's staff than from Carter's," he recalls. "I must have told Carter about his inadequate staff a dozen times or more, but he never acted on my complaints."[54] Ken Duberstein, who served in the Reagan congressional affairs unit (and would become Reagan's last chief of staff), recalled meeting in early 1981 with one committee chairman, a Democrat, who showed him two letters from his counterpart under Carter. The first was dated January 21, 1977, and expressed a desire to work closely with the chairman in the future. The second, dated January 19, 1981, expressed pleasure at having worked with the congressman over the past four years. "The congressman looked at me and said he never saw that person between those two dates."[55]

A number of members of Congress were critical of the way Carter chose to organize the congressional liaison staff. Instead of assigning staff members to groups of legislators (as had been done under Nixon and Ford), the Carter staff was organized according to substantive policy areas; as a result members of Congress had less familiarity with White House lobbyists. One reason behind the change was that it required fewer personnel and thus could meet Carter's goal of cutting the size of the White House staff. As Charles O. Jones notes, it met Carter's "executive management" needs rather than the realities of "legislative politics. Thus, another opportunity was missed to reassure the Democrats in Congress that the new administration was determined to close the gap between them."[56]

Other members of Congress were confused by the unclear lines of authority in the Carter White House. Who's in charge? Who arranges favors? Handles recommendations? Listens to complaints? As Frank Moore told journalist Robert Shogan in the early days of the new administration, "There was a great sense of frustration among the Democrats on the Hill. People wondered, how does it work, who do you need to know? Do we go through Kirbo or do we go through Moore? Does Jordan really have the President's ear, or maybe Mondale is the guy we ought to be talking to. They wanted the game plan."[57]

The Carter game plan, moreover, was a complex one during those early months: a comprehensive energy plan, an economic stimulus proposal, welfare reform, creation of a consumer-protection agency and a new department of energy, reorganization authority, new minimum-wage legislation, a new urban policy, an ethics-in-governmental bill, a hospital cost-containment proposal, and changes in Social Security, to list just the most important items Carter wanted from Congress.

Water Projects and Pork-Barrel Politics

How political calculations factored into the early Carter agenda was a notable sore point in the administration's dealings with Congress. The most noteworthy was a flap over a decision to eliminate a number of federally subsidized water projects. During the transition, some sixty projects had been identified as potential candidates for elimination. To Carter, they epitomized wasteful pork-barrel politics. But to members of Congress, they were the kind of tangible projects that brought benefits to their home districts and state, political credit to them, and in some cases had taken years of lobbying and legislative logrolling.

In late February, just one month after taking office, Carter proposed that funds for nineteen of the projects, in seventeen states, be eliminated or reduced, pending a review of their fiscal and environmental soundness. Their cancellation would save $268 million in fiscal 1978 and some $5 billion over the long run. Carter had failed, however, to consult with congressional leaders or the affected members before announcing his decision, nor had much internal deliberation occurred, particularly about the political consequences of the decision. In Bert Lance's view, it was Carter's "first decision," and it "alienated about as many members of Congress that you can possibly do."[58]

On March 10, as the firestorm from Congress grew, Carter invited a delegation from Congress to the White House to explain his decision. It did little to help the situation; Senator Russell Long of Louisiana, the powerful chairman of the Senate Finance Committee, "shouted and screamed," while Senator Gary Hart of Colorado told Carter he had been "lied to" by White House staff members.[59] That afternoon, the Senate passed an amendment, 65–24, opposing the president's move and requiring the projects be built. The amendment was tacked onto a public works bill that was part of the president's stimulus package, thereby raising the price of a possible presidential veto.

Carter relented—but only a bit—by deleting three of the nineteen projects; then on March 23 he fueled the fires by announcing that fourteen more projects were under review. On April 18, following a White House review, the numbers again changed, with Carter's request that Congress kill eighteen of the previously authorized projects; nine would go forward without change, and five would be scaled back. In July, something of a compromise was reached, with nine of the eighteen projects halted and funds for twelve more new projects dropped. Carter had made his point, but so, too, had Congress.

Against the advice of Stu Eizenstat, Carter signed the compromise bill. "Carter, too often a captive of his southern hyperbole, had initially posed the elimination of the projects as a clear issue of morality and fiscal responsibility," Peter Bourne observes. "He was now compromising with the very forces of evil he had originally condemned."[60] In his memoirs, Carter would steadfastly defend his actions on the projects yet acknowledge that the episode "caused the deepest breach between me and the Democratic leadership."

But the lesson Carter drew was that he should have been more forceful in his opposition, rather than recognize the realities of congressional politics and factor that in as a necessary cost for larger policy goals. The compromise bill, "should have been vetoed. . . . It was accurately interpreted as a sign of weakness on my part, and I regretted it as much as any budget decision I made as president."[61]

A Comprehensive Energy Program

Another artifact of the transition was Carter's comprehensive energy program. Although Carter had spoken in general terms about the need for energy conservation and his desire to create a new energy department during the campaign, during the transition he decided a comprehensive energy program was needed and that it would have to be ready in three months in order to take advantage of the so-called honeymoon with Congress. Operating under Carter's instructions, James Schlesinger and a staff of fifteen labored behind closed doors to develop the plan. But Congress was not the only one kept in the dark; so, too, were agencies and departments and even Carter's own White House staff. Carter first publicized the need for a new policy in a "fireside chat" on February 2, then outlined the now complete plan in a televised address on April 18, followed by a speech before a joint session of Congress two days later.[62]

The proposal elicited some concerns in the administration's inner circles when its details finally became known. Vice President Mondale feared the political repercussions of higher fuel prices, especially on the part of organized labor. Eizenstat was concerned that Carter had abandoned his campaign pledge to decontrol natural gas prices and that the new pricing structures for both oil and natural gas were too complex. Blumenthal also worried about its complexity as well as the economic consequences of the plan.[63] Carter decided to press on.

Congress did adopt, in August, Carter's separate proposal to create the new cabinet-level Department of Energy. And the comprehensive energy plan made it through the House largely intact (with the exception of the standby tax on gas). This was due in no small measure to Tip O'Neill's willingness to create a select committee to handle the legislation rather than send parts of it to existing committees. But the Senate was another matter, and Majority Leader Robert Byrd, sticking to Senate rules, broke the bill up into separate pieces to be reported separately to the Senate following committee action.

At the end of October, five different bills finally passed the Senate, but they were, in a number of ways, quite different from Carter's initial plan and the bill the House had passed. The natural gas pricing plan was defeated, as were the so-called gas-guzzler tax on cars and taxes on crude oil. It took another year, in fact, for the final bill to be agreed on by both houses of Congress; Carter finally signed it on November 10, 1978. Some initial proposals remained, such as tax credits for energy conservation and efficiency standards for home appliances, but the final legislation eliminated the gas tax, greatly reduced the gas-guzzler tax on new cars, and rejected a crude oil equalization tax and taxes on industrial users of oil and natural gas. According to one study, because of these changes, Carter's "quest to redirect the nation's energy policy remained far from complete and in some ways had been compromised almost beyond recognition." In particular, the crucial provisions on oil pricing were defeated in the Senate, "and the plan's most important conservation measure (higher oil prices) was abandoned. . . . [It] served to make more severe the oil shock of 1979."[64]

The $50 Tax Rebate

Another Carter proposal emerged during the transition and ran into difficulty. It was simpler in substance but still controversial: his plan for a $50 rebate for each taxpayer. The plan had been devised during the transition by Charles Schultze, who was picked to head the Council of Economic Advisers. It was the centerpiece of Carter's two-year, $31 billion economic stimulus program announced on January 27; the rebate alone would total over $11 billion, more than two-thirds of the stimulus program's costs in its first year.

The rebate, however, was unpopular with conservatives, who thought it unnecessary, and with liberals and labor, who either didn't think it went far enough or favored instead a public jobs program to stimulate the economy. In March, it passed the House 219–194, but by then the unemployment rate had dropped to 7.3 percent from 8 percent in November, and inflation was showing signs of rising. Within the administration, OMB Director Bert Lance and Treasury Secretary Blumenthal began to have serious reservations about its merits, particularly in light of concerns raised by Wall Street. Even Schultze began to show doubts; in December he was 95 percent certain the rebate was needed, but now his certainty had dropped to 65 percent. Only Walter Mondale still thought the rebate was needed.

On April 14, Carter announced that he no longer favored the rebate in light of changing economic conditions. The decision was met with some relief in the Senate, where opposition had begun to develop (particularly as Carter was pushing the fiscal need to cut all of those water projects). But not all members of Congress were happy. Senator Edmund Muskie of Maine criticized Carter for breaching his promise to the American people and failing to consult with Congress before making his announcement. Congressman Al Ullman, an Oregon Democrat and the powerful chairman of the Ways and Means Committee who had led the fight for the rebate, felt that "I and a lot of other members put our necks on the line." Carter, in his view, "was a little less than fair to those of us who supported the rebate against our better judgment and worked hard to get it passed." Ullman was a particularly dangerous member to cross; as Frank Moore would note in a March senior staff meeting, "We're talking about ten or so major things [in Carter's agenda then before Congress] and eight of them have to go through Ways and Means."[65]

In a memo to Carter in June, Gerald Rafshoon, the president's outside media adviser, listed both the water projects and the rebate as examples of flip-flops that were hurting Carter politically. "Although you still are personally popular," Rafshoon noted, "your performance is perceived as inconsistent" and "the media talks about your flip-flops again." After noting the rebate and the water projects (as well as decisions on the B-1 bomber and inconsistent statements about Carter's energy proposal) as examples, Rafshoon observed that while individually they may mean little, "cumulatively they add up and *can* affect you politically."[66]

Integrating Politics with Policy Analysis

Carter's difficulties with Congress were in part a reflection of Carter's own judgment. He was always suspicious of politics as a motivating factor in his policy choices. As Richard Moe recalls, "He would reject any kind of political argument on any substantive matter. He would go out of his way to make clear that he didn't want to hear political arguments."[67]

According to Eizenstat, "We used to always joke that the worst way to convince the President to go along with your position was to say that this would help you politically."[68]

But Carter's political problems can also be linked to the decision-making processes that had emerged in his administration, particularly the lack of adequate integration of politics and policy analysis. In late March, Jordan sent Carter a memo that raised a number of issues about the policy process to date. Jordan especially raised concerns that Carter was working off written memoranda in domestic and economic policy and that they were "receiving much less of your time and attention than foreign policy questions." Jordan also felt that Carter was too reliant on his Economic Policy Group (EPG, which included Blumenthal, Kreps, Marshall, Schultze, and Lance) and that "they have not yet melded as a group into an effective mechanism for developing policy or presenting you with options on complicated economic issues." They have "different backgrounds and constituencies" and produce policies that are "negotiated out" and that are neither "particularly good nor necessarily right."[69]

Most important, in Jordan's view, Carter had failed to produce "politically credible proposals." The *"dynamics and composition,"* of the EPG, according to Jordan, *"does not lend itself to a balanced political consideration of the economic decisions you must make."*[70]

Jordan was not alone in registering his concerns about political credibility. Other staff members also noted the lack of integration of policy analysis and political strategy during Carter's first year and linked it to problems in Carter's staff system and decisionmaking processes. According to Landon Butler, the "only place where politics and policy at the highest level came together was in the person of Jimmy Carter. There was no point below Jimmy Carter where politics and policy came together." Jordan might have done this, but as Jordan himself later reflected, "It was never done across the board because I didn't have the substantive background to make judgments on these things."[71]

A Sharper, Leaner Policy Agenda

Prioritizing his agenda was another problem Carter faced, and it would have ramifications both within his administration, as policy overload developed, and without in his dealings with Congress and projecting a clear political message. In the same late-March memo in which he raised concerns about political credibility, Jordan also pointed to problems of agenda overload:

We continue to have a major problem in the coordination of the goals and objectives of your Administration. Each cabinet officer is pursuing programs and goals independent of one another and oblivious to the political relationships of their programs. . . . If we have several controversial programs before the Congress at the same time, a coalition of opponents will develop. We have to pace ourselves, relating our goals to a timetable that is sensitive to the problems of Congress and takes into account the need for public awareness efforts.[72]

In Watson's view, problems in establishing priorities directly affected Carter's success with Congress: "We clearly did have a problem in that the president wanted to do so much so fast. . . . We had too many things on our agenda for our own good. We needed to be a little more 'laid back.' We would have been more effective in the long run had we done so."[73] Bert Lance recalls that "we must have had forty or fifty things we were dealing with all at the same time."[74]

As with other problems during Carter's first year in office, his choices about staff organization were linked to his overloaded agenda. According to Eizenstat, the absence of a chief of staff or someone charged with coordinating these efforts was a particular source of difficulty in this regard: "There was no one to say well look now we can't send up hospital cost containment, welfare reform, tax reform, economic stimulus package, energy and so forth, all of which were going to the same committees at the same time. . . . What happened in part is a lack of internal organization."[75]

Change did eventually come, but it took until late 1977 when Mondale was put in charge of a year-end review of policy. The new legislative-priorities group under Mondale's direction, according to Eizenstat, "was done . . . in a very professional way."[76] By that time, however, Carter's honeymoon was over, missteps in his legislative agenda had become apparent, and perceptions about how this White House operated had been well formed.

Foreign Policy Decision Processes and Outcomes

By and large Carter's foreign and national security policymaking operated within a more clearly defined and orderly system, yet it, too, was beset with organizational problems that had consequences on policy decisions and outcomes. That system had been developed by Brzezinski during the transition. In December, he presented Carter with a plan that essentially replicated the elaborate committee structure that had existed under Kissinger, although with the proviso that the secretaries of state and defense, rather than the NSC adviser, would head up the groups. Carter rejected the plan, preferring a newer, simpler structure.

In January, Brzezinski presented a new plan. It created two committees: a policy review committee (PRC), usually to be chaired by the secretary of state; and a special coordinating committee (SCC) to be chaired by Brzezinski himself.[77] The latter would deal with "cross-cutting issues," arms control, intelligence activities, and crisis management. Brzezinski also proposed and Carter approved a procedure for organizing NSC paperwork. Brzezinski and his staff would prepare and organize most of the staff work, including the preparation of presidential review memoranda (PRMs), as well as gathering information for PRC or SCC meetings, preparing agendas, and coordinating the paper flow. If principals agreed on policy recommendations, Brzezinski would submit a presidential directive (PD) to Carter for signature. If no recommendations were forthcoming, Brzezinski, drawing on his own notes or those of his staff, would prepare a summary report for Carter.

It was an orderly process but one that would create difficulties. Secretary of State Vance "opposed this arrangement from the beginning, and I said so to the president." Vance was particularly concerned that participants were kept in the dark, since neither the PDs nor the summaries were circulated back to members, which "meant that the national security adviser had the power to interpret the thrust of discussion or frame the policy recommendations of department principals." Carter, however, backed Brzezinski and was worried about leaks if documents were widely circulated. He did, however, tell Vance he could come to the White House and look at the drafts if he wanted. "Given the enormous pressure on our time," Vance reports, "this was not realistic."[78]

Vance would note in his memoirs that he made a mistake in not pressing his objections more forcefully with Carter: "The summaries often did not reflect adequately the complexity of the discussion or the full range of participants' views." Vance often found discrepancies in the documents he did see, "occasionally serious ones," and sometimes "I had to go back to the president to clarify my views and to get the matter straightened out." When Vance left office, one of the pieces of advice he gave his successor, Senator Edmund Muskie, was that he insist on reviewing NSC-prepared summaries and directives in draft form before they were forwarded to the president.[79]

Vance was not alone in his concerns about Brzezinski's operations. Attorney General Griffin Bell, whom Carter asked to attend NSC meetings as a nonstatutory member, recalls that Brzezinski "imposed an order on the proceedings that took me by surprise. He would always summarize the sessions, and the six or so points he would glean from the discussions often seemed a highly personal view, especially when it came to resolution of problems. This prevented a free flow of ideas to the president in the national security area."[80]

Bert Lance, another nonstatutory member of the NSC, recalls that Brzezinski would try to keep him out of meetings by calling a "principals' meeting" on short notice and, at times, in Lance's view, when he knew the OMB director could not attend. Since they were for principals only, Lance could not send a deputy in his place. Finally, Lance confronted Brzezinski and told him if he couldn't be there, his deputy would, whether or not Brzezinski approved. "And if you don't like it, I suggest you go talk to the president about it and see what he says. I'm telling you this is the way it's going to be." There were no more conflicts between NSC meetings and other meetings Lance had to attend, he reports.[81]

Vance and others could rely on informal channels to get their views across to the president. One of these for Vance was his nightly report, which went directly to Carter for his evening reading. According to Vance, "I used this document to raise policy issues directly and quickly." In June 1977, often in lieu of formal NSC meetings, Carter began to hold weekly breakfasts on Fridays with Vance, Defense Secretary Brown, Brzezinski, and Mondale to resolve key policy disputes as well as to discuss broader foreign policy matters. The breakfast was preceded, however, by a lunch the day before where Vance, Brown, and Brzezinski would hash over the matters to be taken up the next day. According to Vance, these lunches became "somewhat routinized" with a "complex and too lengthy agenda negotiated in advance by the staffs."[82]

It is interesting to note that Carter thought his Friday breakfasts "didn't have a prepared agenda ahead of time."[83] Yet clearly much had gone on at the luncheon the day before. Furthermore, even Vance concedes that if agreement was reached among the three principals, "it would be extremely difficult for another point of view to prevail." Brzezinski notes another problem with the Friday breakfasts: "There was some disadvantage in the casual way some decisions were made and interpreted. For example, each participant would write down for himself the president's decisions as guidance for implementation." This practice would persist until 1980, when Carter finally had Brzezinski prepare a summary document.[84]

Although Vance and Brzezinski would eventually come into conflict, particularly as Brzezinski became a visible and outspoken advocate, during the first months of the Carter presidency consensus seemed to prevail. Both had reservations about Carter's "deep cuts" proposal in strategic arms talks with the Soviets (Mondale and Brown favored Carter's position, which the Soviets quickly rejected). But on most other matters, as Alexander Moens points out in his study of Carter's foreign policy decisionmaking, they "rarely disagreed."

Yet, as Moens observes, they "did not put the difficult questions on the table." "To make matters worse, the consensus more often than not was along the lines of Carter's initial policy beliefs"; as a result "Carter was not fully aware of the limits of his ideals." Moreover, where a John Kennedy could learn from his mistakes in the Bay of Pigs fiasco, "Carter does not seem to have learned anything from his early setbacks. SALT II, human rights, the neutron bomb fiasco . . . are all examples of this lack of self-criticism."[85]

A Lingering Problem of Staff Coordination

During its first year, the Carter administration continued its effort at executive-branch reorganization that had begun during the transition. As part of its work, the reorganization project undertook an analysis of eight early policy decisions, and its findings were highly critical of the decisionmaking process in each instance, citing poor staff work, unbalanced advocacy, and a general lack of administrative coordination.[86] In mid-July 1977, some changes were made in the broader organization of the EOP. Eizenstat's hand in coordinating domestic policy development was also strengthened; his staff was increased and he was given greater control over the memo process and the role of cabinet clusters—at the expense of Watson's cabinet affairs office.[87] Eizenstat finally got the organizational mandate that he thought Carter had agreed to back in late December. But as Shirley Anne Warshaw has pointed out, it had the effect of limiting the cabinet's role in policy development: "The cluster groups continued to meet on minor policy issues and on coordination matters, but had little direct responsibility for major policy initiatives."[88]

The reorganization project, while attentive to defects in Carter's decisionmaking process, did not address the central issue of administrative overload on the president and the problems generated in the absence of a chief of staff. As Hamilton Jordan would recall, "The first year was obviously a learning experience for the President and for the staff. He was . . . dealing with too many things himself."[89]

Effective coordination proved elusive throughout Carter's four years in office. Yet by January 1978, both Carter and his top assistants recognized that one person clearly needed to oversee the staff. Jordan was the natural choice, but Carter only named him staff coordinator, still reluctant to admit the need for and delegate sufficient authority to a full-fledged chief of staff. A year and a half later, in the summer of 1979 and following Carter's "retreat" to Camp David and his "national malaise" speech, Jordan was finally designated chief of staff.

Even then Jordan's efforts may have been too little too late. As Watson observed, "Dick [Cheney, Ford's chief of staff] said to me that he thought the spokes of the wheel model would be unworkable. I agreed with Dick. I knew President Carter wasn't going to start with a chief of staff and that it was going to be a matter of evolving into it. I hoped it would be sooner rather than later, but it turned out to be later."[90]

Even with Jordan's appointment, the problems did not disappear. According to Rubenstein: "When Hamilton came aboard he made a lot to do in the first couple of weeks but they backfired. Staff evaluations backfired, the firings which many wish never occurred [backfired] . . . and Hamilton of course got diverted." Although Jordan was "Carter's closest confidante . . . he had no administrative abilities."[91] In Anne Wexler's view, "nothing changed when Jordan took over. . . . [He] was a very nice, gracious, courteous young man" but "far over his head as anyone I have known."[92] Jordan's own view was that he was a "short order cook" who "sometimes burned the food."[93]

When he became chief of staff, Jordan brought in Al McDonald, who had been on Robert Strauss's staff when he was serving as U.S. trade representative and had been head of the McKinsey management consulting firm, as his administrative surrogate with the formal title of staff director. However, according to Rubenstein, "it didn't work out because Al didn't have the political backing nor did he have the support within the White House staff to be able to carry that function off." Carter "never did have a chief of staff system until Jack Watson became chief of staff [in 1980] but by that time it was too late."[94] And as Watson himself was to note, by the time of his own appointment, "the system had just been in place so long, and the grooves so deeply etched, that there was inertia even after a decisive presidential mandate to go to the chief of staff [system]. We had two and a half years of different operations, command, control, and communication. We were accustomed to our grooves."[95]

* * *

The fact that those "grooves" would prove so deeply etched for Watson provides telling commentary on how early decisions about organizing a presidency, selecting personnel, and crafting policy and decision-making processes can powerfully affect a presidency. Carter's experience is especially notable, not just for the effort that went into these matters starting back in the spring of 1976 but also for how both what is done and what fails to be accomplished can be consequential.

Although the 1976 transition cannot be regarded as one of the more successful of the transitions we will examine, it still had great impact once the Carter administration took office. It set the groundwork for a White House staff that was at best loosely defined and lacked coordination and discipline. Absent forethought and organization, what was hoped to be a collegial operation became compartmentalized. Communication became strained; weighing in on policy matters in an informed and timely manner became difficult; politics and policy lacked integration. The White House Management Committee neither functioned as a committee nor engaged in much management.

Some aides took advantage of the fluidity; Eizenstat, for example, began to exercise a measure of control over domestic policy, while Watson "made a nuisance of himself" and insisted on "crashing the party."[96] Others became bogged down in their jobs (Jordan most notably in those early days). But there were consequences: Eizenstat's effort reestablished a White House–centered domestic policy operation at the expense of Carter's hopes for a cabinet-centered process. As Jordan became enmeshed in personnel matters, his role as a source of political advice suffered.

The absence of much attention to how the cabinet might more productively participate in the policy process rendered Carter's hopes of relying on it as a source of policy advice more difficult, if not impossible, to achieve. Cabinet meetings quickly proved to be unproductive as a forum for collective deliberation. Problems of discipline and loyalty emerged. Relations with the White House often became strained. And policy efforts led by cabinet members proved disorganized and frustrating, such as HUD's urban policy initiative or the inability of Labor and HEW to agree on a welfare-reform proposal. Carter's cabinet would end up not much different from that of his predecessors, and Carter would experience similar frustrations.

As during the transition, Carter himself loomed large over the internal workings of his presidency and what issued from them. But, as earlier, the effects were often negative. He continued to be reluctant to vest real authority in any of his top aides; now that he was in office, that lack of trust yielded a compartmentalized staff. Artificial boundaries were created, with, most notably, policy and political "tracks" meeting only at the very top. Policy detail flowed upward, while staff management and discipline were neglected. Carter's hoped-for collegiality became difficult to instill, not only in the absence of earlier efforts to foster it or ongoing organizational arrangements to further secure it but also because of Carter's own interpersonal style in meetings, particularly his propensity to demonstrate his knowledge of policy detail and his hard work.

Yet in the posttransition period, Carter's freedom to maneuver became more constrained. This is perhaps the most important lesson of the Carter transition experience. The very system that he sought to create now came back to frustrate him. It now fell to him to monitor his subordinates' work—witness his weekly interaction with Eizenstat. Absent better coordination and communication at the staff level, the "tracks" of policy and politics fell to him to bring together. Lacking a chief of staff to whom to delegate some of the dirty work in staff management, Carter faced that task, but it was not one he relished or actively pursued. Carter wanted a collegial system and thought he was good at delegating responsibility to others. Yet what developed was almost exactly the opposite: compartmentalized rather than collegial; micromanagement rather than delegation.

The Carter experience is revealing about how, once in office, those organizational and personnel choices made during the transition create a context in which the president and his advisers must then function. Staff members get used to their compartmentalized niches, and alternative patterns of communication and interaction become difficult to instill. Turning routine staff meetings into a more collegial deliberative process is no easy matter. Coordinating the activities of those involved in the policy process where little existed before becomes a major undertaking. Bringing cabinet members to heel who have become accustomed to a degree of independence is a daunting task.

The fact that many of these were initially the *president-elect's* choices especially complicates the matter. Where the need for staff coordination is not recognized in the first place, it may take years, as it did for Carter, to begin to rectify the situation. Where infighting and conflict have been allowed to fester, collegiality may become impossible to instill. Relations between the cabinet and White House may never fully recover from a bad start, even when there are wholesale cabinet shake-ups as occurred in the summer of 1979. While transitions can offer positive benefits to be reaped, they can also serve as occasions when presidents come to suffer from the opportunities they have squandered.

Notes

1. These were Tim Kraft, special assistant to the president for appointments; James King, personnel; Richard Harden, budget and organization; Hugh Carter, administration; Greg Schneiders, special projects; Joseph Aragon, ombudsman; Martha Mitchell, service problems and D.C. liaison; Peter Bourne, drug issues; and Rick Hutcheson, staff secretary.

2. "White House Office: Organization and Responsibilities, January 1977," January 25, 1977, Staff Secretary Files—Hutcheson, Box 272, CL.

3. Rubenstein, Miller Center Oral History, p. 61, CL.

4. Carter, Miller Center Oral History, p. 9, CL.

5. Edward Walsh, "Central Role for Jordan," *Washington Post,* February 22, 1977.

6. Hedrick Smith, *Power Game,* p. 338. Rick Hutcheson did prepare an agenda for that first meeting. It listed four items for discussion: (1) general comments—Lipshutz, Jordan; (2) personnel, logistical problems; (3) review of policy on salaries; and (4) paper flow guidelines. Staff Secretary Files—Hutcheson, Box 248, CL.

7. Senior Staff Meeting Minutes, Staff Secretary Files—Hutcheson, Box 248, CL.

8. On January 30, 1978, Carter announced at a senior staff meeting that "he has asked Hamilton to hold staff meetings and coordinate things—to discuss developing problems at an early stage." Senior Staff Meeting Minutes, January 30, 1978, Staff Secretary Files—Hutcheson, Box 248, CL.

9. Dom Bonafede, "No One Tries to Roll Over Jordan in the White House," *National Journal,* April 16, 1977, p. 583.

10. Jordan, Miller Center Oral History, p. 20, CL.

11. Moe, Miller Center Oral History, p. 40, CL.

12. Carter, Miller Center Oral History, pp. 7–8, CL.

13. Butler, Miller Center Oral History, p. 21, CL.

14. Dom Bonafede, "The State of Carter's Union," *National Journal,* January 15, 1977, p. 91; Dom Bonafede, "Something Old, Something New, Something Black and Spanish Too," *National Journal,* January 22, 1977, p. 136.

15. Watson, Miller Center Oral History, pp. 5, 34, CL.

16. Kirschenbaum, Miller Center Oral History, p. 19, CL. According to Hamilton Jordan, "The mistake the President made was that he and his staff tended to compartmentalize problems and issues in the White House too much. Our organization reflected that." "Because of the way things were compartmentalized, I along with the rest of the people on the senior staff read about our foreign policy position in the *New York Times* for the first five or six months." Jordan, Miller Center Oral History, pp. 19, 53, CL.

17. Watson, Miller Center Oral History, pp. 5, 34, CL.

18. Bourne, *Jimmy Carter,* p. 372.

19. Kirschenbaum also recalled other instances where the policy process suffered: "We knew much more than Stu's people about the problems, benefits, issues and what you could do with CETA, at the local level. Stu's person for

CETA had come from the Hill, had spent a number of years at the Kennedy Center before, and was very theoretical about CETA. . . . We knew the reality which CETA faced, and we knew a lot more than did Stu's person who was working on that policy." Kirschenbaum, Miller Center Oral History, p. 9, CL.

20. Kirschenbaum, Miller Center Oral History, p. 10, CL.
21. Bourne, *Jimmy Carter,* p. 372.
22. Watson, Miller Center Oral History, p. 10, CL.
23. Eizenstat, Miller Center Oral History, p. 21, CL.
24. Moe, Miller Center Oral History, pp. 31–32, CL.
25. Brzezinski, Miller Center Oral History, p. 64, CL.
26. Bell and Ostrow, *Taking Care of the Law,* p. 45.
27. Warshaw, *Powersharing,* p. 110.
28. Eizenstat, Miller Center Oral History, p. 27, CL.
29. Eizenstat, Miller Center Oral History, p. 27, CL.
30. Moe, Miller Center Oral History, pp. 25, 43, CL.
31. Lance, *The Truth of the Matter,* p. 85.
32. Moe, Miller Center Oral History, pp. 29, 42, CL.
33. Carter, Miller Center Oral History, p. 54, CL.
34. Moe, Miller Center Oral History, p. 27, CL.
35. According to Bruce Kirschenbaum, "The forty or fifty of us below the senior and deputy levels had a harsher view. We thought that the president's major flaw was his paranoia about the Watergate experience." Kirschenbaum, Miller Center Oral History, p. 19, CL. For Eizenstat, the lessons of the Nixon presidency were also an important factor: "He felt the centralization of authority and power and a chief of staff during the Nixon era had been one of the things he had run against and one of the mistakes of the Nixon era." He "truly believed that Nixon had fallen into some of the problems he had because of this over-centralization, because the President was not hearing enough things from enough people, that he was isolated and so forth." Eizenstat, Miller Center Oral History, pp. 21–22, CL. According to Eizenstat, "He wanted to be the one that pulled the pieces together rather than having someone do it for him." "President Carter is a man of great pride. . . . He prided himself on that intelligence and felt that perhaps it exceeded that of the people around him and that therefore he should be the one to pull all these things together rather than having somebody else." Eizenstat, Miller Center Oral History, pp. 21–22, CL.
36. Watson, Miller Center Oral History, p. 19, CL.
37. Kirschenbaum, Miller Center Oral History, p. 19, CL.
38. Watson, Miller Center Oral History, pp. 4–5, CL.
39. Rubenstein, Miller Center Oral History, p. 61, CL.
40. Along with Eizenstat's first report, Hutcheson informed Carter that Eizenstat's effort duplicated his own weekly report to the president: "Mr. President: Virtually everything mentioned in Stu's report is recapitulated once a week in my follow-up report to you." Hutcheson then offered to merge the two reports. Carter agreed, penning in "OK" at the top. But Carter also instructed Hutcheson, "Do not remove items from your list until I personally mark them 'done.'" Memorandum from Stu Eizenstat to the President, "Weekly Status Reports," March 1,

1977, and note from Rick Hutcheson to the President, undated, Susan Clough Files, Box 36, CL.

41. Memorandum from President Carter to Staff, "A Matter of Grammar," September 29, 1977, Susan Clough Files, Box 40, CL.

42. Rubenstein, Miller Center Oral History, p. 28, CL.

43. In fact, Watson had anticipated this problem in his November 3, 1976, transition report, when he noted that Carter may be "one of the smartest men" ever to achieve the presidency, but there is a "potential danger in that circumstance . . . the danger of thinking you know more than you do, of not listening, of not reaching out, of not exposing yourself to vigorous give and take." "You must take time to listen and have different voices to hear." Memorandum from Jack Watson to Jimmy Carter, "The Executive Office of the President," November 3, 1976, Staff Secretary—Handwriting Files, Box 3, CL.

44. Lance, Miller Center Oral History, pp. 37–38, CL.

45. Jordan, Miller Center Oral History, pp. 64, 65, 67, CL.

46. Albright, Miller Center Oral History, p. 50, CL.

47. Carp, Miller Center Oral History, p. 13, CL.

48. At best, Carter told them that "if there are sharp differences among the staff" he would call a meeting to resolve it; that "Ham, Jody, and Frank [are] welcome to involve themselves as much as they wish in the early stages of decision making"; and that "staff should not hesitate to make minor decisions on his behalf. . . . He is happy to trust Stu's judgment—or if in doubt, give him a call." Senior Staff Meeting Minutes, Staff Secretary Files—Hutcheson, Box 248, CL.

49. Moe, Miller Center Oral History, p. 74, CL.

50. Brzezinski, Miller Center Oral History, p. 91, CL.

51. Anderson, *Electing Jimmy Carter,* p. 104.

52. Rubenstein, Miller Center Oral History, p. 76, CL.

53. O'Neill, *Man of the House,* p. 372. Carter also violated a long-standing tradition that, at White House meetings with members before 9:00 A.M., a full breakfast was expected to be served rather than the rolls and coffee that were initially provided. Congressional complaints quickly restored the old eggs and bacon (to which grits were now added).

54. O'Neill, *Man of the House,* pp. 368–369.

55. Kenneth M. Duberstein, "The Reagan Presidency: A Chief of Staff's Perspective," in Thompson, ed., *The Reagan Presidency,* p. 24.

56. Jones, *Separate but Equal Branches,* pp. 179–180. Jones points out that the issue-based system initially used to organize the staff was changed on the House side in May 1977 when William Cable was hired to head up House liaison. Also see Davis, "Legislative Liaison in the Carter Administration," pp. 287–302.

57. Shogan, *Promises to Keep,* p. 208.

58. Lance, Miller Center Oral History, p. 24.

59. Shogan, *Promises to Keep,* p. 214.

60. Bourne, *Jimmy Carter,* p. 415.

61. Carter, *Keeping Faith,* pp. 78–79.

62. The plan included a complex system of oil and natural-gas pricing, increased taxes on domestic oil production, created a "standby tax" on gas when yearly consumption targets were exceeded, imposed penalties on new vehicles with low fuel efficiency, offered tax credits for home-energy conservation, funded development of new energy sources, and offered some tax rebates to consumers due to higher energy costs.

63. John C. Barrow, "An Age of Limits: Jimmy Carter and the Quest for a National Energy Policy," in Fink and Graham, eds., *The Carter Presidency,* p. 162.

64. Barrow, "An Age of Limits," in Fink and Graham, eds., *The Carter Presidency,* p. 175.

65. Shogan, *Promises to Keep,* pp. 197, 230.

66. Memorandum from Gerald Rafshoon to President Carter, June 14, 1977, Chief of Staff Files—Jordan, Box 34, CL.

67. Moe, Miller Center Oral History, p. 63, CL.

68. Eizenstat, Miller Center Oral History, p. 60, CL.

69. This view of the EPG was shared by Bert Lance, one of its members during the first year: "We did not have a cohesive economic policy group. . . . It was beset with the internal fights about who was going to prevail and who in the eyes of the *Washington Post* was going to be the winner. That's really what they were trying to do rather than trying to do what was right and proper economically. So I don't think he was well served by the structure." Lance, Miller Center Oral History, p. 61, CL.

70. Memorandum from Hamilton Jordan to President Carter, undated, but from the end of March, Chief of Staff Files—Jordan, Box 34, CL (emphasis in original).

71. Butler, Miller Center Oral History, p. 36, CL.

72. Memorandum from Hamilton Jordan to President Carter, Chief of Staff Files—Jordan, Box 34, CL. As with other problems in the Carter presidency, Carter himself was also a contributing source. As Hamilton Jordan recalls, "President Carter—and Governor Carter—was almost incapable of seeing a problem and not addressing it. He had difficulty setting clear public priorities." Jordan, Miller Center Oral History, p. 19, CL.

73. Watson, Miller Center Oral History, p. 100, CL.

74. Lance, Miller Center Oral History, p. 39, CL.

75. Eizenstat, Miller Center Oral History, p. 34, CL.

76. Eizenstat, Miller Center Oral History, p. 50, CL.

77. In addition to the two principal committees, there were also lower-level, interdepartmental groups, chaired by senior agency officials, to deal with matters not requiring the attention of the SCC or PRC.

78. Vance, *Hard Choices,* p. 37.

79. Vance, *Hard Choices,* pp. 37–38.

80. Bell, *What Went Wrong,* p. 39.

81. Lance, *The Truth of the Matter,* p. 107.

82. Vance, *Hard Choices,* p. 39.

83. Hargrove, *Carter as President,* p. 26.

84. Brzezinski, *Power and Principle,* p. 68.

85. Moens, *Foreign Policy Under Carter,* pp. 48, 84.

86. President's Reorganization Project, "Decision Analysis Report," June 28, 1977, Jordan Files, Box 37, CL; for further discussion of the decision-analysis project, see Burke, *Institutional Presidency,* pp. 128–130, 132–133. Another report, dated June 3, 1977, noted in particular that "current arrangements don't consistently deliver the kind of staff work the president needed. . . . For each major issue he should receive a decision paper with full set of realistic options, fully developed, with pros and cons, and which advisers stand where for what reasons, all objectively stated." The goal of a "full staffing" of issues required better management of the information process, including drawing more systematically upon resources throughout the government, more timely development of substantive and political information and analysis, and clear opportunities for senior advisers to weigh in. The June 3 report was incorporated into a lengthier document issued on June 29. That report broadened its critique of the decisionmaking process. Jordan's performance was implicitly criticized: "Political analysis within the EOP . . . is not applied to decisionmaking on a systematic basis." The linkage between the White House and the departments was not working: "Departmental specialists have demonstrated high competence in support of EOP decisionmaking, but their involvement is not consistently included, varying widely across policy areas." Economic analysis was also falling through the cracks: "The Economic Policy Group is not fully effective as currently operating. This has resulted in inadequate staffing of the economic aspects of some issues." In addition, the report noted that "there is also insufficient systematic attention to follow-up on presidential decisions." There were some bright spots: Brzezinski and his NSC staff "operate within a tradition which encourages them to distinguish between the role of conveying views and information objectively to the President." In fact, the report recommended that the NSC's policy-review-memorandum process be adopted for domestic and economic policy. As well, the report made suggestions for strengthening political analysis, recommended wider sharing of decision memoranda, particularly with the OMB and the CEA, and proposed a unified system of paper circulation under the direction of the staff secretary. The report especially recommended that Eizenstat, as domestic policy adviser, rather than Watson, as secretary to the cabinet, be given primary responsibility for process management in domestic policy, just as Brzezinski was doing in national security. President's Reorganization Project, "Notes on Process Management and the Domestic Policy Staff," June 3, 1977, Eizenstat Files—Staff Office/DPS, Box 270, CL; President's Reorganization Project, Recommendation Memo No. EOP-1, June 29, 1977, Jordan Files, Box 37, CL.

87. On July 15, the White House sent its first reorganization plan to Congress. Changes in the organization of the EOP were essentially the same as Wellford had proposed back in December. Seven units were eliminated, with their functions assigned elsewhere: Council on International Economic Policy, Office of Telecommunications Policy, Federal Property Council, Office of Drug Abuse Policy, Energy Resources Council, Economic Opportunity Council, and

Foreign Intelligence Advisory Board. The Domestic Council was disbanded, with its policymaking functions assigned to a new domestic policy staff under Eizenstat's direction and as part of the White House Office. The Economic Policy Board was also eliminated, however Carter's message to Congress did not spell out how its responsibilities would be handled. The report proposed combining administrative support operations, about 380 personnel, into a central administrative unit, which would later become the Office of Administration.

88. Warshaw, *Powersharing,* p. 111.

89. Jordan, Miller Center Oral History, p. 36, CL.

90. Watson, Miller Center Oral History, p. 24, CL.

91. Rubenstein, Miller Center Oral History, p. 63, CL.

92. Anne Wexler, White House Exit Interview, CL. According to Wexler, Watson, by contrast, "was a real chief of staff," "far different" from Jordan.

93. Jordan comment at Carter Center conference, "Role of the President's Staff," March 21, 1995.

94. Rubenstein, Miller Center Oral History, p. 63, CL.

95. Watson, Miller Center Oral History, p. 27, CL.

96. Watson, Miller Center Oral History, pp. 5, 34, CL.

3

Ronald Reagan: Hitting the Ground Running?

Recognizing the Task at Hand: Preelection Efforts

Like Carter, Reagan and his advisers began to think about a possible transition to the presidency even before Reagan had been nominated as his party's presidential candidate. "We knew we would have to move decisively if we were to redeem Reagan's pledge of instituting important changes," Ed Meese, a longtime associate of Reagan who would play a central role in the transition, observes in his memoirs.[1]

Yet in many respects the Reagan effort, while beginning early, was to depart markedly from what Carter had done four years earlier. His would be a more successful transition with better organization and policy planning, with a clearer fix on crafting the decisionmaking processes for the new administration. The transition experience would have more positive impact on the early days and months of Reagan's presidency, but as had been the case under Carter, there were limits on what transition planning, in the end, would accomplish and in its ability to fully prepare for a Reagan presidency.

The 1980 preelection effort especially differed from what had occurred four years before. First, Meese (who would oversee the effort while serving as the campaign's chief of staff) set very narrow limits on what would be done before election day. He chose E. Pendleton James to head the effort; James was an old friend and corporate headhunter who had also served a stint in the White House personnel office during the Nixon administration.[2] But unlike Jack Watson's operation under Carter, Meese narrowly defined James's mandate: it was a personnel planning operation, not a full-blown transition that would ambitiously delve into policy planning, agenda-setting, and White House organization and planning.[3]

Second, it relied on a small staff. Initially James operated out of his own Los Angeles office, moving to Alexandria, Virginia, only in September.[4] James assembled a very small group, most of whom had connections to the campaign and had some experience in previous transitions. As Meese would later observe:

> There were a couple of people who had worked on fund raising during the primary campaign—like Helene von Damm—and since there was no need for fund raising during the general election campaign we put them together with Pen. It was a very small group—two or three—and then he had a few people that were working part time and who had been involved in previous administrations' transitions.[5]

Third, the campaign and preelection transition were more closely linked than they had been four years earlier. Meese took steps to carefully monitor James's work, often meeting with him early in the morning or late at night. It provided a measure of oversight and supervision that Jack Watson's efforts had lacked.

Furthermore, better coordination between the transition group and the campaign operation stilled some of the rivalries and tensions that had cropped up four years before. Although James's operation in Alexandria was physically apart from the campaign (the latter was based in Arlington), the facts that Meese was the campaign's chief of staff and deputy to William Casey, its chairman, and that James reported directly to Meese undoubtedly dampened the kind of divisiveness that had quickly formed between Hamilton Jordan's campaign staff and Jack Watson's transition operation in 1976. As Meese himself acknowledges, "The fact that I was one of the two top leaders of the campaign . . . there was a certain amount of good will and deference, that came out of that."[6] Helene von Damm, who had served on Reagan's staff for many years, was appointed to assist James, which may also have alleviated some of the fears among Reagan loyalists about being left out once the election was over.

The 1980 preelection effort was different from Watson's in another important way: although there was a brief announcement in September that a transition team had been formed, its membership was never publicly announced. "As a matter of fact," Meese would later observe, James worked "in total secrecy so that none of it leaked out to anyone in the campaign because we wanted them to focus all their efforts on the election."[7] The fact that James was not readily available to the media was a particular contrast to 1976, when Jack Watson's name and activities figured prominently in press speculation before the November election. Those in the inner circle, such as Meese, Casey, and Michael Deaver, also worked to still any public venting of dissension within the Reagan camp; according to one report, "The architects of the winning Republican's transition have so far clamped a tight lid on outward signs of clamor or disorder."[8]

While James's operation proceeded on personnel matters, the development of policy proposals that might be needed for a new Reagan administration had also been well under way—but under the auspices of the campaign organization, another departure from 1976. In April, under Richard Allen's leadership, some seventy defense and foreign policy experts convened to provide policy advice. By October, their number had grown to 132, and they were organized into twenty-five working groups. In domestic and economic policy, Martin Anderson had enlisted the aid of some 329 advisers, organized into twenty-three task forces.[9] According to one participant, Reagan asked them to begin to develop specific policy proposals because "he didn't want a six-month period of trying to get organized."[10] In fact, Reagan had raised the issue of preparing policy not just for campaign purposes but also for a possible presidency as early as his April meeting with Allen's foreign policy group.[11] Both Allen and Anderson, moreover, were veterans of the 1968 Nixon transition.

Organizing a Transition: The Postelection Effort

Meese had also been at work in the weeks before election day in organizing the transition's postelection operation.[12] His efforts, coupled with the absence of the internal turmoil and squabbles that had engulfed Carter in 1976, enabled Reagan to unveil his transition team at his first postelection press conference on Thursday, November 6. At the top was an executive committee chaired by William Casey, with Anne Armstrong as vice chair. Both had served as cochairs of the campaign. Senator Paul Laxalt of Nevada, a close Reagan friend from their days as governors of neighboring states, was named to chair a congressional advisory group, an effort to signal greater attention to Congress than Carter had undertaken four years before. Meese was named as director of the transition, and it was Meese who became the key figure in the Reagan transition. James Baker, however, was designated as a deputy director and placed in charge of White House planning, a key role in determining the organization and management of the future White House staff. With the exception of Baker, the top layer of the Reagan transition effort replicated his campaign team, thus potentially reducing the jockeying for power and position that had plagued Jimmy Carter. But it also was a leadership group that drew not just on Reagan's California associates but also on veterans of the Nixon and Ford administrations.

Under Meese, and at his suggestion, three senior advisers were appointed to three policy areas: Martin Anderson for domestic and economic issues, Caspar Weinberger for budget matters, and Richard Allen for foreign and defense policy. All three served in the Nixon administration, and all had long been associated with the president-elect. According to Anderson:

> Our responsibilities were sweeping, but not confining. On the organization chart we reported to Meese. But our charter cut across all traditional organizational lines. Our mandate was policy. It was unprecedented and unconventional, but it seemed to work. We had the authority and responsibility to involve ourselves in anything related to our issue areas—whether it was a question of who should get a particular government job, or what policy position we should take on any issue, or a question of government organization or press relations or congressional relations.[13]

The three senior advisers were only part of the highly organized transition effort Meese had crafted. In addition to Baker, six deputy directors were appointed: Michael Deaver, Drew Lewis, Lyn Nofziger, William Timmons, Richard Wirthlin, and Verne Orr. Deaver continued in his role as liaison to the Reagans. Drew Lewis acted as "special liaison" to the Republican National Committee (RNC), women's groups, the business community, and state and local governments. His office also developed a policy briefing program for cabinet-designates and senior staff. During the initial part of the transition, Lyn Nofziger handled press relations, as he had done during the campaign.[14]

Wirthlin used his polling skills to develop a broader strategic plan for the new administration, while Verne Orr was the nuts-and-bolts administrator of the transition. Other key figures in the transition were Peter McPherson, who served as legal counsel, Pen James, who continued to oversee personnel appointments, and Ed Gray and Darrell Trent, who were involved in policy planning.

Timmons's job was to gather information about departments and agencies. It was the most organized effort to date, and five working groups were established,[15] which were broken down into forty-eight task forces of some three to twenty persons. Each team was charged with assessing policy initiatives, budgetary and personnel matters, and pending legislation and legal issues.[16] Team members were cautioned that they held only temporary assignments, and once its final report was in, their work was complete.[17] Performance and effectiveness, however, varied. Some veterans of past administrations were particularly unhappy with the work of their assigned team, including Caspar Weinberger, Terrel Bell, and Alexander Haig.[18] The relationship of transition teams to the independent regulatory agencies was especially rocky.[19]

Although most had worked in the Reagan campaign, the top layer of the group was drawn broadly from various wings of the Republican Party. Some, like Allen and Deaver, were especially close to Reagan, but others, like Baker, Timmons, Armstrong, and Drew Lewis, had worked for Ford or Bush. "They are very competent," said one admiring Carter White House aide. "They're no strangers to Washington. They're experienced. They know their way around and they know what they want. They're more relaxed than we were four years ago."[20] Not surprisingly, reports also began to surface indicating discontent among the so-called New Right with the large number of former Nixon and Ford officials involved in the transition. Special concern was raised about the role—and possible high-level appointment—of George P. Shultz; concerns about Timmons also surfaced.[21]

The 1980 transition was a highly organized affair—in the minds of some it was overorganized—with a spate of committees, task forces, and informal groups. According to David Stockman, "Meese had a massive network of worker bees churning out voluminous reports."[22] The sheer size of transition staff alone was unprecedented. In December, transition administrator Verne Orr conceded he wasn't exactly sure how many people were working on the transition. He estimated that some 1,100–1,200 might be involved, with perhaps four to five hundred receiving some kind of compensation. Orr thought that there were about twice as many people involved as had been initially expected.[23]

The 1980 transition benefited from a concerted effort on the part of the Carter White House to make the transition both successful and amicable—in Carter's words, "to do what's right, to do what's fair for the new administration."[24] Jack Watson and Al McDonald were designated to head up the Carter team, with Harrison Wellford assisting on departmental matters. On November 12, Meese and Casey held their first meeting with McDonald and Watson in the chief of staff's White House office. This would be the first of a series of regular contacts between the incoming and outgoing administrations. Both McDonald and Wellford would later recall that their interactions were highly cooperative.[25]

But problems sometimes cropped up. Most notably, unlike the practice that had been established in the Truman-Eisenhower and Eisenhower-Kennedy transitions, no representatives from the Reagan camp were invited to observe firsthand OMB's preparation of the final Carter budget proposal. Carter's people claimed they were simply following the precedent they faced in the 1976 transition, but, as Laurin Henry points out, "Even so, this represents a deterioration in transition practices from earlier times, and one of considerable importance to an incoming administration placing a high priority on budgetary revision."[26] The final Carter numbers would, as we shall see in Chapter 4, draw Reagan's anger once he was in office and began working on his own budget proposal.

It is especially notable that not only was the transition up and running quickly after election day, but Meese was cognizant of the difficulties Carter had endured four years earlier and sought to instill cooperation and a sense of teamwork within the transition:

> The teamwork concept . . . we tried to carry through the whole transition. We would start each day at seven o'clock and between seven and seven-thirty we would have a meeting on the policy issues, with the policy people and occasionally some of our other advisers. Then from seven-thirty to eight we would have a meeting of the heads of the different divisions of the transition, such as Bill Timmons, Pen James, and others. It was more on the process itself and any problems that there might be. So there were these events on a regular basis to develop a sense of teamwork. Everybody knowing what was going on so that there weren't any mysteries or little antagonisms building up at an early stage, which is not uncommon in that kind of operation.[27]

Filling the Cabinet

Reagan and his advisers were well aware of the need to invest considerable effort and care in selecting the members of the new administration. This was a presidency with a clear ideological vision and a legislative mission, and it followed an administration of the other party (as did the Carter and Clinton transitions). But Reagan and his advisers would more clearly recognize the need to be attentive to a wider range of executive-branch appointments than had Carter. And unlike both

Carter and Clinton, appointments did not crowd out other transition matters, most notably staffing and organizing the White House.

The process for appointing persons to positions in the incoming administration varied according to the location and level of the appointment. Reagan's old California friends and supporters—the Kitchen Cabinet—played a role in cabinet-level (and sometimes sub-cabinet-level) appointments, although their actual influence was less than reported at the time. Pen James and his staff were the central players in lower-level appointments; by November some 30,000 names had been placed in a computer database, with eighty-seven key positions in economic policy areas identified and studied in detail.[28] Meese, Baker, Deaver, and James—sometimes joined by Laxalt, Bush, and Nofziger—made the final call and then forwarded their recommendations to Reagan. Meese and Baker, however, largely controlled appointments to their respective parts of the White House staff.

It is worth noting that the Reagan personnel operation encountered hurdles that had not been present four years before. It was the first administration to fall under a 1978 law requiring detailed financial disclosure procedures for prospective nominees, as well as new restrictions on lobbying and other conflict-of-interest activities both during and after governmental employment. To deal with these matters Meese, on December 8, created five teams of some forty volunteer lawyers to advise the transition on the new laws and help guide its personnel process through the new legal thicket. As Meese would later note, the new rules took their toll: "One of the roadblocks in recruiting people to serve in the administration was the maze of laws that governed federal personnel. . . . Dismayed by these bureaucratic demands, some well-qualified individuals declined to serve; those who persisted were subject to long delays in getting clearances. All of this made filling government slots difficult."[29]

Reagan's Kitchen Cabinet

In filling cabinet positions, Reagan turned not just to James's operation but to his Kitchen Cabinet for advice. The group was composed of longtime Reagan friends and supporters as well as members of the transition team; most began to develop their own short list of candidates. James (whose staff also provided a working short list of possible candidates) recalls meeting at least three times with its members at William French Smith's law firm in Los Angeles.[30] Caspar Weinberger, William Simon, Paul Laxalt, and Bill Casey also attended many of the meetings. Reagan attended two of the meetings, and James Baker and Anne Armstrong attended the November 22 meeting when Reagan was present. Helene von Damm, Reagan's former personal secretary and now a member of James's staff, acted as note taker. The group was especially influential in narrowing down the top nominees for cabinet positions. Pen James's "finished product . . . was our raw material," according to William French Smith.[31]

Yet shortly after the election, when James got wind that the group was meeting, he sought to limit its influence. At the first meeting of the group that he attended, James told them, "I've just talked to the President-elect. He asked me to get three recommendations for each post." According to Helene von Damm, who was there with James, "Now it would be clear that we were there to receive recommendations, not marching orders."[32] The Kitchen Cabinet would suggest, not dictate; Reagan would be presented with no fait accomplis, even from his oldest friends and political supporters.

The Kitchen Cabinet followed the instructions and tried to narrow the choices to a short list of three candidates, which were then presented to Reagan. The final choices, however, were made by Reagan and his senior advisers, meeting at Reagan's Pacific Palisades home. In fact, Reagan himself had essentially already decided on four appointments: Weinberger at Defense, Senator Richard Schweiker (R.–Penn.) at Health and Human Services, Smith as attorney general, and Casey as director of the CIA. The Kitchen Cabinet was also less influential in the selection of the secretaries of treasury and state. George Shultz emerged as the favorite for the State Department, but the fact that he, as well as Weinberger (already picked for Defense), were executives at the Bechtel Corporation worked against him. Reagan personally sounded out Shultz for a position, but, according to Michael Deaver, he never explicitly told him he was thinking about secretary of state: "I think Shultz would have been secretary of state except for the way Reagan handled it."[33] Al Haig (who may have been Reagan's choice all along) was next on the list. Former President Richard Nixon had lobbied Reagan on Haig's behalf, but some of Reagan's staff were concerned about Haig's own presidential ambitions, his role as chief of staff to Nixon during Watergate, as well as concerns about his ability to be a team player. Casey, James, Baker, and Meese met with Haig, who evidently alleviated their reservations; Reagan appointed him.

That William Simon (who was touted as the top choice—if not unanimous choice—of the Kitchen Cabinet) did not become secretary of the treasury is also indicative that the Kitchen Cabinet was less powerful than thought. Simon, who was strongly backed by the group, was blocked by former President Gerald Ford and Senator Bob Dole. Both reportedly felt that Simon was not a team player and too abrasive.[34] Donald Regan, the chairman of Merrill Lynch, eventually was offered the job, probably due to the support of Bill Casey, who knew Regan from New York financial circles and had appreciated Regan's efforts to save several faltering brokerage houses in the 1970s when Casey was chairman of the Securities and Exchange Commission.[35]

Some of the others who ended up with cabinet positions got them through the influence of a powerful patron, rather than the Kitchen Cabinet per se. Laxalt, for example, was influential in the choice of James Watt as secretary of the interior. According to Watt, Reagan had made two promises to Laxalt: one, that he could play tennis on the White House courts, and second, "that he could pick the secretary of the interior."[36] Senator Strom Thurmond successfully pushed the candidacy of South Carolina Governor James Edwards, a former dentist, for the Department of Energy. Bob Dole lobbied for John Block for agriculture secretary. In this instance, Reagan met with the two finalists, Block and Richard Lyng (who had been Reagan's state secretary of agriculture) and selected Block. On December 28, the *New York Times* noted that "roughly half" of Reagan's ultimate choices for the cabinet were "people he wanted from the beginning." The other half were persons his close advisers met and interviewed and then "agreed upon among themselves." The Kitchen Cabinet, on which much public attention was focused, proved to be "secondary."[37]

By Christmas Eve, the Reagan cabinet was in place, with the exception of secretary of education.[38] While reports had circulated about possible nominees, Reagan and his advisers had played the game more closely to the vest than Carter did four years earlier. According to the *Washington Post,* "The president-elect has managed to maintain a substantial degree of secrecy about the way he is going about the selection of cabinet members, even if he has not been able to keep all of the names confidential."[39] According to Pen James, cabinet selection was so closely held, not even his own secretary was aware of what was going on.[40]

Subcabinet Appointments

Reagan and his advisers also departed markedly from the Carter experience by keeping tighter hold on subcabinet positions. Whereas Carter turned over these appointments largely to his cabinet-designates, James and Reagan's senior advisers recognized the critical role of assistant secretaries, deputy secretaries, and other political appointees in the actual running of their departments and implementing the Reagan agenda. James's operation focused its attention on these appointments and offered lists of suitable candidates—sometimes even just one name—to incoming cabinet members.

But it also brought further conflict with the Kitchen Cabinet.[41] According to Joseph Coors, "We met with cabinet members a number of times to help guide them and give them suggestions for sub-cabinet posts. But there was some difference among the various secretaries as to their receptiveness to our suggestions."[42] The Kitchen Cabinet's involvement also caused difficulties within the Reagan camp. Following one of its November meetings, the group expressed a desire to move on to subcabinet appointments. According to von Damm, "Pen James was thunderstruck. 'Do they think they are actually going to choose the cabinet and the sub-cabinet?' 'No, no,' I assured him. 'They're just an advisory group.' But the truth was, I wasn't so sure."[43]

The issue of the Kitchen Cabinet's role came to a head in late December. William Wilson, who had taken over as chair of the group following William French Smith's nomination as attorney general, summoned Meese and James to a meeting of the group that he convened in Washington two days after Christmas. According to Helene von Damm's account, their complaints "were simple, and at least partially true. We did not take their recommendations as commands. We had not given them the feedback they wanted. Now we were not including them in the selection of the sub-cabinet."[44] Wilson told the group he was planning to move to Washington and help with the staffing, particularly at the subcabinet level.

James grew frustrated by their interference and, according to von Damm, quit and flew back to California. A few days later, James was persuaded to return to Washington.[45] Reagan and Meese, however, did not directly address the mounting tensions. Wilson, in fact, was able to get White House credentials and a suite of offices in the Old Executive Office Building. It was not until late February that the Kitchen Cabinet realized its advice was no longer wanted. According to Deaver's account, it was James Baker who finally figured out how to resolve the problem. Baker invited Wilson, Justin Dart, Alfred Bloomingdale, and Holmes Tuttle to meet with White House counsel Fred Fielding. At the meeting, Baker told Fielding that these were all friends of the president but needed to know the rules and regulations if they were to stay on. Fielding then passed out the financial disclosure forms. Tuttle said,

"You mean I gotta put all my financial assets down?" Dart, recognizing the situation for what it was, then said, "Fellas, I don't know about you, but they don't want us here. I'm going home."[46] Although its members would continue as social friends of the Reagans, the Kitchen Cabinet would never again exercise the influence it had wielded, or perhaps thought it had, while Reagan was in Sacramento.

The Reagan Cabinet and Presidential Decisionmaking

Reagan's attention to the cabinet did not stop with appointments. The Reagan transition offers the only recent example of an effort to think about the role the cabinet might play in the decisionmaking processes of the new administration. While other presidents-elect have spent much time and effort in selecting cabinet members, only Reagan and his advisers thought about and began to organize ways of making productive use of them.

Reagan's experience as governor provided the backdrop for what emerged. As governor, Reagan's practice was to delegate authority to his agency heads while using them as a collegial body to provide input and advice. At the time, some forty or fifty departments within California state government were divided into four major agencies; their four heads, plus the state director of finance and the executive assistant to the governor (essentially a chief of staff and a position Meese himself had occupied),[47] composed Governor Reagan's cabinet. The six cabinet members met regularly with the governor; following their joint deliberations, Reagan would make his decisions. This arrangement, in Meese's opinion, "had worked very well for the governor and really had been the forum for his decisionmaking. Virtually every major policy decision went through that process. So he liked that idea and wanted to bring it to Washington."[48] But Meese also recognized that the greater number of cabinet-level departments at the federal level, as well as the broader scope of their policy responsibilities, made simple adoption of the California system unworkable. An alternative model would have to be crafted, one that, while similar in operation, would provide the kind of smaller group that Reagan found more comfortable.

Executive Committees and Supercabinets

That alternative model began to develop during the transition. Reports that Reagan would rely heavily on his cabinet members in his policymaking emerged very quickly after the November election. At least initially, there was evidence that some kind of supercabinet, not unlike that proposed during the Nixon years, was envisioned. On November 8, the *Washington Post* reported that Meese had spoken of the need to streamline the cabinet by creating a smaller grouping of its members that would function as a "cabinet within the cabinet."[49] On November 13, the *New York Times* noted that plans were circulating to create a "Cabinet Executive Committee," which would include the president, the vice president, the attorney general, the secretaries of state, defense, treasury, agriculture, and health and human services, as well as the chief of staff and the White House secretary of cabinet affairs. According to William French Smith, who would later become attorney general, "An executive committee of the cabinet provides a diversity of viewpoints but is not so large as to be unmanageable. The idea is to defuse the role of the cabinet secretary as the advocate of his own department and to have him play a broader role."[50] In fact, in the Meese-Baker memo of understanding dividing up their respective responsibilities, both Baker and Meese were listed as "members" of such a "Super Cabinet Executive Committee." And Ed Meese would later recall that the recommendations of the Nixon-era Ash Council (which had proposed a supercabinet) weighed importantly in their early deliberations, as did the alternative idea of some kind of executive committee.[51]

The question of size was not the only one to figure into these deliberations; so did the question of teamwork—avoiding the parochialism of cabinet officers too closely tied to departmental perspectives and curbing the competitive relationships between cabinet members and the White House staff that had plagued previous administrations. In William French Smith's view, an executive committee would "defuse" departmental advocacy. Furthermore, press reports indicated that cabinet members would be given office space in the White House, "so that they might work beside the next president as members of a policy-making 'board of directors'" and so that friction with the White House staff "might be avoided by drawing major department heads into the inner circle of the president's closest advisers."[52] On December 1, in an op-ed piece in the *Washington Post*, Caspar Weinberger noted that such proximity would facilitate the "necessary coordination between departments and the White House," and—as did develop—"the whole operation would be served by a cabinet secretariat run by the counselor to the president to whom the National Security Council would also report."[53]

As weeks passed, the idea of some type of supercabinet began to fade. Appearing on ABC's Sunday-morning show *Issues and Answers,* Meese said that the Reagan team was still working on plans to restructure the relationship between the White House staff and the cabinet: "Plans are being studied to use the cabinet in new ways."[54] On December 4, Meese announced that the role of the cabinet had not yet crystallized. Appearing again on television on December 28, Meese suggested that instead of a supercabinet of a few top officials there would be something more akin to a task-force approach: "I think there will be various working groups within the cabinet so that you can focus on key ideas." At the same time, another transition official viewed the proposal to place key cabinet members in closer proximity to the president as a "symbolic" statement rather than as a proposed change. By January, Meese backed off from any predictions about a set plan: "In California, where we had a similar problem, [the solution] evolved over a period of eight years and I expect this one to evolve here."[55]

The issue of how the cabinet was to figure into Reagan's policy process also provided a major point of contention between Meese and Jim Baker—each of their own respective roles hinged on the outcome—and reports indicated that Baker opposed the creation of a supercabinet. On December 17, Baker told reporters at a breakfast meeting that it had not been decided whether cabinet officers would have offices in the White House, as some Reagan aides had previously suggested. Neither was Baker sure that some kind of supercabinet would be created: "Up in the air," he said. "I've been the one most outspoken against it." In Baker's view, such an arrangement would cause the remaining cabinet members to feel demoted, and it would have grave political consequences.[56]

Baker especially had reservations about the role of a select group of cabinet officials presiding over issue clusters: "What that does is necessarily downgrade the importance of the other departments. It makes their constituents mad and it makes [the] committee chairman up on the Hill mad. . . . Someone else—a deputy—will run that department and he'll become a strong lobbyist of that department no matter what his title is."[57] Left unsaid was its effect on the White House staff (and, by implication, the chief of staff): lessening its impact on policy and placing it in more a coordinating, if not subordinate, role.

Baker preferred the Ford model of more informal working groups, citing the Ford Economic Policy Board as a good example: it nominally had fourteen members and was chaired by the treasury secretary, but it operated through smaller, ad hoc groups of key officials, with the White House retaining a great measure of control over its agenda and deliberations.[58]

What would emerge in February as the cabinet council system was an amalgam of the Meese and Baker views. But its development during the transition is noteworthy, not just for the fact that extensive thought and analysis was put into the effort but also for the kinds of considerations brought to bear. There was a recognition of Reagan's own prior practice of delegation and group deliberation, coupled with a realization that what had transpired in Sacramento needed to be adjusted to the realities of Washington. This was not just a matter of size and manageability—the greater number of federal departments—but also a recognition of the problem of departmental advocacy and a tendency toward parochialism, a need to instill teamwork, a recognition of potential tensions with the White House staff, and the need to develop good coordination. As well, the deliberations and discussions—particularly between Meese and Baker—provide an early example (despite a strong difference of views) of mutually working out an acceptable alternative. It was a far cry from Jimmy Carter's experience four years before: a similar desire to make use of the cabinet but with little thought or even recognition of ways that might be put in place to do so productively. As we shall see in the next chapter, while the cabinet councils sometimes delivered less than promised, it was at least an effort to which some thought about organization and process had been given.

Crafting a Policy Agenda

Developing the policies of the new Reagan administration was an especially important part of the transition effort. Although Bill Clinton would also use his transition as a time for defining policy choices, the Reagan case is the only one among the four most recent to both undertake policy development and link it to a broader strategic plan. There were some difficulties along the way, most notably David Stockman's efforts to come to terms with the budget priorities of the administration-to-be. But overall it was an effort during which the groundwork for the Reagan revolution, for better or worse, at least had been laid.

In Ed Meese's view, the instructions here came from the very top: "One of the things [Reagan] wanted to do before taking office was to have those policy issues that were ready for decision—or at least tentative decision—presented to him at a briefing so that he could sit down with some of the major players. Welfare reform was one of them, some of the tax ideas." Reagan "did not want to wait until the twentieth of January to get into some of the preliminary briefings if not decisions."[59]

Reagan quickly benefited from the extensive array of task forces that had been assembled to advise him during the campaign. In Martin Anderson's view, "By election day the overall economic policy plan was set firmly in principle; during the transition our focus shifted from idea[s] and strategy to implementation and programs."[60] Over the weekend of November 15, Reagan convened a full-dress economic review meeting. George Shultz headed the thirteen-member economic policy coordinating group, a committee that Meese created to flesh out an economic plan. Following the meeting, Shultz publicly stated that Reagan would stick to the 30 percent, three-year tax reduction plan that had been announced in the campaign.[61]

Policy planning also benefited from Meese's initial efforts in thinking about and organizing the work of the transition. Early on, Meese established a policy research and development team led by Ed Gray. According to Meese, the group "produced position papers on subjects from welfare reform to crime, energy, the economy, and many others. Ed had served as Reagan's press secretary during the gubernatorial days and knew his mind very well. He was later to become director of the office of policy development in the White House."[62]

Meese established another group to oversee the policy work going on in all these various groups and committees. "With all the policy planning and research going on, someone had to keep track of the whole process, so I created the Office of Policy Coordination and placed Darrell Trent in charge."[63] Trent had been Martin Anderson's deputy during the campaign, overseeing domestic policy research at campaign headquarters while Anderson was traveling with the candidate. He, too, had served in the Nixon administration and was a senior fellow at the Hoover Institution. Trent's ostensible job was not to make policy but to analyze the information coming from the various policy groups, from Wirthlin's office, from Timmons's teams, from Laxalt, Evans, and Tom Korologos (who oversaw congressional relations), and other sources and to present it for review by the senior transition advisers: Meese, Anderson, Allen, and others. Martin Anderson notes, however, that Trent's real contribution lay not just in coordinating policy but in fostering its implementation by those who would be part of the president's team: "What was not written down [in the description of Trent's duties] was the real purpose of the Trent group: to educate incoming cabinet and other key members of the administration on exactly what Ronald Reagan's policies were."[64]

Building Bridges

Reagan and Meese clearly sought to strengthen their links to Capitol Hill, especially attempting to avoid the sometimes strained relations that bedeviled Carter four years earlier. Senator Paul Laxalt became

Reagan's representative to the Senate, while Congressman Tom Evans, a Republican from Delaware, brought together a group of Republican House members. According to the administration's subsequent self-study of the transition, Laxalt and Evans acted in a kind of "Godfather" role, "serving as a sounding board for ideas, visits, meetings and events dealing with Congress."[65] Meese also sought to bring some members of Congress directly into the transition by making them members of Timmons's executive-branch teams. This effort was blocked by the OMB, which saw congressional involvement as a violation of the separation of powers, particularly the access it might give to information that fell into the domain of executive privilege.[66]

Reagan had more luck in bringing several key members of Congress on board as foreign policy advisers. Shortly after the election, he established a bipartisan committee of four senators (Democrats Henry Jackson of Washington and Richard Stone of Florida, and Republicans Howard Baker of Tennessee, soon to be the Majority Leader, and John Tower of Texas, slated to become head of the Armed Services Committee) to advise him on foreign policy developments in the period leading up to his inauguration.[67]

Meese was successful in implementing one important linkage to Congress early on. An office of congressional relations, headed by Tom Korologos, was established on the first day of the transition, November 5, and worked closely with Laxalt and Evans. Unlike Frank Moore four years earlier, Korologos was a veteran in Hill matters, having served on the Nixon and Ford congressional affairs staffs and having spent a number of years as a lobbyist. The mission of Korologos's unit was "to make sure that during the transition, the president's congressional relations would get off to a start that would set the basis and tone for his relations with the Congress far into the future." The congressional-relations office handled all résumés and job referrals coming from the Hill, set up the many courtesy calls and visits by Reagan with members of Congress, and handled the confirmation process. It also conveyed information and set out Reagan's positions on matters that came up in the lame-duck session of Congress. While overall direction on the "big issues" was set in Meese's 7:00 A.M. senior staff meeting, the unit handled many of the "little things" that the Carter transition had ignored four years before: "tickets to the Inaugural, positions on minor bills, special thank-you's and the like."[68]

One organizational change that Baker, working with Wirthlin, made during the transition was to move the congressional-relations staff from the Old Executive Office Building back into the White House proper. The move, according to the report on the transition prepared later in the year, "indicat[ed] the importance the Reagan administration wanted to place on relations between the Congress and the White House."[69]

Reagan's own efforts to establish good relations with Congress were also an important part of the transition's efforts. As the administration's postelection transition report concluded in 1981, "The biggest successes . . . were in [Reagan's] visits to the Hill, the lunches in Blair House, the one-on-one visits set up with leaders early on and the excellent work of the staff in getting the Cabinet aboard."[70] On November 17, Reagan made his first visit to Washington, the primary purpose of which was to meet with President Carter. But while in the capital that week, Reagan also called on Republican and Democratic leaders as well as many other members of Congress, including a private meeting with Senator Ted Kennedy. The Reagans also hosted a dinner for all of the Republican senators and their spouses.

Reagan met with members of the Supreme Court and made a special visit to the headquarters of the Teamsters labor union, which had backed him in the campaign. Returning to the East Coast in early December, Reagan met with Terence Cardinal Cooke in New York, as well as a group of African American supporters. Throughout these weeks, the members of the Reagan transition—especially Nancy Reagan—also sought to introduce themselves to "social Washington," many of whom, while Democrats, had been ignored by the Carter administration over the past four years.

Strategic Planning: The Initial Actions Report

One major innovation in the 1980 transition was the creation of the Office of Planning and Evaluation under the direction of campaign pollster Richard Wirthlin and assisted by Richard Beal and Roger Porter. One task of the group was to determine "how best to allocate the president's time to achieve policy objectives." A series of memos was also written on the organization and function of presidential "councils" for policy planning and decisionmaking, as well as exploring changes in the domestic policy staff that would operate in this revised context.[71] It was yet another channel of information and advice about the administration's decisionmaking processes.

The efforts of Wirthlin and his staff were especially directed at planning an overall strategy for the new administration. Their recommendations were encompassed in an "Initial Actions Report." The report had been commissioned by Meese and Baker in a memorandum of December 12, 1980, to senior transition staff members. "All of us have given a good deal of individual thought to the initiatives that ought to be taken in the early days of a Reagan Presidency. Now we need to pull together these elements into a comprehensive action plan for the first 90 days. . . . We have asked David Gergen and Dick Wirthlin to work with each of you (and others as appropriate) over the next few weeks and from that effort, they are to draft a proposed action plan that can be reviewed with the President-elect by January 10."[72]

The report recognized the need to act quickly to take advantage of the honeymoon with Congress, but unlike Carter four years earlier, it stressed the need for a more focused and limited agenda, largely directed at enacting the president-elect's economic program.[73] Not surprisingly, Wirthlin was particularly attentive to public expectations about the new presidency and the need to carefully craft policy initiatives so that they met those expectations. Based on a 3,000-person survey conducted on the heels of the election, Wirthlin detected a public that was concerned about the direction of the country, was "hoping for change" and a "restructuring and redirecting of public policy," but was "yet to be convinced that Mr. Reagan's policies will work. The President's substantial communication skills are required to generate the public and congressional support necessary for their success."[74]

As part of this effort, David Gergen supervised a study entitled "The First 100 Days." The first part of the study was a fifty-five-page chronology of the various activities undertaken by newly elected presidents from Carter back to FDR. Use of constitutional powers, actions in foreign affairs, meetings with domestic political groups, travel and public appearances, and media activities were listed for each president; a comprehensive day-by-day chronology of all significant presidential actions during the first hundred days was presented for each president; and a twenty-page comparative matrix of each activity over the first twenty days was included.[75]

Wirthlin and his associates also developed a detailed personal schedule for the president covering his first four weeks in office. Although their suggestions do not exactly match Reagan's actual daily calendar, many of the recommended actions and meetings with congressional, business, interest group, military, and other leaders were in fact held.

Welfare Reform

One piece of the Reagan policy agenda was a direct product of the transition: welfare reform. It is one of the few cases in recent transitions where a major policy effort was developed and approved de facto before the president took office. Both as governor and as presidential contender, Reagan had strongly advocated turning control of welfare back to the states. During the campaign, Robert Carleson, who had been state director of welfare under Reagan and then served as U.S. commissioner of welfare under Nixon, headed a task force that developed an ambitious plan to transform some eighty categorical federal programs into six block grants for each state. Carleson then served as head of the transition team at the Department of Health and Human Services (HHS) and, early in January following his appointment to the White House domestic policy staff, met with Reagan. "In effect," Carleson recalls, "I received my own report," and with Ed Meese's consent, he made a comprehensive presentation to President-elect Reagan at Blair House. According to Carleson:

> I had a decision book prepared for him. There were eight or nine people in the room from time to time, but the only people who knew what was going were Reagan, myself, and my deputy, Carl Williams. It was about a two-and-a-half hour decision meeting. I remember one of the things Reagan said, as we were part way through, was, "Boy it's fun to be making decisions again!" I would go down through each item in the welfare proposal and he would approve them. He knew what I was talking about because we had been through the whole welfare thing in California for two hectic years, so he knew the subject very well. In fact I would come upon an item and say: "Remember this governor? When we couldn't do it because of federal law or regulations?" And he would say, "Oh yes, I remember that."
>
> I got a decision made on each of the pages. Thirty-some-odd items. I indicated that the first thirty or so would be for a welfare-reform program we would start in April of 1981 with a big announcement. The other three were for the following year or two, which would be block grants for AFDC [aid for families with dependent children], Medicaid, and food stamps. He approved all of those. Then he approved a recommendation that this be put together, the legislation written, and the regulations written and so forth.[76]

Carleson then told Stockman about Reagan's decisions, and the fiscal savings were promptly incorporated into Stockman's budget estimates.

At one level, Carleson's efforts indicate a more active and informed decisionmaker on Reagan's part than is commonly assumed, a matter we will discuss in Chapter 4. More important, it illustrates the advantages of moving early in a policy area where the president-elect and some of those around him already had a great deal of expertise and commitment. In Carleson's case that was especially needed, since welfare reform was likely to generate some opposition from those on the White House staff who were less-committed Reaganites.

In fact, that is what happened. On February 1, the *Washington Post* published an article on the administration's proposed changes, and Carleson recalls that when "I saw that story hit, I knew there might be a problem."[77] The next day, Carleson made copies of the key pages of the welfare proposal with Reagan's initials on them and "waited for the stuff to hit the fan":

> Sure enough I got called over—I think it was Darman and Gergen. They were very upset. They said, "You went around the system and you didn't get any approval from the president before you put this in the budget." And I said, "No, I had approval from the president," and I slid out my approval papers with his initials on them and the minutes of the meeting. They said, "When did this happen?" and I told them January 6 or 8. They said, "Well that was before he went into the White House and doesn't count." So I said—we were in the Roosevelt Room at the time—"Well, he's over there in the Oval Office, why don't we walk in there right know and find out if he approved of this." They said, "No, it's too late now, it's already in there."[78]

Reaganomics: Stockman's Transition Efforts

The transition also was a period in which Reagan's economic program took further shape. The groundwork had been laid by some of the task forces Martin Anderson had organized during the campaign, as well as by Reagan's own commitment to cuts in domestic spending and significant tax reductions (the latter was also embodied in the tax-cut proposal offered by Congressman Jack Kemp of New York and Senator William Roth of Delaware). During the early weeks of the transition, Weinberger had continued work on budget matters, while Shultz's economic coordinating group sought to pull the pieces together, particularly in reaffirming Reagan's commitment to tax relief. Wirthlin's strategic plan had also reemphasized the importance of budget and tax issues as the centerpieces of the Reagan policy agenda.

But it was David Stockman's efforts during the transition that would prove most significant. In November, Weinberger had sounded out Stockman for the position of energy secretary. Stockman, however, told him his real interest was in Weinberger's old job at OMB. On December 3, Reagan contacted Stockman and offered him the job.

Stockman "soon discovered," as he relates in his memoirs, that it would be up to him to "design the Reagan Revolution." He quickly found that while "everything was getting attention, nothing was getting priority."[79] He decided that he would fill the vacuum, and on December 19 he sent Meese and Baker a memo sketching out an action plan for moving quickly after the inauguration. Both agreed, and Stockman "had the ball." As Stockman realized, time was of the essence—a plan would have to be devised within ten to fifteen days of the inauguration—but "Meese had by now entombed himself beneath a pyramid of paper and disorganization. He never met a committee he didn't like." Meese, in fact, had created an economic policy coordinating committee that was designed to set policy. "The government's technical 'budget and auditing' work, as [Meese] called it, would go on in OMB. What [Meese] didn't fathom was that policy and the budget are inextricable. He granted me a much greater charter than he realized."[80]

One difficulty Stockman faced early on was in obtaining accurate forecasts crucial in determining revenues on the supply side and entitlement demands and cost of living increases on the demand side. Yet by January, no appointments had been made to the Council of Economic Advisers, the usual in-house source of such projections. Stockman attempted to muddle through, drawing on an interim forecasters' group, but they, too, could not reach agreement on the five-year scenario required by the congressional budget process. "This meant we would be flying blind for a while as to the precise size of the spending cut needed to balance the equation. We'd be scrambling to assemble the budget cut package while working against a moving target."[81]

On January 7, 1981, a meeting was convened at Blair House (with Reagan, Bush, Regan, Meese, Baker, Anderson, and Stockman attending) to take the first serious look at the economic choices that would have to be made. The first hour was spent on the "obligatory speeches" and questions to Alan Greenspan (whom Stockman had invited to attend) about how the Federal Reserve Board worked.

Stockman's budget presentation took the second hour. He came well prepared with copies of the first of his many briefing books. Using a chart, he showed that Jimmy Carter's FY 1981 "balanced budget" was already $20 billion in deficit in September, $38 billion by November, and, now, $58 billion by January—the latter without even figuring in the cost of the proposed tax cuts. Before Stockman could move to the centerpiece of his presentation, a lengthy session of Carter-bashing ensued, led off by Reagan's exclamation, "Damn it, I knew they were going to do

this to us. It just proves what we've been saying all along." Finally, near
the end of the meeting, Stockman hurriedly discussed the need for $75
billion in cuts per year, with perhaps more needed if the Kemp-Roth tax
cut plan, which was the congressional legislation that was the vehicle for
Reagan's tax proposal, were enacted. "I thought this would have a sobering effect. My message was that far more sweeping and wrenching
budget cuts than we had told the public about would be needed." "But
they didn't grasp that. . . . With the exception of Marty Anderson and
Alan Greenspan, no one in the room betrayed any comprehension of
what the federal budget looked like or how it was calculated."

Returning to his office, Stockman looked at Reagan's schedule and
discovered he had already used up a quarter of the time Meese had allocated between then and inauguration day for discussions with Reagan
present on the upcoming budget. "We hadn't even scratched the surface." The Reagan revolution "would not be a simple matter of 'limiting the rate of increase in federal spending,' as Meese kept phrasing it.
It would involve drastic reductions in dozens of programs."[82]

The fact that Stockman had begun so early enabled him to grasp
the difficulties of the task ahead. But his experience during the transition, particularly in getting others to take seriously the enormity of the
job, was a harbinger of the difficulties. The absence of reliable economic indicators and the delay in naming the CEA, a primary resource
on such matters, were areas where the transition process had not been
up to full speed.

Yet the transition had moved the Reagan policy agenda forward,
not only in beginning to shape key policies but in building bridges to
Congress and prioritizing a policy agenda. Whether it would work out
would remain to be seen.

Shaping the White House Staff

Even before the first cabinet appointments had been announced, Reagan moved quickly to firm up his top staff. Of the three recent transfers
of power to the opposite party, the Reagan transition, by far, was most
attentive to the organization and functioning of the White House staff.
How the top members of the staff came to their positions and how
those positions were defined offer an interesting glimpse into the internal dynamics of the Reagan entourage, as well as Reagan's own role
in one of the most important sets of decisions made during the transition period.

On Saturday, November 14, Reagan announced that Edwin Meese would serve as "counselor to the president" with cabinet rank. In addition to coordinating the input of the cabinet in the policy process, Meese was assigned supervision of both the domestic and national security policy staffs, the first time both had been placed under one aide.[83]

At the same press conference, Reagan announced that James Baker would serve as White House chief of staff. At least initially, press reports downplayed Baker's duties as largely "administrative"; according to one account, "his job, by design, appears to involve less power than traditionally associated with the title."[84] On November 15, the *Washington Post* described the division of labor as something of a "Mr. Outside, Mr. Inside" arrangement, with Baker handling press, Congress, and patronage while Meese handled the cabinet as well as policy development. Few were surprised at Meese's appointment; Reagan himself on one occasion had named Meese as one of the first persons he would appoint to his new administration. The choice of Baker was more noteworthy. He emerged as chief of staff, according to one account, "to prevent the suggestion that Reagan would rely on a tight circle of old California friends."[85] In actuality, the story was more complex.

Baker Becomes Chief of Staff

How the division of labor between Meese and Baker was worked out remains something of a controversy. Although he provides an extensive discussion of the transition in his memoirs, Meese is silent on how he came to be counselor to the president with Baker as chief of staff. In his book, Martin Anderson simply notes their respective appointments as "deputy presidents."

Several members of Reagan's inner circle apparently had doubts about Meese. According to one source, Bill Casey took a keen interest in who would be chief of staff since it would affect his access to the Oval Office as a likely high-level appointee. Although he "liked Meese" and "had become close to him," Casey did not feel that Meese had the managerial talents to be chief of staff. Casey reportedly told columnist William Safire, "Ed's too disorganized. He'll stuff everything in his briefcase. He'll take it home and lose it." Instead of Meese, Casey supported Baker, whom he had brought to the attention of Reagan as someone who could help him prepare for his debates.[86]

In his memoirs, Michael Deaver reports that he had spoken to Reagan about the possible appointment of Baker ten days before the November election while the two were alone enjoying cocktails at Reagan's rented farmhouse in Middleburg, Virginia. Reagan asked about the suitability of Richard Allen as NSC adviser. Deaver replied that he might want to think about a chief of staff first. That seemed to surprise Reagan: "I've always assumed Ed Meese would fill that role." Meese may be more valuable in another role, Deaver replied. "You need to think about someone who knows Washington, knows the way the town works." Reagan asked if he had anyone in mind, and Deaver replied, "Jim Baker." "That's an interesting thought," Reagan said.

Later that same day, Deaver called William Clark (who, like Meese, had served for a time as Reagan's executive assistant in Sacramento) and told him of the conversation and the need for someone like Baker rather than Meese as chief of staff. The problem in Deaver's mind was what to do about Ed Meese. "That's easy," Clark told him. "You make Meese chief counsel to the president." Deaver then went back to then-candidate Reagan and told him about the suggestion. Reagan thought it made sense.[87]

In their discussion of the events, Bob Schieffer and Gary Paul Gates indicate that Deaver had been working for months to get the job for Baker. An important ally was Stu Spencer, the California campaign strategist who had been instrumental in Reagan's first campaign for governor in 1966. By 1976, Spencer had strayed from the Reagan camp, running Gerald Ford's election campaign that year. In early September 1980, Spencer rejoined the Reagan team, largely at the suggestion of Nancy Reagan. While Meese and Casey planned campaign strategy from their Arlington, Virginia, headquarters, Spencer and Deaver traveled on Reagan's campaign plane, swapping stories, planning his schedule, and crafting his performance.

In early October, Spencer dined with the Reagans in Dallas and offered Baker's name as a possible chief of staff: "You're going to be in a new place and you need someone in there who knows the ropes. Washington is not Sacramento." Spencer then approached Baker. As Baker recalled, "Stu said he thought it was really important for the governor to have somebody who had been through the 'Washington experience' and he said he was going to talk to Deaver about it and then at one point . . . the three of us talked about it."[88]

Spencer also encouraged Baker to take over the job of preparing Reagan for his debate with Carter, and he lobbied for Baker to get the assignment. It was a crucial move. Not only did Reagan perform well—thereby alleviating some predebate jitters in the Reagan inner circle about how their candidate might appear at perhaps the most crucial moment of the campaign—but it also established Baker's skills in the minds of the Reaganites, particularly Nancy Reagan, ever mindful of those who were of service to her husband.

According to longtime Reagan watcher Lou Cannon, it was on the evening of October 29, following that very debate with Carter, that Spencer really began to press his campaign against Meese with Reagan. Spencer again ran down a list of possible candidates for chief of staff, including Deaver. Reagan, however, thought Deaver was better suited as the "number-two guy." Meese's name came up, and it was Reagan, not Spencer, who made the case against him: "Ed cannot be chief of staff. He's not organized." Spencer, who thought he might have a hard time dissuading Reagan from appointing Meese, simply agreed and offered Baker's name as an alternative. Reagan's response was, "Do you think he'd do it?"[89]

Reagan's role in the chief of staff decision may indicate a willingness to acquiesce to the machinations and court politics of those around him. Neither did he proactively explore alternatives to Baker. Yet Reagan, too, had a grasp of Meese's strengths and weaknesses, and he pragmatically knew that the fit would not be good.

Moreover, Reagan's positive response to Baker is a bit unprecedented in American politics and is revealing about Ronald Reagan. Baker had been George Bush's campaign manager only a few months before and had served as Ford's delegate-hunter in 1976. Yet for Spencer it was no surprise: Reagan pragmatically selected his aides for what he thought they could do for him rather than what they had done for others, even his rivals.[90] Spencer's own history with Reagan was testimony: he and associate Bill Roberts had been selected as Reagan's campaign strategists in 1966 because they were viewed as the best firm in California even though they had run Nelson Rockefeller's primary bid there against Barry Goldwater in 1964 and were anathema to conservatives.[91] Reagan's own ideological commitments notwithstanding, he wanted achievers, not just believers, and he had the self-confidence to enlist the services of even those who had supported his political opponents.

For his part, Meese began to think about the White House staff as election day approached. According to Deaver, during their last campaign stop in Pacific Palisades, Meese had asked him to join him for breakfast. Deaver describes the meeting as "a tense one," in which Meese came armed with an organizational chart listing himself as chief of staff, with Deaver placed in charge of scheduling, press, and politics. Deaver put Meese off, telling him they needed to get through election day first.

Deaver was further alarmed when he met with Richard Wirthlin, who confided to him that he would be on the White House staff and in charge of communications and political operations, functions that had appeared under Deaver's name a few days earlier. "I asked Wirthlin where he had gotten his information. He said from Ed Meese."[92] (In 1998, Wirthlin told me that he could not recall any such conversation with Deaver.)[93]

The day after the election, Meese called Deaver and said they ought to meet with Reagan to set up the White House staff.[94] Deaver knew what was coming and tried to duck out, but to no avail. Deaver and Meese met with Reagan for lunch, and Meese brought along the chart with his name penned in as chief of staff.[95] According to Deaver, Meese produced his chart, Reagan glanced at it, then told him the bad news: "Ed, I have really thought about this a lot, and I have decided to divide the White House responsibilities. I plan to make Jim Baker the chief of staff and you my chief counsel. Jim will run the White House and deal with legislation. You will have the policy shop." According to Deaver, Meese was deeply disappointed by the decision. As they left Reagan's home, Deaver told Meese, "Ed, I think this is the best for everyone and you ought to sit down with Jim Baker and work it out."[96] To his credit, Meese did precisely that.

An Agreement Is Worked Out

The next day, Reagan met with Meese and Baker and began to sort out their respective roles. Baker came prepared to the meeting and had drafted an agreement detailing their respective responsibilities. By November 13, Meese and Baker worked out a modus operandi and initialed a two-column list identifying their respective duties. Their appointments were announced the next day. Four days later, the memo was initialed again after the phrase "attend any meeting which President attends, with his consent" was added to each of their respective columns.

Although Meese would have a role in the cabinet and coordinate both domestic and national security policy development, Baker would coordinate and supervise all White House staff functions, have the ability to hire and fire all White House staff members, preside over meetings of the White House staff, coordinate the White House paper flow, and set the president's appointments and schedule. Baker would also occupy the traditional office of the chief of staff, while Meese would be housed in the NSC adviser's office that Kissinger and Brzezinski had occupied. Both had "walk-in" rights to see the president, but, as Schieffer and Gates observe, "with Baker's aides' monitoring who entered and left the Oval Office, Meese was never there without Baker's knowledge, yet it was easy for Baker to drop in without Meese's knowledge." Meese may have been given control over development of domestic and national security policy, but "he had been stripped of the necessary tools to make policy, to turn theory into reality. . . . Baker had given himself the levers that are necessary to manage the compromises" that would produce the real policies of the Reagan White House.[97] Baker kept his copy of the agreement with Meese locked in his office safe, while the more easygoing and trusting Meese kept his in a desk drawer.[98]

News of Baker's appointment as chief of staff was tightly held within the Reagan inner circle. As late as November 11, the *New York Times* reported that the consensus favored Meese as chief of staff, with Baker occupying a high-level position, possibly attorney general.[99] The reports proved unfounded.

Baker as Chief of Staff–Designate

News reports notwithstanding, Baker lost no time in beginning to organize the immediate White House staff. Even before his responsibilities had been formalized in the joint memorandum of understanding with Meese, Baker had already been placed in charge of White House planning. Baker thus immediately assumed responsibility for organizational matters that would have direct bearing on his job as chief of staff.

Baker moved quickly to assemble his personal staff. His chief assistant was David Gergen, who served as his deputy director, and Baker appointed Frank Hodsoll and, a bit later, Richard Darman as executive directors, with responsibilities for day-to-day coordination and, especially, White House planning. Both Darman and Hodsoll had worked with Baker when he was in the Ford administration. Baker also brought on board Margaret Tutweiler, who would become an important Baker aide through the Bush presidency, and Gergen enlisted John Rogers, who would eventually be placed in charge of White House management and operations. Baker undoubtedly had given early thought to assembling a transition staff. Frank Hodsoll, for example, had been working on the campaign staff and had helped Baker with the debates. Shortly after Reagan won and even before Baker's appointment was official, Baker told Hodsoll that "I want you to come in with me, so don't go anywhere."[100]

By November 12, 1980, Gergen had already forwarded to Baker a "variety of materials relating to the staff structure and professional staff positions of the Carter White House." Gergen's summary of the material clearly implied that changes would be needed: "One of the most striking features of the current structure is how many people have a direct reporting relationship to the President. They apparently do not report through the chief of staff but copy him on papers. In the past this has proved to be highly unsatisfactory."[101]

Three days later, on November 15, following his consultations with Jack Watson and Al McDonald of the Carter White House, Baker set up twenty transition teams to examine each of the units in the EOP. These teams provided him with management and organization information, as well as recommendations for appointments, and identified both long- and short-term policy issues. John Rogers interviewed most of the career White House staff, and a decision was made to replace most of the career appointees. On December 5, Diane Brokaw was placed in charge of White House personnel. She collected all résumés for White House jobs and maintained complete files for each individual. A personnel report was prepared for Baker each week and reviewed at weekly staff meetings. Any files not used were returned to James's operation.[102]

For his own White House staff, Baker turned to Hodsoll and Darman; both would hold positions as deputy chiefs of staff, with Darman principally serving as staff secretary. But for other top White House positions, Baker cast his net more broadly. He appointed Elizabeth Dole to head public liaison operations; Rich Williamson, an associate of Senator Paul Laxalt, was brought on to direct intergovernmental relations; and Lyn Nofziger was finally persuaded to join the administration and placed in charge of the political affairs office. Nofziger had been passed over as press secretary in November, and it was widely reported that he would be returning to California. When asked if he were surprised that he hadn't been asked for his advice about the incoming administration's press operations, Nofziger replied, "I'm never surprised by anything in this organization."[103] In January, as Baker was facing criticism from right-wing Republicans disappointed with the appointments to date, Baker jotted in the margins of one report that criticized him: "I . . . believe in political loyalty. Nofziger—my idea. Not loading up with Ford-Bush types."[104]

By the third week in November, Baker had begun meeting with former Republican chiefs of staff and other former White House officials, as well as with Jack Watson, Hamilton Jordan, Alonzo McDonald, and Hugh Carter from the outgoing administration. Donald Rumsfeld, Ford's former chief of staff, provided Baker a copy of his infamous "Rumsfeld's rules," and in his handwritten notes of their meeting on

November 20, Baker recorded several other important pieces of advice: "Make sure the 'other side' of an argument is always presented to the [president]; "Make the [president and cabinet] understand that the fail safe system exists, how it works, and that he breaches it at his peril."

Dick Cheney, another Ford chief of staff, was especially forthcoming with suggestions in his meeting with Baker on November 19. Some were organizational in nature: "Strong cab[inet] and strong staff in WH—not 'either or' proposition. Have to have both"; "orderly schedule and orderly paper flow is way to protect the [president]. Got to be brutal in scheduling decisions. Most valuable asset in DC is time of RR"; "Stay away from 'Oh, by the way decisions.' It's not in anyone's interest . . . and all have to understand that. Can hurt the [president]. Bring it up at a [cabinet] meeting. Make sure everyone understands this."

Cheney also offered Baker some suggestions on how to define his own role as chief of staff: "Be an honest broker. Don't use the process to impose your own policy views on Pres."; "Keep a low profile. You've got good credibility w/ press. Husband it carefully. If you become a major public figure—quoted all the time in papers—you lose credibility—feathering your own nest rather than serving Pres."; "talk to press—always on background."

Cheney also made some personnel recommendations, several of which would come to fruition: "Darman—good staff secretary—familiarity with gov't,"—advice that Baker would take; "Maybe Gergen as asst. to Pres. for Comm[unication]"—a post that Gergen would eventually occupy; "talk with [congressional] leadership re person for Congl. relations"; "Press secty: Doesn't have to be a reporter or journalist. Better off if not! What press really wants is someone who 1) speaks for the Pres.; 2) they can trust what he says. Not a press guy in Oval Office but a Pres[ident's] guy in press room."

Cheney also stressed with Baker the importance of obtaining full FBI field investigations on all White House staff (a problem that would plague the early Clinton presidency), as well as the importance of developing a code of ethics: "*Publish them*, conflicts of interest, blind trusts, etc."

On November 21, Baker met with Jack Marsh, who had served as a senior member of the Ford White House and was a former member of the House of Representatives. Marsh especially stressed moving the congressional liaison office back into the White House proper. It was another good piece of advice Baker would follow.

Jack Watson, in his meeting with Baker, especially emphasized the role of chief of staff. Watson offered four pieces of advice:

1. *Resolve disputes* that don't need to go to the Pres.
2. *Be an honest broker*. Make sure everything is staffed out.
3. [Chief of staff] is place where politics and policy come together. Make sure the political aspect, the p.r. aspect is looked at.
4. *Administer the place*. Run it.[105]

Baker closely studied the organization of the Carter White House and, together with Gergen, Darman, and Hodsoll, began to plan in December the organization of the chief of staff's own office. In one meeting with Watson, Baker went down the list of personnel in Watson's office, jotting down their duties and Watson's advice about how such functions might be changed in a Baker chief of staff operation. Baker noted, for example, that there would be a need for an assistant to the president for intergovernmental affairs and that he would "need someone to take charge of all the special assistants" to the president. Baker also noted that he would need an "overall deputy [who] keeps watch over meetings, makes sure they're held, really administers the place," but that Watson felt that he didn't "need both a [Landon] Butler and an [Al] McDonald." Watson also advised Baker, "Don't use this as a model, reduce it considerably!" And, "Don't try and be an alter-[president]. Don't build up a big personal staff."[106]

Al McDonald, Watson's deputy and the Carter staff director, also met frequently with Baker. McDonald prepared several memos for Baker and Meese on organizing the presidency, which drew upon his own experiences since August 1979 in attempting to bring better order to the Carter White House.[107] As McDonald would later recollect: "I indicated to them [Baker and Meese] that we were at an unusual historical moment and that if they wanted to get under way in an effective manner they needed to sit back and do some serious thinking about what kind of presidency they wanted and how they would organize it."[108] In his handwritten notes of a meeting with Baker at the Georgetown Club on December 5, 1980, McDonald recorded that Baker was "opposed to big 3 cabinet types but he hadn't talked to Weinberger—whose idea it is." McDonald also noted that with respect to the "division of responsibilities" between Baker and Meese it was "all to Baker except cabinet [secretary]." McDonald also "urged process/issues" management for the chief of staff.[109]

Baker drew upon a wide range of advice not only in thinking about his own role as chief of staff but more broadly on how the Reagan White House would function and the presidency would be organized. His job as deputy director of the transition in charge of White House planning granted him a broad venue—both the immediate White House Office and the encompassing EOP—even extending into parts of the staff system that had been placed under Meese's direction, such as the NSC and its staff.

Frank Hodsoll, a recently retired foreign service officer and now Baker's deputy, met with members of the Carter NSC to learn more about how policy papers were circulated, what kinds of staffing was undertaken, how the meetings of the NSC were organized, and even how cable traffic was reported to the White House.[110] Discussion and analysis was also undertaken about how the domestic policy staff had functioned under Carter and what changes might need to be made.[111]

Hodsoll was especially impressed (and surprised) by his work with the outgoing staff secretary under Carter:

> I have never forgotten what he told me when I asked him how he served his papers to the president, the process and that kind of thing. He said the president gets up very early, works very hard, and reads everything. He likes to "rake"—and that is a quote—"rake" through his in-box. I said, "No kidding," and went back to Baker and said evidently this is what is going on and that's what we've got to change. Ronald Reagan won't want to read through his in-box.

Hodsoll, along with others, interviewed members of Carter's OMB, Office of Science and Technology Policy, Council on Environmental Quality, and other EOP units, and a series of reports was prepared on those units. Hodsoll said: "Here's what they do, here's some things you may want to consider as you proceed in order to assure that the president is properly staffed." "Basically my job was to find out what the current situation was," he would later emphasize. "I was not looking at it from the point of view of what policy items needed to be addressed"—although Hodsoll, as a former foreign service officer, was centrally involved on the Iran hostages problem—"but more from the point of view of what did these groups do, how did the paper flow go, how could we assure that the president-elect when he did become president would have proper staffing and options and that there wouldn't be end runs."[112]

Baker also was kept abreast of the role George Bush would play in the upcoming administration. Following a meeting with Vice President Mondale, in late November Bush forwarded to Baker a typewritten list of "points to discuss per my visit with Mondale." It included such items as keeping Mondale's current office, access to domestic policy, "weekly scheduled lunch—*alone* with President"; "sit in on any meeting???"; "[troubleshooting] role as opposed to line authority"; and "lots of Hill action."

Dean Burch, a longtime Republican Party operative now adivising Bush, discussed the items with Meese and, in a November 21 memo to Bush, noted that Meese agreed to four key items: (1) "You and the President will have a scheduled weekly luncheon—no staff, no agenda"; (2) "you will automatically be invited to all presidential meetings"; (3) "you will receive a copy of all memoranda going to the President"; and (4) "you will have the Vice-President's office" (Meese also said Bush could have Brzezinski's office, which Meese was going to take, if he preferred that instead). On December 2, Bush sent Baker a handwritten note: "JAB III: Dean talked to Meese on his own, this is the result. I like it. In haste, GB."[113]

On January 3, 1981, Gergen, Darman, and Hodsoll forwarded to transition director Ed Meese a memo detailing their work to date on planning for the Reagan White House staff. They noted the staff appointments that had already been made and announced (including Deaver, Allen, Anderson, Dole, Nofziger, and Max Friedersdorf, who had been picked to head the congressional relations unit) as well as those decided but not yet made public (Darman as staff secretary, Joe Canzeri as assistant to Deaver, and Richard Beal as director of the office of planning and evaluation).[114] Allen, Anderson, Dole, and Friedersdorf, they added, were also in the process of selecting staff.[115]

The memorandum also outlined some of the management and organizational issues they were exploring. These included the organization and role of the public liaison and intergovernmental relations staffs; the organization of the domestic policy staff; continuation and/or reorganization of the Council on Environmental Quality and the Office of the U.S. Trade Representative. The memo also noted that "through various subterfuges" the Carter administration had increased the size of the staff and that while some staff reductions might be possible (particularly with the elimination of the Council on Wage and Price Stability and, perhaps, the CEQ [Council on Environmental Quality]), significant reductions did not seem likely. The report also noted that while the "Carter people cooperated well," they had not provided detailed staffing patterns for use by the Reagan transition teams.[116]

By January 12, 1981, Baker and his staff had produced a detailed checklist of actions to be taken so that the new White House staff would be up and running on inauguration day. The checklist outlined what hiring decisions remained, established a timetable for filling vacancies and processing the array of paperwork for those appointed, and set out what steps still needed to be taken in interviewing and possibly retaining career White House personnel. Each of the items was assigned to a specific member of Baker's staff for action with a set deadline date for completion. These jobs included both important issues (memos on paper flow and meetings, briefings on security classifications) and mundane matters (handing out office diagrams, changes in the phone system, and preparation of a packet on the White House mess and motor pool).[117]

Integrating Policy and Politics

Although Meese's and Baker's respective responsibilities had been divided up, the issue remained as to how they would be integrated and coordinated as part of a broader decisionmaking process. By December, it became clearer both within the transition and to outside observers that Baker's duties were more than merely administrative; in fact they were "political," broadly defined. In an organizational chart prepared on December 6, 1980, an arrow clearly shows that "appointments and paper flow" would go from Meese's operation to Chief of Staff Baker. As well, the chart indicates that Baker would control a number of White House units with important political (and at times implicitly policy-related) responsibilities: congressional liaison, legal counsel, public liaison, communications, political affairs, intergovernmental affairs, press secretary, speechwriters, and personnel.[118]

By mid-January, Meese and Baker had begun to think about how their respective responsibilities would operate on a day-to-day basis. Members of both groups would take part in White House senior staff meetings; following those meetings, Baker, Deaver, and Meese would meet daily with Reagan.

The ability to integrate policy and politics (which in theory, at least, partly divided their respective job descriptions) would prove crucial to the arrangement, especially in facilitating the smooth working of the Reagan staff system. So, too, would the role played by Mike Deaver—the third member of what would be labeled the "troika"—who was given responsibility for the president's scheduling, appointments, and travel and was liaison to Nancy Reagan and her staff.

Furthermore, the ability to pull policy and politics together in a coherent manner would turn on the working relationship among Reagan's three top aides. In public, Baker defined his role accordingly: he saw his mission as one of making the system "run smoothly" and his role as a "neutral broker," rather than as a policy advocate who would tread on Meese's turf. Baker also expressed sensitivity to the potential divisions and rivalries within the White House: "I am going to be concerned that those staff fights not occur."[119]

But the issue of whether in practice harmonious coordination would take place would await the new administration. It was no small matter, especially since some of Baker's tasks were not only more political but at times policy-related. To take just two examples, congressional liaison would involve him in the bargaining and negotiation processes with Congress that can directly affect the particulars of policy outcomes, while communications, speechwriting, and scheduling would draw him into the process in which the broader themes of this presidency would be developed, marketed, and sold.

The Reagan Team Meets

The efforts of Meese, Baker, Wirthlin, James, and others appeared to pay off when, in early January, Reagan returned to Washington to meet with his key advisers and his newly designated cabinet. As Ed Meese notes, "The culmination of the transition process occurred on January 7, 1981, when Reagan convened a series of meetings in Washington to review the work of the transition teams, as well as Wirthlin's plans, and to prepare for the incoming administration."[120]

On January 8, Reagan convened his first meeting with his cabinet-designates, an all-day affair held in a conference room at the State Department. Reagan told them to "speak openly" even if their views differed from his and, further, that they should "not feel constrained to speak only about something from their own department."[121] Yet he emphasized that he would be the one making final decisions. The meeting also included briefings by Meese and Baker on how the White House staff would operate, introductions of its key staff members, a presentation by Pen James on the personnel process, and remarks by Senate Majority Leader Howard Baker and House Minority Leader Bob Michel on congressional matters.[122]

Reagan again assembled the cabinet on January 19, the day before his inauguration. The agenda for the meeting included seven items: (1) an update on the Iranian hostage situation by Alexander Haig; (2) an update on succession issues by Ed Meese; (3) a report on the Freedom of Information Act by Peter McPherson; (4) a presentation on the Initial Actions Project by Wirthlin; (5) reports by Stockman on the budget; (6) a presentation on energy targets by James Edwards; and (7) discussion of the schedule for cabinet activities by Ed Meese.[123]

As the administration's in-house report on the transition would later note, these preinaugural sessions had "two primary purposes: to allow cabinet members to meet and commence working relationships and to commence building a schedule for the first part of the Administration. The Economic Recovery Program was a major topic of many of the cabinet meetings as well as briefings by various staffers."[124] By inauguration day, the new Reagan administration appeared to have "hit the ground running."

* * *

The Reagan transition bore some similarities to Carter's transition four years earlier. A significant effort had been undertaken to plan for a possible transition before the election was even over, extensive study had been undertaken of White House organization, management teams had been created to look at agencies and departments, a personnel operation was set up, and great effort was put into the process of appointing a cabinet. Yet in the particulars there were crucial differences. The preelection period was marked by more harmonious relations between the transition and campaign staffs, as well as more direct oversight and communication, largely through the work of Ed Meese. Pen James's tasks were limited to personnel, unlike the broader mandate Watson enjoyed, and James's efforts operated out of the media limelight. No press interviews were given, and few reports of his activities appeared; the various alarm bells that had disturbed the Carter campaign's inner circle about Watson's intentions did not ring.

There were developments brewing that might have generated considerable controversy, most notably the effort among Reagan's top advisers to make Baker rather than Meese chief of staff. But while it may have caused some personal disappointment, it did not trigger internecine warfare or lead to more permanent damage; differences were worked out, much to the participants' credit.

Meese had himself produced a plan for the transition, and immediately after the election Reagan did not delay putting it into effect. Although unwieldy at times, it created a structure that would, for the most part, facilitate the tasks at hand. Reagan's interest in using his cabinet as a source of policy advice, coupled with a concern for teamwork, manageability, and an avoidance of parochial advocacy, led to a lengthy deliberation and analysis of various models that culminated in the cabinet-council system. Whether they would deliver in practice, however, would remain unknown until after the inauguration. At the very least, Reagan and his advisers had given much thought to the cabinet's role in the administration's decision process, unlike the situation four years earlier, when there was much rhetoric about cabinet government but little deliberative reality. The cabinet selection process was also given due attention—but not to distraction. Reagan's longtime supporters were given input, but Reagan and his most trusted circle of advisers retained control (although not at some price to Pen James).

Baker's job of White House planning enabled him to get a head start on crafting an effective staff system. His efforts here, including assembling a staff, touching base with his opposite numbers in the outgoing administration, and drawing on the experiences of others who had been similarly placed, are perhaps a model among recent transitions. But his division of labor with Meese still needed to be worked out in practice, particularly in its apparent organizational separation of policy from politics and day-to-day management.

The Reagan policy agenda began to take definite shape during the transition as well. It was aided by a fleet of task forces that had been at work during the campaign and by committed Reaganites with a bent for policy matters, Martin Anderson most notably. The transition was attentive to policy issues, and it began the process of prioritizing the agenda and setting a strategic plan in the work Wirthlin and his associates undertook. It was a far cry from the laundry list that Carter presented upon taking office. Reagan also began the process of building bridges to Congress and the Washington establishment, another difference from his predecessor. Internally, the transition's congressional affairs office facilitated this effort; there would be no Frank Moores or seats for the Speaker in the upper balcony.

Yet the Reagan agenda was far from complete. As Stockman's travails suggest, general principles did not easily translate into concrete budget proposals. Neither did all of the principals, at that point, have a full sense of the enormity of the task ahead. The process had begun, but it was far from complete.

The Reagan transition is notable, compared to what occurred before and after, because the president-elect was most clearly its centerpiece but not its driving force. Reagan had provided broad policy direction, he had enlisted the commitment of true believers while also reaching out to more establishment Republicans, and he was the reference point as some of the decision processes were cut and tailored during the transition, the cabinet-council system most notably. Yet he was a less active force compared to other presidents-elect in the same situation. He had recognized the merit in appointing Jim Baker yet had not searched for alternatives; he was certainly willing to delegate authority but did not exhibit, at least during the transition, an awareness of the limits of delegation or the managerial needs that arise in its wake. We see little imprint of Reagan, in particular, on the Meese-Baker division of labor or on the ways each man organized his respective operations. For Reagan, the test would be, first, whether the arrangement itself was fundamentally sound in the way staff responsibilities had been parceled out; and second, whether he could rely on the skills and expertise of those he had selected and whether such trust would be repaid in competence and in securing the policies to which he was so deeply committed.

Notes

1. Meese, *With Reagan,* p. 57. Meese had worked in Reagan's political campaigns and in his gubernatorial administration; most notably he served for a time as his executive assistant, in effect his chief of staff.

2. Late in 1979, Meese and James met for lunch at the California Club in Los Angeles. Meese told him that "there was one thing that I felt we ought to do, and that was that in the event we won, the one task that couldn't just be put together on election day was planning the whole personnel aspect [of the new administration]." Burke interview with Ed Meese, May 27, 1998. According to James, Meese didn't want to ask, the day after the November election, as most presidents-elect had done, "What do we do now?" James, White House Exit Interview, Reagan Presidential Library, Simi Valley, California (hereafter cited as RL). In the spring of 1980, as Reagan locked up the Republican nomination, James and Meese again chatted, and the subject again came up. "He asked if I were serious," Meese later recalled. "I assured him that I was, and he began quietly to plan for a personnel operation from his Los Angeles office." Meese, *With Reagan,* p. 57.

3. According to Meese, "Their purpose was to identify the appointments that would have to be made. Secondly, to look at what prior administrations had done, to see what were the problems, what were the techniques that might be helpful, and then to plan a process for the handling of personnel." Meese was quite aware of the difficulties generated four years earlier by Watson's broader mandate. "We were cognizant," he recalled, "that in the Carter administration there had been a certain amount of jockeying for positions even before election day," which detracted from the election campaign. Yet Meese also knew, from talking to Martin Anderson and Richard Allen (then serving as policy advisers), of the problems they had experienced in the Nixon transition of 1968: "They said that one of the major problems they had was dealing with all the personnel appointments. They got all kinds of résumés, all kinds of congressmen calling, and they had to get these positions filled. There was a lot of confusion." So Meese "talked it over with Bill Casey [the campaign's director], and we agreed that this was one thing [a personnel operation] that ought to be an exception, so that at least we had a plan in place and weren't in the

same position that some of the other administrations were in." Burke interview with Ed Meese, May 27, 1998.

4. Over the summer of 1980, the Reagan campaign was successful (unlike Carter four years earlier) in obtaining a favorable ruling from the Federal Elections Commission allowing it to raise private funds for the transition, as long as its operations were kept separate from the campaign. In September, the Presidential Transition Trust was formed and housed in the former headquarters of the Bush campaign in Alexandria, Virginia.

5. Burke interview with Ed Meese, May 27, 1998.

6. Burke interview with Ed Meese, May 27, 1998.

7. Burke interview with Ed Meese, May 27, 1998.

8. Dick Kirschten, "The Reagan Team Comes to Washington, Ready to Get Off to a Running Start," *National Journal,* November 15, 1980, p. 1924.

9. In the area of economic policy, which was to emerge as central during Reagan's first two years in office, Reagan drew on an impressive array of advisers. Indeed, as far back as 1975, Anderson had organized a group of leading economists to advise Reagan: Milton Friedman from Chicago, C. Lowell Harriss from Columbia, Hendrick Houthakker from Harvard, Arthur Laffer from Chicago, J. Claburn LaForce from UCLA, Richard Muth and Ezra Solomon from Stanford, Murray Weidenbaum from Washington University, and William Niskanen from Ford Motor Company. Only Marina von Neuman Whitman, a professor at the University of Pittsburgh and former member of Nixon's CEA, declined Anderson's invitation; Whitman threw her lot in with Jimmy Carter. In 1980, Anderson created six task forces in economic policy and a comprehensive economic policy coordinating committee, chaired by George Shultz. The chairs of each of the six policy task forces were Arthur Burns (international monetary policy), Alan Greenspan (budget policy), Paul McCracken (inflation), Charles Walker (tax policy), Murray Weidenbaum (regulatory reform), and Caspar Weinberger (spending control). Reagan, according to Anderson, had seventy-four advisers on economic policy alone, including Milton Friedman, Jack Kemp, William Simon, and Walter Wriston. Anderson, *Revolution,* p. 171.

10. Dick Kirschten, "The Reagan Team Comes to Washington, Ready to Get Off to a Running Start," *National Journal,* November 15, 1980, p. 1925.

11. Laurin Henry, "The Transition: From Nomination to Inauguration," in David and Everson, eds., *The Presidential Election and Transition, 1980–1981,* p. 198. The Reagan policy effort also benefited from the efforts of the conservative Heritage Foundation, to which a number of them were connected (especially Meese). Over the summer, Heritage prepared a 3,000-page report on policies, programs, and personnel that it hoped would serve as a blueprint for the new administration; the Heritage study was widely disseminated among Reagan advisers.

12. Before the election, Meese also began the process of locating space for a possible postelection transition operation. Washington attorney Peter McPherson was assigned the task, and he obtained seven floors of an office building at 1726 M Street, NW. The General Services Administration also provided space

for the vice president–elect's transition in a building at 734 Jackson Place, NW, and in unused office space in the New Executive Office Building. Perhaps not coincidentally, the building selected was located next to the headquarters of the American Enterprise Institute, often regarded as the conservative counterpart to the Brookings Institution. On November 4, election day, phone-company workers began to install equipment even before the returns came in. Since Reagan would likely remain in California during much of the transition, Meese also began to set up a West Coast branch of the transition, which was eventually housed directly across the street from Reagan's Pacific Palisades home.

13. Anderson, *Revolution,* p. 204.

14. However, Meese combined all press functions together and designated Robert Garrick as director of an office of public affairs. This included the press operations on the East Coast run by James Brady and in California by Joe Holmes. Press briefings were held by both Holmes and Brady on a daily basis, and they were supplemented by press briefings given by Meese approximately every third morning.

15. The five groups were: economic affairs, national security, resources and development, human services, and legal and administrative.

16. David Abshire, a former assistant secretary of state under Nixon and head of Georgetown University's Center for Strategic and International Studies, was assigned national security. Stanton Anderson, a former Nixon White House official and deputy assistant secretary of state, was assigned economic affairs. Elizabeth Dole, the wife of Kansas Senator Robert Dole and a former federal trade commissioner, was given human services. Richard Fairbanks, a former associate director of President Ford's Domestic Council, was assigned natural resources and development. Lorne Smith, a law professor at Widener University and counsel to the Reagan campaign committee, was assigned legal and administrative agencies. Assisting Timmons were Montana businessman Frank Whetstone as senior adviser, Stanley Ebner, a vice president of Northrop Corporation and former counsel to the OMB, as coordinator, and John Nugent, a business associate of Timmons, as assistant. Team leaders were also selected for each of the cabinet departments: State—Robert E. Neumann; Defense— William R. Van Cleave; Treasury—Gerald Parsky; Justice—Richard Wiley; Interior—Richard Richards; Commerce—Calvin Collier; Agriculture—Richard Lyng; Labor—Richard Shubert; HHS—Robert Carleson; Transportation— Arthur Teele; Energy—Michael Halbouty; Education—Lorelei Kinder; HUD—Gerald Carmen. T. R. Reid, "Transition Office Chooses 13 Team Leaders," *Washington Post,* November 14, 1980.

17. Each team was instructed to prepare three reports. The initial report was due November 24, 1980. Given the accelerated deadline, it was seen as a "test run" and "was used to gauge the level of information available from the departments and agencies." It also "provided a measure of the competence of each team and the individuals on the team." The second report was due on December 8 and stressed budget and personnel issues. The final report was due on December 22 and contained team recommendations. "It was this report

which was used by the Cabinet designees since many of them were formally announced at this time." Draft Report, "Transition of the President and the President-Elect," Meese Files, OA 5097, p. 37, RL.

18. Weinberger, *Fighting for Peace,* p. 41; Terrel Bell, *The Thirteenth Man,* p. 41.

19. According to the administration's transition study, "When the Reagan transition team first appeared at the Federal Commerce Commission, it was told, politely, that it had no business being there." Others were more cooperative: "The CPSC [Consumer Product Safety Commission] felt threatened by the new administration, especially with its organic legislation up for renewal in the spring of 1981. They provided space, secretarial help, and full access to all public information." "The change of leadership in the Senate . . . increased the feeling of vulnerability among the independents." Draft Report, "Transition of the President and the President-Elect," Meese Files, OA5097, pp. 47, 49, RL. Danny Boggs, who headed the team for the Federal Energy Regulatory Commission (FERC), felt his counterparts at the agency were quite cooperative. Boggs's situation may have been unique, however; Boggs had been assistant to the chairman of the old Federal Power Commission, which had been reorganized into FERC, and knew a number of staff members there. Burke interview with Danny Boggs, June 17, 1998. Transition teams also encountered some resistance from lower-level Carter administration officials. At the Energy Department, for example, Carter officials reportedly refused to provide information about pending enforcement cases to a transition team headed by oil producer Michael Halbouty. At Agriculture, Assistant Secretary Carol Tucker Foreman refused to divulge pending regulatory rules and papers dealing with legal strategy in pending litigation concerning labeling pork products to Donald Van Houweling, a lobbyist for the National Pork Producers Council then serving on the transition team headed by Richard Lyng, a past president of the American Meat Institute. Related concerns were raised in the Defense and Labor Departments. Dick Kirschten, "Spinning the Revolving Door," *National Journal,* December 13, 1980, p. 2128.

20. Hedrick Smith, "Transition Shaping Up as a Very Fast Pit Stop," *New York Times,* November 16, 1980.

21. Hedrick Smith, "Reagan Loyalists Are Wondering About Their Champion's Loyalty," *New York Times,* November 20, 1980.

22. Stockman, *Triumph of Politics,* p. 75.

23. James Perry, "Reagan's Transition: It's Computerized, Crowded, and Chaotic," *Wall Street Journal,* December 11, 1980. As it was, when the transition was over, an official administration study indicated that there were some 1,559 staff members, of whom 311 were salaried employees; 331 staff members received a token salary of $1, and the remaining 917 received no remuneration from Transition Act funds. From its $2 million allotment in federal funds (the same amount as in 1976, despite an almost 50 percent increase in inflation), the transition spent slightly less in government funds ($1.75 million) than Carter had four years before ($1.78 million). The 1980 transition was able, however, to use an additional $1 million raised from private sources.

Draft Report, "Transition of the President and the President-Elect," Meese Files, OA5097, p. 24, RL.

24. Al McDonald handwritten notes, November 12, 1980, "Meeting of President with Senior White House Staff," 10/22/80–11/12/80, McDonald Donated Papers, Box 15, CL.

25. Burke interview with Harrison Wellford, June 3, 1998; Burke interview with Alonzo McDonald, July 15, 1998. According to McDonald, "My concern was that the transition be handled in the most effective way possible and on the most amicable basis. That's the tone we established at the beginning." "Ed Meese, Jim Baker, and I met from the outset and we got along fine. They were invited to keep in touch with me by telephone or personally whenever they needed to discuss something or whenever they wanted to review something with me. In addition to the regular sessions we had together, it was typical that when President-elect Reagan was staying at Blair House in Washington that both Ed and Jim would have breakfast with me at some early hour. . . . We talked just as openly as if we were in the same administration or in the same professional law firm. I think we developed a strong mutual respect for each other as individuals."

26. Laurin Henry, "The Transition: From Nomination to Inauguration," in David and Everson, eds., *The Presidential Election and Transition, 1980– 1981,* p. 214.

27. Burke interview with Ed Meese, May 27, 1998.

28. Following the election, James's staff expanded enormously—eventually reaching about a hundred in size. Like Timmons's executive-branch teams, it was organized into five functional areas: human services, legal and administrative services, natural resources and development, national security, and economic affairs.

29. Meese, *With Reagan,* p. 61.

30. Among those involved, in addition to Smith and James, were Los Angeles auto dealer Holmes Tuttle, Colorado brewer Joseph Coors, Alfred Bloomingdale, businessman Jack Wrather, Lockheed executive William Wilson, Colorado businessman Daniel Terra, Dart Industries executive Justin Dart, businessman Charles Wick, supermarket executive Theodore Cummings, oilman Henry Salvatori, steel executive Earle Jorgensen, and W. Glenn Campbell, head of Stanford's Hoover Institution.

31. Dom Bonafede, "Reagan and His Kitchen Cabinet Are Bound by Friendship and Loyalty," *National Journal,* April 11, 1981, p. 609.

32. Helene von Damm, "Out of the Kitchen, into the Cabinet," *New York Times Magazine,* November 27, 1988.

33. Strober and Strober, *Reagan,* p. 68.

34. Steven Weisman, "The Reagan Cabinet: A Selection by Negotiation and Compromise," *New York Times,* December 28, 1980.

35. Hedrick Smith, "Staunch Conservatives Opposed Choice of Regan for Treasury," *New York Times,* December 13, 1980.

36. Strober and Strober, *Reagan,* p. 70.

37. Steven Weisman, "The Reagan Cabinet: A Selection by Negotiation and Compromise," *New York Times,* December 28, 1980.

38. On December 11, Reagan announced the first round of eight cabinet nominees: Regan at Treasury, Weinberger at Defense, Smith at Justice, Drew Lewis at Transportation, Casey at CIA, Stockman at OMB, Schweiker at HHS, and Malcolm Baldrige at Commerce. Although in Washington at the time of the announcement, Reagan did not personally appear before the media to introduce the nominees, perhaps to avoid questions about delays in appointing a secretary of state. On December 16, while in Los Angeles, Reagan issued a statement nominating Haig to State as well as Ray Donovan to Labor. On December 23, Reagan announced—with the exception of the Department of Education—his remaining cabinet choices: Watt at Interior, Block at Agriculture, Pierce at HUD, Edwards at Energy, and Kirkpatrick at the UN. On January 6, Terrel Bell's appointment as secretary of education was announced.

39. Robert G. Kaiser and David Broder, "6 Key Nominations by President-Elect Are 'Quite Certain,'" *Washington Post,* December 4, 1980. Yet on December 10, the *Washington Post* reported that "some transition aides privately expressed criticism that the way the Cabinet selection process has gone on has allowed prominent Republicans' names to be dangled embarrassingly in public and sometimes subjected to harsh public criticism. 'Reagan . . . is inviting guerilla warfare' over his choices, one aide said." Robert G. Kaiser, "Haig Once Again Key Candidate to Head State Department," *Washington Post,* December 10, 1980.

40. James, White House Exit Interview, RL.

41. The Kitchen Cabinet was successful in urging Al Haig to take Judge William Clark as his deputy at State. Clark had been Reagan's chief of staff and then was appointed to the California Supreme Court.

42. Dom Bonafede, "Reagan and His Kitchen Cabinet Are Bound by Friendship and Ideology," *National Journal,* April 11, 1981, p. 609.

43. Helene von Damm, "Out of the Kitchen, into the Cabinet," *New York Times Magazine,* November 27, 1988.

44. Von Damm, *At Reagan's Side,* p. 147.

45. Von Damm, *At Reagan's Side,* pp. 147–148; see also Bob Colacello, "Ronnie and Nancy, Part II: The White House Years and Beyond," *Vanity Fair,* August 1998, p. 117.

46. Bob Colacello, "Ronnie and Nancy, Part II: The White House Years and Beyond," *Vanity Fair,* August 1998, p. 120.

47. The executive assistant was also in charge of some of the departments that didn't neatly fit in the other agencies, such as military affairs, criminal-justice planning, and emergency services.

48. Burke interview with Ed Meese, May, 27, 1998.

49. Lee Lescaze, "Reagan, Advisers Plan a Quick Shift," *Washington Post,* November 8, 1980.

50. Hedrick Smith, "Reagan Moving to Trim Budget by $13 Billion," *New York Times,* November 13, 1980.

51. Burke interview with Ed Meese, May 27, 1998.

52. Dick Kirschten, "Accentuating the Differences," *National Journal,* November 15, 1980, p. 1944; and Dick Kirschten, "Reagan and the Federal

Machinery," *National Journal,* January 17, 1981, pp. 88–89. See also Hedrick Smith, "Reagan Seeks to Emphasize Role of Cabinet Members as Advisers," *New York Times,* November 8, 1980.

53. Caspar Weinberger, "Yes, Washington Can Have Cabinet Government," *Washington Post,* December 1, 1980.

54. Lee Lescaze, "Several Chosen for the Cabinet, Meese Says," *Washington Post,* December 1, 1980.

55. Dick Kirschten, "Reagan and the Federal Machinery," *National Journal,* January 17, 1981, pp. 88–89.

56. Steven Weisman, "3 Key Deputies Will Head Reagan White House Staff," *New York Times,* December 18, 1980.

57. Dick Kirschten, "Reagan and the Federal Machinery," *National Journal,* January 17, 1981, pp. 89–90.

58. Dick Kirschten, "Reagan and the Federal Machinery," *National Journal,* January 17, 1981, pp. 89–90.

59. Burke interview with Ed Meese, May 27, 1998.

60. Anderson, *Revolution,* p. 204.

61. Steven Rattner, "Reagan's Economic Program," *New York Times,* November 16, 1980.

62. Meese, *With Reagan,* p. 59.

63. Meese, *With Reagan,* p. 59.

64. Anderson, *Revolution,* p. 203.

65. Draft Report, "Transition of the President and the President-Elect," Meese Files, OA 5097, p. 155, RL.

66. Laurin Henry, "The Transition: From Nomination to Inauguration," in David and Everson, eds., *The Presidential Election and Transition, 1980–1981,* p. 201.

67. Stone and Jackson, along with Washington lawyer Edward Bennett Williams—a Democrat who had attempted to deny Carter renomination—also joined Reagan's foreign policy advisory board of Gerald Ford, Henry Kissinger, Alexander Haig, Texas Governor Bill Clements, Weinberger, Allen, Armstrong, and Senator John Tower of Texas.

68. Draft Report, "Transition of the President and the President-Elect," Meese Files, OA 5097, pp. 63, 66, RL.

69. Draft Report, "Transition of the President and the President-Elect," Meese Files, OA 5097, p. 155, RL.

70. Draft Report, "Transition of the President and the President-Elect," Meese Files, OA 5097, pp. 63, 66, RL.

71. Draft Report, "Transition of the President and the President-Elect," Meese Files, OA 5097, p. 159, RL.

72. Memorandum from Jim Baker and Ed Meese to R. Allen, M. Anderson, J. Brady, R. Garrick, T. Korologos, D. Murphy, D. Stockman, B. Timmons, D. Trent, "First 90 Days Project," December 12, 1980, Hodsoll Files, 90 Days Project, Baker VII-C, Baker Papers, Rice University. In addition to Wirthlin, Gergen, and Hodsoll of Baker's staff, other participants in the planning meetings for the report included Garrick, Allen, Trent, Beal, and Harper.

Hodsoll's handwritten notes, 12/16/80 and 12/18/80; Hodsoll Files, 90 Days Project, Box VII-C, Baker Papers, Rice University.

73. Four criteria were used to determine these strategic considerations: (1) The expressed wishes of the president-elect as to what he wanted to accomplish during his administration; (2) issues identified that the public expressed it wanted the president to accomplish during his administration; (3) major legislative issues in which current legislation would lapse, necessitating additional and immediate action; and (4) a creative list of accomplishments to be achieved in the future. With its emphasis on both budgetary and strategic issues, the office was "then able to judge the impact that budget considerations would have in each of these areas." Draft Report, "Transition of the President and President-Elect," Meese Files, OA 5097, p. 162, RL.

74. "Final Report of the Initial Actions Project," January 29, 1981, Wirthlin Private Papers, pp. 1, 4.

75. "First 100 Days," Richard Beal Files, Boxes 12, 390, RL.

76. Burke interview with Robert Carleson, April 21, 1998.

77. Spencer Rich, "Reagan Due to Propose Wiping Out Two Social Security Benefits," *Washington Post,* February 1, 1981. Carleson also adds that "when I watched the news that evening, as Reagan came back from Camp David and got out of his helicopter, the reporters [asked] if it were true that he was going to propose workfare in the budget. I saw the look on his face and there was a slight bit of surprise and he said, 'I'll tell you one thing, I'm all in favor of workfare.'" Burke interview with Robert Carleson, April 21, 1998.

78. Burke interview with Robert Carleson, April 21, 1998. Furthermore, according to Carleson, "I had anticipated that there would be trouble from those guys because they were never a part [of the Reagan campaign team]. In fact Darman had worked for Elliott Richardson [when he was secretary of HEW under Nixon], and they opposed very strongly our California welfare-reform program because they were trying to push the family-assistance program, which Reagan was opposing. That was why I decided to follow this thing to the White House and keep my hands on it, and it got in there." Carleson, who not only had worked for Reagan and Nixon on welfare matters but also had worked for the Senate Finance Committee, proved adept at securing passage of the proposed changes: "I had anticipated a long struggle, particularly in the [Democratic-controlled] House. There were several items in there that were duplicative, several items I was willing to throw away, and several items that did the same thing two different ways. But because of the work I had been previously doing with the Senate Finance Committee over the years, with Senator Russell Long [the former chair of the committee], and with the Republicans, it went right through the Finance Committee and the full Senate real fast. They made only a couple of minor changes." Carleson then advised David Stockman to adopt the language in the Senate's version of the bill as it moved over to the House: "Don't change a word of it. Take out our original language, which had only been slightly changed, not very significantly, and make sure the thing you get through the House is identical to what got through the Senate. If they were successful in rolling the Speaker and the leadership

in the House, which was the plan, I wanted the language to be identical so that, when it went into conference, the Senate side could insist that it not be conferenceable, the part relating to welfare." Stockman followed the advice. "So all these provisions where I tried to do the same thing two different ways, even the items that we were willing to give up in negotiations, all got enacted into law and nobody really knew that it was in there. The media didn't know about it, so that was how we got our 1981 welfare in."

79. Stockman, *Triumph of Politics,* p. 75.

80. Stockman, *Triumph of Politics,* p. 83.

81. Stockman, *Triumph of Politics,* p. 85.

82. Stockman, *Triumph of Politics,* pp. 87–90.

83. Meese was also placed in charge of a small planning and evaluation staff headed by Richard Beal, an associate of Richard Wirthlin, that would deal with long-range planning.

84. Dick Kirschten, "Reagan Moving Quickly to Name White House Board of Directors," *National Journal,* November 22, 1980, p. 1994.

85. T. R. Reid, "Reagan Picks 2 Top Staff Aides," *Washington Post,* November 15, 1980.

86. Persico, *Casey,* p. 204.

87. Deaver, *Behind the Scenes,* p. 124.

88. Schieffer and Gates, *The Acting President,* p. 81.

89. Cannon, *President Reagan,* p. 71.

90. Cannon, *President Reagan,* p. 71.

91. Rockefeller's 1964 primary fight also enlisted another future Reagan associate, Caspar Weinberger. In fact—and this is an interesting commentary on Reagan's own personality—Weinberger and William French Smith would both support Reagan's challenger for the GOP nomination for governor two years later, San Francisco Mayor George Christopher. So, too, would two members of what would become Reagan's early Kitchen Cabinet: tire manufacturer Leonard Firestone and MCA record producer Taft Schreiber. After the primary was over, any wounds were quickly healed, and all became influential Reagan supporters and advisers.

92. Deaver, *Behind the Scenes,* p. 125.

93. Burke interview with Richard Wirthlin, June 5, 1998.

94. That morning Baker and Meese met for breakfast, and Meese told Baker that Reagan would be talking with him about matters that would involve them working together. Baker did not tell Meese, according to one account, that he had received a call from Reagan the night before telling him that he wanted to meet with Baker on a matter of importance, one that Baker assumed would be the chief-of-staff appointment. That same day, Reagan offered Baker the position. At the meeting, Baker realized that he would have to work out some position for Meese and proposed that Meese be designated "counselor to the president" with cabinet rank—a title, interestingly enough, that others had bandied about. Schieffer and Gates, *The Acting President,* p. 81.

95. Schieffer and Gates, *The Acting President,* p. 82.

96. Deaver, *Behind the Scenes,* p. 125. Schieffer and Gates indicate that Meese may have had some inkling the night before that he wasn't going to be chief of staff—hence his discussion with Baker about the two of them working together. Schieffer and Gates, *The Acting President,* p. 81.

97. Schieffer and Gates, *The Acting President,* p. 85. A copy of the agreement is reproduced on page 83.

98. Dom Bonafede, Hofstra University Conference on the Reagan Presidency, April 22, 1993, taped remarks, RL.

99. Douglas Kneeland, "Aides to Reagan Guessing Who Will Get Which Job," *New York Times,* November 11, 1980.

100. Burke interview with Frank Hodsoll, January 26, 1999.

101. Memorandum from David Gergen to James Baker, "The Carter White House," November 12, 1980, James Cicconi Files, Presidential Personnel (James), Box 9107, RL.

102. Draft Report, "The Transition of the President and the President-Elect," Meese Files, OA 5097, pp. 135–138; see also Memorandum from David Gergen, Richard Darman, and Frank Hodsoll to Ed Meese, "White House/Executive Office of President (WH/EOP) Transition," January 3, 1981, Office/Desk Files 1981, Box 30, Baker Papers, Rice University.

103. Lee Lescaze, "Reagan's Press Secretary Takes His Leave," *Washington Post,* December 1, 1980.

104. Baker handwritten notes, January 1, 1981, Box 30, Baker Papers, Rice University.

105. "Office Descriptions," Box 30, Baker Papers, Rice University.

106. Notes of Meeting with Jack Watson, undated, Box 30, Baker Papers, Rice University.

107. Memorandum from Al McDonald to Ed Meese and Jim Baker, "Organizing the Presidency," December 8, 1980, McDonald Donated Papers, Box 15, CL; Memorandum from Al McDonald to Ed Meese and Jim Baker, "Suggestions of Structure of the President's Staff," December 17, 1980, copy provided to author by Mr. McDonald.

108. Burke interview with Alonzo McDonald, July 15, 1998.

109. McDonald handwritten notes, December 5, 1980, Box 15, 12/12/80–1/19/81, McDonald Donated Papers, CL.

110. Hodsoll, handwritten meeting notes, no date, NSC, Hodsoll Files, OA9107, Box 1, RL.

111. "Notes on National Policy Development and Coordination—Possible Ideas for Discussion," January 14, 1981, Hodsoll Files, Policy Development Organization, Box VII-C, Baker Papers, Rice University.

112. Burke interview with Frank Hodsoll, January 26, 1999. Frank Hodsoll's notes of a December 13, 1980, meeting with Baker are indicative of the range of staff and organization matters that Baker and his associates were working on at such an early date. Hodsoll lists items such as the effect of "Friedersdorf leaving the FEC," "detailed breakdown admin.," "classified system," "perk notebook," "Budget—role, materials in advance," "inner office," "attendance and staff rep.," and "space." Hodsoll, notes of "Baker Mtg., 12/13/80," Hodsoll Transition Files, Box VII-C, Baker Papers, Rice University.

113. George Bush to James Baker, handwritten note, Box VII-B, Baker Papers, Rice University.

114. They also noted that Ed Schmults had been chosen as counsel to the president, although Schmults was not in the end appointed to the job.

115. On January 13, appointments in the chief of staff's office were announced: Richard Darman was appointed as staff secretary, Frank Hodsoll, who had served as a deputy assistant secretary of commerce, was named principal deputy to Baker, and Richard Williamson, an aide to Senator Paul Laxalt, was named principal political deputy to Baker. Williamson's initial responsibilities were in the areas of economic policy, with a special focus on deregulation, and reorganization and reduction of government programs. The announcement of Williamson's position was premature: he would end up serving as special assistant for intergovernmental affairs rather than as one of Baker's lieutenants.

116. Memorandum from David Gergen, Richard Darman, Frank Hodsoll to Ed Meese, "White House/Executive Office of President (WH/EOP) Transition," January 3, 1981, Box 30, Office/Desk Files, 1981, Baker Papers, Rice University.

117. "Checklist for WH/EOP Transition," January 12, 1981, Office/Desk Files 1981, Box 30, Baker Papers, Rice University.

118. James Cicconi Files, EOP, Box 9107, RL.

119. Dick Kirschten, "Reagan and the Federal Machine," *National Journal,* January 17, 1981, p. 93.

120. Meese, *With Reagan,* p. 69.

121. Burke interview with Ed Meese, May 27, 1998.

122. For versions of this meeting see Terrel Bell, *The Thirteenth Man,* pp. 15–20; Haig, *Caveat,* p. 76; and Stockman, *Triumph of Politics,* pp. 85–89.

123. "Cabinet Meeting Agenda," January 19, 1981, Box 30, Office/Desk Files 1981, Baker Papers, Rice University. The meeting was held this time in the New Executive Office Building.

124. Draft Report, "Transition of the President and the President-Elect," Meese Files, OA 5097, p. 154, RL.

4

Reagan in Office

The Reagan transition had clearly thought through several organizational and decisionmaking matters, including ones that pose important tests for determining the impact of the transition on his presidency. Formal mechanisms for linking the cabinet and the White House staff had been explored, particularly in designing a system to meet Reagan's own needs. But providing a way for the cabinet to have input has not been an easy matter since the Eisenhower years, particularly given the forces at work centralizing policymaking within the White House staff.[1] Would Reagan succeed where others, Carter most notably, had failed?

Like Carter, Reagan and his advisers had also focused on the White House's role in the policy process. But in 1980, the issues were not staff size or the lessons of the Nixon presidency. The work of the transition had a much better fix on how the various parts of the White House staff operated and what changes might be needed. But the Reagan transition posed its own challenges. The difficulty for Chief of Staff James Baker would be in handling his status as a Reagan outsider and, more important, in making the division of labor he had settled with Meese work. In theory, a workable arrangement with Meese had been crafted, but would it become a working relationship able to link politics and policy, able to reconcile ideological commitment and pragmatic compromise? Would the commitment to the cabinet-council system gel with Baker's own White House–centered political and policy units?

For Meese, the question of day-to-day management lingered, beginning with the specter of his briefcase-as-black-hole. Would the policy apparatus under his control—the cabinet councils and the White

143

House Office of Policy Development (OPD), most notably—have their intended role in the policy process? The fact that Richard Allen and the NSC staff reported through Meese was an especially important artifact of the transition. How would the NSC adviser, placed in a weaker organizational position, relate to a secretary of state who fashioned himself as the vicar of foreign policy? For both Baker and Meese, would an amicable relationship at the top extend downward?

With respect to Ronald Reagan, did the organizations and processes crafted during the transition in fact meet his needs as a decisionmaker? Did they provide a means that allowed him to delegate without losing broader control? Did he have the skills as a manager to make it work?

Finally, how did all of these pieces of the policy process affect policy outcomes? This was an agenda-driven presidency, and it was a transition in which policy matters had received early attention. Would key policies of the early Reagan presidency be linked to what had gone on before?

Decisionmaking Processes

Cabinet Councils

What would emerge in February as the cabinet-council system was one of the more important innovations of Reagan's presidency and drew from both Baker's and Meese's positions on how the cabinet members might productively contribute to the administration's policy decisions. In accord with Baker's own experience with the Ford administration's Economic Policy Board (he had been undersecretary of commerce and a participant in its operations), the councils were organized along functional policy lines with a heavy reliance on staff support from the White House. For Meese, the councils provided cabinet members' input on policy without reliance on the cabinet as a whole. Moreover, following Meese's notion of a "supercabinet," five cabinet officers were designated individually as the chair pro tem of each of five proposed councils and thus would have more authority than their cabinet counterparts.[2]

On February 13, 1981, Meese issued a memorandum outlining how the system would operate. Five councils were proposed: (1) economic affairs (CCEA), (2) commerce and trade (CCCT), (3) human resources (CCHR), (4) natural resources and environment (CCNR), and (5) food and agriculture (CCFA). In January 1982, a sixth council, on legal policy, was created, and in September 1982 a seventh council, on management and administration, was added. The president was the chair of each council, although when not in attendance (as was usually the case), meetings were led by the chair pro tem—the cabinet officer in each lead department: Treasury Secretary Don Regan (CCEA), Commerce Secretary Malcolm Baldrige (CCCT), Health and Human Services Secretary Richard Schweiker (CCHR), Interior Secretary James Watt (CCNR), and Agriculture Secretary John Block (CCFA). Vice President George Bush, Meese, and Baker were designated ex officio members of all councils, as was Martin Anderson after October 1981, following his practice of attending almost all council meetings up to that point.

Cabinet members were assigned to councils based on the policy areas within their administrative domains. All meetings, however, were open to any interested cabinet officer—an invitation Meese extended in his memo to the cabinet outlining the new system.[3] In announcing the council system, Meese emphasized that the whole cabinet would continue to meet three or four times a month on matters that "cut across the board."[4] However, most policy discussions would take place in the smaller council meetings.

A staff secretariat was created for each council and was chaired by a member of Martin Anderson's OPD staff (Anderson, in turn, reported to Meese). In the early days of the Reagan presidency, these so-called executive secretaries were Roger Porter (CCEA), Dennis Kass (CCCT), John McClaughry (CCFA), Robert Carleson (CCHR), and Danny Boggs (CCNR). According to Boggs, their respective assignments were somewhat fortuitous: most had already been appointed to policy positions in the OPD, and then "the policy chieftains became, as part of that assignment, the executive secretaries of those cabinet councils. It was something that was thrashed out within the office. The office arrangements [within the OPD] had already been made and it was a one-to-one correspondence with the councils."[5]

The staff secretariat, however, was not just a White House staff operation: each cabinet member on the council designated a staff member from his or her department to serve on the secretariat, and there were representatives from the OMB and other White House units. The staff secretariat played a crucial role in establishing the agendas of each council and, working with OPD and the departments, preparing the working papers that would form the basis of a council's deliberations.[6]

According to Martin Anderson, the staff system "worked very well." Members of the cabinet never complained about not knowing what was going on in the secretariat. And the OPD and the staff secretariats experienced very little difficulty in getting information from the departments and agencies "because we were dealing with the secretary or his designees" on the secretariat. Each executive secretary coordinated with the respective chair of each council, Anderson, and Meese's office to set an agenda. The executive secretaries also made sure that papers were distributed ahead of time through Craig Fuller's Office of Cabinet Affairs "so that when people came in and sat down at meetings they had a fully developed [view] of what was going on."[7]

Most of the work in preparing position papers for each council was undertaken prior to council meetings by ad hoc working groups, set up as a policy issue came up on the agenda. Use of working groups had been suggested by Anderson to Meese, who adopted the proposal. They were temporary in nature, and at any one point forty to forty-five working groups would be at work. Unlike the secretariat, which had a set roster of members, a working group could be drawn from any department or agency, even outside experts.

The council system promised a number of benefits. One was a strong measure of White House control. Existence of working groups and the designation of a chair and the group's membership required White House approval, for example. Meese and Baker also had the power to decide which council had jurisdiction over what issues and when full meetings of the council would be scheduled with the president presiding as chair. As Craig Fuller pointed out at the start: "We will function as a rules committee."[8]

Within the councils, according to Danny Boggs of the natural resources council, "everything got some kind of imprimatur" from the highest levels of the White House. It was not "we've done it and that's the way it's going to be." If everyone "was in agreement, then the sign-off might be more perfunctory." In other cases, where disagreements surfaced, the view of the council was "here's what we have discussed and you write up a paper for the president or for the cabinet that would reflect this." "In fact that was one of the most interesting things I did: write papers where the people were very contentious and try to be honest and accommodating as to their views."[9]

The councils also served as a reality check. William Niskanen, a member of the Council of Economic Advisers, would later observe that the system "had the effect of thinning out proposals and focusing on real alternatives. In most cases, it gave the president genuine options to select from rather than 'choose my proposal' versus 'chaos,'" which Niskanen felt sometimes emerged in the administration's budget deliberations. "Many things never came up through the process because people knew down the line they would not fly once they reached the White House."[10]

Both cabinet meetings and the cabinet-council system also facilitated teamwork, a factor that Reagan, as governor and now as president, felt was an important part of his policy process.[11] The collegial nature of the process reinforced Reagan's hope that cabinet members would not simply reflect the views of their own department but think of themselves as providing more general advice and serving as *his* advisers. "That was the whole idea," in Meese's opinion, "and the president himself mentioned this at the first meetings, that people should not feel constrained to speak about something from their own department. He wanted their general knowledge and their general input on matters whether they were directly related to their function or not."[12] Similarly, Richard Wirthlin, who made a number of presentations to the cabinet in his role as Reagan's outside pollster and adviser on overall political strategy, recalls Reagan specifically instructing the assembled cabinet that they "should not withhold their opinions even if they ran counter to their department's view."[13]

The system had wider political benefits. The mere existence of working groups, for example, could be politically useful since the administration could point to their ongoing work as evidence of its concern in various policy areas yet not be required to bring forth a recommendation. During the first year, this was especially important in not deflecting attention away from the administration's economic program. Also, Martin Anderson recalls, "by not establishing a working group, we were able to submerge certain issues until we were ready to deal with them." As a result, the White House "had a clear picture of what policy issues were developing, how urgent they were, and when they were coming before the cabinet councils for discussion. I knew, Ed Meese knew, and so did Jim Baker . . . and Michael Deaver."[14]

Similar political benefits obtained as issues moved to the cabinet councils or the cabinet as a whole. In David Gergen's view, the cabinet served as a useful lightning rod to deflect criticism away from the White House and the president. Speaking at the 1981 annual meeting of the American Political Science Association, he noted that with the council system it was "the people out in the departments . . . the lieutenants who can easily give blood." "You'd better have someone out there on the front line who is willing to take the shots on the really controversial issues and to save the president and not let him get enmeshed and be a commentator on everything that goes on or be out front on every issue." Gergen especially saw a contrast to the Carter presidency, where everything was brought into the Oval Office, with notable consequences, often negative, for the president.[15]

Meetings of the cabinet councils were intentionally held in the White House (usually the Roosevelt Room) rather than in the home department of the council chair, which brought additional indirect benefits. It reinforced the presidential nature of the endeavor, and it facilitated better communication and linkages, especially informally, to the White House staff. According to Anderson, the time before and after meetings allowed council members to meet with the White House staff for further discussion. "These short impromptu discussions among and between the president's policy advisers were probably as important to the advancement and development of his policy as the meetings themselves. Valuable pieces of information were exchanged, disagreements worked out privately, and Reagan's advisers got to know each other personally, intimately."[16]

The council system also facilitated policy implementation. According to Meese, "When the President does make his decision, cabinet and staff alike know what that decision is. They also know, each of them having had their chance at input, that they are now accountable for carrying out that particular decision."[17] In his study of the councils, Chester Newland found that they helped "to keep the entire administration focused on the president's general direction."[18]

All of these effects, in varying degree, were felt by a number of cabinet members. For HHS Secretary Richard Schweiker, "I thought it was very good because we were able to get into more detail and specifics than you would at a cabinet meeting." Schweiker also felt that "it made the work go smoother and probably provided better policy solutions than just going in and having a shoot out in the cabinet room." And for Schweiker, "Because of that camaraderie coming out of those meetings, you could invariably pick up the phone and work out differences . . . you had a better working relationship."[19] For Agriculture Secretary John Block, the process ensured that cabinet secretaries weren't "blindsided and all of a sudden find out that some decision was made and that they were hanging out in the cold." While you "might win some or you might lose some, everyone did get their chance to put their oar in the water." Block specifically recalls that the system allowed him to get issues discussed: "If there was something that was going on and I felt resistance from another department, or someone in the Reagan administration, or even OMB, I would talk to [Cabinet Affairs Secretary] Craig Fuller about it and we would sit down and get everyone together."[20]

But perhaps the most important benefit of the councils was to its principal: they met Ronald Reagan's needs. In the view of Ralph Bledsoe, the system "suited Reagan's style. Reagan liked to have things bubble up, dealt with by task forces, work groups, and all that." "He liked to have papers put together, ideas from a lot of places, and then brought together and put in front of him with a reasonable number of people present." Thus, unlike Kennedy's collegial ExCom, policy options (at least in theory) had been well staffed and thought about beforehand; and unlike Carter's initial hope to use his whole cabinet as a collective decision body, you "didn't have a complete roomful of people" but rather a "more reasonable number." "You had as many cabinet members who wanted to come, but also a core group of cabinet members on each of those councils."[21] At least in theory, therefore, the transition had served to devise a way of bringing the cabinet in on policy deliberations in a workable and organized way.

Cabinet Councils: Action or Inaction?

But did theory and design meet reality? As the Reagan presidency progressed through its initial hundred days and then through the remainder of the first year, the track record of each of the councils varied greatly. According to Ed Harper, who served as David Stockman's deputy at OMB and then Anderson's replacement as head of OPD, "Some of the cabinet councils worked very well, others didn't work."[22]

The newly established Office of Planning and Evaluation (OPE)—another Meese innovation—undertook several studies of the council system and carefully monitored its progress. In mid-July 1981, the OPE issued its first report summarizing the cabinet councils' activities. Through July 7, the councils had met a total of fifty-five times covering fifty-eight different topics. By far the most active council was economic affairs, which had met thirty times (54 percent of all meetings) and handled twenty-seven (47 percent) of the total number of topics. Among its most frequent agenda items were the thrift industry (ten meetings), budget issues (six meetings), Polish debt (five meetings), and "economic outlook" (five meetings). Commerce and trade met seven times, handling eight topics, of which enterprise zones had been the most frequent (three meetings). Natural resources and the environment met twelve times, handling fifteen topics, including the Clean Air Act (seven meetings), oil exploration (four meetings), and natural gas decontrol (four meetings). The two other councils barely registered: human resources met just three times—once to organize, once to review social security reform proposals, and once to review a proposal dealing with Vietnam veterans; food and agriculture met three times to cover six topics, and its last meeting—as of July 1981—was held on May 20.

The report further indicated that only five presidential policy directives had emerged from the system by mid-July. Three related to commerce and trade issues (Ottawa summit, trade relations with Mexico, and shoe import restrictions), one had emerged from economic affairs (youth differential minimum wage), and one from human resources (social security reform). As to the disposition of agenda items, "two-thirds of the time, items were simply reviewed and discussed, directed for further study, or postponed," the report concluded. Of the fifty-five total meetings, the president had attended only five (three for commerce and trade, once for human resources, and once for economic affairs—a discussion on the budget), while the vice president had attended nineteen meetings.[23]

Some of these differences in levels of activity undoubtedly reflected the different emphases and priorities of the Reagan agenda rather than a failure of the council system as a whole; one would not expect the council on food and agriculture to be as proactive as economic affairs. Variations among the councils may also have been related to the skills and efforts of its participants. The CCEA, while most closely linked among the councils to the economic agenda of Reagan's first year, also benefited from a chair pro tem, Don Regan, and an executive secretary, Roger Porter, who ran the council smoothly and efficiently and was a veteran of the Ford administration's Economic Policy Board. According to Ralph Bledsoe, "They were always on top of whatever was the current economic issue. They were good meetings, there was some excellent stuff discussed." In particular, "Don Regan was a terrific manager of those meetings, a good chairman pro tem. Everybody got a chance to say something, then he would summarize it. He was a real asset to the way that the economic policy should work. Regan would let those voices come in." Meetings were studiously kept to one hour and "were very well organized" in contrast to some of the other councils; Porter also "kept the meeting flowing."

In contrast, "Jim Watt's meetings," which Bledsoe also attended, "were kind of wild affairs; people would say anything they wanted and so would Watt." Particular council members also varied in their influence; Regan, Commerce Secretary Malcolm Baldridge, and U.S. Trade Representative Bill Brock were especially influential in Bledsoe's view. "When Baldridge spoke, people listened. And he always spoke very slowly, very thoughtfully. Brock was like Baldridge. The two of them were well respected as people who had something to say and had good ideas. Very respected by their colleagues."[24]

At one level, the council system was useful as a forum for deliberations for what might be regarded as second- or third-tier policy issues. It was thoughtfully crafted and, in the view of a number of participants, operated well and met their expectations. But at another level, it was surely not some form of cabinet government, and it did not wholly replicate the way department heads had provided input during Reagan's years as governor. During the transition, it was recognized that adjustments would clearly have to be made to take account of the realities of Washington, the most important of which were the greater number of federal departments and the existence of a large-scale staff at the White House.

While influential on some issues, the councils were not the only channel of information and advice to the president. Indeed, several significant policies during Reagan's first year were sometimes worked out outside its bounds—welfare reform, proposed changes in social security—or input and influence were shared with other sources—some of the critical parts of the first-year economic program.[25] The operations of the Reagan White House staff would still remain central to the decisionmaking processes of this administration.

The Troika in Operation

In contrast to the Carter transition, not only had the Reagan transition been a time when the question of how to use the cabinet had been considered; it also had the benefit of clearer thought about and organization of White House operations. The division of labor among Baker, Meese, and Deaver was particularly central to the planned operation of the White House staff. In theory, it played to their respective strengths, but in practice, the separation of politics from policy, pragmatism from ideology, might prove more difficult to bridge.

One challenge stemming from the transition was a need to make the arrangement work at the top. By most accounts, Baker, Deaver, and Meese—the so-called troika—recognized this challenge and sought to create among themselves the kind of working relationship necessary to bridge separations of policy and politics, ideological commitment and pragmatic adjustment. In Ed Meese's view, "There was plenty of work to go around," and "by having Jim Baker join Mike and myself, we had someone with considerable Washington experience that complemented our experience in knowing President Reagan and working with him."[26]

During 1981, the troika met regularly for breakfast before the 8:00 A.M. senior staff meeting and then would usually meet with Reagan at 9:00 A.M. and perhaps again during the day as the situation demanded. Meese, Baker, and Deaver also convened weekly "issue lunches" with the president to provide him a chance to review more broadly what was happening on the policy front. During the first months of the new administration, they also convened at 5:00 P.M. in Baker's office to go over personnel appointments with Pen James.

Frank Hodsoll, Baker's deputy during the first year, later observed that "Baker made a very big effort to make sure that the relationships among those three were good, and he went out of his way to make sure he never did anything without making sure everyone was a part of it."[27] James Cicconi, who succeeded Hodsoll as Baker's deputy, recalls that the three "worked very hard on their relationship and by and large did well. . . . Baker, I think, would tell you that he got along well with Ed Meese and Mike Deaver, and worked very well with them. I think Ed Meese would tell you the same thing."[28]

Hodsoll especially recalled the distinct contributions each of the three made: Meese with his close working relationship with Reagan and his connections with longtime Reagan supporters, Deaver with his close personal ties to both the president and Nancy Reagan. Baker, for his part, "was looked to by the president, Mrs. Reagan, and some of the people who had been with Reagan a lot longer as someone who could help them work the Washington system." Having served as undersecretary of commerce for Rogers Morton and later working directly for President Ford in the 1976 campaign, "he had really gotten a feel for how Washington operates," according to Hodsoll. "The Meeses and Deavers of the world, and the president himself, relied on, to a great degree, Jim's judgment."[29]

Cleavages Develop

But the same effort to make the situation work at the top did not always extend to members of the troika's respective staffs. As months passed, reports began to filter into the media of divisions and infighting within the staff. In a January 1982 interview with Howell Raines and Steven Weisman of the *New York Times*, Baker noted that "when we are able to stay in close communication, the system works pretty well. Where it begins to break down is when we are not in close communication." Baker also conceded that "because it is a triumvirate system . . . there are bound to be some tensions at the staff level; lower and middle level staff people who for reasons of turf or for bureaucratic reasons tend to get at odds with each other."30

There were also disagreements, if not a "split," between the "true believers," the ideologically committed Reaganites who "believed there was a revolution," Hodsoll later noted, and those with Washington experience "who were trying to end up with the best deal possible." "There were periodic complaints by those who would have preferred to stick on issues longer and without compromise and those who didn't."31

Yet Baker and his associates in the White House realized that their newcomer status, plus their Washington ties in an administration with a decidedly anti-Washington ethos, presented a challenge to be overcome. According to Hodsoll, one of the ways they attempted to do this, "and this was true of Baker and all of us on the Baker team, was by being scrupulously fair," even to "people we didn't agree with." And at least in Hodsoll's mind, "eventually we were respected and trusted. Once you get there, all good things are possible."32

From Policy to Politics

The transition also had impact on the administration once in office in the way particular responsibilities had been parceled out. The transition's division of the troika's labor was not perfectly balanced in terms of influence and power, and Baker benefited from the fact that power gravitates to those most directly involved in day-to-day politics. Baker's control of the press operations, the communications apparatus, and the congressional and other liaison groups placed him in a position of influence over day-to-day, more immediate decisions of the Reagan White House, even though Ed Meese supervised the policy-development units. For example, while Baker's legislative strategy group (LSG)33—which met several times a week in Baker's office—did not make decisions about what the broad policies of the Reagan administration might be, the "adjustments" and compromises it crafted in trying to gain their approval by Congress clearly had an impact on the final product; increasingly it was, in the words of one participant, "more of a driving force."34 For Martin Anderson, the Baker group's "recommendations for compromises with Congress could have a significant effect on that policy."35

The economic agenda of 1981 and the legislative politics required to achieve it especially shifted power away from those parts of the staff system and decisionmaking processes under Meese's direction. The OPD was increasingly viewed as being less than aggressive; at best its impact on policy was filtered through the complex cabinet-council structure and Martin Anderson's involvement in the budget working groups and the economic policy group that met every Tuesday at the Treasury Department. In January 1982, one White House aide reported that "there is no domestic policy shop. The domestic policy shop is in two places—the Baker political operation and OMB."[36]

Not surprisingly, over time Baker's staff came to be perceived as more efficient and politically adept—the center of political action in the Reagan inner circles. As William Safire noted in October 1981, "Mr. Meese's men . . . are generally contemplative types who prefer low profiles. Mr. Baker's men . . . are aggressive doers who expand their authority as a matter of course. . . . As a result, Mr. Baker and his hard-driving crew appear to be running things."[37] As for Meese, even a longtime associate such as Martin Anderson felt he was overcommitted; "his briefcase earned the nickname of the black hole because it was reputed that anything that disappeared inside it never came out." "The trick to work effectively with Meese," even Martin Anderson felt, "was to make sure you got to spend time with him, personally."[38] By early 1982, according to the *New York Times,* White House aides had "gradually learned to turn to Mr. Baker to get issues resolved because Mr. Meese moves more slowly. Mr. Baker crisply manages the day to day White House operation, quarterbacks legislative strategy, oversees the press office, the political office, relations with governors and mayors, sits on the budget review board, and plots strategy for the 1982 [midterm] election."[39]

Baker's organizational skills and those of his deputies were another force at work that bolstered his position. Little of the confusion in how information was to be processed, advice tendered, option papers prepared, events scheduled, and policies implemented that had bedeviled Carter occurred in the first months of the Reagan presidency. Baker's morning staff meetings particularly contrast with what transpired during the early Carter years, and they were more adept at both long- and short-term planning. According to Baker,

> One of the things we do in our morning sessions is to talk about how we think the president's time is being allocated and spent in a macro sense, not just for that day but for the month or the month to come. Are we doing enough outreach stuff; are we doing enough policy stuff; do we have enough time built into the system for national security decisions; are we doing enough consensus building and constituency work?[40]

Both Baker and President Reagan also benefited from a smooth-flowing system of staffing and paperwork that had been developed by

Richard Darman during the transition and then quickly implemented. Within a week of taking over as staff secretary, Darman issued a lengthy memo outlining how memoranda were to be prepared and routed through the White House and on to the president. Darman outlined procedures covering six different types—briefing papers, decision memoranda, signature memoranda, information memoranda, telephone call recommendations, and schedule proposals—and different protocols and formats were set out for each and samples were provided. Briefing papers for meetings, for example, required not only names, dates, location, and time but also purpose, background, participants, press plan, sequence of events, outline of agenda, president's role, and talking points (where appropriate). "*All* papers for the President," Darman noted, "should be routed through the staff secretary."[41] Darman also established a system for eliciting advice from White House staff members on policy issues percolating through the system. The cover sheet of these staffing memoranda listed the names of some twenty-five staff members (and the vice president), which Darman would then check off for either "action," "FYI," or both. A due date for comments was indicated and a space for remarks was provided; relevant memos and other information were then attached.[42] Although, as Frank Hodsoll later noted, there are ways of getting things through a White House apparatus "from old friends that you can't prevent, the vast majority, anything important, went through the Darman apparatus." According to Hodsoll, "He did an excellent job of making sure the right people" had been involved in policy deliberations.[43]

How does this shed light on the transition's impact on the decisionmaking processes of the Reagan presidency? One might attribute Baker's success to the skills and expertise of its principal—Baker himself. At some level this is no doubt true. But the transition also had important effects beyond Reagan's willingness to reach outside his inner circle and tap Baker for chief of staff. Baker's work during the transition in understanding the operations of the White House and in planning for his own work as chief of staff gave him a head start in crafting a well-organized and smooth-running operation. Even the shift in influence away from Meese and toward Baker could be linked back to their original division of labor in November: Meese's position looked strong—even the media thought so at the time—but Baker's duties proved more influential.

The other strength of Baker's operation arose from the personnel choices that had been made. Its smooth workings depended not just on its organization but also on the skill of the participants—Deaver, Darman, Gergen, and Baker himself, most notably. Meese's operation, by contrast, suffered to some extent from his own difficulties as an efficient manager, as well as some personnel choices that were less adept than Baker's.

As they had during the transition, Meese and Baker (plus Deaver) worked hard to make their arrangement work. But that did not always extend down the chain of command. The tension between the Reagan loyalists—largely on Meese's side—versus staff members with wider experience and a more pragmatic orientation—largely in Baker's operation—that began during the transition persisted once the Reagan presidency got under way. Making this part of the system work was not just a job for Meese and Baker; it also was a job for Ronald Reagan, the one person above it all who commanded respect and was in a position to resolve differences. Could he rise to that task?

Reagan as Manager and Decisionmaker

A Passive President?

In regard to Ronald Reagan's role in the decisionmaking processes of his presidency, the conventional wisdom is that he was a passive participant. Compared to Carter, there is no doubt that he didn't enmesh himself in detail. And unlike Carter, he was more comfortable delegating responsibilities to his subordinates, whether on his staff or in the cabinet. Much of the work of the transition, while attentive to Reagan's needs as a decisionmaker, was a product of the efforts of others and bore little evidence of his personal attention or direct involvement.

It is tempting to buy the view of Reagan as passive participant, which meshes neatly with the notion that the transition was highly consequential for this presidency: it was then that the decisionmaking processes of his presidency largely took shape. As a result, and absent an active decisionmaker, the policy processes crafted during the transition determined policy decisions that would come later.

Yet it would be a mistake to assume that much of what went on in the Reagan presidency, particularly in its first year, simply passed by this president. Thus how the transition and the decisionmaking processes meshed with Ronald Reagan's role as a decisionmaker and manager is more challenging to sort out.

At one level, this sense of passivity may have been a deliberate ploy on Reagan's part. On his desk in the Oval Office was a small brass plaque with the inscription: "There's no limit to what one man can accomplish as long as he's willing to let someone else have the credit." During the cabinet selection process in December, according to Lyn Nofziger, Reagan met with Texas Governor Bill Clements, who was trying to derail a possible nomination of Senator John Tower for defense secretary and was pushing for Caspar Weinberger in his place:

> Reagan was very noncommittal but listened. When Bill Clements had gone, Reagan turned to me and said, "You know, I didn't want to tell him this, but it had already occurred to me to name Cap Weinberger secretary of defense. I didn't want to tell him. He would think that I had stolen his idea. . . . " To this day, as far as I know, Bill Clements thinks it was his idea.[44]

But Reagan's tactic could also bear costs. In Ed Meese's view, Reagan "did not try to grandstand. As a result of this, many people in the government, particularly some on the White House staff, tried to magnify their own positions and importance with the press."[45]

Several participants in internal administration debates reveal a president who not only articulated a broader vision for his presidency and his political agenda—which many have noted—but also placed his mark on its particulars. In February 1981, Reagan personally rejected a request by Energy Secretary Edwards to continue funding some federal synthetic-fuels projects, and he pushed his advisers to cut 25 percent in federal aid to schools rather than the recommended 20 percent. He also overruled Stockman's plan to eliminate the urban development grant program. According to one account, Reagan "told his advisers that he was impressed with the arguments of mayors and Congressmen that the program generated billions of dollars in private investment in cities."[46]

The significant increases in defense spending, particularly in the first years of the Reagan presidency (which would contribute greatly to the developing deficit problem), were also in great measure Reagan's doing. Murray Weidenbaum, the chair of the Council of Economic Advisers, repeatedly urged Reagan to be more cautious and to make more cuts. Yet in Weidenbaum's view,

> In the battles on the military budget, the president would intervene most often on the side of Cap Weinberger. For example, when we urged a 90 percent increase in the defense budget over the first four years, instead of the defense department's desired 100 percent increase, Cap replied that our lower number would send the wrong signal to the Russians. The president said to me, patiently and sadly, "Murray, we don't want to send the wrong signal to the Russians."[47]

In fact, Weidenbaum notes, Reagan was generally "too nice of a guy to say 'no' often enough to his key people." When department heads appealed cuts, "President Reagan overruled us time and time again. . . . It never was a question of who was in charge." "Contrary to prevailing mythology," Weidenbaum observes, "the budget process would have worked much better if he had delegated more responsibility to his key subordinates. We came in with large budget cuts, and he did not agree with them."[48]

Reagan was also directly involved in the second prong of his economic program: decisions about what the administration would accept on the tax-cut bill. At a meeting with the legislative strategy group in May and facing increasing congressional opposition to the Kemp-Roth 10–10–10 formula (10 percent for each of the subsequent three years), it was Reagan who made the final decision to scale back the formula (to 10–10–5) in hopes of selling the plan to a reluctant Congress: "Twenty-five percent is as low as we can go. I don't want you fellas asking me to go under that figure. We'll take it to the people if we have to," he told the group. Reagan also indicated a willingness to accept some "ornaments" to the bill in the way of changes in the tax code to placate special interests and gain the support of their advocates in Congress; although some would prove costly, they were necessary to win support. According to Stockman, Reagan had made the key decisions that became the "LSG's negotiating charter in all the negotiations that followed." Even Baker came to the understanding, Stockman notes, "that this was a genuine presidential decision—beyond the ministrations of even the Chief of Staff."[49] In Murray Weidenbaum's view, Reagan's decision on the formula was instrumental in scuttling a Democratic alternative: "If the president had gone along with that, the bill would have passed. His response, however, as I recall very clearly was: 'I can win this,' and he did. The Democrats in the House became scared of him because they saw he could beat them, so he won that battle and many others." But Weidenbaum adds, "I wonder if we would have those remaining triple-digit budget deficits if he had compromised."[50]

Reagan, while prone to compromise in some areas, also held firm as the budget battle heated up. In June, Stockman urged Reagan to fight the congressional Democrats' attempt to gut the initial omnibus resolution mandating cuts through a variety of budget gimmicks. Baker, nervous that a loss on the floor of the House would jeopardize both the budget effort and the upcoming battle over tax reform, urged caution. Stockman, however, laid the out the problem before Reagan and told him that he couldn't live with the meager cuts that had been made. Reagan asked for the numbers and studied them carefully. "As he read it, the muscles in his jaw started to grind," Stockman recalls. But Reagan held firm: "Well, if that's the case," he told his aides, "we can't accept it." Meeting with congressional leaders later that day, Reagan did temporize a bit: some of the phony cuts would be accepted. But they would be contained within a more acceptable alternative to the Democrats' effort, and the Reagan-backed plan (Gramm-Latta II) passed later in the month.[51]

Terrel Bell, Reagan's secretary of education and a moderate who was often at odds with the more committed Reaganites, specifically notes in his memoirs that Stockman's characterization of Reagan as a passive spectator to his presidency is off the mark:

> David Stockman, in his book *The Triumph of Politics,* claimed that the president wandered in circles on policy matters, not giving direction with respect to decisionmaking. I never saw evidence of this. He often made decisions on budget and other matters that I did not like, some of which made me angry. But I never felt his policies were aimless or wandering or lacked clear focus. . . . Ronald Reagan made decisions that David Stockman did not like. Maybe this was the source of Dave's complaints. . . . Reagan was a decisive leader, and it is inaccurate to portray him otherwise.[52]

Another area where there is evidence of a more active Reagan is in the preparation of his speeches and other public remarks. Here, too, conventional wisdom has it that Reagan was heavily "scripted" by his advisers, yet Reagan's own level of involvement belies such accounts. For example, Reagan took an active role in preparing his crucial February budget address to Congress. The speechwriting staff prepared a draft, but Reagan himself added material on a weekend trip to Camp David just before the speech. On his return to the White House the day before the address, he met with his aides and went over the speech paragraph by paragraph. "It was a major editing session, with Ronald Reagan playing editor-in-chief," according to one aide.[53] Two months later, it was Reagan who drafted, in his own handwriting, a proposed address to the nation outlining the need for social security reform. Reagan also drafted remarks on the occasion of his firing of the air-traffic controllers, communiqués to Soviet leader Leonid Brezhnev, and some of his other major speeches later in the year.[54] He even edited the infamous index cards that his staff prepared for his meetings.[55]

Reagan valued meetings with his top advisers as a way of helping him think through problems. According to Ed Harper, "He liked to hear the positions discussed in his presence and to make a decision after having heard the various points of view."[56] For some, this was further evidence of his passivity. In John McClaughry's experience with the food and agriculture cabinet council, Reagan "did not like conflict among his lieutenants" and preferred that a consensus be reached. And Meese, in McClaughry's view, was the loyal lieutenant most skilled at producing that consensus. His "great talent" was "sitting at the table with conflicting staff or cabinet members and getting everyone to agree."[57]

But in Donald Regan's view there was a method behind Reagan's style in meetings:

> The man had a technique of sitting quietly. A lot of people thought he was dumb because he did this. They would say, "The President never spoke up." Why should he? He's got a panel of experts around him. Why not listen? Reagan took from them more than he put in because they knew the subject. He would hear their views, and most of the time they were opposing views. Then he would make up his mind. . . . Invariably the man had good instincts and judgments.[58]

Others have noted that Reagan would, on occasion, be a more active participant. According to a report on one of the first meetings of the CCEA that Reagan attended, the discussion got bogged down in technicalities. The president asked Don Regan for an explanation "in terms a layperson can understand." "You don't need to know the detail on that," Regan replied. "Yes I do," the president replied firmly and was given the explanation.[59]

Reflecting on meetings with congressional leaders and party officials, which he attended in his capacity as head of the Republican National Committee, Frank Fahrenkopf would later recall that "I saw him more than once take off his reading glasses and throw them on the table so hard that they would go up and hit the top of the ceiling in the cabinet room. He was very forceful. He knew what he believed in, and he knew what he wanted to see accomplished. He was a strong leader in that regard." According to Fahrenkopf, Reagan did have notes on small cards that he would refer to during the course of meetings, but the notion that he was wholly reliant on them was "unfounded." He may have used the cards to open or close a meeting, but in between "it was an open to-and-fro discussion. Reagan did not need the cards to make clear his position on such issues as increased taxes or whether he was going to veto something."[60]

Whether active or passive in meetings, a number of Reagan associates agree on his capacity to make a decision when called upon to do so. According to Bill Brock, "He didn't hesitate to make a decision [even if the cabinet was fairly divided]; he would make it and that was it. The nice thing about him was that he didn't make the loser feel like he was totally out of favor. He would be so gracious, yet firm . . . you didn't feel as though he was saying 'You're an idiot.'"[61]

But there were aspects of Reagan's decisionmaking that clearly made him dependent on the work of his staff and others in the administration. As in the transition, Reagan was the recipient of advice but not an active force in how what was presented to him had developed. In particular, Reagan's decisions as president were the end product of a process in which he was largely uninvolved in the crucial, initial stages of policy formulation, where controversies and divisions would be most apparent and differences on issues not papered over by consensus. Neither was Reagan prone to reach out and solicit information and advice beyond that provided him. According to one adviser, "He loves it when you call him, but he never calls you."[62]

Reagan's broad philosophy and vision, even if he was uncertain about the specifics of policies or how they had come about, created a sense of energy and commitment, at least in the first year. But over time, his philosophical views and principles could sometimes make him vulnerable to manipulation. According to one report, "Reagan can be induced to change his mind, but it is a complex and tricky process. The key, by unanimous consent of all who work for him, is to argue that a new position is as compatible with his fundamental beliefs as the one he is urged to abandon. Then Reagan can justify a switch as a mere tactical adjustment rather than a reversal of his conservative philosophy."[63] While a more active participant at the end of the decisionmaking process, Reagan was still beholden to the quality of work produced by those around him and to the good faith of their deliberations, both of which largely escaped his purview or concern.

A Problem of Management

Given Reagan's lack of attention or curiosity about how and what was percolating through his White House, it is not surprising that more general management of his White House staff could cause him problems. His lack of attention here carried over from the transition, where management issues were usually handled by Meese, Baker, or others in the Reagans' inner circle. By all accounts he was well liked and respected by his associates, not prone to temper tantrums or petty pique. But he also trusted too much in those around him. According to Lyn Nofziger, who observed Reagan throughout his political career, "He has this funny problem. He's too trusting. He thinks that if you work for him you'll like him and be loyal to him. He's right about 90 percent of the time, but unfortunately the other 10 percent can create problems."[64]

Managing personnel was a particular problem. According to Bill Brock, "He didn't like [to fire people]. He was very uncomfortable chewing people out."[65] More generally, in Brock's view, there was a "lack of willingness to direct the White House staff. There were too many games being played beneath him, and they did not involve real issues or basic principles, but rather petty stuff."[66] In the view of Helene von Damm, who had served Reagan throughout his political career, "He had innumerable strengths," but management "wasn't one of them. In fact never in his whole life did he understand how to manage a staff or appreciate the importance of staff work." "He always seemed oblivious to any infighting in the White House or to existing tensions."[67]

Even Ed Meese would later observe that success, given Reagan's penchant for delegation, "depends on the assumption and the reality that the people on whom he relies to share his vision will indeed carry out that decision . . . especially that he as president receives full and accurate information." In Meese's experience, there were some staff members who, pursuing their own policy goals, "could deprive him of needed information or dilute it after the fact." Moreover, Meese shared the view that Reagan trusted his staff and was reluctant to impute bad motives or to fire transgressors. But some "took advantage of this," and it "led to some of the darker days of his administration."[68]

Both in his general decision processes and in the management of those processes Reagan would be able to stave off those "darker days" if, as had been the case during the transition, those processes were well designed and the personnel selected to fill positions within them were skilled and committed but avoided the temptation to pursue their own agendas or engage in intramural turf battles. But even in Reagan's first months as president, there were signs—as we now turn to policy outcomes—that the decision-making process did not always fulfill its promise.

Policy Outcomes

What were the effects of the transition and the various decisionmaking processes that had been crafted on the early policies of this administration?

We have already seen one case—welfare reform—where a major policy proposal made during the transition prevailed despite subsequent staff opposition. The two cases I discuss here illustrate how the transition placed the administration in a more difficult position. One—social security reform—had not figured in the transition's agenda planning at all, and it is indicative of what happens when a transition *fails* to prepare for a major policy effort. Moreover, it was thwarted by an inability, stemming from the division of labor made during the transition, to integrate policy change (Meese's operation) with political considerations (Baker's shop) as decisionmaking unfolded. The second—the development and passage of Reagan's first-year budget and tax proposals—had begun during the transition. But the transition had not adequately served to explore the assumptions underlying the proposals or grappled with their long-range implications. Once Reagan took office, the decisionmaking process did not yield the critical scrutiny that was needed.

Social Security Reform?

The ill-fated social security proposal of 1981—delaying Consumer Price Index–based increases and more heavily (and immediately) penalizing those retiring at age sixty-two—was one of the major policy embarrassments of the early months of the new presidency. It particularly reflects a number of weaknesses in the administration's decision-making process. First, unlike Reagan's economic plan, it had not figured in the earlier agenda planning of the transition. By March, however, congressional Republican leaders as well as David Stockman recognized that changes in social security might be needed to meet budget-cut targets. It cost $200 billion per year, nearly one-third of the entire domestic budget, and it was fast approaching insolvency.

Second, absent prior planning, policy deliberations were hastily undertaken. An ad hoc working group was created, and it quickly generated a complex set of options, including an increase in the payroll tax, reductions in unearned benefits, and increased penalties for early retirement.[69] On Monday, May 11, President Reagan chaired a meeting of the cabinet council on human resources at which fifteen changes in social security were on the agenda. The hour-long meeting was the first and last opportunity the council members got to discuss the proposal, and it was held only one day before the reform package was presented to Congress. The ad hoc group's final recommendations were not made available to the council's participants until the Saturday (two days) before the meeting, and a clean copy of the final proposal was circulated only on Sunday, the day before.

Third, the policy deliberations that did take place did not adequately factor in political considerations that were likely to be critical with such a politically charged program. Unlike welfare reform, it was a popular middle-class entitlement, and charges had been made in the campaign that Reagan intended to balance the budget and get his proposed tax cuts "on the backs of the elderly." HHS Secretary Richard Schweiker was one of the prime movers of the effort and a member of the working group. Schweiker felt he had assurances from his former colleagues on Capitol Hill that the reforms would go through. It was a mistaken assumption that went unchallenged.

Jim Baker, heading the political side of the Reagan staff system, chose not to make his concerns felt during the working group's deliberations. Carleson and Schweiker, both members of the working group, attribute a good measure of the ensuing political controversy to the absence of Baker or one of his chief lieutenants at meetings. According to Carleson, the "Baker chair" at the meeting remained empty; Schweiker recalled that it was occupied by a very low level aide.[70]

Baker's operation had not been caught off-guard. Social security reform, in fact, had appeared on the agenda of the senior staff meeting as early as March 30 ("HHS looking at long-term social security financing. Question of whether we need private task force to look at this. Anderson will check"). On April 8, Martin Anderson, a member of the social security working group, reported back ("Social security funding issues to be surfaced through Human Resources Cabinet Council. Anderson notes 3 problems: specific administration positions on bills on Hill; social security system could run out of money as early as FY '83 and '84; Need long term legislation"). On Monday morning, May 11, the first agenda item of the senior staff meeting was the cabinet council meeting later that day ("Decisions include a number of sensitive items designed to bring social security financing into balance. These include reducing the amount payable on early retirement, eliminating widows with children over twelve, and eliminating dependents of early retirees").[71]

Fourth, the way policy had developed played into Ronald Reagan's weaknesses as a decisionmaker. At one level, he was prepared to make a decision and did so. He did reject several of the proposals—one to cut off survivors' benefits to children at age twelve, another to require new federal employees to participate in social security, and another by Schweiker to raise payroll taxes—but he approved the rest of the changes "just a few hours after they had been presented to him."[72] But he had received, as did the other council members, the final package only the day before the meeting.[73] And given his general lack of curiosity about how proposals had been crafted, Reagan was not likely to probe into the weaknesses of the proposals now in front of him. Unlike welfare reform, social security was not a policy area with which he had much familiarity; nor was he likely to know about the weakness in the political vetting that had taken place. In fact, at the council meeting on May 11, neither Baker nor Darman, who were in attendance, chose to raise questions of political feasibility (Stockman: "There wasn't really time").[74]

Baker may also have misguessed Reagan's willingness to make a decision so quickly; it was his usual practice not to do so at the meetings themselves. In his account of the meeting, Lawrence Barrett notes that Martin Anderson may have been particularly persuasive in urging the president to act with speed, which in turn caught Baker by surprise since "he thought Reagan would follow his custom and refrain from making a decision on the spot. In the interim, the proposals might be modified or tactics for presenting them worked out."[75]

Although Reagan had embraced most of the reforms, the political logistics of selling the package remained unresolved. But that afternoon, following the meeting, Baker convened his legislative strategy group. Unlike other occasions where Baker's group would modify proposals to attain their passage, this effort of the LSG was tantamount to scuttling the whole program. As soon as the group gathered, Baker told them (according to Stockman's version of the meeting) that the economic package would come first and that they needed to be concerned whether "we screw up the agenda" with this proposal. Baker then announced that "this isn't Ronald Reagan's plan. It's Dick Schweiker's . . . has everybody got that?" It would be an HHS proposal generated as a kind of ministerial response to an earlier request by a House committee.

Schweiker adamantly defended the proposal and recognized that it would be dead on arrival if it wasn't perceived as having complete White House backing. Baker backed off a bit and did permit Schweiker to present the proposal as an administration bill, but it still came from HHS—for all that signaled.[76] To be fair to Baker's position, the proposed changes not only made social security solvent over the immediate future; as Lawrence Barrett has pointed out, they added up "to twice what was necessary. Put another way, Reagan would now be open to the charge that he wanted to 'balance the budget on the backs of the elderly,' which is exactly what he had promised not to do."[77] Yet by not weighing in sooner, Baker had let the decision process run a course that was now politically costly.

Once the package was announced, the proposed changes in the penalties for early retirement proved particularly controversial. In Stockman's account, the date at which the proposed penalty (from 20 percent to 45 percent of age-sixty-five benefits) for retiring at sixty-two had slipped through the cracks (Stockman again: "We had run out of time").[78] Technicians in HHS, in his view, had simply inserted January 1, 1982, in the blank, thus upsetting the plans of people who were planning to retire in the immediate future. Bob Carleson disputes this account and recalls that Stockman knew full well the proposed date and was one of its proponents—the presumed savings were needed for Stockman's budget calculations for the upcoming fiscal year, set to begin in October.[79]

But whether Stockman or Carleson is right as a matter of historical record, or whether Baker's group had sandbagged the Reagan loyalists by their earlier absences, or whether those with good political radar missed an important opportunity or were reluctant to speak out at the May 11 evening, the episode does suggest that policymaking and political reality had not meshed well.

Congress's response was not surprising: social security reform was dead in the water. The Senate eventually voted 96–0 against any proposal to "precipitously and unfairly penalize early retirement." As it was, the resolution was something of a Pyrrhic victory for the White House, since it represented a compromise from much harsher language offered by Senator Daniel Patrick Moynihan that would have denounced the administration's package entirely.

Reagan, for his part, wanted to fight on. He drafted, in his own handwriting, a speech he proposed to give on national television defending his social security program.[80] But he eventually was dissuaded by his staff from doing so. The whole episode was one of the few occasions that first year in which the administration had been put on the political defensive.

The Reagan Economic Program

Reagan's economic program, which would emerge as the hallmark of his first year, was also affected by the transition, but less for its positive contributions and more for what it failed to prepare for. The Wirthlin group's "Initial Actions Report" had targeted budget reduction and tax reform as key administration priorities, and it identified the need to move forward quickly with proposals during the honeymoon.[81] Yet the report was lean on budgetary specifics. That job would fall to OMB

Director David Stockman. "Few of the plan's actual details," Richard Darman recalls, "were developed until Stockman began to provide them in December after the election."[82]

The transition had given Stockman something of a head start in his work. At that time, Stockman had devised the broad strategy of forcing Congress to agree early—and be constrained by—the reconciliation process set forth in the 1974 Budget and Impoundment Control Act. It was the first time its complex steps, procedures, and timetables were fully used, and it strategically positioned the administration well in its dealings with Congress.[83]

But the transition also complicated Stockman's efforts. Meetings with Reagan, Stockman, and the cabinet-designate had been set up in early January, but Stockman found he only "scratched the surface" in outlining the drastic budgetary actions that would be needed. Most important, Stockman, despite his own congressional experience in budget matters, lacked reliable indicators of future economic conditions—particularly revenue projections—that would be crucial in determining the impact of budget and tax changes on the federal deficit. Neither could Stockman turn to the CEA for input; not yet designated, its selection had been one of the few in the Reagan transition that took more time than expected.

A need to move quickly had been set out in the administration's "Initial Actions Plan." But that, coupled with the absence of reliable economic projections, put Stockman in an especially difficult position. It was not until February 7 that, in Stockman's words, the "warring economic sects"[84] in the Reagan administration could agree on an economic forecast. Yet that left only three days before they would meet with Reagan (February 10) and only another eight days before Reagan appeared before a joint session of Congress to present his economic package.

After inauguration day, following the plan for cabinet government (which Stockman regarded as "naive"), Meese scheduled a full cabinet meeting for each day of the first week; the budget was one of the principal topics for discussion. But Stockman found the reception less than satisfying: "I was faced with cabinet colleagues who were ill-schooled in even the basic tenets of the Reagan Revolution. Most were carrying their own do-it-yourself policy formulation kits."[85]

If the Reagan plan had been incrementalist in nature, then the "low level of fiscal literacy" at the top of the Reagan White House might not have mattered. "But a plan for radical and abrupt change required deep comprehension—and we had none of it." The Reagan plan involved raising defense spending and cutting taxes on a multiyear basis. When complete, the increase in defense spending plus the lost revenue due to the tax cuts would amount to 6 percent of gross national product (GNP). How much of the remaining 15 percent of GNP that went to domestic spending—including entitlements—had to be cut so that the deficit didn't swell? "History cannot blame the President for not considering this crucial question: I never provided him with a single briefing on this. There simply wasn't time. . . . No one raised any questions about what wasn't being reviewed and what wasn't being learned. . . . We thus recklessly charged ahead."[86]

The story about how Stockman's group eventually agreed to the economic numbers in their forecast is revealing about how reckless the deliberative process proved to be. The final hurdle was getting the new head of CEA, Murray Weidenbaum, to sign on. Weidenbaum felt that the forecast for inflation was too low. Finally, he and Stockman came up with a number they could agree on. Someone asked, "What model did this come out of Murray?" Weidenbaum replied, "It came right out of here," slapping his belly, "my visceral computer." The Weidenbaum number, although more cautious than Stockman's projections, added $700 billion in projected GNP over five years, building in $200 billion in phantom revenues. Although pleased at the time with the projections, Stockman would later admit that the "massive deficit inherent in the supply-side fiscal equation was substantially covered up. Eventually it would become the belly-slap that was heard around the world."[87]

Stockman, while a key figure, did not fly solo on budget matters in the early months of 1981. In Murray Weidenbaum's view, "Key budget and economic policy decisions" were made "by an informal group of White House officials during the first term": President Reagan, Vice President Bush, Baker, Meese, Anderson, Regan, Weidenbaum, as well as Stockman.[88] Some budget matters also made their way through the CCEA, and they were regular fare at the weekly Tuesday breakfasts at the Treasury Department that Regan, Stockman, Weidenbaum, and Anderson attended.[89]

But budget matters, particularly budget cuts, were not suited to fit the decision process that had been set up. Cabinet members, operating in their councils, were not likely to put their own departments and programs on the chopping block, and Meese and Baker did not have the budgetary expertise to exercise White House control. For his part, Stockman created an ad hoc "budget working group" (himself, Anderson, and Weidenbaum) that dealt directly with cabinet members. It was designed as a sort of appeals court, according to Martin Anderson, "that directly reviewed disputed budget cuts with individual cabinet members."[90]

But in his haste, Stockman sometimes made mistakes of monumental proportions, particularly in dealing with more experienced and skilled cabinet members. Caspar Weinberger, who had once held Stockman's position in the Nixon administration, was a particularly adept adversary. Defense was the one area slated for a budget increase, and any amounts added would mean deeper cuts elsewhere. Stockman and Weinberger finally were able to reach a compromise that increased defense spending by 7 percent a year using Carter's 1980 defense budget as the baseline. Only later did Stockman realize that the numbers were based on two very different estimates of Carter's budget. Stockman thought the figure was $142 million, the number used in the campaign; Weinberger, however, used a figure that included a 9 percent increase Congress had voted in response to the Iran hostage crisis and the FY 1981 rather than FY 1980 figure, for a baseline of $222 million. Weinberger's numbers stuck, and as a result the defense budget increased by a real growth rate (inflation factored in) of 10 percent rather than the 5 percent that Reagan had recently campaigned on.[91]

Stockman was also "rolled" by the politically skilled and bureaucratically wily Al Haig. Where only ten to fifteen people were usually present for the meetings Stockman convened to go over a department's budget, forty to fifty showed up for Stockman's meeting with Al Haig on the State Department's budget. Haig complained: "I can't make decisions in a roomful of people." Yet in Stockman's view, "It was surreal . . . they were his people, he had brought them." Cuts in State Department programs would be made later in private meetings between Haig and Stockman, where Haig's domineering personality would overwhelm any opposition. Haig finally agreed to some modest cuts, but even then, Stockman notes, he managed to send up to Congress "supplemental requests" about every other month to gain back his modest losses.[92]

Stockman's impact was not just felt in budget negotiations; it was his numbers, projections, and analysis—begun during the transition and set out in myriad black books—that bolstered the administration's case for deep cuts in domestic spending. Stockman's "magic asterisks" indicated "unspecified cuts to come," and his projections of inflation and the growth of GNP were, at best, educated guesswork. Coupled with his continued belief in and efforts to secure the significant tax cuts of Kemp-Roth, this would set the Reagan administration on a perilous course (unprecedented in its magnitude) of skyrocketing deficits.[93]

But also remarkable is that the White House was not kept in the dark on all that was transpiring. Economic and budget matters were at least discussed at the early-morning meeting of the troika, at the 8:00 A.M. meeting of senior staff (budget matters regularly appear on its daily agenda), and at the meeting of Meese's own staff that followed the 8:00 A.M. meeting (which included Anderson and Stockman deputy Ed Harper).[94] Baker's late-afternoon LSG also tracked developments in Reagan's economic program, particularly those stages where legislative strategy was required and when congressional negotiations were under way.[95] And though the administration was about to embark upon a course based on Stockman's rosy estimates and magic asterisks, no alarm bells sounded.

Reagan's role in the decision process was also crucial. Like social security, the federal budget was not an area where he had deep expertise; nor was he likely to delve into the minutiae of economic forecasts and revenue. Furthermore, it was a matter that often required *his* decision; any appeals of Stockman budget-group recommendations came to him. And as we saw earlier, decisions Reagan made were often guided only by his gut instincts and anecdotal information: mayors who told him urban development grants worked; or support for Weinberger's defense increase because of the signal it might send to the Russians.

On February 18, Reagan stood before Congress and unveiled his economic plan. By that time, Stockman had estimated that the tax cuts and the defense buildup would cost $900 billion. Yet he had identified only some $450 billion that might be cut (including many magic asterisks of unspecified cuts), all of which had yet to run the gauntlet of Congress as well as the power politics of Washington lobbyists and special interests. Moreover, the real deficit that might emerge would likely be even worse: the numbers were based on an economic forecast that painted a "rosy scenario," a label Weidenbaum applied "in jest." "If I had known then what I know now," Weidenbaum observed years later, "that is one wisecrack I would not have made."[96]

In his memoirs, Stockman observes that using the same forecast over a five-year period and plugging in the numbers for Jimmy Carter's budget (less defense, no Kemp-Roth) yielded a $365 billion surplus.[97] During his eight years as president, by contrast, Reagan managed to accumulate more federal debt than all of his predecessors—over two hundred years of the American Republic—*combined.*

The transition had allowed Stockman to begin his work, but it had not fully prepared him for the task ahead. And in its haste to hit the ground running, the transition had not provided Stockman sufficient time. Moreover, the process—in which a number of groups and actors participated—offered little in the way of a reality check that could question assumptions, particularly future revenue and growth projections and magic asterisks. The pragmatism and politics that had scuttled social security reform (albeit late and at a costly point in the game) either could or would not challenge the central tenets of the Reagan economic agenda or the weak economic assumptions on which they were built. Stockman's own reservations would build, but by that time it was too late; Reaganomics was in place.

Foreign Policy Decision Processes and Outcomes

Decisions made during the transition also had repercussions for foreign and national security policy once Reagan took office. Two in particular stand out. The first was the selection of Alexander Haig, who had publicly and privately touted himself as the "vicar" of foreign policy, as secretary of state. The second was the decision to have NSC Adviser Richard Allen report through Meese rather than directly to the president. Problems began on inauguration day when Haig presented a memorandum to be signed by Reagan that outlined a process that would give Haig preeminence over foreign policy; the vicar-designate would become the vicar-triumphant. Entitled "National Security Decision Directive No. 1," it immediately raised concern among Reagan's top aides that it constituted a "power grab" by Haig.[98] Although Haig did not get to see Reagan, he met with Meese, Baker, and Deaver, who subjected it to, as Haig later phrased it, a "dogged critique."[99] Reagan never signed the document, and Meese instructed Haig to work with other agencies and departments involved in foreign policy on a revised document.[100]

On February 26, Chief of Staff James Baker unveiled the basic structure of the national security and foreign policy process that the Reagan administration would use. Haig's responsibilities were much less than he had hoped for in his inauguration-day memorandum. But the terms of the agreement, which had been finalized in a meeting in Ed Meese's office, gave Haig more authority than his predecessors under Carter. The agreement also called for the creation of interdepartmental groups that would be headed by representatives of the secretaries of state and defense and the director of the CIA.

The NSC assistant and his staff continued to play a secondary role in the setup, with Allen reporting through Meese and with the departments

rather than the NSC staff taking the lead in the new committee structure. However, Meese and Allen would decide what issues fell within
the jurisdiction of which interdepartmental committee—no small matter.

Allen's role clearly departed from the pattern set by his immediate
predecessors. He did not have cabinet rank. Also, unlike Brzezinski,
who had chaired the interagency special coordination committee
(which enabled him to wield great influence over Carter's foreign policy), Allen was simply part of a departmental-dominated apparatus. For
Allen, his role model was Gordon Gray of the Eisenhower years rather
than McGeorge Bundy, Kissinger, or Brzezinski, who had used their
positions, access to the president, and NSC staff to put their own imprint on day-to-day policy developments. Selling policy, in Allen's
view, was the "White House press secretary's job, not mine." "If you're
looking for action in terms of day-to-day operations, sending out cables and circulating memos," he told colleagues, "this is not the place
for you." Instead, Allen felt that long-term planning and initiatives
were within his domain. According to some former NSC staff members, "The system's been emasculated. Allen isn't going to be able to
coordinate policy. He's too busy getting out of everyone's way."[101]

While Allen may have modeled himself after Eisenhower-era NSC
advisers, he operated in a White House that lacked the smooth machinery and orderly processes of the Eisenhower system. As Lou Cannon notes, based on an interview with Allen, "Much of Allen's time
was spent vainly trying to shove decision documents and position papers through the funnel-like management system that Meese had created to spare Reagan from decision-making." Allen's paperwork ended
up on Meese's desk or in his infamous briefcase, "and too many of
them stayed there. At one point in Allen's year-long tenure, fourteen
separate papers requiring presidential decisions were blocked by the
Meese bottleneck."[102]

By October, reports indicated that Allen and his assistants played a
"clearly secondary staff role and not the traditional role of adjudicators
and coordinators of different departmental views." "With some exceptions, Mr. Allen's staff is seen by other officials as bureaucratically un-
skilled and highly ideological."[103] Ed Meese was not much help, either:
"Meese is said to have veto power and to be a kind of traffic police-
man, . . . but he does not have the background, the time or the staff to
run the system on a day-to-day basis. However, they say he will not
delegate the power to anyone else."[104]

With no strong NSC staff and with groups under departmental rather
than NSC control, issues moved immediately from the interdepartmental

groups to the NSC for deliberation. In July, Meese sought to bridge the gap by creating the National Security Planning Group. Its aim was to freely discuss national security issues, similar in purpose to the NSC but without the presence of the chair of Joint Chiefs or any staff aides. Its members were Haig, Weinberger, Casey, Bush, and the troika, with Reagan presiding. Allen's role was described as that of "note taker." There was no memorandum formally establishing the group, and its operations were likened to a larger-scale version of Johnson's Tuesday lunches. According to one member of the NSC, "Since no one is in charge, everyone has to be there."

As Leslie Gelb reported in the *New York Times,* "The system is pictured as a highly informal, word-of-mouth one, riddled with somewhat more than the usual number of personality conflicts but with somewhat less than the usual differences over philosophy." "Preparations for meetings at the White House are described as erratic. Sometimes there are papers prepared, sometimes not, and sometimes the papers are prepared no more than 12 hours in advance of the meeting." In July, the National Security Planning Group met to discuss terrorism, but the option paper they had been given had not even been approved by the relevant assistant secretaries. According to Gelb, "As participants tell it, this means that White House meetings often occur without agreed papers by key aides and experts on the issues, the facts and the alternatives." After meetings, "subordinates rarely see minutes of what has been discussed or a memorandum of decisions. The net effect, according to virtually all those interviewed, is that the participants often return to their departments with more than the usual number of conflicting interpretations of what happened and what was decided."[105] As late as October 1981, the administration had issued only twelve national security decision documents and had yet to review almost all standing decisions from prior administrations on a broad range of foreign policy matters.

Conflict and Controversies Emerge

Although Reagan had hoped to avoid some of the turf battles and infighting over foreign policy that had occurred in the Carter years, his administration seems to have fared much worse. Haig continued to be a source of irritation, not just to others in the foreign policy circle but also to the White House and eventually the president himself. In just the first two months of the new administration, Haig had feuded with Stockman over foreign aid; then with Transportation Secretary Lewis and with Bill Brock, the special trade representative, over Japanese auto imports; and then with Agriculture Secretary Block over the Soviet grain embargo. According to a first-hundred-days recap in the *New York Times,* "Haig's biggest disagreements have been with Defense Secretary Caspar W. Weinberger over statements about the neutron bomb, arms negotiations with the Russians and—most embarrassingly—over who was in charge in the Situation Room at the White House hours after Mr. Reagan had been shot."[106] In his tiff with Weinberger, Haig had advised European allies to disregard the defense secretary's statement on the neutron bomb. In the aftermath of the publicity, the State Department publicly released a cable informing U.S. embassies that the news stories were wrong.

Haig lost an important battle in late March 1981, when the White House named Vice President Bush rather than Haig as its foreign policy crisis manager. A crisis management committee had been outlined in Haig's infamous inauguration-day memo—with Haig as chair. Haig reportedly threatened to resign if he were not given the job, but Bush was appointed instead.

Haig then came in conflict with the White House staff. On March 25, 1981, Reagan met with Haig. Although Reagan denied that Haig threatened to resign, White House officials said that "Haig did speak of resigning to senior White House aides." A State Department source also said Haig gave that impression to subordinates before his meeting with Reagan. According to the *Washington Post,* Haig "was not entirely satisfied with the outcome," and there was "continuing concern about the future of working relationships between Haig and senior presidential advisers and a sense that much remains unresolved."[107]

In another article in the *Washington Post,* Lou Cannon reported that "a related problem from a White House perspective is that Haig had failed to grasp the preferred Reagan style, which is collegial and harmonious rather than confrontational." The public dispute began following Haig's March 24 testimony before a House subcommittee in which he expressed a "lack of enthusiasm" over reports that Bush, not he, would be placed in charge of crisis management. The incident also brought to the fore criticism of Haig's style in cabinet meetings: according to one official who attended most cabinet meetings, "Haig's attitude was aloof and uncooperative. The only way he knows to come on is full bore—he's too much a military man."[108]

In June, UN Ambassador Jeane Kirkpatrick became the latest Haig target, with the "State Department" expressing concern over how she had handled a UN resolution condemning but not punishing Israel for an attack on Iraqi nuclear reactors. According to one report, "Mr. Reagan was reportedly so annoyed by the criticism that he threw down his copy of the *New York Times* and immediately telephoned Mrs. Kirkpatrick to reassure her of his support."[109]

Meanwhile, Richard Allen reportedly had been photocopying articles that contained criticism, coming from State Department sources, of himself and other top White House aides, which he then passed around at meetings in order to rally support against Haig. Top White House aides were also described in the press as regarding Haig's personality as "volatile" and "unusual." By July, they were telling the press that strained relations with Haig were a "fact of life" in the Reagan administration and that "frustration" had been felt at the highest levels of the administration.[110] Haig's view of the White House staff was that they were "second-rate hambones."[111]

In early November, Haig told columnist Jack Anderson (who was preparing a column that characterized Haig as being on Reagan's "disappointment list" and having "one foot on a banana peel") that an unnamed Reagan aide (presumably Allen, according to some reports) "has been running a guerrilla campaign against him for nine months."[112] At Haig's request, Reagan himself was drawn into the controversy and called Anderson to deny the allegations. On November 5, Reagan called Haig and Allen into a private, one-hour meeting in the Oval Office and ordered them to end their feuding.

Although nine months earlier Reagan had pledged to end the pattern of the administration speaking with conflicting voices over foreign policy, there still was "no disciplined system for making decisions in these areas," a lengthy study by the *New York Times* concluded. "Sometimes the process is so centralized, so tightly held among the President and his political advisers that no one with expert knowledge is present and little staff work is done." Reagan's foreign policy choices, in turn, were affected: "This was the case in the recent decision to deploy the new MX missile in fixed silos." At other times, "The operation is so disorganized that the President risks his whole leadership position," as in the failure for months to prepare for a battle with Congress on the proposed sale of AWACS (early warning radar aircraft) to Saudi Arabia. "Other decisions are made at the top in the White House without proper regard for the consequences on other matters," the analysis continued.[113]

In December, it was Allen's turn to face the political heat. Reports surfaced that in January he had received $1,000 from a Japanese magazine to arrange for an interview with Mrs. Reagan. Allen placed the cash in his office safe and said he had forgotten about it. It also came to light that Ed Meese had ordered a management review of the NSC apparatus, fueling speculation that Allen's departure was imminent and that major changes were planned. Although a Justice Department investigation cleared Allen of wrongdoing, the expected shake-up in the NSC did take place, and he was forced to resign his position on January 4, 1982. His replacement was William Clark, a longtime Reagan associate who had been serving as Haig's deputy at the State Department. In addition, Clark was given direct access to Reagan, thus ending Meese's supervision of the NSC system.

Although Clark's relationship to Reagan and to Haig, as well as his reputation as a mediator, were thought to bring stability to the Reagan foreign policy system, difficulties persisted. While serving as Haig's deputy, Clark had worked diligently to smooth the troubled waters between Haig and the White House staff. But reports now surfaced of Haig's feuds with Clark, which even included alleged shouting matches between Haig and the mild-mannered Clark.[114] According to one White House aide, "It's untenable to have a Secretary of State who feels the President's role is subordinate to his." For his part, Haig told his aides that he was "tired of having four of five people running foreign policy" and intended to "straighten things out" or quit.[115] In a surprise announcement on June 25, 1982, President Reagan announced Haig's resignation and his replacement by George Shultz.

Yet in Baker's view, problems persisted. Reagan's foreign policy apparatus "was often a witches' brew of elbows, egos, and separate agendas. From day one, the level of suspicion and distrust was utterly out of control among many of the major players. I can't remember any extended period of time when someone in the National Security cluster wasn't at someone else's throat." Even in cases where Reagan had "decided a major policy issue, his subordinates would ignore his wishes and pursue their own policy schemes. . . . The chaos and backbiting served him and the country poorly."

At one point Baker and Deaver even concocted a plan to move Baker into the NSC adviser slot and Deaver to chief of staff. According to Baker, "The abortive plan to make me National Security Adviser was advanced by Mike Deaver and me in an effort to inject some sanity and cohesion into the national security process." They even thought they had Reagan's assent to the move, but at the last minute others in the Reagan inner circle intervened. In Baker's view, "Predictably, it was torpedoed by some of the very same principals whose small-bore behavior had given rise to the proposal in the first place."[116]

Yet the rest of the White House was not without problems. Toward the end of the first year, reports began to surface—fueled by unnamed sources—that Meese's power was dwindling while Baker's was on the ascent.[117] Other stories detailed infighting and competition between their respective staffs. The situation got worse, not better, over time.

In 1982, the *New York Times,* for example, reported, "'What do they do?' has been the stiletto-like question brandished for some time in White House corners about counselor [Meese] and his sizable staff of planners. . . . In the past year, the sniping has become ingrained in White House circles as Mr. Meese's power has waned."[118] In 1983, the *Los Angeles Times* reported that "Baker, Deaver, and Meese long ago ceased functioning as a collective management team, and now operate, as one administration official described it, as 'individual lords, each possessing his own fiefdom, with middle-level people often brandishing swords.'" According to one White House aide, "I've never worked in an organization like this. There is no one person to give orders, except the president. This lends itself to jockeying for position and not letting anyone else get too far ahead. Pretty soon you have a lot of walking wounded."[119]

In the view of Martin Anderson, "Unfortunately, the kind of systematic and tough staffing that took place during the transition was not sustained. Slowly, gradually, one by one, people less talented and less completely committed to Reagan's policy agenda began to fill the ranks of the administration. The results were disastrous."[120]

* * *

The Reagan transition contrasts markedly with the Carter experience four years earlier. It managed to avoid the conflicts that had marked Carter's effort and carried over into his presidency. Partly this was due to a better sense of teamwork, oversight, and organization and an ability of some of the principals to bear their own personal disappointments. Yet there was also an earlier and more clearly defined effort to establish jobs and responsibilities in the upcoming administration.

More attention was also paid to the broader organization of the Reagan presidency, especially in designing the various processes that would impact presidential decisionmaking. Of particular note were the efforts made to make better use of the cabinet through the cabinet councils and to attempt to tailor that system to Reagan's own decisionmaking style and experience. The experiment was only a partial success; key policy decisions were either made largely outside the system—welfare and social security reform—or drew only in part on its operations—Reagan's budget and tax proposals. But the councils did handle a number of second- and third-level policy issues. At least from the participants' perspective, they fostered teamwork and provided an organized way for coordinating the input of cabinet members as well as the White House staff.

White House organization had also been well explored during the transition by Meese and Baker; there was no vacuum or void, as with Carter. Baker's appointment as deputy director of the transition in charge of White House planning gave him a formidable head start in crafting the staff he would lead. He took full advantage of the opportunity. The difficulty for Reagan's top advisers was in making their division of labor work. Both Meese and Baker were able to settle on a working relationship, but in the end it was one that would yield a shift in influence toward Baker's operation. Here, the efforts of the transition failed to anticipate the end results of separating policy from politics and day-to-day management.

The arrangement was largely successful in the first year of the Reagan presidency, which points not just to the merits of settling matters of organization and process early on but also to the importance of the skills and commitments of those who would occupy key positions.

But those skills and commitments, and the organizational arrangements in which they operated, did not perform well in the two policy cases—both important—that we examined. In social security reform, Baker's impact was not felt as proposals were initially fleshed out; neither did it register at the May 11 meeting where Reagan made his decisions. It was only afterward that Baker swung into action, and the response doomed the fate of social security reform in 1981. On budget and tax proposals, neither the policy operation nor the units under Baker's control were in a position to question the fundamental assumptions underlying Reaganomics. Budgetary matters in particular did not fit neatly in the decisionmaking structure that had been crafted. Baker's operation could foster their political success—as it did—but it was not equipped to question their soundness.

Yet even as these policy areas do not exhibit a decision process operating at its best, foreign policy fared even worse. What Baker and Meese had worked out for domestic policy did not occur in the relationships among Reagan's foreign policy principals. Conflict, competition, and infighting were the order of the day, and it registered in a number of policy areas. But here, too, the transition had some effect: the decision to make Richard Allen's position subordinate to Meese made him less of an equal than his predecessors as NSC assistant. Working out a suitable national security process not only eluded the transition planners; it would continue to vex Reagan throughout his presidency.

From Ronald Reagan's perspective, the work of the transition yielded a process that seemed to fit his felt needs as a decisionmaker: one that would match how he had operated as governor, one that allowed him to delegate, one that—in theory, at least—would generate the kind of deliberative processes he felt comfortable with. He could provide broad direction, and he was a more active participant than is common lore.

Unlike Carter, a process had at least been organized and crafted. But like Carter, it sometimes operated in ways that played to weaknesses rather than strengths. In both social security reform and in the budget and tax proposals, Reagan made final decisions but relied on a process that had not adequately vetted the political implications of his choices or made clear the questionable assumptions underlying policy proposals.

As a decisionmaker reliant on delegation, Reagan depended on the trust of those serving him and the integrity of a process that would produce well-crafted and thought-out policy choices. For Reagan, the arrangement could work if those entrusted with the power vested in them rose to the task. It is an important feature of the Reagan transition and early presidency that an effort so directed at organizational matters would rely so heavily on the trust and shared commitment of its principals. It was, as Meese, Anderson, and others came to realize, a feature of the Reagan presidency that could pose potential problems. Reagan, moreover, did not possess the managerial skills of an Eisenhower, able to detect and compensate for shortcomings; nor was he willing to reap whatever benefits a Jimmy Carter might have obtained from enmeshing himself in policy details.

As the Reagan administration wore on, the situation became worse, not better. As those he relied on for managerial practice became enmeshed in their own turf battles, Reagan lacked the ability and will to exercise control himself. Difficulties especially emerged in his second term with Don Regan's appointment as chief of staff and the internal machinations of Robert McFarlane, John Poindexter, and Oliver North.

But in 1981 Reagan and his advisers had at least come prepared to the presidency with a policy agenda. In contrast to the Carter experience, strategic planning and prioritizing had been undertaken, and better relations with Congress had been established from the start. Reagan's efforts had reoriented the national political agenda. Whether that agenda—particularly in its budget and tax proposals—was a wise course is another matter.

Notes

1. For further discussion, see Burke, *The Institutional Presidency,* pp. 35–40, 90–98.

2. Other factors also played a part in the development of the councils. The particular functional groupings of the five councils, for example, may have drawn from the experience of the transition itself: Timmons's executive branch management teams had been broken down into five groups. According to Danny Boggs, who would serve as executive secretary for one council, Martin Anderson was an important source of inspiration. Anderson's experience in the Nixon administration had taught him that "serious decisions from scratch in the full cabinet was not very likely," and yet "he felt strongly that there was a need both for a way for having people air things and a way for keeping decisions closer to the White House orbit as opposed to letting the agencies run wild." Burke interview with Danny Boggs, June 17, 1998. In his exit interview from the White House staff, Anderson also noted that Nixon's attempt to solve the problem "by setting up a Domestic Council was still too big and unwieldy. Nixon's meetings were dominated by staff." Martin Anderson, White House Exit Interview, RL. Caspar Weinberger, whom several participants cited as an important adviser to Meese in establishing the councils, may also have brought his own experience in the Nixon cabinet to bear; Weinberger had served both as OMB director and secretary of HEW and thus observed Nixon's increasing frustration with his cabinet firsthand. Burke interview with Ralph Bledsoe, June 23, 1998, and Burke interview with Richard Wirthlin, June 5, 1998. Weinberger himself acknowledges a role in working on such a proposal: "We tried to set up a similar situation in Washington, but a number of people who were more favorable to the basic idea of presidential staff versus the cabinet were able, in one way or another, to make sure that the more traditional form was established—that is, that the president would have his own staff, and the cabinet would more or less run the departments." Caspar Weinberger, "Reagan and International Arms Agreements," in Thompson, *Foreign Policy in the Reagan Presidency,* p. 48. Furthermore, although Meese was cognizant of and favorably disposed to the recommendation of the Ash Council for the creation of a supercabinet during the Nixon administration, both Meese and Weinberger were aware of the congressional opposition that had developed to the proposal as well as the problems that had emerged when Nixon created a single Domestic Council under the direction of John Ehrlichman. Burke interview with Ralph Bledsoe, June 23, 1998.

3. Memorandum from Ed Meese to the Cabinet, "Cabinet Councils," no date, Khachigian Files, Box 4689, RL.

4. Meetings of the full cabinet continued to be regularly held. In his first five months as president, Reagan presided over nineteen meetings of the cabinet, and by June 1982 some fifty full cabinet meetings had been convened. However, these sessions were less than final decision points; rather they served to familiarize cabinet members with policy issues that might be beyond the scope of their particular responsibilities or the councils in which they had participated, as well as an assortment of management issues. As Chester Newland notes, they were "sessions noted for presidential focus through stories on his philosophy of self governance and limited government" and for the need for "disciplined work on [his] priorities." Newland, "A Mid-term Appraisal," p. 9; see also Dick Kirschten, "Reagan's Cabinet Councils May Have Less Influence Than Meets the Eye," *National Journal,* July 11, 1981, p. 1242.

5. Burke interview with Danny Boggs, June 17, 1998.

6. The staff secretariat was apparently a late addition to the structure of the council system. As late as February 9, Frank Hodsoll, one of Baker's deputies, reported to him that some understanding of "where the staff of such a cabinet cluster will be" remained to be worked out. The particular issue of the memo concerned a bit of organizational politics between Martin Anderson and Don Regan. Anderson wanted to convene a lunch group of his "outside economists"; Regan would "go along" provided that the cabinet cluster on economics was announced first. According to Hodsoll, Treasury thought that the staff of the cluster would be at Treasury. In Hodsoll's view, "I don't think that would work; going this way on economics prejudices how you go with State and DOD." Hodsoll noted that there were boundary issues still unresolved; there needed to be some understanding of "how the economic group relates to other groups; e.g., international economic issues, resources, social, etc." Memorandum from Frank Hodsoll to James Baker, February 8, 1981, Policy Research (Anderson), Hodsoll Files, OA 9107, Box 1, RL.

7. Martin Anderson, White House Exit Interview, RL. From the very start of the Reagan presidency, care was taken to ensure an orderly and organized process of information gathering, distribution, review, and implementation. On January 27, 1981, Craig Fuller, director of the Office of Cabinet Affairs, sent to all cabinet members a lengthy memo describing the procedures to be used for submitting agenda items and distributing material to other cabinet and White House staff members; the memo also set out a time frame to be used and a standard format in which information was to be presented. Memorandum from Craig Fuller to Cabinet Members, "Cabinet Procedures," January 27, 1981, Khachigian Files, Box 4689, RL. In addition, Fuller's office prepared briefing memos for President Reagan prior to each meeting of the cabinet or its councils, and Richard Darman, as staff secretary, assembled the final set of materials that went to the president. Fuller's office also issued weekly tracking reports for each item on every council's agenda (and followed them afterward); the reports briefly summarized the "forcing action" of each item (e.g., a congressional hearing, or a statutory or administration deadline), current status, to what council or White House unit the item was staffed to, and the particular

official assigned to take action. For an example, see "Office of Cabinet Affairs, Issue Tracking Report," November 30, 1981, Meese Papers, Office of Cabinet Affairs Tracking Summaries, OA 2825, RL.

8. Dick Kirschten, "Circles Within Circles," *National Journal,* March 7, 1981, p. 399.

9. Burke interview with Danny Boggs, June 17, 1998.

10. William Niskanen, "Organizing the Government for Policy Making," in Thompson, ed., *Reagan and the Economy,* p. 30.

11. Meese also contributed to the cabinet's sense of teamwork and an emphasis on frank discussion by convening monthly breakfast meetings without the president or any staff present. We would "just talk about how the cabinet was going, whether there were any problems anyone was having, any feeling that they were being shut out or any other difficulties of communication. We tried to solve them there among us." It was "similar to what I had done in Sacramento; if you have just the members of the cabinet there, without the president and without the staff, you can hash these things over and it's a very different atmosphere." "We designed it not to be an agenda-driven meeting, but a meeting where people could feel free to bring things up. . . . It was probably one of the most free-flowing meetings." Burke interview with Ed Meese, May 27, 1998. In the view of Education Secretary Bell, "These were off-the-record sessions that enabled all thirteen cabinet members to meet with Ed to talk over problems and to ventilate issues that were particularly galling to us. It was a very effective procedure, and Ed performed his role well." But Bell, who was becoming increasingly disaffected, notes that "I seldom had much to say. . . . I doubted that there was much value in expressing my frustrations to my twelve colleagues, and I didn't care to unload on Meese." Bell, *The Thirteenth Man,* p. 99.

12. Burke interview with Ed Meese, May 27, 1998.

13. Burke interview with Richard Wirthlin, June 5, 1998.

14. Anderson, *Revolution,* pp. 228–229.

15. Dom Bonafede, "Generation Gap," *National Journal,* October 24, 1981, p. 1914.

16. Anderson, *Revolution,* p. 225.

17. Meese, "The Institutional Presidency," p. 196.

18. Newland, "A Mid-term Appraisal," p. 10.

19. Burke interview with Richard Schweiker, May 6, 1998.

20. Burke interview with John Block, April 15, 1998.

21. Burke interview with Ralph Bledsoe, June 23, 1998. Bledsoe was a member of the Office of Planning and Evaluation, then executive secretary of the cabinet council on management and administration, and, finally, executive secretary of the Domestic Policy Council—one of the two remaining councils when they were all combined in Reagan's second term.

22. Harper, "The Reagan White House: The Approach, the Agenda, and the Debt," in Thompson ed., *Leadership in the Reagan Presidency II,* p. 128.

23. Based on the data in the OPE report, the average attendance for each council was twenty-two attendees for economic affairs, twenty-five for commerce

and trade, seventeen for human resources, twenty-two for natural resources, and twelve for food and agriculture. With the exception of the Council on Economic Affairs, attendance tended markedly to go up when the president or vice president was present. Memorandum from Richard Beal to Edwin Meese, "Strategic Evaluation Memorandum #1: Summary of Cabinet Council Activities," July 16, 1981, Beal Files, CFOA 465, Box 1, RL. In early November, the OPE issued a second report (less comprehensive than the first) that brought the analysis through the end of September. Only two presidential policy decisions had been issued since early July, one on synthetic fuels and one on nuclear policy, both issuing from the cabinet council on natural resources and the environment. Although the report did not track presidential or vice presidential attendance, the average attendance figures for each council was almost exactly the same as it had been in the earlier report. The one noticeable difference was a widening in the gap between the most active and the least active councils: economic affairs had met fifteen more times, commerce and trade sixteen times, natural resources nine times, while food and agriculture met only once and human resources had not met at all. From February through September, the councils had handled eighty agenda items (not counting repeats at subsequent meetings); of these, forty-one (51 percent) were in economic affairs, eleven (14 percent) in commerce and trade, twenty-one (26 percent) in natural resources and the environment, seven (9 percent) in food and agriculture, and three (4 percent) in human resources. OPE did a third study of the council system, tracking its work from February 1981 to May 1982. As in the first report, CCEA and CCCT were the most active councils and continued to meet on a regular basis. CCEA met six to nine times a month for a total of a hundred meetings, and CCCT met from once to four times each month for a total of thirty-one meetings. CCHR met only three times from February to June 1981, did not meet for five months, and then met twelve times from November through April 1982. CCNR met twenty-six times in 1981, but only once a month thereafter. CCFA met only ten times through the whole period. "Action on Cabinet Council Agenda Topics" and "Summary Data on Cabinet Council Meetings," Office of Policy Evaluation, November 3, 1981, Beal Files, CFOA 465, Box 1, RL. In terms of attendance, Reagan participated in twenty-six of the 191 meetings (14 percent), Anderson in 124 (65 percent), Weidenbaum in 114 (60 percent), Regan in 113 (59 percent), Baldridge in 100 (53 percent), Drew Lewis in ninety-three (49 percent), Vice President Bush in eighty-eight (43 percent). Those infrequently attending were, among the cabinet, Haig at only nine meetings (5 percent), Weinberger at thirteen (7 percent), and, among the staff, Baker at only thirteen (7 percent). Meese attended only thirty-five meetings (18 percent). Newland, "A Mid-term Appraisal," pp. 7–8.

24. Burke interview with Ralph Bledsoe, June 23, 1998.

25. Walker and Reopel, "Strategies for Governance," p. 753.

26. Burke interview with Ed Meese, May 27, 1998.

27. Burke interview with Frank Hodsoll, January 26, 1999.

28. Burke interview with James Cicconi, April 29, 1998.

29. Burke interview with Frank Hodsoll, January 26, 1999.

30. Steven Weisman and Howell Raines, "Reagan's Staff Is Like-Minded but Not Always of One Mind," *New York Times,* January 17, 1982.

31. Burke interview with Frank Hodsoll, January 26, 1999.

32. Burke interview with Frank Hodsoll, January 26, 1999.

33. In addition to Baker, its members included Darman, Gergen, Friedersdorf, and Duberstein from congressional affairs, Craig Fuller, Meese, Anderson, and Stockman and his deputy, Ed Harper. Others would attend as the situation demanded, such as Treasury Secretary Regan, who was a frequent participant when budget and tax items were under consideration. Darman, *Who's In Control?* p. 84.

34. Burke interview with James Cicconi, April 29, 1998.

35. Anderson, *Revolution,* p. 239.

36. Howell Raines, "Policy Office Is Short on Clout and Long on Critics," *New York Times,* January 11, 1982.

37. William Safire, "Of Meese and Men," *New York Times,* October 22, 1981.

38. Anderson, *Revolution,* p. 238.

39. Hedrick Smith, "The Making of a Chief of Staff," *New York Times,* February 8, 1982.

40. Steven Weisman and Howell Raines, "Reagan's Staff Is Like-Minded but Not Always of One Mind," *New York Times,* January 17, 1982.

41. Memorandum from Richard G. Darman for White House Senior Staff, "Memoranda for the President," January 28, 1981, Staff Secretary (Darman), Hodsoll Files, OA 9107, RL. Emphasis in original.

42. Examples of these can be found in Martin Anderson Files, Staffing Memos, CFOA103, RL.

43. Burke interview with Frank Hodsoll, January 26, 1999. Darman, in fact, "was totally fair because Darman was more subject to suspicion than Baker or me. Darman had worked for Elliott Richardson; Darman had to get over that." However, in contrast to Hodsoll's positive assessment of Darman, one high-level member of the OPD would later recall that Darman was "aggressive and smart" and not above attempting to influence the process. Burke interview with John McClaughry, October 21, 1997.

44. Nofziger, "Reagan: The Person and the Political Leader," in Thompson, ed., *Leadership in the Reagan Presidency I,* p. 85.

45. Meese, "The Reagan Presidency," in Thompson, ed., *Leadership in the Reagan Presidency II,* p. 225.

46. Steven Weisman, "Reagan's Moves Hinting at Style for a Presidency," *New York Times,* February 23, 1981.

47. Murray Weidenbaum, "Reagan and Economic Policy Making," in Thompson, ed., *Reagan and the Economy,* pp. 9–10.

48. Murray Weidenbaum, "Reagan and Economic Policy Making," in Thompson, ed., *Reagan and the Economy,* p. 9.

49. Stockman, *Triumph of Politics,* pp. 239, 246.

50. Murray Weidenbaum, "Reagan and Economic Policy Making," in Thompson, ed., *Reagan and the Economy,* p. 7.

51. Stockman, *Triumph of Politics,* p. 213.

52. Bell, *The Thirteenth Man,* p. 31.

53. Steven Weisman, "Reagan's Moves Hinting at Style for a Presidency," *New York Times,* February 23, 1981.

54. Examples of these drafts can be found in James Baker's papers at Rice University.

55. Examples can be found in the President's Handwriting File at the Reagan Library. The Reagan Library also has an extensive collection of the speech drafts he edited.

56. Ed Harper, "The Reagan White House: The Approach, the Agenda, and the Debt," in Thompson, ed., *Leadership in the Reagan Presidency II,* p. 128.

57. Burke interview with John McClaughry, October 21, 1997.

58. Don Regan, "The Reagan Presidency: Atop the Second Tier," in Thompson, ed., *Leadership in the Reagan Presidency I,* p. 53.

59. Steven Weisman, "Reagan's Moves Hinting at Style for a Presidency," *New York Times,* February 23, 1981.

60. Frank Fahrenkopf, "Reagan as Political Leader," in Thompson, ed., *Leadership in the Reagan Presidency II,* p. 25.

61. Bill Brock, "The Reagan Presidency: Leadership Revisited," in Thompson, ed., *Leadership in the Reagan Presidency II,* p. 117.

62. George Church, "How Reagan Decides," *Time,* December 13, 1982.

63. George Church, "How Reagan Decides," *Time,* December 13, 1982. In 1982, for example, the $99 billion, three-year package of revenue measures crafted by Senator Bob Dole was accepted by Reagan under the rubric of "tax reform" rather than as a tax increase. Transportation Secretary Drew Lewis, moreover, got him to accept a five-cent-per-gallon increase in the federal gasoline tax as a "user fee" rather than as a tax increase.

64. Lyn Nofziger, "Reagan: The Person and the Political Leader," in Thompson, ed., *Leadership in the Reagan Presidency I,* p. 85.

65. Bill Brock, "The Reagan Presidency: Leadership Revisited," in Thompson, ed., *Leadership in the Reagan Presidency II,* p. 117.

66. Bill Brock, "The Reagan Presidency: Leadership Revisited," in Thompson, ed., *Leadership in the Reagan Presidency II,* p. 118.

67. Von Damm, *At Reagan's Side,* pp. 184, 320.

68. Meese, Hofstra University Conference on the Reagan Presidency, April 22, 1993, taped remarks, RL.

69. The group included HHS Secretary Schweiker, OMB Director Stockman, and Martin Anderson and Carleson from OPD.

70. According to Schweiker, "Baker's office was invited to participate in working through the proposal. For reasons I don't understand, they sent a second- or third-level . . . person there, and eventually we all signed off after a lot of lengthy debate on the whole thing. And then Baker's office ambushed it. They either got cold feet or changed their minds, after agreeing that this is what they wanted to do. It was probably Darman. They shot it down internally and then put us out there to be the fall guy. I didn't object to that . . . but it was

clear they had shot it down and I was to be the fall guy. And I took the fall. What ticked us off was that their guy was in on the whole thing right from the beginning, approved it all along the way, and signed off on it. That's what ticked us off. They got cold feet at the last minute or they weren't paying attention to what their guy was saying. One way or the other, that's what happened." Burke interview with Richard Schweiker, May 6, 1998.

71. "Agenda for Senior Staff Meeting," Baker Papers, Box VII-B, Rice University.

72. Dick Kirschten, "Reagan Cabinet Councils May Have Less Influence Than Meets the Eye," *National Journal,* July 11, 1981, p. 1246.

73. Lawrence Barrett notes, however, that the package went to Reagan "along with caveats drafted by Darman." Barrett, *Gambling with History,* p. 156.

74. Stockman, *Triumph of Politics,* p. 188.

75. Barrett, *Gambling with History,* p. 157. Stockman also notes that Anderson realized that Baker et al. would try to dissuade the president from some of the more controversial proposals being made once the meeting was over, and that Anderson was instrumental in selling Reagan on the package at the meeting. Stockman, *Triumph of Politics,* p. 188.

76. In the days following Schweiker's announcement on May 12, the White House began to further distance itself from the proposal. In his notes of legislative-strategy group meetings he attended, Ed Harper recorded on May 20 that "we're not backing off on this, but the president will not lead." On May 21, he wrote: "Social Security—need to get this off of front page. Only submitted to Hill in response to request from a Congressional Committee for a position. No presidential involvement." Harper's notes are quoted in Stockman, *Triumph of Politics,* p. 192.

77. Barrett, *Gambling with History,* p. 156.

78. Stockman, *Triumph of Politics,* p. 190.

79. Burke interview with Robert Carleson, April 21, 1998.

80. The handwritten speech can be found in James Baker's papers at Rice University.

81. Burke interview with Richard Wirthlin, June 5, 1998.

82. Darman, *Who's In Control?* p. 82.

83. Technically, the reconciliation process was first used in 1979, but it led to such wrangling in Congress that the reconciliation instructions were removed from the final budget resolution. It did provide, however, an interesting example of how the White House might use the process to force substantive cuts.

84. Stockman, *Triumph of Politics,* pp. 91–92.

85. Stockman, *Triumph of Politics,* p. 103.

86. Stockman, *Triumph of Politics,* pp. 91–92.

87. Stockman, *Triumph of Politics,* p. 97.

88. Also, Weidenbaum cautions, a "Roshomon effect" needs to be factored in to understand the decisionmaking processes of the Reagan presidency: "We all tend to overestimate our roles and underestimate the other fellow's contribution. The problem facing historians will be that some people during that

period were publicly very vocal, while others respected the confidence of the President to a greater degree." Murray Weidenbaum, "Reagan and Economic Policy Making," in Thompson, ed., *Reagan and the Economy,* pp. 5, 18, 24.

89. Anderson, *Revolution,* p. 237.

90. Anderson, *Revolution,* p. 243. According to Anderson, while it originally had eight members—Stockman, Weidenbaum, Anderson, Meese, Baker, Don Regan, Tim McNemar (Regan's deputy), and Bill Brock—after a few meetings only the first three regularly attended.

91. Weinberger, in his memoirs, states that Stockman's account of the meeting "is most politely described as fanciful." Stockman "made a few notes," "asked one or two questions," and "agreed with our recommendations." Weinberger, *Fighting for Peace,* p. 49.

92. Stockman, *Triumph of Politics,* p. 119.

93. It is also useful to bear in mind Martin Anderson's admonition that Stockman's book is "marked by gaping holes in the telling of how Reagan fashioned his economic program," and that "crucial parts of the story [are] left out." Anderson, *Revolution,* p. 237.

94. Anderson notes that it was his idea to invite Harper to the meetings: "As a senior member of the White House staff, Harper attended all the daily senior staff meetings and served as an invaluable bridge to the OMB, keeping them informed about the president's needs and keeping the White House staff informed about OMB's activities." Anderson, *Revolution,* p. 247.

95. Stockman, Regan, Anderson, and Weidenbaum would often be invited to LSG meetings when budget issues were under consideration, although they were not regular members.

96. Murray Weidenbaum, "Reagan and Economic Policy Making," in Thompson, ed., *Reagan and the Economy,* p. 8.

97. Although the deficit numbers are mind-boggling, the Reagan administration was remarkably successful in getting Congress to approve its economic program, albeit with a heavy dose of compromise and congressional politics as usual. In May, a successful coalition of Republicans and conservative Democrats passed the omnibus first budget resolution (Gramm-Latta I) that instructed committees to cut almost $37 billion from the proposed budget. In June, the same coalition overturned the work of the Democrat-controlled House committees and passed Gramm-Latta II, which led to specific cuts of $37.7 million. Although the degree of cuts was remarkable, Stockman and the administration had to compromise heavily to get its winning margin (only six votes). Deal-making had gone on until the very morning of the House vote, figures were crossed out, pages misnumbered, and in haste even a congressional aide's name and phone number had found its way into the final bill (her name was Rita Seymour, and her number was 255-4844). It was also ridden with congressional budgetary gimmickry. In late July, the tax package passed. The original proposal of a 10 percent cut for each of three years was changed to a 5 percent cut the first year, with the 10 percent cuts to follow. Changes were made in business depreciation rules. But as with the budget bill, normal congressional politics was not absent—it contained numerous "Christmas tree"

tax provisions that benefited a variety of special interests. When all was said and done, the modified 25 percent Kemp-Roth tax cut was estimated to yield a loss in revenues of $983 billion from 1982 to 1990, while changes in the depreciation formula yielded a $402 billion loss and the congressional "ornaments" added another loss of $468 billion, for a projected total revenue loss of $1.853 trillion—a figure that would never be met by spending cuts and yielded the deficits of the Reagan-Bush years.

98. Don Oberdorfer, "Reagan Aides See Power Grab: Haig Starts Fast and Strong," *Washington Post,* February 8, 1981. In late March, the *Washington Post* reported that Haig's attempt sowed "the seeds of Haig's difficulty with the White House." Lou Cannon, "Pitfall for Strong Men," *Washington Post,* March 26, 1981.

99. Haig, *Caveat,* p. 76.

100. In his version of the episode, Haig claims that NSDD-1 had already been worked out by State, Defense, and the NSC and had been reviewed by Weinberger, Casey, and Allen. Haig, *Caveat,* p. 74.

101. Hedrick Smith, "A Scaled Down Version of Security Adviser's Task," *New York Times,* March 4, 1981.

102. Cannon, *President Reagan,* p. 189.

103. Leslie Gelb, "Foreign Policy System Criticized by U.S. Aides," *New York Times,* October 19, 1981.

104. Leslie Gelb, "Foreign Policy System Criticized by U.S. Aides," *New York Times,* October 19, 1981.

105. Leslie Gelb, "Foreign Policy System Criticized by U.S. Aides," *New York Times,* October 19, 1981.

106. Steven R. Weisman, "Reagan's First 100 Days: A Test of the Man and the Presidency," *New York Times Magazine,* April 26, 1981.

107. Don Oberdorfer and Lee Lescaze, "Reagan Reassures Haig," *Washington Post*, March 26, 1981.

108. Lou Cannon, "Pitfall for Strong Men," *Washington Post,* March 26, 1981.

109. Steven Weisman, "Reagan Aides Call Strains with Haig 'Fact of Life,'" *New York Times,* July 2, 1981.

110. Steven Weisman, "Reagan Aides Call Strains with Haig 'Fact of Life,'" *New York Times,* July 2, 1981.

111. Cannon, *President Reagan,* p. 195.

112. Bernard Gwertzman, "Haig Charges a Reagan Aide Is Undermining Him," *New York Times,* November 4, 1981.

113. Leslie Gelb, "Foreign Policy System Criticized by U.S. Aides," *New York Times,* October 19, 1981.

114. The development of their tensions was summarized, shortly before Haig's resignation, in Leslie Gelb, "Haig-Clark Feuds Emerging Over Foreign Policy," *New York Times,* June 22, 1982.

115. Steven Weisman, "Haig Resigns Over Foreign Policy Course," *New York Times,* June 26, 1982.

116. Baker, *Politics of Diplomacy,* pp. 26–27.

117. Murray Weidenbaum, the chairman of the CEA, would later observe: "Over the years there seemed to be an undramatic but steady shift of power to the White House staff, especially to Jim Baker's side of the House as opposed to Ed Meese's. I did not get the feeling that the President was interested in these organizational matters. This certainly became evident when Jim Baker and Don Regan switched positions." Murray Weidenbaum, "Reagan and Economic Policy Making," in Thompson, ed., *Reagan and the Economy,* p. 6.

118. Francis X. Clines, "Reagan Counselor Seen as Displaying New Vitality," *New York Times,* September 23, 1982.

119. George Skelton and Sara Fritz, "The New White House Buzzword—Burnout," *Los Angeles Times,* December 19, 1983.

120. Anderson, *Revolution,* p. 205.

5

George Bush:
A Friendly Takeover?

Recognizing the Task at Hand: Preelection Efforts

George Bush's transition to the presidency in 1988 offers a somewhat different challenge than the cases of Carter, Reagan, and Clinton. This was a "friendly takeover" by a vice president who had served the outgoing administration for eight years, and so Bush was presumably in a much better position to take the reins of power. Bush's prepresidential career also was of potential benefit: he had spent most of his political life inside the Washington Beltway, and he did not face the difficult range of adjustments that the others had to in coming from Atlanta, Sacramento, and Little Rock. This was no political outsider and local entourage arriving at the White House steps. But as we shall see, the preparation for the Bush presidency resembled those of Carter and Reagan, and it would face some of the same tests. The decisions made and actions taken, in turn, would carry over into his presidency.

Like Jimmy Carter and Ronald Reagan, Bush began to think about his transition to the presidency well before the November election. Indeed, he began the process almost a year before the actual transition was to take place, an all-time record. In late 1987, Chase Untermeyer, a longtime Bush associate,[1] approached the vice president with a proposal to begin planning for a possible Bush presidency. Untermeyer posed the idea to George W. Bush, the vice president's son, at a Christmas party at the Bush home. George W. immediately informed his father, and by the end of the party the vice president told Untermeyer that it "was a little early to think of such things but that he would contact me later to discuss it."

191

In January 1988, Bush met with Untermeyer and told him he wanted him to conduct the project. They discussed the broad outlines, but Bush cautioned that he did not want any work undertaken until it was clear he was going to be the Republican nominee. By April, the presidential nomination was secure, and Bush asked Untermeyer to prepare a memorandum outlining the project, which Untermeyer promptly did. By then, Untermeyer had resigned from the Pentagon and, following a brief trip to South America, returned home to find a copy of a memo from the vice president to his campaign staff. In the memo, Bush, using essentially the same language Untermeyer used in the memo to him, informed staff that Untermeyer would undertake a transition planning project. Untermeyer and Bush again met in Kennebunkport, Maine, over Memorial Day weekend, and Bush gave the final go-ahead.

Through the summer months, Untermeyer worked alone out of his apartment in Washington. Although Bush had agreed to Untermeyer's efforts, he set strict limits on his mandate. Unlike Jack Watson, Untermeyer did not begin drafting an extensive array of memos on the organization of the White House or assemble a staff that would begin to compile policy proposals or develop a broader thematic policy agenda. And unlike Pen James, who in 1980 also had a limited mandate, he did not even put together a team that would begin the process of reviewing positions and commence a personnel process. "My charter was simply to prepare a plan for the transition and for a transition headquarters, but do nothing in the way of personnel," Untermeyer later recalled. "Bush was deeply concerned that such work, when inevitably it became public, might make him appear overconfident and presumptuous." Untermeyer did begin to have conversations about the transition with various people "but otherwise operated under cover."[2]

But public it became just before the Republican convention, when Bush himself told columnist David Broder of Untermeyer's efforts.[3] Untermeyer thought initially that Bush's comment to Broder was an accident, but on reflection he later concluded that Bush "wanted to have a lightning rod apart from the campaign, apart from his own vice presidential office" that would attract office seekers and deflect them away from the business of the campaign. At the same time, Untermeyer also felt that Bush still wanted Untermeyer to run a low-key, one-man office: "George Bush, politician, rather than George Bush, government executive, knew that if there is an alternative center from the campaign where all the goodies are being studied and passed out, that is where those [who] are ambitious and energetic are going to gravitate," rather than to the campaign.[4]

In one of the few media reports of his efforts, Untermeyer acknowledged the limits on his organization mandate: "My charter was firmly set out by George Bush. It is to deal with the structure for making personnel and policy decisions in an orderly way after November 8. I am to come up with a plan for a transition, not to make any job-placement decisions or recommendations, not even to suggest key people for transition team posts."[5]

Unlike Jack Watson's operation, one Bush aide noted, Untermeyer's "planning and what he developed was not really a blueprint that excluded people. Moreover, I don't think [Bush] would have wanted such a system to exist. Chase had been doing some work but very quietly."[6] In the view of J. Bonnie Newman (who would join the transition and later serve in the Bush White House), the effort was "very reflective of George Bush." "He was trying to do this smaller, more quietly, using a rifle rather than shotgun approach, trying to maintain, in the positive sense of the word, some kind of dignified yet reflective control of the process."[7]

From mid-August through the end of October, Untermeyer had five meetings with Bush and his chief campaign strategists, James Baker and Governor John Sununu of New Hampshire, and the group discussed several of Untermeyer's recommendations. According to Untermeyer, "The VP made various decisions after these deliberations, in effect authorizing me to proceed immediately toward their implementation. I cannot overemphasize how valuable these secret pre-election sessions were." One of the decisions made during this time was that Untermeyer would become director of presidential personnel if Bush won the White House.[8]

Help from Some Friends

In contrast to the more cautious approach prevailing within the Bush camp, the Reagan administration was undertaking a series of steps to prepare for an orderly transfer of power, whether to Bush or Democratic candidate Michael Dukakis. Its efforts in this regard far exceeded those of recent outgoing administrations. In fact, Raymond Fontaine and other representatives of the General Services Administration (GSA) met with representatives of both the Dukakis and Bush campaigns to go over the logistics of the transition and the new rules about public disclosure.[9]

Yet within the Reagan White House, less bipartisan expectations prevailed and preparations were under way in the event of a hoped-for

Bush election. On November 1, 1988, Robert Tuttle, director of the White House personnel office, forwarded a memorandum to Chief of Staff Kenneth Duberstein entitled "Transition Planning." Item 2 of the memo stated, "I have met on approximately a half dozen occasions with Chase Untermeyer for in-depth discussions and have thoroughly briefed him on the operation and organization of Presidential Personnel." (No mention is made of briefings with members of the Dukakis campaign.)

Tuttle goes on to note that he, his associate directors, and Untermeyer's deputy, Ross Starek, have reviewed "in depth the approximately 550 presidential appointments requiring Senate confirmation." "We [Untermeyer and Starek] have given them an appraisal of each position the Bush Administration will have to fill, an outline of the budget and staff requirements for each position, a candidate profile, an appraisal of the incumbent, and an indication of the incumbent's interest in remaining in the position." At the bottom of the memo, Tuttle concludes, underlined, that "this project was done entirely within PPO [Presidential Personnel Office]; no calls were made to the agencies, the incumbents or any other organization to assist in the planning for these meetings."[10]

J. Bonnie Newman, who would shortly use many materials developed by the Reagan White House, found these volumes "very, very helpful." Newman also had access to the personnel descriptions she had worked on as a member of the Reagan personnel office in 1981. In addition, Dick Kinser of the White House developed a helpful how-to guide for personnel, which set out qualities to look for in prospective candidates, interviewing techniques, advice on how to organize personnel work, and other matters relevant to the effective screening of candidates. To have all of this "during the Bush transition really gave us a head start," Newman would later observe.

Chase Untermeyer recalls that his preelection meetings with Tuttle at the White House were "extremely valuable." Half of his sessions with Tuttle and his assistants were lengthy affairs in which they proceeded "department by department, agency by agency, job by job, as to what the various positions and responsibilities were, what kind of people were there now, and candidly assessing who would be good to retain, who would be good to move to another position, or who would be good to terminate."[11]

And the briefing books were extremely useful, according to Untermeyer. "Each book contained the 'authority sheets' for each presidential appointment, with the staffer's experienced judgment as to which jobs were the most important, the most difficult, the hardest to fill, etc. These books became the hour-by-hour bosom companions of my own personnel staff after the election."[12] Untermeyer would later recall that "none of this was available to my counterpart in the Dukakis campaign, nor could it have been." "In a normal transition of one party to the other, all that would have been delayed until the actual transition, and even then it would have been shared grudgingly at best."[13]

On November 5, three days before the election, John Tuck of Duberstein's staff prepared a memo for the chief of staff outlining ten "checklist" steps to be taken in the coming days. The first item in the report was: "Brief Jim Baker/Craig Fuller by phone on transition plans." Item number two: "Brief the President on Tuesday regarding transition plans" under either a Bush or Dukakis electoral victory. Duberstein also had the White House executive clerk's files scoured for information about past transitions.[14]

Colin Powell, the NSC adviser, also had been preparing for the transition in his area. On November 3, five days before the election, Powell forwarded to Duberstein a report outlining what transition preparation his staff had undertaken. According to Powell, the NSC had prepared a volume of briefing materials on the organization, staffing, and budgeting of the NSC staff, a volume on specific issues likely to come before the NSC during the transition and the first six months of the presidency, and a set of papers surveying what Powell described as the "family jewels": intelligence programs, commitments to foreign governments, and "other matters of special sensitivity."

Powell reported that there had already been contact with the (yet to be elected) Bush camp. At the request of Bob Kimmitt of the vice president's staff, material had been compiled on the diplomatic meetings held by Reagan, Carter, and Nixon during their first year in office. The material was provided "some weeks ago for informal planning purposes."[15]

Organizing a Transition: The Postelection Effort

A Team Bush Could Trust

The postelection transition benefited from two developments: first, it was quickly up and running; second, its personnel were longtime Bush associates. Although Untermeyer's efforts had been restricted in scope, the Bush transition was in full stride one day after the election. In fact, on election night Untermeyer handed Bush a twenty-page memorandum that asked him to make a series of decisions. One of them was to establish a significantly smaller transition operation—numbering fewer than a hundred people—even though five hundred staff positions had been prepared for at transition headquarters.[16] Although Untermeyer's estimate was off a bit—225 persons were ultimately to serve on the transition staff—the "friendly takeover" was clearly a much leaner operation compared to the 1,500 involved in the Reagan transition eight years before.

At his first press conference, on the day after the election, Bush unveiled the key people who would head his transition. While Untermeyer's mandate may have been limited, Bush had clearly been thinking beforehand about what his transition would look like. Craig Fuller, his vice presidential chief of staff, and Robert Teeter, his pollster and campaign strategist, would serve as codirectors of his transition. Two deputy directors were also announced: Untermeyer would continue to head the personnel operation, and C. Boyden Gray—Bush's legal counsel as vice president—would serve as legal counsel for the transition. In fact, Bush also announced that Untermeyer and Gray had been tapped to serve in corresponding positions on the White House staff: Untermeyer as director of presidential personnel, Gray at the helm of the White House legal counsel's office. Their appointments not only brought two friends on board; the offices they would hold were crucial to the appointments process and gave them a head start.

Bush set the record in making the earliest postelection White House staff appointments—one day. Rounding out the announcements was the appointment of Sheila Tate, Bush's campaign press secretary, as transition press secretary. No mention was made, however, as to whether she would occupy the position after the inauguration.[17] Not one to be boxed in by any formal organization, Bush also indicated that Jim Baker would serve as an adviser on "key aspects" of the transition, further sign of Baker's influence within the Bush inner circle.[18]

All of the appointees, with the exception of Tate, were longtime associates of Bush and not just campaign veterans. All were generally regarded as moderates; Fuller, Tate, Teeter, and even Untermeyer (who once reported for the *Houston Chronicle*) had prior experience in the news media. As Bonnie Newman would later recollect, a close connection with Bush was pervasive among those involved in the transition: "Most of us were known quantities to the president-elect, and I think he wanted to keep the process small, within a group he could trust."[19]

The choice of Fuller and Teeter alleviated some of the tension that had developed in previous transitions—most notably Carter's—between the campaign staff and those with the political-governmental experience that would likely land them a White House position. As David Bates explains: "Fuller had come from the vice president's office and Teeter had come from the campaign, so you had one guy representing more the governance side and the other guy representing more the campaign. I don't think the campaign felt left out. I think there was a real nice melding."[20]

By now Fuller and Teeter had officially opened the transition office in Washington and held a brief sidewalk news conference. Fuller said that they were preparing a list of three to five names for each major appointment and that there was no timetable for the announcements. Teeter noted that the vice president wanted not only to look at a list of names but also "to examine some of the criteria and some of the issues that will be facing each of those departments, so that he can consider people in that context."[21]

Two days later, Fuller and Teeter again briefed the press, emphasizing once more that Bush would play an active role in the process. Both indicated that they would meet with Bush daily to review names for top positions. According to Teeter, the process was designed to help Bush feel "totally familiar with the issues facing these departments [so that] he knows exactly what kinds of people he wants." Fuller signaled, as Bush had at his first press conference, that the transition would seek fresh faces: "[We are] actively seeking and recruiting people to come in the government who may not have served before."[22] While friendly, the transition was a takeover nonetheless, and few Reagan appointees were likely to keep their positions.[23]

Not surprisingly, Bush and his aides reached out to core Bush supporters. Early on, a special group had been put together, headed by son George W. Bush, to ensure that those who had demonstrated political loyalty would be considered for positions.[24] According to one member, "We were to make sure that old supporters didn't get left out, didn't get forgotten about."[25] J. Bonnie Newman, who was working under Untermeyer at the time, recalls that she would receive coded resumes from George W. as well as from Jim Baker and Robert Mosbacher. But the operation was quite informal and in no way resembled Reagan's Kitchen Cabinet, which "literally came right into town and set up a separate office."[26]

Meetings were also held with Bush campaign workers and Republican party leaders in every state, and fifty "recruiters" were identified

to come up with the fresh faces.[27] Bush and his advisers also announced that three top-level transition aides had been specifically
charged with the recruitment of blacks, Hispanics, and women.[28] Bush
was especially concerned with increasing the number of female appointments, and he reportedly telephoned Untermeyer on several occasions asking him, "Where are the women?"[29] Yet a strong personal connection to George Bush was the most valuable currency.

While the Bush transition made efforts (or at least publicized a desire) to search far afield for personnel, the large teams that Reagan
dispatched to the agencies and departments eight years earlier were
not mustered. In fact, several top aides felt that the information-gathering activities of the Reagan transition teams were unnecessary. On
November 15, Fuller told the press that "volunteers will serve, but we
are not going to send large teams of people around town." Boyden
Gray called the Reagan teams a "waste of time and money."[30] Even
before the election, while speaking at Harvard on October 23, Richard
Darman observed that the 1,500-person Reagan transition in 1980,
particularly with its extensive array of teams, did not operate all that
effectively: "If there has been a more colossal waste, I'm not aware
of it."[31]

Instead, the Bush transition relied on the good graces—and perhaps career concerns—of incumbent Reagan officials by having Ken
Duberstein, Reagan's chief of staff, send a memo to each department
and agency head on November 21, requesting the kind of information
that the Reagan teams had assembled on their own. The memo requested a response by November 25, and Jim Pinkerton, director of the
transition's policy planning office, was to be contacted should questions arise.[32]

Although Bush was running a leaner transition with respect to the
advice and information gathered for incoming secretaries, this did not
mean they were operating in a data vacuum. "Voluminous books have
been written for appointees to read. And in case they don't, face-to-
face briefings are held on the same transition subjects. A formal briefing with transition representatives is the first scheduled meeting of a
newly designated secretary," one press report observed. "They were
handed a thick sheaf of single-page instructions on transition behavior,
from parking spaces to the costs of inaugural tickets. They were given
inch-thick black binders containing information about their new jobs or
departments, and guidance on what Bush promised during the campaign about the areas under their jurisdiction."[33]

Filling the Cabinet

A Cabinet of Friends

Bush lost little time in filling most of his top-level appointments, and it would culminate in a cabinet that had a high degree of Washington experience as well as close personal connection to Bush. At his first press conference, the day after the election, Bush announced, as predicted, that his friend and alter ego, Jim Baker, was his choice for secretary of state. Two days before the election, over cocktails at the vice president's residence, Bush had asked Baker—"out of the blue," according to Baker—if he would serve assuming Bush won. Baker accepted on the spot.[34]

For other appointments, Bush turned for advice to a small group of his closest advisers, including Baker, Treasury Secretary Nicholas Brady, Sununu, Teeter, Fuller, and Vice President–elect Dan Quayle with Untermeyer serving as rapporteur. Dubbed the Cabinet and Sub-Cabinet Advisory Group (CASAG), they met regularly with Bush to go over potential nominees. According to one of the participants, the sessions were "relaxed." "No one person dominates the discussion and there have not been any knockdown, drag-out fights." In the first meetings few names were discussed; talk focused instead on what role was envisioned for a particular department, what initiatives might be forthcoming, and, in the words of one aide, "more generally about the sort of individuals needed." In subsequent meetings, Teeter would often remind the group of what Bush had said about a particular policy area during the campaign, with the discussion then focusing on who might be likely to best achieve those objectives.

Throughout, Bush was described as an active participant: "He keeps the discussions going, asking questions, saying 'Let's move to this,' or 'Let's move to that.' He is quite involved."[35] Yet at times, Bush was prone to act on his own: the appointments of Baker to the cabinet and John Sununu and Brent Scowcroft to the staff were clearly his decisions and apparently made without much internal debate.

On November 15, Bush announced that he would retain Nicholas Brady at Treasury and, a week later, that Attorney General Richard Thornburgh and Education Secretary Lauro Cavazos would be continuing in the Bush cabinet.[36] In the ensuing weeks other Bush friends and associates were named: Robert Mosbacher for the Commerce Department, Carla Hills as U.S. trade representative (a position with cabinet

rank), and Clayton Yeutter for Agriculture.[37] One former and one outgoing member of the House of Representatives—Edward Derwinski at
Veterans Affairs (a newly created cabinet department) and Manuel
Lujan at Interior—were tapped; Samuel Skinner, a former federal pros-
ecutor and Chicago transportation executive, was selected as secretary
of transportation; and Elizabeth Dole, former head of Transportation
under Reagan and the wife of Kansas Senator Bob Dole, was named
secretary of labor. On December 19, the appointment of Congressman
Jack Kemp as secretary of HUD was announced by Bush.[38]

Two other appointments were also settled at this time; both generated some controversy. The first was Louis Sullivan, who was named
head of HHS. Sullivan, an African American and president of Morehouse College School of Medicine, aroused controversy from antiabor-
tion groups who charged that Sullivan was soft in his positions and was
not fully committed to the prolife cause. However, Fuller and Teeter
met with Sullivan in late December and were satisfied that his views
were consistent with those of the president-elect. The second controversial nomination was not so easily sidestepped.

Potential Trouble: The Tower Nomination

It had been rumored as early as mid-November that former Texas Senator John Tower would get the nod for defense secretary. But his possible nomination generated controversies within and outside Bush's
inner circle. One point of contention was prolonged negotiation with
the transition team over control of subcabinet appointments. On November 23, the *Washington Post* reported that "more than a week ago,
Tower was told by a close Bush associate that he could name the three
service secretaries—for the Army, Navy and Air Force—but that Bush
would select the No. 2 Pentagon appointee, the deputy secretary of defense, and the two undersecretaries who direct acquisition and administer defense policy issues." Bush aides were concerned that Tower
would fill all the defense slots with his wide circle of friends and associates in the defense field, thus making the department less responsive to the White House. In his memoirs, however, Tower indicates that
the story "overstated the situation to a considerable degree," but he
adds this caveat: "In discussing my views on the way I would organize
the Pentagon's leadership structure, I made it clear that I intended to
recruit several former Senate committee aides and staff members."[39]

Tower's reputation (as a member and former chairman of the Senate Armed Services Committee) of not being fully committed to the

reforms proposed by the Packard Commission, particularly in the area of procurement reform, was another source of controversy. As well, a letter sent by the ranking members of the committee, Georgia's Sam Nunn and Virginia's John Warner, stressing that they would particularly scrutinize the qualifications of Pentagon nominees, caused further concern.[40] Fuller and Teeter were reported to have urged Bush to look at corporate executives who might be more capable at achieving management reforms at the Pentagon.[41] In his memoirs, Tower notes that Teeter in particular preferred a manager at the Pentagon and "seemed to be the one who was pushing the idea the hardest."[42] Tower also notes that Treasury Secretary Brady, who had served a brief interim stint in the Senate, "apparently did warn the president-elect's top advisers that it would not be as easy as everyone thought."[43]

Tower's nomination was also delayed due to allegations of improper personal conduct (based on evidence presented in his recent divorce case), as well as concerns about his lobbying activities after leaving the Senate. But Bush and his advisers decided to go ahead, and on December 16, following the completion of what Bush termed an "extensive" FBI investigation, the Tower nomination was announced.[44]

During the campaign, Bush had signaled that he would be his own president with "new faces" and "wholesale change." Yet only three appointments hailed from outside the Beltway. Even more important, almost all the cabinet members had close personal and political associations with Bush (Baker, Mosbacher, Brady, Tower), had worked in his campaign (Skinner), were well known from their service in Congress (Kemp, Derwinski, Lujan), or had served in various capacities along with Bush in prior Republican administrations (Elizabeth Dole, Yeutter, Cavazos, Watkins). Sullivan could even claim a strong link to both George and Barbara Bush: he first met George at a dedication of a new building on the Morehouse campus in 1982, traveled with both of them on a state visit to Africa, and appointed Barbara (whom he had introduced at the Republican convention) to his medical school's board of trustees. Neither Reagan nor Carter had been so closely linked in one way or another to such a large number of their appointees.

On January 12, Bush held his first meeting with the cabinet-designates. He encouraged them to "think big," "be frank," and "fight hard" for their positions but also to support the president once a decision was made—not voice their disagreement publicly. Bush warned them to adhere to the "highest ethical standards" and cautioned them that he didn't like the "kiss and tell" books that had proliferated in the Reagan years.[45]

Subcabinet Appointments

In filling subcabinet positions, Bush and his aides sought to establish what Untermeyer termed a "cooperative" relationship.[46] While the transition staff prepared lists of candidates for top positions, they were "suggestions" or "strong suggestions." "Nobody is trying to cram guys down secretaries' throats," said one Bush aide.[47]

Two incoming cabinet members were exempted from the system: Jim Baker and Nicholas Brady. The State Department transition team that Jim Baker assembled only days after the election—Bob Zoellick, Margaret Tutweiler, Dennis Ross, and Robert Kimmitt—filled that department at its highest levels.[48] By mid-February, as the approval process dragged on, several cabinet secretaries were reported to have bypassed Untermeyer's system: "Some have gone straight to Bush for decisions; some have bypassed the wait for White House personnel paper work; some have gone to congressional Republicans to ask them to pressure the White House to move."[49]

Yet while Bush may have permitted them greater leeway to select their own senior associates, he and the transition operation retained control over lower-level appointments. The latter was similar to the efforts of the Reagan transition—but with a difference: Bush was less concerned with ideological purity than with getting jobs for Bush supporters.[50]

The Bush transition faced a particular difficulty that the Carter, Reagan, and Clinton transitions did not: since it was a "friendly" rather than a "hostile" takeover, some Reagan administration incumbents might have thought they would remain in the new administration, despite the fact that Reagan had ordered their resignations. As Andrew Card recollects, "I think hostile takeovers may be easier. In a friendly takeover you have all of your friends who believe that nothing has changed and they are going to keep their jobs. The reality is that the new president will put in his people. So we did have some tension that was less than constructive."[51]

But the Bush transition also had some advantages. Many of those involved in the Bush transition had prior White House experience that was especially useful in fully understanding the positions and personnel under consideration. As J. Bonnie Newman notes, "Familiarity with the system is very helpful." The government "plum book isn't good enough"; it "doesn't tell you anything about the real responsibilities of a position and what qualities you might be looking for." Newman recalls that she, Untermeyer, Boyden Gray, and Andrew Card, in screening prospective candidates, would have several informal discussions where they would "get into organizational roles" as well as discussing the qualifications of prospective candidates. "So many of us had previously worked together and were known to one another that it was easy to have informal discussions. . . . There was a trust level, a familiarity that existed among the group that benefited those kinds of conversations."[52]

Once selections had been made, the Bush operation also benefited from close cooperation with the Reagan White House in navigating through the increasingly dense and complicated array of disclosure forms and clearance procedures. According to Newman, "They really provided us with a road map, which streamlined the process. Boyden must have worked really closely with them because he had ready to go, hot off the press, a lot of memoranda providing guidance and instructions regarding the various clearance procedures. . . . We had all of the necessary forms ready." Gray's office was able to inform prospective appointees about the ethics requirements and disclosure forms, "so if anyone wanted to screen themselves out early and not have to reveal all of that very detailed information, there should not have been any misunderstandings."[53]

The Bush Cabinet and Presidential Decisionmaking

As the appointment process unfolded, Bush and his advisers made several decisions that would affect the organization and the role of the cabinet in his decisionmaking. One set concerned which of the nondepartmental appointees would be given cabinet rank. Bush decided that OMB Director Darman and Trade Representative Hills would hold the rank, as had been the case under Reagan. But in early December, it was announced that Bush had decided not to give the UN ambassador (a position Bush once held) cabinet rank, as had been the case previously; the director of the CIA (another position that Bush had held) would not have cabinet rank. According to one account, "Bush's decision, conveyed recently to subordinates, reflects his preference that the two posts be less visible in internal policy-making debates." Bush was especially concerned that "the CIA should not attempt to influence policy as was the case with the late director William J. Casey."[54]

Bush's new drug czar, former Education Secretary William Bennett, also would not be formally designated a member of the cabinet. Bush announced Bennett's appointment at the same January 12 ceremony where Watkins was also introduced, and Bennett had said he was looking forward to working with "my colleagues in the cabinet." But the lack of cabinet rank apparently came as a surprise to Bennett, who learned about it after he was not invited to the first official meeting of the cabinet after inauguration day. Bennett's position as director of the Office of National Drug Control Policy had been recently established by Congress as part of the EOP in order to raise the visibility of the drug issue and bring organizational stability to what had been an informal arrangement; Bennett's salary, moreover, was deliberately set by Congress at the level of a cabinet member. When the issue became public in late January, the White House press office noted that "the president's preference was to limit the number of cabinet members. . . . Secretary Bennett will attend cabinet meetings as appropriate."[55]

Bush and his advisers also decided to continue with the cabinet-council system that had been established in the Reagan presidency. But instead of creating the five (at one point, seven) councils in Reagan's first term, the two-council arrangement—one for domestic policy, the other for economic policy—used in the second Reagan term was followed. Furthermore, the attorney general (Thornburgh) and the treasury secretary (Brady) were placed in charge of each of the councils. Both, of course, were veterans of the Reagan cabinet. According to Andrew Card, the placement of Thornburgh and Brady as heads of each of the councils continued assignments that had developed in Reagan's second term. At the start of Reagan's second term, Attorney General Edwin Meese had been put in charge of the newly combined domestic council, and when Thornburgh replaced Meese at the Justice Department he took over that assignment as well. Since "Thornburgh was a holdover from the Reagan administration, he wanted to keep that role. And the same with Nicholas Brady."

Card remembers that there had even been some discussion of whether two councils were needed or just one and that even Bush himself may have "favored just the domestic council." But a decision was made to continue with the two councils.[56]

Another decision made at the time was that the councils—particularly their staffs—would be placed under the direction of the secretary to the cabinet (David Bates) rather than the White House domestic policy operation. This was an important but little-noticed change that had been made during Reagan's second term, and Bush continued the practice. According to David Bates, "There was some discussion about the pros and cons of that, but Andy [Card] and Governor Sununu decided to leave it under the cabinet secretary."

In Bates's view, there was not much difference in the way the councils operated from what had gone on under Reagan: "It was pretty similar to the system we inherited." Bates discussed his new position with both Sununu and Bush, and in thinking about what changes he might make once he was in office, he recalls that he just wanted to "continue with the model that had worked effectively toward the end of Reagan's term. I thought that had worked pretty well and wanted to continue on with that." Bates also benefited from the close network of prior association among Bush's top aides: "I had worked for Craig Fuller [who had been secretary to the cabinet in Reagan's first term], so I had a sense of how it worked." Bates also conferred with Reagan's outgoing cabinet secretary, Nancy Risque.[57] But Andrew Card recalls that Bates wanted his office to have a stronger role in the policy process than had been the case in Reagan's second term: "He had been a party to a relatively weak cabinet affairs office in the Reagan administration and he did not want it to be weak in the Bush administration."[58] The potential problem with the setup was the fact that cabinet affairs had a relatively small staff, while the domestic policy shop was much larger. For the arrangement to work, Bates would need to establish a good working relationship with the person selected to lead the domestic policy operation, a post that had yet to be filled.

Crafting a Policy Agenda

The Beginnings of an Agenda—or Missed Opportunities?

As we have seen under Carter and Reagan, the transition period is important not just for getting a team in place; it is also the time to translate campaign promises into policy priorities and begin to establish a legislative agenda. In Bush's case, this was especially necessary, as the campaign was comparably devoid of policy specifics, relying instead on the vagaries of "a thousand points of light," "a kinder, gentler nation," and "no new taxes" and such specifics as requiring the pledging of allegiance, banning the burning of the American flag, and enacting tougher laws to deal with the likes of Willie Horton.

Foreign Policy Comes First

Early efforts were made in the area of foreign policy, where Bush had clearer commitments and great personal interest. As Andrew Card recollects, Bush "was very active with Brent Scowcroft and Jim Baker getting up to speed as secretary of state. Brent Scowcroft is a seasoned national security person, and the president had latent interest in those areas. So there was lot that went on in the foreign policy side."[59]

On December 7, 1988, Bush met with Reagan and Soviet Premier Mikhail Gorbachev at Governors Island in New York Harbor, following the latter's address to the United Nations. The day after the meeting, Bush reports that he sat down with Scowcroft at the vice president's residence in Washington, and "I told him I wanted to come up with something dramatic to move the relationship with Moscow forward," "something bold and dramatic." In Scowcroft's view, one goal was to loosen Moscow's grip on Eastern Europe; the other was ongoing arms-control talks. According to Scowcroft, "I thought these were opportunities for dramatic cuts to not only strengthen strategic stability but also to reduce the conventional forces Moscow relied on to control Eastern Europe." Bush recognized that "I came into office with a vision of the world I wanted to see, but I had no fixed 'ten-point plan.' Brent would more than make up for my failings. . . . He fit the bill perfectly. He was someone who would hit the ground running."[60]

The other principal member of the foreign policy team, Jim Baker, had by December moved his office from transition headquarters to a suite of rooms in the State Department. During the transition, Baker "talked to every ex-president and most ex–secretaries of state." "I spent November 1988 through January 1989 assiduously studying the issues," Baker reports, and "I sat through a briefing by every sitting undersecretary and assistant secretary of state and many prospective ones." Baker's immediate staff prepared strategy papers on a range of issues. While recognizing that "the central focus of my job initially had to be U.S.-Soviet relations," Baker began to take steps during the transition to forge a bipartisan solution to the crisis in Central America, especially by gaining congressional assent to a plan for extending humanitarian aid to the contras in Nicaragua for one year. "I knew we had to find a way to get Central America behind us if we were to be able to deal aggressively with the decline of Soviet power. . . . Without doubt, it was my first priority." Bush and Baker had agreed to get Central America off the political agenda by no longer asking for military assistance.

Baker was instrumental in arranging Bush's meeting with President Carlos Salinas of Mexico at a Houston air force base, thereby setting the stage for what would become the North American Free Trade Agreement (NAFTA). During the transition, Bush and Baker also wanted to change the tone of foreign policy in their dealings with Capitol Hill: "As we discussed foreign policy plans during the transition, the President made it clear that he wanted to move away from the politics of confrontation between the executive and legislative branches."[61]

Another foreign policy problem that Bush began to tackle during the transition concerned Latin American debt. Bush convened a working group composed of Baker, Brady, Scowcroft, Darman, and Federal Reserve Chairman Alan Greenspan. Together they developed what came to be known as the Brady Plan for restructuring the region's increasingly mounting debts. The plan, which Brady presented in March, provided for U.S., International Monetary Fund, and World Bank resources to provide collateral backing the debt. While parts of the plan were controversial, it came at no cost to the U.S. Treasury and was instrumental in reviving economic stability, if not growth, in the nations affected.[62]

Budgets and Taxes

The most important policy area where work was well under way during the transition concerned the budget, particularly what strategy the new administration would take in tackling mounting deficits.[63] Bush faced not only the traditional expectation of putting his imprint on the budget that had been under preparation by the OMB. Doing so by mid-February, he also faced a triple-whammy. As Richard Darman would later note, first, spending was running about 22 percent of gross domestic product (GDP) while revenues were running at 19 percent, hence deficits continued to loom large; second, without significant reductions the automatic cuts set by Gramm-Rudman-Hollings would require reductions in areas, such as defense, that ran against the new administration's priorities; and, third, most of the easy cuts had already been made in the Reagan years. Neither would a flexible freeze—that is, freezing total spending (with some adjustment for inflation) while flexibly increasing or decreasing particular programs—work, at least as Darman saw it.[64]

Throughout December and January, Darman worked to craft a solution. He met with congressional leaders and members of the bipartisan National Economic Commission that had been created in 1987 to address the budget deficit. He received input from former presidents Ford and Carter (both of whom thought tax increases were necessary) and was even the recipient of advice from Richard Nixon, who, in Darman's words, "neatly straddled the no-new-taxes problem." "I don't know whether the flexible freeze will work," Nixon told him. "If it doesn't, then, and only then, is it appropriate to debate a tax increase."

In a later fax to Bush, Nixon would reiterate his two-step approach, adding "to roll over on [Bush's well-known "read my lips" pledge] would guarantee oblivion."[65]

Starting on December 4, Darman commenced an internal review process and met with Bush, Quayle, Brady, Baker, Teeter, and Sununu on a regular basis. "Slowly but surely, I did what the campaign staff had been unable to do. . . . I forced the group to focus on the hard budget realities."[66] The group met several times over subsequent weeks, and something of a consensus emerged: the administration would fashion a budget that contained limited revisions, frame the revisions in terms of a flexible freeze, propose no new taxes, and encourage bipartisan cooperation "in order to help the *Congress* reach agreement on a budget resolution."[67] While setting fiscal and budgetary parameters, the burden to cut specific programs was kicked into Congress's court.

The matter of what to do about taxes was particularly vexing. While Brady and Teeter thought that the tax increases proposed by the bipartisan commission would provide political cover for Bush to abandon his "read my lips" pledge, Baker felt that option was not feasible in the first year. Bush was inclined to go along with Baker. On December 21, prior to a meeting with the group, Bush invited Darman to share lunch. Darman raised the key issues: he could produce a budget that might get by in the first year, but it was going to be near impossible, with the Democrats controlling Congress, to craft a program of long-term deficit reduction without some concession on taxes. Bush responded with something like the Nixon two-step: "Only if it's after we have tried our best."[68] The groundwork had been laid: Bush would "muddle through" in his first year, with the "big fix" to come— if needed—in the second.[69] It was a decision that would lead to the 1990 budget agreement and have repercussions on Bush's chances for reelection.

Domestic Policy

In contrast to the budget, other areas of domestic policy lagged during the transition. "As for the traditional cabinet departments," Andrew Card notes, "I did not find a lot of policy deliberation. . . . The most active practical area of debate was over the personnel who would head these departments and agencies." Some discussion of issues did take place, but it was largely as a reactive effort to stave off the efforts of incumbent Reagan officials to stay in their positions. Some of them, Card remembers, "started to feed a policy decision as a red herring as to why they should not be asked to leave. . . . That generally triggered some kind of policy planning session—if we tell that person he is going to be replaced and he is the champion of X policy, is he going to claim we are not interested in X policy? We better do something to show we are in favor of X policy even though we are going to replace this person. Mostly department people; but a little bit at the White House, too."[70]

Jim Pinkerton's assignment to direct policy planning during the transition might have been another place where domestic issues could begin to percolate. But according to Pinkerton, while it was "a great title, a great office . . . I don't recall doing a lot of policy planning. I recall doing a lot of 'Thank you for your position paper on this.' 'Thank you for your agenda.' 'Thank you for this, thank you for that.'" "Most of the time it was just gathering paper [from] people who had been involved in the campaign and/or people who wanted to be involved in the administration. . . . It was more of a paper-gathering function, meeting-holding and paper-gathering."

Pinkerton and his staff did put together a book containing all of Bush's campaign promises, organized both by issue and time frame. Pinkerton also "helped a little on the inaugural speech, but only a little." "I met Arnold Schwarzenegger and helped him get launched on being the chairman of the President's Council on Physical Fitness, probably the most productive thing I did during that two-month period."

The wrangling over Bob Teeter's role in the new administration and the delay until almost mid-January in appointing Roger Porter to head the domestic policy staff also contributed to the problem. "Somewhere in there, Roger Porter got hired to be the director of policy," Pinkerton recalls, "but I don't remember him being in Washington much before Bush got inaugurated. He was the policy guy."[71]

Building Bridges

For his part, George Bush sought at least to convey the image of a president-elect who took domestic issues seriously. He held well-publicized meetings with erstwhile rivals Senator Bob Dole and Michael Dukakis, breakfasted with Senate Democratic Leader George Mitchell, and attended a dinner honoring Jack Kemp sponsored by the Heritage Foundation and the Institute for Free Enterprise Development. As part of his effort to be more inclusive, Bush had lunch with Jesse Jackson on November 30, convened a meeting with sixty African American Republicans on December 8, and met with Benjamin Hooks, director of the

National Association for the Advancement of Colored People, on December 9.

Efforts were made to depict a more congenial, relaxed Bush. He was photographed fishing, dining in a Chinese restaurant in a Washington suburb, mailing a silver foot to Texas Governor Ann Richards,[72] and showing reporters around his home in Kennebunkport. The Bushes and Quayles even went to the movies (*My Stepmother Is an Alien* was the feature that night).

Like the Reagans eight years before, the Bushes were attentive to the contributions that social events at the White House might make to political success. In the second week of January, Susan Porter Rose of Barbara Bush's staff forwarded to the president-elect and future First Lady a memo on the social activities that had been undertaken in the Nixon, Ford, Carter, and Reagan presidencies during their first ninety days of office. The memo had been requested by the president-elect.[73]

One area where attempts were made to show a substantive commitment concerned the environment. Here, C. Boyden Gray took the lead and met on at least four occasions with representatives of six environmental groups. According to one account, "They discussed issues they could agree on (specifically, improving energy efficiency and reducing vehicles' carbon monoxide emissions)" as well as "suggestions for Republican environmentalists who might grace Bush's transition and administration."[74] On November 30, Bush himself convened a breakfast meeting with the group. At least for the moment the efforts paid off: after the meeting one participant told the press, "We will be on his team now."[75]

Shaping the White House Staff

Like Reagan eight years earlier, Bush recognized that the organization of his White House staff—particularly the appointment of a chief of staff—would be an early priority of his transition. John Sununu would later tell reporters that Bush had discussed the possibility of his appointment as early as two weeks before election day.[76] The day before the election, Bush recorded in his own diary that he discussed announcing Sununu's appointment as chief of staff with Jim Baker, "but that will come later."[77] In fact, Bush did not announce Sununu's appointment until November 17.

Rebuilding the Troika?

In the intervening days, there was considerable jockeying among Bush's top aides about how the responsibilities of the chief of staff would be defined, what top-level positions others would occupy, and even whether the choice of Sununu was a fait accompli. Sununu personally entered the fray. The day after the election, he held a press conference in Concord, New Hampshire, and stated he was not interested in serving as secretary of education or energy, perhaps forestalling any last-minute effort to shunt him off into a cabinet position (though Sununu did say he might be open to a White House position).

While Bush traveled to Florida for a short vacation, Baker and the other top transition officials met, and one of the first items on their agenda was an examination of how the top level of the Bush White House would be organized. Baker favored bringing all three—Fuller, Teeter, and Sununu—into top positions, replicating to a great degree the troika of Reagan's first term.[78] Fuller would handle the day-to-day decisionmaking process, Teeter would continue in his role as strategic planner, and Sununu would oversee domestic policy, perhaps serving as senior counselor to the president, much as Meese had done during Reagan's first term. According to the *Washington Post*, it was felt that this division of responsibilities would play to the respective strengths of each: Fuller, "known for his effort to impose discipline on Bush decisions and for creating a staff system that operates smoothly"; Teeter, "known for his professorial manner and skilled approach to public opinion and policy issues" as well as his "longstanding ties to Bush and Republicans on Capitol Hill"; and Sununu, "known for his quick grasp of policy issues and his ebullient self-confidence in articulating his views." The arrangement would also avoid, it was reported, perceived weaknesses with each: Fuller "at times had bumpy relations with old-timers in the Bush entourage and he is not a trained political strategist"; Teeter was "not regarded as the most efficient manager"; and Sununu lacked Washington experience.[79]

But Baker's efforts did not come to fruition. According to reports, Fuller and Teeter were opposed to making Sununu chief of staff. Fuller, who had served four years as Bush's vice presidential chief of staff and, earlier, as secretary to the cabinet in the Reagan White House, was reluctant to serve under Sununu in a deputy position. Sununu, for his part, was reported to be reluctant to come to Washington if Fuller got the senior position. According to one Bush aide, there was considerable "tension" and "jockeying" over the proposed arrangement; Fuller was described by one friend as fighting hard for the chief-of-staff job and was "not a happy camper."[80]

On November 14, Sununu flew to Florida to meet with the vacationing president-elect, and reports surfaced that Bush was leaning toward Sununu. Media accounts of the process indicated that many in the Bush entourage were not happy with Sununu and that he was viewed as a risky choice. Among the worries expressed were whether he could impose discipline on Bush and keep him focused on his principal policy objectives, whether he was able to delegate authority, whether he could work well with members of the Bush inner circle, and particularly whether he could curb his pronounced ego and aggressive nature. They would not prove to be unfounded concerns.

To his credit, Bush was not prone to let the matter slide or unduly permit bickering among his aides, as Carter had done under similar circumstances in 1976. "I'd like to make the decision soon," he told reporters on November 15, "because that person can start working towards staffing the whole White House for what will be a very important beginning."[81]

Bush was not happy with the idea of a "troika." In fact, according to the *New York Times,* Bush was "alarmed by reports that he was considering a troika." Further, Bush was "enraged by the notion that some associates wanted a less assertive chief of staff to make sure that there was no rival" to Jim Baker and Richard Darman, should the latter become OMB director. "What is clear about the incident, some Bush associates said, is that it shows Mr. Bush will operate with a firm hand, despite the loyalty he feels for some aides."[82]

As Andrew Card later recalled, while "there certainly were Jim Baker, Bob Teeter, Craig Fuller discussions that suggested that [a troika] might be something they were looking at," these talks "did not include the president." "I received a phone call just a matter of days after the election . . . from Florida that gave me a good indication of what was likely to happen [i.e., that Sununu would get the nod]." Card, who would not be formally named as Sununu's deputy until December 16, got another call the very next day, asking him to help organize the White House staff: "Even well before John Sununu was announced publicly, I spoke to the president, I spoke to John Sununu, and I started along with Ed Rogers, who was close to Lee Atwater but knew John Sununu."[83] Rogers would soon join Card as one of Sununu's two deputies.

Furthermore, although Fuller might have had Baker in his corner, the efforts on Fuller's behalf might also have run up against the opposition of another Bush intimate, Boyden Gray. According to one report, "It was widely known in the campaign that Mr. Fuller and Mr. Gray did not get along and that Mr. Fuller sought to force Mr. Gray out. In the end, Mr. Gray stayed and Mr. Fuller went."[84]

Sununu as Chief of Staff, Further Negotiations

On November 17, nine days after the election, Bush announced the appointment of Sununu as chief of staff. While the president-elect might have been willing to let the opposition to Sununu among his inner circle run its course, he was neither dissuaded from his choice, nor did he unduly delay announcing what had apparently been his decision all along. Bush clearly wanted Sununu—and it was Sununu he got.

Bush particularly valued Sununu's political stature: "You want someone who's run for sheriff," Bush stated at the press conference announcing Sununu's appointment. Bush also noted that "I decided to send a signal that I have a strong chief of staff who in my view will be able to work with the Congress and the various strong secretaries that we will have in the Cabinet departments."

Responding to a press question about his own "combative personality and hot temper," Sununu told the assembled reporters, "I'm a pussycat." He went on later to note that "I have two responsibilities. One is to be an honest broker and present the views on the various sides of the issue, and if—after I fulfill that—then have an opportunity to indicate my recommendations." But that should not come "until after all the options have been presented, until all parties have had a chance to present their views on it. It's the only fair way to allow the person on whose desk the buck really does stop to make the best decisions." Sununu also laid down an interesting challenge to reporters: "I suspect that the way I'll measure my success is that after a few years of George Bush—as seen as having a great presidency—people [will] wonder who the chief of staff was—struggle hard to remember his name."[85]

But the selection of Sununu also meant that Fuller would depart once the transition was over, an outcome that was announced that same day. Bush likely delayed the Sununu announcement because he wanted, if possible, to find a position for Fuller (a cabinet post, most likely), then announce the two appointments at once.[86]

As for Teeter, reports continued in November and December that Bush wanted him to serve as Sununu's deputy but also with the title "counselor to the president." And Teeter had an extended discussion with Bush about the position on December 15. Teeter, one transition official said, would have "an ideas mandate," with Sununu in charge of the "operations mandate."[87]

While Sununu was willing to have Teeter serve as one of his deputies, Teeter envisioned broader responsibilities, including counselor to the president—the title that Ed Meese had been given under Reagan—thus making him more of an equal to Sununu. "The Sununu deputy thing [was] a problem," according to one transition official. "He envision[ed] himself at the same level as Sununu." Teeter also wanted to have direct access to Bush, which Sununu was reported to have opposed.[88] (Only three people were, in the end, to have direct, independent access to President Bush: Sununu, NSC Adviser Scowcroft, and press secretary Marlin Fitzwater). Finally, like Meese, Teeter wanted to have cabinet rank, which proved to be a particular sticking point in the negotiations.[89]

On January 9, Teeter announced that he would not be joining the new administration, and he cited concerns about moving his family to Washington (a reason one transition member also noted in an interview with me). According to the *Washington Post,* however, differences with Sununu over his position remained the real impediment: "A source close to Sununu said that he does not intend to have a deputy overseeing policy development and communication, areas that Teeter was to handle, and he believes he can oversee all aspects of White House operations without another deputy." The newspaper concluded that this left Sununu "the unrivaled center of White House staff operations."[90]

As negotiations with Teeter dragged on, Sununu did not neglect to think about how his own role as chief of staff would be defined and how a Bush White House might be structured. In an interview with Maureen Dowd of the *New York Times,* Sununu said, "I'm trying to take the basic structure of the last three or four White Houses and digest them"; "I really think George Bush's style is different from Ronald Reagan's or Jimmy Carter's or even as far back as Dwight Eisenhower's that I want to try and tailor the structure to suit his particular style of working"; "Am I to be visible or invisible? I prefer to be invisible for a while. But if he wants me to be visible that's his choice. The level of detail he wants presented to him he will determine. The frequency of meetings that he wants to frequent."[91]

But in other interviews with reporters, Sununu indicated a more aggressive style as chief of staff. In an interview with the *Boston Globe* in early December, he described himself as a "strong doorkeeper," deeply interested in domestic policy, and he indicated that he would take the lead in setting the day's agenda at the White House. He also said he would be a "tough critic" of Darman and would review budget proposals before they reached the president.[92] When other media picked up on the story, Sununu backpedaled on his statements, saying that Bush will determine the structure of the White House and that it will serve the president's needs, not Sununu's.[93]

But behind the scenes, Sununu labored to put his imprint on the White House staff. The failed negotiations with Teeter would have repercussions later on, as the communications strategy and the public selling of the Bush presidency came to occupy a lesser position in the staff system. There would be no high-level man like Mike Deaver in this administration; neither would there be an Ed Meese–type of figure, with cabinet rank and counselor status, to push a Bush policy agenda at the highest (other than Sununu) levels.[94]

A Different Approach at the NSC

As with the appointment of his chief of staff, Bush took an active and direct role in the appointment of his other major in-house policy adviser—the NSC assistant. On November 23, six days after the Sununu announcement and a bit more than two weeks after election day, Bush announced that Brent Scowcroft would serve in the post, a position he had held under Gerald Ford.

Scowcroft had been an important and influential adviser to Bush for some time and was, in Bush's words, "a trusted friend." Scowcroft's appointment brought several other strengths. His closeness to Bush fit the president-elect's hope that the NSC adviser could provide his views "unvarnished" (as Bush phrased it at the press conference) and enjoy direct and frequent access to the Oval Office. At the same time, his earlier stint in the job indicated that he would be no Henry Kissinger but rather an "honest broker" (again, Bush's words) who would be a fair manager, particularly in calming the waters among the various participants in the process. According to one report, Bush especially wanted to avoid the "friction and gridlock between cabinet members that characterized the Reagan years."[95]

While Bush stated at the press conference announcing Scowcroft's appointment that he saw little need for changes in NSC staff operations, Scowcroft's experience in the post, as well as his more recent assignment as one of the three principal members of the Tower Commission investigation of Iran-contra, indicated that he could make any necessary changes in a unit that had been much troubled during the Reagan years. At the very least, there would no revolving door at the top. Scowcroft promised stability compared to the seven NSC assistants who had occupied the job during the eight years of the Reagan presidency.

According to press reports, Scowcroft's appointment was a "deliberate surprise." Sununu had been informed of his appointment but did not "know the announcement was to be made so quickly, the sources said." The fact that Sununu was out of the loop might have been a signal that Sununu's responsibilities would not extend into the area of national security, as Meese's did eight years earlier.

In announcing Scowcroft's appointment, Bush implicitly indicated that as president he would be more involved in foreign and national security policymaking than his predecessor. He told reporters that he planned to "personally read" the daily intelligence briefing every morning and that he expected Scowcroft to keep him fully abreast of developing events even during the night. "Shake me and wake me," were Bush's instructions. As well, Scowcroft would have, according to Bush, "direct access, day and night."

In his memoirs (jointly written with Scowcroft), Bush recalls that he had toyed with the idea of appointing him to the CIA or as secretary of defense. But the more Bush thought about it, the more he recognized that Scowcroft was the "perfect honest broker I wanted. He would not try to run over the heads of cabinet members or cut them off from contact with the president, yet I also knew he would give me his own experienced views on whatever problems might arise." But Bush also realized that Scowcroft's appointment would indicate that the NSC staff still counted: it would "send a signal to my cabinet and to outside observers that the NSC's function was to be critical in the decision-making process."[96] Although not explicitly saying it, Bush recognized that Scowcroft would provide an able and skilled counterweight to Baker at State and (at the time) Tower at Defense.

Further Staff Appointments: Familiarity and Experience

As he had with Sununu and Scowcroft, Bush took a direct role in selecting the third person who would play a major role in his administration and have direct access to the Oval Office: press secretary. On November 28, Bush announced (again, it was the president-elect who did the announcing) that Reagan press secretary Marlin Fitzwater would continue in that position. Like Scowcroft, Fitzwater brought obvious expertise by continuing to serve in a position he already held, and he was a known and loyal commodity, having served a stint as Bush's vice presidential press secretary before returning to the West Wing in 1987 following Larry Speakes's departure.

As Fitzwater recounts in his memoirs, he had assumed the job would go to Sheila Tate, who had been press secretary during the campaign and was serving in that capacity during the transition. But Bush and Craig Fuller were concerned that her relations with the press had deteriorated. According to Fitzwater, "The press had turned on Sheila during the campaign. They accused her of never being available to them for questioning and for spending too much time in the cushioned embrace of the presidential entourage."[97] Tate may also have been concerned about the reports she was hearing that some in the Bush inner circle thought she was unqualified to be the first female press secretary and preempted the criticism by taking herself out of the running for a job she may not have wanted in the first place. According to one person familiar with Tate's thinking, "If you don't really want the job, then why should you let people make you feel bad about yourself?"[98] Even in the usually civil Bush camp, the knives might sometimes flash.

During this period, Bush also settled on the key members of his White House economic team. Again, Bush personally unveiled his choices to the press. On November 21, he announced the appointment of Richard Darman as OMB director[99] and Stanford economist Michael Boskin as chair of the CEA. On December 6, Carla Hills, the first woman appointed to a high-level position, was presented as his choice to head the Office of U.S. Trade Representative. Both Darman's and Hills's positions would continue to hold cabinet rank.

By mid-December, the appointments of the remainder of the top White House positions were nearing completion. Although press reports indicated that "Bush's choices are mostly unknowns" and "not Washington insiders," indeed most had past associations with Bush and several had served in the Reagan administration.[100]

On December 16, Andrew Card, David Bates, J. Bonnie Newman, and James Cicconi were named as assistants to the president. Card, who also would serve as Sununu's deputy, had been active in the 1980 and 1988 Bush campaigns, had been a member of the Massachusetts legislature, and was a candidate for governor in 1982. Card also served as director of the intergovernmental affairs office and in the political affairs office in the Reagan White House. David Bates, who was placed in charge of cabinet affairs, had been a friend of son Jeb Bush and, after law school, became George Bush's personal assistant. During the Reagan administration, Bates served in subcabinet positions in the Commerce and Treasury Departments, then rejoined the Bush vice presidential staff as an assistant to Craig Fuller. During the 1988 campaign, Bates had been one of the "gang of six" top advisers to Bush, along with Teeter, Roger Ailes, Mosbacher, Fuller, and Atwater.

Jim Cicconi was designated as staff secretary. He had worked on James Baker's losing 1978 campaign for Texas attorney general and as an aide to Texas Governor William Clements. When Baker became chief of staff in 1981, Cicconi joined his staff as one of his deputies. Cicconi then returned to private law practice (at Robert Strauss's law firm) but was brought back during the campaign to help craft (along with Sununu) the 1988 Republican platform and then to serve as issues director for Dan Quayle. As staff secretary, Cicconi was in charge of all the paper flow to and from the Oval Office. In a departure from past practice, Cicconi was also placed in charge of Bush's scheduling, and another Bush associate, Joseph Hagin, directed that operation under Cicconi.

J. Bonnie Newman, who was placed in charge of White House management and administration, had come to know Bush in the late 1970s when he had begun to campaign in her native New Hampshire. Newman was tapped to serve as associate director of White House personnel and as an assistant secretary in the Commerce Department during the first Reagan term, then served a stint as chief of staff to U.S. Senator Judd Gregg of New Hampshire. In 1988 she was brought on board the transition to help out with personnel. Like Card, Newman was also close to John Sununu.

But not all White House slots were filled so smoothly. The transition team had some difficulty with the position of head of the congressional relations office, critical to Bush's lobbying efforts on Capitol Hill. Former Congressman Tom Loeffler, a Texas Republican, was reported to have turned down an offer, and two others were approached but said they were not interested.[101] Finally, on December 22, Frederick D. McClure's appointment as assistant to the president for legislative affairs was made public. McClure, a native Texan and an African American, had worked for Senator John Tower, served in the congressional relations operation during the Reagan years, and had been the Washington lobbyist for Texas Air Corporation.

The same day that McClure's appointment was announced, David F. Demarest was tapped to be assistant to the president for communications. Demarest got his political start at the Republican National Committee and later served as deputy to RNC Chairman William Brock. During the Reagan years, Demarest joined Brock at the Office of U.S. Trade Representative and later at the Labor Department, where Demarest became an assistant secretary for public and intergovernmental affairs. In July 1988, he was placed in charge of the Bush-Quayle campaign's speechwriting and communications operation. In another change from past practice, Demarest was given jurisdiction over the public liaison staff, and the speechwriting unit was placed under his control.

One position that remained unfilled at the top level was head of domestic and economic policy. On January 11, 1989, Sununu announced that Roger Porter had been asked to serve as assistant to the president for both policy areas. It was Porter's third White House tour: he had served as a special assistant to Gerald Ford and managed the Economic Policy Board; then during the first Reagan term he had been executive secretary of the Cabinet Council on Economic Affairs and director of the Office of Policy Development before returning to his professorship at Harvard's Kennedy School. Porter's appointment was a bit abrupt; he had been slated to serve as a deputy in the Office of U.S. Trade Representative.

That same day, Sununu announced another set of staff appointments. Most followed the pattern of having had previous White House service as well as prior association with George Bush. James Pinkerton was named to serve under Porter as a deputy assistant for policy planning. Pinkerton had worked in the Reagan policy development and political offices, then served as a research director for Bush's precampaign political action committee. The new directors of the White House political and public liaison offices were also announced. These had been downgraded to the deputy-assistant level. Bonnie Kilberg, who had served in the legal counsel's office under Ford and was active in Virginia political circles, was placed in charge of public liaison; Jim Wray, a former RNC political operative and national field director of the Bush campaign, was slated to take over political affairs. Wray's appointment suggested that the real center of political affairs in the Bush administration would be in the RNC, where Lee Atwater had been named party chairman. Sununu also announced that longtime aide David Carney would serve as deputy director of the political office.

Other Bush associates found themselves appointed to newly crafted, special-purpose units. C. Gregg Petersmeyer, dubbed the "thousand points of light man," was placed in charge of a new national service unit that was designed to encourage volunteerism, a Bush campaign theme. Petersmeyer, a Colorado oil executive, had been an aide in the Nixon White House and had known Bush for twenty years (even spending a month with him in 1975 while Bush was serving in Beijing). Richard Breeden, who had been on Bush's vice presidential staff and was a partner in Houston's prestigious Baker and Botts law firm, was appointed as assistant for issues analysis. Breeden would essentially serve in a troubleshooting/special projects role, and he immediately began to work on addressing the savings-and-loan crisis. Stephen Studdert was placed in charge of "special activities." Studdert had served in the Reagan advance office and was given that responsibility under Bush, but he also was placed in charge of Petersmeyer's operation. Studdert would direct the 1989 inauguration and was reputed to have a talent for organizing and staging events.

All told, Bush had assembled a White House team that, unlike his two predecessors, had close links to him. Moreover, given Bush's own career path, many had worked with him in different governmental positions. He was thus able to bring together personal loyalty as well as a degree of Washington expertise, both critical ingredients but often hard to find in one person. There was also a third trait present in many who served in the Bush White House: a kind of low-key, understated personal style. As J. Bonnie Newman explains, both George and Barbara Bush were quite cognizant of the kind of persons they wanted to serve: "Both . . . had been around government in enough different types of positions that they had a very good view of the city, the culture, the good, the bad. They had a real sense of the type of person they wanted. . . . They would be less than tolerant of young staffers that would overexercise their position and rights. They were really looking for an understated White House staff. They didn't want a lot of cowboys." Did that message come directly from George Bush? "I know it did. And Barbara Bush."[102]

Newman especially remembers the appointment, on her own staff, of the person who would handle White House perks and direct White House operations: Rose Zamaria (whom Newman had not met before Bush appointed her). Zamaria had worked for Bush when he was a member of Congress; in Newman's view, Bush knew she "was the kind of no-nonsense person who was not going to be dealing or double-dealing or taking advantage of having that kind of responsibility." Whereas the Carter administration became immobilized over tennis-court privileges, "that didn't happen to us because Rose is Rose and she took care of it, as the president knew she would. . . . George Bush wanted people in positions who could do the job. George Bush wanted a Rose Zamaria who is very tough. He wanted a Rose Zamaria in there whom he knew could say no."[103]

Yet the Bush staff was in no way a preexisting team that had worked together with Bush before he entered the White House, as had been the case in the Reagan administration with Meese, Deaver, William Clark,

Helene von Damm, and Nancy Reynolds. Bush's inner circle had some dyadic links with one another, but their strongest connections were the links—developed at different points in his career—with George Bush. According to one participant, "A team didn't come in here as came into the Reagan White House. . . . There were many different sets of relationships [with George Bush], different kinds over many years."[104] The relative newcomer, it might further be noted, was John Sununu, who had worked closely with Bush only essentially during the 1988 primaries. Sununu's opposite number on the national security side, Brent Scowcroft, was by contrast the "closest soul mate the president had in this particular structure."[105]

Organizational Changes

With respect to the White House staff, Bush "gave pretty firm direction," Card observes. He was very clear about what "decisionmaking funnels" he wanted reporting to him. Furthermore, he wanted fewer people at the top of the White House organizational pyramid. As Card relates, "He wanted fewer people in the hierarchy in the Bush White House than were in the Reagan White House. He also wanted to leave room for advancement. In government you cannot often give people a promotion that results in more money, so you give them a promotion that results in a better title." Bush also decided that the public liaison unit on the staff would be downgraded to the deputy-assistant level, and it would be structured in three subunits: one for economic groups, one for "constituency" groups, and one for what he called "heritage" (ethnic) groups.[106]

Marlin Fitzwater's recollections of his discussions with Bush about becoming press secretary, especially the kind of access to meetings he would have, are revealing not only about Bush's direct role in the matter but also what it says about his thinking and decisionmaking once in office. In discussing his appointment with Bush, Fitzwater sought to establish the same access to the new president and to meetings that he enjoyed under Reagan. In fact, the vice president had been instrumental in seeing to it that Fitzwater was a participant in every major Reagan meeting. Yet in discussing Fitzwater's role in the new administration, Bush was now a bit reticent. "Do you have any questions?" Bush asked him. "Just the one you advised me to ask when I joined President Reagan," Fitzwater replied. "Will I have access to you, and to all meetings?" Although Bush frowned, he thought it would work out. Fitzwater then asked about NSC meetings, which he attended under Reagan.

"Well I don't know," Bush pondered. "Some of those might not be appropriate." Sensing trouble, Fitzwater pulled back and told Bush, "Let's wait and see how it works out."

In Fitzwater's view, the exchange typified Bush's "penchant for secrecy." "His personality was naturally prone to compartmentalization, which means secrecy. He asked people for advice on their specialty— economics, foreign policy, press, etc.—but seldom held open discussions. This later proved to be a weakness, especially in considering the country's economic conditions. . . . It meant he would never think to invite me to a nonmedia meeting."[107]

Following his appointment as chief of staff, John Sununu took over from Teeter the responsibility of dealing with the White House staff and its organization. As Jim Pinkerton relates, "Whenever Sununu got appointed, at that point it became clear that Sununu was running things. Somewhere along there I realized my reporting funnel now is Sununu and [Sununu deputies] Andy Card and Ed Rogers. Whatever that date was, that's when Pinkerton read the tea leaves power-wise."[108]

Sununu's appointment by November 17 also gave him time to work on White House matters. Although he was still the New Hampshire governor, Sununu commuted regularly between Washington and his home in Salem. By that date, he had already begun to think about his own staff, and his daily schedule shows numerous meetings over the following weeks with some of the persons who would come to occupy staff positions, as well as meetings with outgoing Reagan Chief of Staff Ken Duberstein and Congressman Dick Cheney, who held the same position under Ford.[109] Sununu convened periodic meetings on "White House organization," and he met with several members of Congress. He also participated in the budget working group, was part of the CASAG personnel process, and met with various constituency groups.

Sununu could rely on the able services of deputy Andrew Card. Card was not only close to Bush but also came to know Sununu starting in the early 1970s, when both were involved in politics in their local communities (Card in Massachusetts, Sununu in New Hampshire). "I was picked by both President Bush and John Sununu, and that distinction was relatively unique among the White House staff."[110]

Card's experience served him well. Even before Sununu's appointment (much less Card's) was formally announced, Sununu had asked him to help out. Card quickly began to assemble information useful to planning the new staff system:

> I knew where to go in the White House, and I went to the executive
> clerk's office in the White House and got copies of all of the flow

charts of presidents going back to Eisenhower. Then I drew a list of all of the responsibilities I knew of in the White House from my days there and from talking to policy people and the career staff. And then we just went through, deciding whether or not those responsibilities appropriately rested in the White House and what structure would best serve the president to meet those policies.[111]

Experience and personal ties in the Bush network also helped other top aides both understand and adapt to their new positions. Just as David Bates could go to Craig Fuller for advice about the job of secretary to the cabinet,[112] Jim Cicconi could turn to Richard Darman. In Cicconi's case, since Darman had done "an exceptional job in that position, one of the first things I did was sit down with Dick and get his advice."[113]

But Cicconi, whose position as staff secretary handled "everything going to and from the president," also recounts that some changes were made: "I had slightly different responsibilities than Dick. He had the administrative operation of the White House reporting to him; I did not. But I had scheduling, which he did not have. That had been reporting to Deaver while Darman was in there." Adjustments were especially made to fit George Bush's desired working ways: "But the biggest difference was that we worked for very different presidents who approached the job and their workload differently. Just as he had to adjust to Ronald Reagan in the way Reagan preferred to work, I had to adjust to the way George Bush preferred to work."[114]

A number of the incoming Bush White House staffers could also rely on the good auspices of the Reaganites they were replacing. David Bates had been able to turn to his outgoing counterpart, Nancy Risque. Cicconi could rely not just on Darman but also on Rhett Dawson, as did J. Bonnie Newman, whose duties in White House management also overlapped with Dawson's job as director of White House operations. As head of the transition personnel operation, Untermeyer developed a close relationship with Robert Tuttle, whom Untermeyer was slated to replace after the inauguration, as did Boyden Gray with Arthur Culvahouse, his opposite number in the Reagan White House. The Bush transition also enjoyed good cooperation in assembling information pertinent to the White House staff.[115]

Some organizational changes and parceling of responsibilities were based "on the personalities that came in," according to Andrew Card. Some resulted from job negotiations: "As with any kind of job search, there were some people who said 'I will come and work at the White House, but I want this condition met.' It might be a title, it might be an added area of responsibility, or it could have been 'I want my office in the West Wing or whatever.'" There were "some suggestions that came from potential employees that were outrageous, some that were reasonable. Some were disruptive to the original flow-chart thinking and some weren't."[116]

Jim Pinkerton's experience in being hired as domestic policy adviser in charge of policy planning is revealing about the informal process of determining positions and responsibilities. According to Pinkerton, one day Jim Cicconi

> sat me down and said, "Here's the way it works. There is an assistant to the president, and it won't be you. There will be a deputy assistant, and that will be you. So we will also make you director of OPD." That's the way it usually works. The assistant is theoretically at the president's elbow, sitting there helping him. As a sort of sop they say the deputy assistant is director of the office [of policy development].

But Pinkerton was reluctant to take the position, largely because the person who would be at the assistant-to-the-president level had yet to be named:

> I kind of figured since I don't know who it is going to be, don't make me director of the office either, because Mr. Big will get in there and take one look at me and say, "Pinkerton, you're obviously the right guy to run things" or "Pinkerton, you're obviously the wrong guy to run things." In which case I would hate to have the title taken away. So I sort of went for a lateral kind of thing. I said, "Look, we don't know who it is going to be; for better or worse I am sort of a loose guy, a speculative type. Just put me in charge of, give me the title of policy planning. I like the deputy-assistant part, that will be fun, but don't make it for policy development, make it for policy planning. In that way if the guy comes in and doesn't like me, it will be "pretend I don't work for him." That's actually the way it kind of worked.[117]

In sum, as one press report notes, "Through a succession of stylistic touches, [Bush] succeeded, in the month since Election Day, in nearly extinguishing the memory of his ungentlemanly campaign and forging instead a relaxed, spontaneous image."[118]

The president-elect had assembled a cabinet and staff populated with longtime friends, most with a high degree of prior governmental experience. Yet the question remained whether imagery and friendship would translate into policy substance; whether Bush and his associates would be able to establish policies and programs under difficult budgetary circumstances; and whether Bush's own considerable background and experience would yield the kind of leadership needed for his presidency.

* * *

In many respects, the 1988 transition had all the appearances of an effective effort that would culminate in a successful early administration. Although Untermeyer's initial assignment was, by design, comparably modest, Bush had given some thought to what his administration might look like even before his election was secure. He and his associates also monitored and otherwise provided oversight to Untermeyer's operation, and none of the tension that had plagued Carter (and even the preelection jockeying for position in the Reagan inner circle eight years before) emerged.

The day after the election, Bush moved immediately to set up his transition operation and was ready to announce several key appointments: Baker at State, Untermeyer and Gray in the White House. The transition clearly benefited from the good auspices of the Reagan administration, both before and after the election. Advice and information of various sorts were quickly conveyed, giving members of the transition both an easy start and a head start. Many of them also could draw on their own experiences in past Republican transitions and presidencies. This was not just a friendly takeover—it was a familiar takeover.

Like Jimmy Carter, Bush had a propensity to draw on trusted associates. As a political insider, however, Bush could tap a pool of talent—for both his cabinet and his White House staff—that had prior White House or executive-branch experience (sometimes both). Where it was lacking, something else valuable usually was there in its stead: congressional experience or, as in Governor Sununu's case, other forms of executive leadership. But there was also one particular feature of that personal relationship: their links were to George Bush, not necessarily to each other, as had been the case with Reagan's lieutenants.

By all accounts it was a well-organized and -managed transition. The prospect of Sununu's appointment as chief of staff did generate a bit of intramural politicking, but Bush let the Sununu matter play out for a few days, then announced what had been his decision all along. The negotiations over Teeter's role in the new administration did linger, which had some effect on getting the domestic policy staff up and running, but most of the other pieces of the transition fell into place. Throughout, Bush played an active role, quite different from some of Reagan's indifference to staff and organizational matters and Carter's preference for letting his fellow Georgians work differences out among themselves. Bush played a direct role in selecting both staff and cabinet members, and he was directly involved in determining some of the organizational matters and processes in which they would operate: retention of the Reagan cabinet-council system and a White House staff that had fewer assistants to the president at the top. Bush was especially determinative in Sununu's selection as chief of staff and Scowcroft's as NSC adviser.

Policy, too, had begun to be formed during the transition. Foreign policy clearly was moving forward due to the efforts of Baker, Scowcroft, and Bush. The budget, taxes, and the deficit had already begun to bear Richard Darman's considerable imprint. Steps had also been taken to deal with the savings-and-loan bailout. But on other domestic matters, the agenda had yet to coalesce; it was one soft spot, but clearly a major one.

Although for the most part the Bush transition was well managed, well organized, and attentive to personnel and organization issues, the open question for the Bush transition—and for Bush himself—was whether the judgments and choices made in these matters would prove to be the right ones.

Notes

1. Untermeyer had first met Bush in 1966 when Bush was running for Congress in Houston. Untermeyer later served as his executive assistant (1981–1983). In 1983, he was appointed deputy assistant secretary of the navy for installations and facilities, and from 1984 to 1988 he served as assistant secretary of the navy for manpower and reserve affairs.

2. Correspondence with Chase Untermeyer, December 9, 1998.

3. Untermeyer's one-person operation was then deluged with phone calls and résumés. He began to put the résumés into an empty box that had once held a smoked turkey that friends from Texas had sent the previous Christmas; Untermeyer appropriately dubbed it the "turkey box." Correspondence with Chase Untermeyer, December 9, 1998.

4. "The Reagan to Bush Transition: A Miller Center Panel and Colloquium," in Thompson, ed., *Presidential Transitions*, pp. 176–177. By September, Untermeyer had moved to space at RNC headquarters. The RNC also funded Untermeyer's operation; Bush had decided neither to tap into campaign funds nor to raise funds independently, as Reagan had done. Untermeyer began to meet with a number of persons who had been involved in past transitions, Pendleton James most notably. Untermeyer also did a lot of reading on transitions and the presidency. Correspondence with Chase Untermeyer, December 9, 1998.

5. Dick Kirschten, "As Reagan's Presidency Fades Out," *National Journal*, September 3, 1988, p. 2202.

6. Burke interview with David Bates, October 5, 1998.

7. Burke interview with J. Bonnie Newman, September 29, 1998.

8. Correspondence with Chase Untermeyer, December 9, 1998. Although Bush had instructed him not to do any recruiting, Untermeyer also "took the risk" (in his words) of asking Ross Starek, who had been the State Department's personnel liaison to the White House, to serve as his assistant. Untermeyer, moreover, intended to make Starek his deputy at presidential personnel if Bush won.

9. An internal Reagan White House memorandum indicates that while representatives from the Dukakis camp were invited by the GSA to attend meetings, they never did: "GSA has assured us the Dukakis organization was invited to every meeting, but they never attended." Memorandum from Gordon Riggle to Rhett Dawson, November 3, 1988, FG001–04 606669, RL. Raymond Fontaine even ordered stationery well before the election, and he got the two campaigns to agree that it would have the neutral letterhead "Office of the President-elect" so that half would not have to be thrown away the day after the election. The GSA secured space for a transition headquarters at a Commerce Department building at Connecticut and Florida Avenues. Judith Havemann, "Rules of Transition Start with 'No,'" *Washington Post*, October 21, 1988. The 1988 transition benefited from better financial resources. Under new rules passed by Congress, the transition operation of the incoming administration was allocated $3.5 million, $1.5 million more than had been appropriated in 1980. The new funding arrangement, however, carried with it a new requirement: public disclosure of staff, salaries, and expenses. As it was, all of the additional resources were not needed: only $2,209,000 was spent. The Bush transition was "as clean as a hound's tooth" Fontaine, the comptroller of the GSA and its "transitions czar" since 1968, would later pronounce. Judith Havemann, "Transition Leaves Substantial Change," *Washington Post*, May 2, 1989.

10. Memorandum from Robert H. Tuttle to Kenneth M. Duberstein, November 1, 1988, "Transition Planning," FG001–04 606669, RL.

11. "The Reagan to Bush Transition: A Miller Center Panel and Colloquium," in Thompson, ed., *Presidential Transitions*, p. 180.

12. Correspondence with Chase Untermeyer, December 9, 1998.

13. "The Reagan to Bush Transition: A Miller Center Panel and Colloquium," in Thompson, ed., *Presidential Transitions*, p. 180.

14. Jack Watson's 1980 memo to the Carter administration department and agency heads was attached to the checklist memo, and some of the language in it would appear verbatim in Duberstein's own memo issued to Reagan administration officials on November 21. Indeed, both the Watson and Duberstein memo bear the title "An Orderly Transition of the Presidency." Duberstein's memo, however, contained more detailed instructions on making sure that those purporting to represent the Bush transition were in fact on the list of authorized representatives, a problem that had come up in 1980. As well, Duberstein outlined

steps to avoid actual and potential conflicts of interest regarding any information that might be transmitted, and he issued more detailed instructions about the handling and transmittal of nonpublic or otherwise confidential information. Memorandum from John Tuck to Kenneth Duberstein, "Chief of Staff Duberstein Checklist," November 5, 1988, FG 0001–04, FG 0006–01, 606669, RL; Memorandum from Ken Duberstein to Cabinet and Agency Heads, "An Orderly Transition of the Presidency," November 21, 1988, FG0001–04 606627, RL.

15. Memorandum from Colin Powell to Ken Duberstein, "NSC Transition," November 3, 1988, FG001–04 606669, RL.

16. Steven Roberts, "Bush Personnel Team Aims for Stiff Scrutiny," *New York Times,* November 12, 1988.

17. On November 16, the appointments of the remaining transition deputies were announced. Janet Mullins was tapped to head congressional liaison. Mullins had been deputy national political director during the campaign and had been chief of staff to Senator Mitch McConnell of Kentucky and Senator Bob Packwood of Oregon. Jim Pinkerton was placed in charge of policy development. Pinkerton had been director of research during the campaign and had served on Reagan's domestic policy staff. David Demarest was named to head public affairs, the same job he had done during the campaign. Fred Fielding, a former Reagan White House counsel, was assigned to look after the vice president–elect's office, as well as that of the First Lady. David J. Ryder, a former Bush aide who had directed operations at the Republican convention, was selected to direct management and operations. J. Mike Farren, a former undersecretary at Commerce, was chosen to serve as deputy director under Fuller. Internal Reagan White House memoranda indicate that several of the newly appointed deputies had already been at work for some time before the November 16 announcement. Both Farren and Ryder had met with representatives from the White House before that date, and one internal memo indicates that Farren "appears to be the Deputy Director of the Transition, reporting directly to Fuller-Teeter." The memo also notes that "there will be four lines reporting to Fuller-Teeter in the transition organization: Management, Public Affairs, Personnel, and Policy Development." Memorandum from Rhett Dawson to John Tuck, "Transition Effort Update," November 15, 1988, FG001–04 100467, RL.

18. David Hoffman, "Bush Names Baker Secretary of State," *Washington Post,* November 10, 1988.

19. Burke interview with J. Bonnie Newman, September 29, 1998.

20. Burke interview with David Bates, October 5, 1998.

21. David Hoffman, "Bush Said to Favor Sununu for Chief of Staff," *Washington Post,* November 15, 1988.

22. Maureen Dowd, "Bush Narrowing Field for Top Cabinet Posts," *New York Times,* November 17, 1988. Fuller also told the press that each member of the staff had been required to sign a pledge to prevent conflicts of interest and stop unauthorized leaks to the press. The pledge requires that staff members "hold in confidence any non-public information provided" and requires them to disqualify themselves from any transition matter that appears to be a financial conflict of interest.

23. At his postelection press conference, Bush clearly indicated that changes in personnel would be made. Bush noted, echoing the campaign, that he would "for the most part bring in a brand new team of people from across the country." Martin Tolchin, "Bush Prepares to Share the Fruits of Victory," *New York Times,* November 11, 1988. On November 10, President Reagan facilitated the process by requesting that all political appointees submit their resignations "effective at the pleasure of the president." The order had been agreed upon by both Reagan and Bush before the election and was done at the request of both, according to one senior aide. Gerald Boyd, "Reagan Asks the Cabinet to Resign to Give Bush Flexibility in Choice," *New York Times,* November 11, 1988.

24. Other members of the unit were Bush, Peter Teeley, David Bates (who would be tapped as secretary to the cabinet), Ron Kaufman, Rich Bond, and Don Rhodes of the vice president's staff. Mary Matalin, who had headed the RNC's Victory '88 effort and was slated to become a top aide to Atwater at RNC, was placed in charge of an operation to keep track of fund-raisers and political operatives at the state and local levels for possible positions in the incoming administration.

25. Burke interview with David Bates, October 5, 1998.

26. Burke interview with J. Bonnie Newman, September 29, 1998.

27. Frank Swoboda and Judith Havemann, "Bush Transition Team Embarking on Search for New Talent, Diversity," *Washington Post,* December 3, 1988.

28. Bernard Weinraub, "Bush Plans a Drive to Recruit Minorities," *New York Times,* December 4, 1988. Brought on board were: Betty Heitman, a former president of the National Federation of Republican Women, Jose Martinez, a former aide to John Tower, and Constance Newman, an African American and former HUD official.

29. Maralee Schwartz and Frank Swoboda, "Bush Assistant Describes Trouble Recruiting Women," *Washington Post,* January 12, 1989.

30. Judith Havemann, "Veteran Aides Leading Bush's 'Friendly Takeover,'" *Washington Post,* November 17, 1988.

31. Judith Havemann, "After Jan. 20, How Soon Will the Honeymoon End?" *Washington Post,* October 24, 1988.

32. The memo requested (1) basic organizational information, including statement of resources, goals, and functions of each unit ("Limit: Chart plus 1 page per organizational unit"; (2) "management," including chain of command, regulatory authority ("Limit: 1 paragraph per program"), and review of recent management studies ("Limit: 2 paragraphs per study"); (3) "external process," including key interagency relationships, congressional committee jurisdictions, oversight and legislative issues, and a list of the top-ten anticipated legislative goals for the upcoming 101st Congress ("Limit: 1 page per issue, 1 page of summary discussion"); (4) budget details, trends, and issues; (5) personnel; and (6) policy-development process and goals, including "a calendar of major events, decisions, and milestones that present challenges and opportunities for the Bush administration in calendar year 1989 (Limit: Use basic calendar format—1 page per month)." Memorandum from Ken Duberstein to

Cabinet and Agency Heads, "Transition Organization and Briefing Materials," November 21, 1988, FG0001–04 606627, RL. In addition, C. Boyden Gray also sent a memo to department and agency heads, as well as to heads of White House units, asking them to designate a transition-team person. Gray also requested that the designee sign a confidentiality statement. Memorandum from C. Boyden Gray to Department, Agency, and White House Officials, November 14, 1988, FG0001–04 60627, RL.

33. Judith Havemann, "Helping Bush's Cabinet Get Its Footing," *Washington Post,* January 17, 1989.

34. Baker, *Politics of Diplomacy,* p. 17.

35. Gerald Boyd, "Circle of Senior Aides Helps Bush Fill Top Posts," *New York Times,* December 8, 1988.

36. Brady's reappointment was not unexpected; he was a longtime Bush friend and supporter. Thornburgh's retention was more of a surprise, and there had been some discussion of other possibilities, including former EPA Administrator William Ruckleshaus and Illinois Governor Jim Thompson. Cavazos, a former Texas university president and the first Hispanic member of the cabinet, easily filled Bush's promise during the campaign to have a Hispanic in his cabinet, although it would not be among Bush's more successful picks. Bush in fact would have two Hispanics in his initial cabinet (with the appointment of Lujan at Interior).

37. Mosbacher was a longtime Bush friend and Texas oilman; Hills was a well-known Washington lawyer and former HUD secretary under Ford; Yeutter had been serving as U.S. trade representative.

38. Kemp had been considered for several cabinet positions, but transition officials and the Bush inner circle were concerned that the outspoken conservative would not be a team player.

39. Tower, *Consequences,* p. 36.

40. Walter Pincus, "Bush Team, Tower Negotiate on Filling Key Pentagon Slots," *Washington Post,* November 23, 1988. The *Washington Post* also noted that these negotiations over subcabinet personnel were "at odds with Bush's often repeated statement during the campaign that he would name his Cabinet and then allow them to pick their subordinates without interference from transition personnel."

41. David Hoffman, "Bush Selects Tower as Defense Secretary," *Washington Post,* December 17, 1988.

42. Tower, *Consequences,* p. 33.

43. Tower, *Consequences,* p. 83.

44. "The Reagan to Bush Transition: A Miller Center Panel and Colloquium," in Thompson, ed., *Presidential Transitions,* pp. 179–180. By Christmas Day, the cabinet appointments were essentially complete, with one exception. That exception was the appointment of an energy secretary, which was delayed until January 12. Bush apparently had been wavering between naming an energy secretary familiar with oil and gas issues or one familiar with nuclear power. He eventually settled on the latter, with the appointment of retired Admiral James Watkins, who had been chief of naval operations and was a

protégé of Admiral Hyman Rickover. Untermeyer had come up with Watkins's name, but "my feeling at the time, however, was not one of great pride, but one of anger with myself because I hadn't thought of him a month earlier, since he was such an obvious choice and someone I had known when I was in the Navy Department" (quote at p. 180).

45. David Hoffman, "Watkins, Bennett Named to Cabinet," *Washington Post,* January 13, 1989.

46. Ann Devroy, "Slow Pace of Appointments Irks Some Cabinet Officials," *Washington Post,* February 14, 1989.

47. Ann Devroy, "High-Level Government Jobs Reserved for Bush Supporters," *Washington Post,* January 14, 1989.

48. Burke interview with James Cicconi, April 29, 1998. Jack Kemp at HUD was given only one "strong suggestion" by the transition—that he hire a former aide to Senator Mitch McConnell of Kentucky, an early Bush supporter.

49. Ann Devroy, "Slow Pace of Appointments Irks Some Cabinet Officials," *Washington Post,* February 14, 1989.

50. To further this effort, Bush aide Ron Kaufman was selected to serve as Untermeyer's deputy.

51. Burke interview with Andrew Card Jr., September 17, 1998.

52. Burke interview with J. Bonnie Newman, September 29, 1998.

53. Burke interview with J. Bonnie Newman, September 29, 1998.

54. David Hoffman and Maralee Schwartz, "CIA Director, Envoy Won't Be in Cabinet," *Washington Post,* December 3, 1988.

55. Michael Isikoff, "Drug Czar Won't Be a Cabinet Member," *Washington Post,* January 25, 1989.

56. Burke interview with Andrew Card Jr., September 17, 1998.

57. Burke interview with David Bates, October 5, 1998.

58. Burke interview with Andrew Card Jr., September 17, 1998.

59. Burke interview with Andrew Card Jr., September 17, 1998.

60. Bush and Scowcroft, *A World Transformed,* pp. 8, 16, 19.

61. Baker, *Politics of Diplomacy,* pp. 28, 29, 38, 41–43, 47, 49.

62. David C. Mulford, "The Bush Presidency and International Economic Issues," in Thompson, ed., *The Bush Presidency I,* pp. 127–142.

63. On Sunday, November 13, Fuller indicated that decisions on Bush's economic policy team have "got to be priority one" and that they would prepare a plan for dealing with Congress "in the early days of the Bush administration," as Bush had promised during the campaign. While not indicating the particulars of a Bush budget plan, Fuller noted that Bush would come to the negotiating table with a "flexible freeze" requiring spending to be held to the rate of inflation. Teeter said that "cuts would be likely in domestic spending programs that have grown in recent years." David Hoffman, "Bush Team Acts to Calm Markets," *Washington Post,* November 14, 1988.

64. According to Darman, the Reagan budget projections had been based on fairly rosy projections of economic growth (hence revenues produced) and interest rates. As he would point out to Bush in an early December memo, "If interest rates were merely 1 percent higher than forecast, and real growth 1

percent lower, the deficit would be about $135 billion higher than it was sup-
posed to be balanced. The picture got worse, not better, from there." Moreover,
in order to meet Gramm-Rudman targets, spending growth had to be no more
than 2.8 percent, less than the flexible freeze had called for. Darman, *Who's
in Control?*, p. 207.

65. Darman, *Who's in Control?* pp. 200, 210.

66. Darman, *Who's in Control?* p. 206.

67. Darman, *Who's in Control?* p. 208. Emphasis in original.

68. Darman, *Who's in Control?* p. 210.

69. There is some archival evidence that the budget discussions were not
just at the tax/no tax, freeze/no freeze level. On January 10, the budget group's
meetings focused on health care; on January 11, education and drug control; and
on January 12, enterprise zones, problems of the homeless, and other Bush initiatives. Sununu's Daily Schedule, FG006–03, Box 110, Bush Presidential Library, Texas A&M University, College Station, Texas (hereafter cited as BL).

70. Burke interview with Andrew Card Jr., September 17, 1998.

71. Burke interview with Jim Pinkerton, October 15, 1998.

72. At the Democratic convention the previous summer, Richards delivered a speech with a line that said that Bush "wasn't born with a silver spoon
in his mouth, George Bush was born with a silver foot in his mouth."

73. Memorandum from Susan Porter Rose to Vice President and Mrs.
Bush, January 13, 1989, Chief of Staff Files—Sununu, OA 11322, Box 30,
BL.

74. Burt Solomon, "Getting Ready," *National Journal,* November 19,
1988, p. 2927.

75. Carol Matlack, "Political Math May Explain Bush's Environment Push,"
National Journal, December 10, 1988, p. 3145.

76. Gerald M. Boyd, "Sununu Answers His Critics: I Have to Be Tough
Enough," *New York Times,* November 19, 1988.

77. Bush, *All the Best,* p. 403. Other reports indicated that on election day,
Bush had privately told Craig Fuller—a possible contender for the job—and
others in his inner circle that he wanted Sununu for the position. David Hoffman, "His Political Stature Gave Sununu Edge," *Washington Post,* November
18, 1988.

78. According to Sidney Blumenthal, Baker "wanted even more power.
His political allies reflected the thinking in his circle by openly talking of
Baker as 'deputy president.'" The key would be chief of staff: a more pliable
Craig Fuller rather than the independent and abrasive Sununu. According to
one Republican operative, "Bush hauled Sununu in there to keep Baker from
having influence on that position, and left Fuller in the lurch as a result." Sidney Blumenthal, "I, Baker," *New Republic,* November 2, 1992.

79. David Hoffman and Ann Devroy, "Fuller, Teeter, Sununu Eyed as Top
Bush Team," *Washington Post,* November 12, 1988.

80. Bernard Weinraub, "Amid Tension, Two Vie for White House Chief,"
New York Times, November 15, 1988; Maureen Dowd, "Bush Narrowing Field
for Top Cabinet Posts," *New York Times*, November 17, 1988.

81. Gerald Boyd, "Bush Is Reported to Have Chosen Gov. Sununu as His Chief of Staff," *New York Times,* November 16, 1988.

82. Gerald Boyd, "Top Aide Reticent on Sununu Choice," *New York Times,* November 18, 1998.

83. Burke interview with Andrew Card Jr., September 17, 1998.

84. Bernard Weinraub, "Gray-Baker Vendetta: A Long-Running Tale of Potomac Intrigue," *New York Times,* March 29, 1989.

85. "Transcript of Bush and Sununu Remarks at News Conference," *New York Times,* November 18, 1988.

86. Gerald Boyd, "Bush's Political Engineer," *New York Times,* November 17, 1988.

87. "Under the proposed division Teeter would be in charge of helping formulate domestic policy and promote it politically and publicly." Ann Devroy, "Bush Picks Kemp as HUD Chief," *Washington Post,* December 16, 1988.

88. Gerald Boyd, "Sununu and Teeter Differing on Access," *New York Times,* December 8, 1988.

89. Burke interview with Jim Pinkerton, October 15, 1998.

90. Ann Devroy, "Teeter, Citing Family Concerns, Says No to White House Post," *Washington Post,* January 10, 1989.

91. Maureen Dowd, "Sununu Sees Himself in Background," *New York Times,* November 29, 1988.

92. John Milne, "Sununu Hints at a Run for Senate," *Boston Globe,* December 8, 1988. As the title of the article indicates, Sununu also discussed the possibility that he would return to New Hampshire and run for the U.S. Senate in either 1990 or 1992. The article noted that "such an announcement could reduce his power by making him a 'lame duck' before he is sworn." The *Globe* also reported that Sununu had a political war-chest of $232,000 left over from his last campaign, and that he had spent $12,000 for a voting list that the Bush primary campaign had compiled. He had purchased the list on June 15, a month after he had announced he would not run for a fourth term as New Hampshire governor.

93. Ann Devroy, "Sununu Swiftly Backpedals on Size of His White House Role," *Washington Post,* December 9, 1988.

94. Interestingly, Clayton Yeutter would be appointed as counselor to the president, with cabinet status, in Bush's fourth year as president. By that time Sununu was no longer chief of staff.

95. David Hoffman, "President Scales Back National Security Council," *Washington Post,* February 3, 1989.

96. Bush and Scowcroft, *A World Transformed,* p. 19.

97. Fitzwater, *Call the Briefing!,* p. 173.

98. Lois Romano, "Bush's Team and the Avalanche of Applications," *Washington Post,* December 23, 1988.

99. The prospect of Darman's appointment led to some "inside baseball" speculation in the press. According to the *New York Times,* "Under one plan being considered, Mr. Baker would extend his reach into budgetary and domestic matters through the appointment of his former deputy at the Treasury

Department, Richard G. Darman, as director of the White House Office of Management and Budget." Bernard Weinraub and Peter Kilborn, "Baker Will Wield Broad Influence, Aides to Bush Say," *New York Times,* November 13, 1988.

100. Ann Devroy, "White House Staff May Have New Cast," *Washington Post,* December 17, 1988.

101. Ann Devroy, "White House Staff May Have New Cast," *Washington Post,* December 17, 1988.

102. Burke interview with J. Bonnie Newman, September 29, 1998.

103. Burke interview with J. Bonnie Newman, September 29, 1998.

104. Burke interview with J. Bonnie Newman, September 29, 1998.

105. Burke interview with J. Bonnie Newman, September 29, 1998.

106. Burke interview with Andrew Card Jr., September 17, 1998.

107. Fitzwater, *Call the Briefing!* pp. 173–174.

108. Burke interview with Jim Pinkerton, October 15, 1998.

109. Bush Library records of Sununu's schedule begin on November 21. Chief of Staff Files—Sununu, FG006–03, Box 110, BL. But there is also some evidence of his activities before this date. For example, on November 18, he received a letter from Bobbie Kilberg outlining her thoughts on the White House public liaison office and reminding him of an upcoming meeting with her in New York City; Kilberg later got the job. Letter from Kilberg to Sununu, 1988, Chief of Staff Files—Sununu, OA 1806, Box 1, BL.

110. Later, in 1982, as they campaigned for governor of their respective states, they often ran into each other at radio stations in the overlapping radio markets of the region. Card had also served as the Reagan administration's liaison to the governors and had worked on a number of projects with Sununu in that capacity. As he would later recall: "So we became, I would say, pretty close friends, certainly political allies. I know his wife and children and all that kind of stuff." Burke interview with Andrew Card Jr., September 17, 1998.

111. Burke interview with Andrew Card Jr., September 17, 1998.

112. There is also some evidence that Fuller provided information to Sununu. For example, in late December 1988, Fuller sent Sununu a memorandum that he and Darman had put together in November 1981 setting up a weekly-update briefing system for President Reagan. Memorandum from Richard Darman and Craig Fuller, November 30, 1981, Chief of Staff Files—Sununu, OA 11322, Box 30, BL.

113. Burke interview with Jim Cicconi, April 29, 1998.

114. Burke interview with Jim Cicconi, April 29, 1998.

115. Joe Hagin, who would do Bush's day-to-day scheduling, obtained a list of Reagan's daily and weekly meetings from his counterparts in the outgoing administration, which he then forwarded to Sununu. Memorandum from Joe Hagin to John Sununu, "Regularly Scheduled Meetings," Chief of Staff Files—Sununu, Box 49, BL. Although the memo has no date, it was attached to Sununu's daily "items for discussion" agenda for January 11, 1989.

116. Burke interview with Andrew Card Jr., September 17, 1998.

117. Burke interview with Jim Pinkerton, October 15, 1998.

118. Burt Solomon, "Bush's Transition in Tone," *National Journal,* December 10, 1988, p. 3144.

6

Bush in Office

As the beneficiary of both a friendly and a familiar takeover, Bush was in an enviable position upon taking office in 1989. On the surface, much looked promising. Yet beneath, possible fault lines could emerge. The services of a skilled and experienced staff had been enlisted, but the White House was headed by a potentially powerful chief of staff in John Sununu. During the transition, Sununu had pledged allegiance to the philosophy of being a "neutral broker" as chief of staff, yet his own public comments indicated that he also saw himself on occasion as a policy advocate. Where would his allegiance fall once the administration was under way? Could advocacy be successfully merged with the more custodial and managerial functions of the neutral-broker role? How would Sununu's own career experience as a long-serving state governor accustomed to making his own executive decisions and as someone new to the Washington scene meld with his now quite different responsibilities? Were his critics right about the potential risks in his ability to delegate, be cooperative, and curb his own ego?

Both Bush and Sununu had put great thought into the operations of their White House staff. But again, the effects of some of these changes would await the new presidency. Understandably, Bush had sought to reduce the "title creep" over the eight years of the Reagan White House. But some of the units that were downgraded—especially the political affairs and public liaison offices and the speechwriting staff—could affect the selling of the Bush agenda and the place of politics in its crafting. Did the Bush White House possess the ability not just to formulate policy but also to communicate those policies, to market and sell them, in the absence of a Mike Deaver, David Gergen, or, in this case, Bob Teeter?

Bush and his advisers also sought to follow the pattern set in the Reagan years for melding White House and cabinet input into the policy process: two cabinet councils with the cabinet affairs office in a coordinating role. That may have worked in 1985 when Donald Regan became chief of staff and the system was designed to accommodate one of his chief lieutenants from the Treasury Department, Alfred Kingon, who was brought over to direct cabinet affairs. But would it work with a different cast of characters—David Bates and Roger Porter in particular? Were Thornburgh and Brady the best choices to continue in their roles as the chair pro tems of those councils?

Within Roger Porter's operation, Jim Pinkerton had been hired to direct a domestic policy planning unit, but that decision was made before Porter came on board. Could creative policy planning thrive in such an environment—not just Porter's, but one where Sununu and Darman were major players? Also, how would Roger Porter's own late arrival on the scene, plus his well-deserved reputation as a coordinator rather than a maker of policy, play out?

The cabinet contained members with close personal associations, of various sorts, with Bush. Perhaps that, coupled with his own informal and direct style, indicated a cabinet that would have great influence in this presidency. But did it also portend a legacy of individual contact, of informal wheeling and dealing that might suffer absent proper organization and staff work?

In foreign affairs, Bush had assembled a particularly close and experienced team. Scowcroft had the stature and hands-on knowledge that none of his counterparts during the Reagan administration could match. The deep-seated conflicts of the Reagan years were not likely to erupt, but would Baker, Scowcroft, and George Bush be able to craft a new foreign policy in the waning days of the Cold War and avoid the mind-set that often can settle in on a small group of personally close and sometimes like-minded associates?

As for George Bush, the transition revealed an engaged president-elect, far more prone to immerse himself in what was transpiring in the days leading up to his presidency than was Reagan. But some questions remained: Would his sense of loyalty to those around him be repaid in kind? How would his emphasis on collegiality meld with the sense of some of his associates that he could be secretive at times or at least prone to keep his own counsel? Although a very different type of political actor than Reagan, would Bush muster the abilities to sell his programs to Congress and the public? In particular, with respect to the policies of his presidency, would his willingness to be engaged in foreign policy matters be matched by a concern for domestic affairs, which at least comparably had received less attention, especially the details, both during the campaign and in the transition? Would his vision here, even if a bit dim at the start, yield accomplishments?

Decisionmaking Processes

Taking the Cabinet—but Not Cabinet Government—Seriously

Although George Bush had not publicly articulated a desire to employ his cabinet as a central component of his policymaking, it played a significant role nonetheless. In part, this was an artifact of the transition: all of the cabinet members had some connection to Bush, in many instances a close personal connection going back years. It also was a reflection of George Bush: from the start, Bush made it clear to the White House staff that cabinet members would have access to him. As David Bates, his secretary to the cabinet, observes, "He was very involved with his cabinet and made that very clear to me. He wanted to keep the lines of communication open to his cabinet and wanted his cabinet to feel a part of the administration."[1]

Yet Bush did not have any illusions about using the cabinet as some collective decisionmaking body, as had been the case under Carter. While Bush would convene a meeting of the whole cabinet every three of four weeks, they were "more informational," according to Bates, and a "sounding board," in the view of Edward Derwinski, Bush's veterans affairs secretary.[2]

Bush's usual mode of communicating with cabinet members or soliciting their advice was more informal and individualized: telephone calls, personal notes, meetings with individual members or small groups. According to Bates, "He didn't want to see them cut off . . . from him. So we did a lot of things to make sure that didn't happen." One thing he did was to invite each cabinet member to the White House for a luncheon meeting: "Usually once a week or every couple of weeks he would have a lunch with a cabinet secretary, just to make sure they were staying in touch. And it would give the guy an opportunity to explain what was going on in their portfolio." Both Sununu and Bates would attend as well.[3]

But Bush's penchant for more contact with his cabinet members was not without problems.[4] Most cabinet members "exercised the president's invitation for direct access," Andrew Card notes, but they "didn't necessarily respect the chain of command and wouldn't always report on it, which created tension." Bush "didn't get permission from John Sununu to talk to Jack Kemp." Sometimes that would prove unsettling to Sununu: "I can remember Sununu saying, 'How the heck did he get in there?' 'How did the president get that note?' But the president was always quick to say, even when he heard a rumor that Sununu was upset, 'Look, my cabinet can talk to me anytime they damn well please. They're giving information to me.'" Yet for his part, Bush understood Sununu's position, his need to know what might have transpired, and, in Card's opinion, "never blindsided" his chief of staff. "If he had a conversation with the secretary of HUD, he let John Sununu know about it."[5]

Cabinet Slipups

Although the transition had produced a cabinet that was close to Bush, and Bush himself had sent signals about his openness to their input, on several occasions cabinet members crossed the line and exercised a degree of independence from the White House that would prove damaging. In the early months of the Bush presidency, the White House had difficulty in coordinating the activities of cabinet departments, particularly in establishing control of policy initiatives that might emanate from outside the White House. Sometimes these were efforts that the White House might have liked to take credit for, whereas others were errors and missteps that the White House might have preferred to avoid.

One of the latter occurred during the first week of the new administration. It concerned a proposal that Treasury Secretary Nicholas Brady had floated in closed testimony before the House Banking Committee to levee a fee of thirty cents on every $100 deposited in savings and checking accounts, with the revenues going to fund the bailout of the savings-and-loan industry. Although the proposal was only one of a range of possible options to fund the bailout, Brady's testimony was leaked to the press and led to what one report called a "wave of protest" among members of Congress and within the financial community.[6]

Brady's remarks also led to a confused response on the part of the administration, particularly as to whether it violated Bush's no-new-taxes pledge. Press Secretary Marlin Fitzwater called it a "trial balloon," and he and Sununu emphasized to the press that it was only one option under consideration and had yet to be presented to the president.[7] Bush likened it to an entrance fee charged to a visitor at Yosemite National Park but declined to say whether he would accept it.[8] CEA Chairman Michael Boskin called it an "insurance premium."

OMB Director Darman said it would be considered a tax by the new administration, regardless of whether it was labeled a "user fee" or anything else. William Seidman, the chairman of the Federal Deposit Insurance Corporation, dubbed it the "reverse toaster theory": "Instead of the bank giving you a toaster when you make a deposit, you give it one."[9] (Sununu was reported to have been particularly upset by Seidman's characterization. According to one senior aide, Seidman "would be uncomfortable if the governor [Sununu] did with that toaster what he suggested" in remarks at his morning staff meeting.)[10]

The episode figured centrally in the postmortem of Bush's first week that Sununu conducted with his aides. Sununu confided to one reporter that "probably the most important thing we did not do well was that we could have more discipline in the packaging of the message."[11]

Over the next several months, several other actions taken by cabinet members would occur that the White House would find out about only after the fact: an announcement by the attorney general about the possibility of drug testing in public housing,[12] an effort on drug czar Bennett's part to ban the import of assault rifles,[13] a decision by Veterans Affairs not to appeal a negative verdict regarding the military's liability for using the defoliant Agent Orange,[14] a decision by Commerce Secretary Mosbacher to lift a ban on computer sales to Eastern European nations, and an Environmental Protection Agency (EPA) decision to ban all use of asbestos by 1997.[15]

In the opinion of one administration official, the cabinet had become "undisciplined. . . . Strong members of the cabinet are taking charge." In part, Bush was a source of the problem: "Bush's own style is kind of reactive, not to lay down priorities for these guys. The President wants leadership to come from the cabinet. . . . So he's letting the cabinet do their own thing."[16] But part, too, was a cabinet of friends and longtime associates that made efforts at control difficult.

The Cabinet Councils Continue

During the transition, Bush and his advisers had decided to retain the economic and domestic council system of the second Reagan term as a device for channeling information and advice and for resolving policy disputes. According to the staff secretary, Jim Cicconi, "Although we juggled the chairs a little bit," the councils operated "about like the way they did during the Reagan years." "They played a useful role since you have to have some means for structuring your decisionmaking on major areas of policy, and just about every major area of policy cut across formal departmental lines."[17]

Some reports indicated that the councils were slow to get started and by March had held only perfunctory organizational meetings.[18] But over the next several months, the pace picked up. The Domestic Policy Council (DPC), with nine departments represented, handled amendments to the Clean Air Act, proposals dealing with the Americans with Disabilities Act, and a national drug-control strategy. The Economic Policy Council (EPC), with eight departments at the table, took on the minimum-wage issue, a steel restraint agreement, the FSX fighter agreement with Japan, and a national energy policy. By July, each of the councils was meeting every other week, more when issues were pressing, such as the ten meetings the domestic council held to consider the Clean Air Act.[19]

In February 1990, Bates prepared a year-end report on the DPC. In it he listed the number of DPC meetings—twenty-six in all—from January 20, 1989, to January 20, 1990. Bush attended six of them, but they were only on two policy areas: three meetings on the Clean Air Act, two meetings on drug policy, plus the first organizational meeting of the DPC.[20] Sununu also attended a number of the councils' meetings.[21]

As with the Reagan councils, much of the work was done by working groups. During 1989, there were fourteen DPC working groups or task forces under way, with two more proposed.[22] They were chaired by a variety of persons, with six of them headed by departmental personnel and eight by White House officials (usually a member of Porter's policy development staff).

Unclear Boundaries and Ad Hoc Participants

Not all issues, however, were routed through the cabinet-council system, and there was a good measure of informal policymaking outside its bounds. Bush's child care tax credit and campaign finance proposals were handled in other venues. His educational proposals unveiled to Congress in his February 9 speech had been largely developed by a group led by Education Secretary Cavazos.[23] And the important matter of Bush's budget proposal was debated within a five-member "budget team," which included Sununu, Brady, Darman, Boskin, and Porter. The group met with the president two and sometimes three times a day in the weeks leading up to his February 9 budget message to Congress.[24] Some of the trade issues were not routed through the economic council. According to Cicconi, "We didn't use those [council] meetings for major discussion of trade policy; we would get the people at the table who were relevant to that decision."[25]

The Clean Air Act offers another case in point. Although the act did not require immediate reauthorization, the White House was worried that Congress would write unacceptable legislation, forcing Bush to be in the politically difficult position of having to veto it. According to Andrew Card, "Several individuals in the administration wanted to have a role in formulating policy on this issue." "Roger Porter had expertise in the issue" and had participated in the deliberations that occurred during the Reagan years. "Boyden Gray provided needed expertise on the issue as did John Sununu. William Reilly [head of the EPA] was passionately trying to get a Clean Air Act passed. Some cabinet members had ambivalent views, while others even held hostile views about altering the clean air statute."

But while the DPC discussed the act at a number of its meetings, the difficult decisions in amending the act were developed "through ad hoc dialogues—sometimes late at night by Roger Porter, John Sununu and Boyden Gray." In particular, it was "Sununu and Gray who made the tough policy and strategic calls during that process," although "President Bush was called upon to make the particularly tough decisions."[26]

Whether issues were routed through the councils and, if they were, to which council they were assigned, "was a call that Sununu made," according to David Bates. "Not every issue ended up in the DPC or EPC." Bates's own 1989 annual report on the DPC even acknowledged that "several meetings have been held on an ad hoc basis with only interested council members."[27] Sununu's own daily schedule lists several meetings on policy matters with two or three key officials in attendance, a likely venue for policy differences to be worked out.[28]

Another important policy body outside the EPC or DPC structure was the regulatory review board—the Presidential Council on Competitiveness—headed by Vice President Dan Quayle. Established by Bush in February 1989, it was similar to the regulatory body Bush headed during the first couple of years of the Reagan presidency, and it would have important repercussions later in the Bush administration in trying to reduce antibusiness regulations. During the transition, Quayle himself had brought up with Bush his willingness to lead such an effort, and Bush quickly agreed to put Quayle in charge.[29]

Staff Support: Bates and Porter

Throughout the Reagan years, the staff support provided by the White House was critical to the cabinet councils' operations. The Bush transition, however, had generated a potential problem: Bates's smaller cabinet affairs staff was placed in charge of the councils, yet it would still need to rely heavily on Porter's larger policy development staff for support. The councils' executive secretaries reported to Bates, but many of the working groups were led by a member of Porter's staff.[30]

Bates and Porter, however, were able to work through this organizational impediment and develop a cooperative relationship. Andrew Card recalls that "the personalities of Bates and Porter helped to overcome problems that might have existed with some other people in those positions." But Card does note, despite the efforts of the two to avoid turf battles, that "there was some friction between their staffs." Card also remembers problems in identifying organizational boundaries: "Is it the staff of the domestic policy office, or is it the staff of the cabinet affairs domestic policy group? I don't know if we overcame that entirely." Furthermore, in Card's view, "there were redundancies, where one staffer might have been able to do the job, we had two at the deputy level. . . . I don't think it was as efficient as a business plan written at the Harvard Business School might have suggested it should be." But Card observes that in the end it did not "undermine the development of policy that made its way to the president."[31]

White House Policy Development

Porter brought his considerable skills to bear in coordinating the domestic and economic policy process of the Bush administration. But the transition had one marked impact: the head of its long-term policy planning unit, Jim Pinkerton, had been picked before Porter came on board in early January. Pinkerton and his small staff might have been just the place to develop the "vision" and more creative agenda that the Bush administration seemed to lack. Yet according to Card, Pinkerton's operation was "disconnected" and "kind of floating around without a lot of attention from Roger Porter. Jim Pinkerton was appropriately frustrated at his lack of access." Pinkerton "was also discounted by Dick Darman, witness the famous paradigm speech."[32] As one Bush staff member told it, Darman might have found Pinkerton's intellect and creativity a bit challenging: "When he became a threat to Dick Darman's think-tank—which essentially consisted of only Darman himself—Pinkerton was not invited to participate in the process."

For his part, Pinkerton recalls that "Roger Porter and I got along fine," but "I was noncentral to the workings of the Bush administration. I was on my own little tangents most of the time." Some of Pinkerton's concerns during the transition about his working relationship with the as yet unnamed head of domestic policy in the Bush administration thus proved correct.[33]

Following Bush's February 9 address to Congress, Pinkerton sought to nudge the White House in a more proactive direction, away from the "managing," "ordering," and "maintaining" rhetoric of the speech. Pinkerton put together a memo outlining the need not just to maintain the status quo but also to "gain ground." "I never got a response," Pinkerton would later recall.[34]

Pinkerton's predicament is also indicative of some of the informal, often back-channel policy efforts that can go on in every White House.[35] In this administration, that might have especially emerged because of the ties a number of them had developed during the Reagan presidency. Pinkerton had a close connection to Ed Rogers of Sununu's staff (both had worked in the Reagan political affairs office), and he regarded Card, Sununu's deputy and another Reagan White House veteran, as an ally. According to Card, Sununu "did not ignore the Pinkerton missives. But he would get the Pinkerton missives without Roger Porter's knowledge. And that's because I was close to Jim Pinkerton and Ed Rogers was close to Jim Pinkerton."[36]

Pinkerton also arranged with Jim Cicconi to get on the list of those to whom Bush's speeches were circulated. In Pinkerton's view, the speechwriters were "avant-garde conservative types whom I looked to as allies." "Somewhat bypassing Porter, I was on the bucksheet for Bush speeches, so I would see them and send in my own comments to the speechwriters independent of Porter." This gave Pinkerton a needed "pipeline" into policy debates: "It matters a lot what the president's words are from a staff point of view." Was Porter aware of what was going on? "I don't think he and I ever talked about this in three years. I think he must have known but chose not to make an issue out of it." "I figured if I did make an issue out of it, it would only get worse from my point of view."[37]

Porter also had a back channel of sorts—to the president himself, who was also a sometime tennis partner. Although policy papers developed by the cabinet councils would go to Sununu and then to the president, according to David Bates, "Roger's people would be involved in developing the options paper, and I am sure that if Roger felt strongly about a particular option, he could certainly make that known to Sununu, and I think he could make that known to the president, too, which option he felt should be picked."[38]

Such efforts on Porter's part may have been needed because, according to one participant, "Darman and Sununu often conveniently kept Porter out of the game. They knew the President would reinstate him, but they tried to manage debates so that Porter came in late." Darman, in particular, "frequently cut [Porter] out of the process in a Machiavellian way." But Porter "did have the confidence of President Bush, however, and Bush would frequently ask for his opinions on issues, especially the tough ones."

Sununu could also weigh in. "He would look at the memo to the president that would be the options memo," according to Bates. Did he make his own recommendations? "I am not sure formally on the position paper. But I am sure the president sought his counsel." Both Sununu and Darman, in Bates's view, had significant impact on Bush's domestic and economic policy decisions.[39]

Sununu: A Strong Chief of Staff

Sununu's role as a policy advocate and, at times, gatekeeper would prove to be a distinctive hallmark of his tenure as chief of staff. The rhetoric during the transition about a "neutral broker" role proved to be just that—rhetoric. Sometimes acting alone, sometimes in concert with Darman (with whom he had developed a close relationship), Sununu played a major role in budget negotiations with Congress (eclipsing the role of Treasury Secretary Brady), weighed in on the Clean Air Act and Medicare catastrophic coverage, and prevented extension of federal funding for abortions in cases of rape or incest. In 1990, he would weaken an EPA agreement on rules for filling wetlands, urge Bush to veto parental-leave legislation, attempt to derail a Bush speech on global warming, and make a final effort to weaken the Clean Air Act as it neared passage.[40] In several of these cases, Sununu's position was at odds with proposals that had been developed in the DPC, EPC, or by individual departments and agencies. Most notably, both Sununu and Darman were instrumental in getting Bush to abandon his no-new-taxes pledge in 1990.[41]

In making his policy views known, Sununu did not just shuffle his feet and whisper in the president's ear. His views on policy often translated into a tough, if not at times intimidating, posture toward those who disagreed with him. Jim Cicconi, David Demarest, and Andrew Card, Sununu's own deputy, recall that he "didn't suffer fools gladly."[42] Even Barbara Bush used the phrase in her memoirs: "Unfortunately, John does not suffer fools gladly and is sometimes his own worst enemy."[43]

The key issue is whether Sununu's behavior and demeanor provided discipline to a process that, given its emphasis on collegiality, required a certain level of control and direction. Or did it have a more negative impact on policy deliberations? According to Jim Cicconi, Sununu provided just what Bush wanted: "I would even go further. I think George Bush needed that in a lot of ways, too. Especially in the first couple of years. Was it off-putting to some people? Yes. Did it shut out some cabinet members? Yes. Were there a couple of cabinet members who deserved to be shut out? Yes, at times, because a president's time is pretty valuable and there are people who want to spend it with him who don't have a whole hell of a lot to say."[44]

Yet Sununu "did bring discipline to the process."[45] "He really demanded quality. When you are operating at that level and with that level of responsibility you damn well better be good, better know your stuff, better work hard, better put in the long hours, and you also better be pretty smart. He did demand those things, and I credit him for it. For the most part, he served the president well."[46]

In Andrew Card's opinion, there was a certain element of fairness even when Sununu sought to influence the outcome of a policy debate: "The fairness might be that he would admit he was skewing the process. . . . He would carry a bias into a meeting, but he would never try to hide the fact that he had a bias, and he would let you make your case." Did this limit the president's options? In Card's view, it didn't: "The president knew John Sununu's personality, so I don't think he allowed the bias to necessarily carry the day without having input from others. I don't think the president ever got duped in the process."[47]

At least at the start of the Bush presidency, Sununu's interpersonal style did not appear to affect the collegiality that Bush sought to instill among his subordinates. As J. Bonnie Newman observes, "At the assistants level it turned out to be a fairly cohesive group." Sununu deputy Card may have particularly offset the more abrasive Sununu. According to Newman, "Andy really did represent the kinder and gentler."[48]

Yet others in the Bush administration had less positive regard for Sununu's demeanor. In the view of one staff member, Sununu "knew the answer to the question before you finished posing it. And sometimes he didn't necessarily know the answer but in his mind he knew the answer. So there were a lot of people who were intimidated by him or afraid of him or insulted by him." And that, in turn, may have affected the free flow of information in the Bush policy process: "People who might have had an opinion might have been reluctant to raise it since they didn't want to be challenged by Sununu. So the intimidation factor might have had an impact."

Yet by the same token, Sununu relished a good argument, as long as his adversary was well prepared. As Cicconi explains:

Did he sometimes play a tough-guy role? Sure. Did I have arguments with him? Absolutely, we used to have knock-down, drag-outs on different things. . . . I think John is an intellect, a very well developed intellect. But I think he is respectful of other views provided they are well based. Would he let a fool argue with him? Probably not very long. But if you knew what you were talking about, if you had done your homework, and you raised valid points, you could have a good argument with him and turn him around.[49]

But there were also reports of a more abrasive Sununu emerging, not just in his dealings with underlings but with cabinet members and even congressional leaders. According to one report, when Bob Michel, the Republican House leader, took a position on housing and capital-gains taxes that Sununu didn't like, "He dressed Mr. Michel down in terms that many in the House found insulting." "Our relationship with Sununu has been no bed of roses," a member of Michel's staff said at the time. "He can be a very hard man when he wants to be."[50]

Phillip Brady, who succeeded Cicconi as staff secretary, would later observe that while Sununu's "decisiveness" and knowledge may have been assets at the start of the administration, "those same qualities, however, became less productive as time passed. Sununu came to be viewed by some as being overly dismissive of other people's points of view and somewhat aloof."[51]

The Sununu-Darman relationship especially rankled many in the administration. "They enjoyed matching wits" and the "gamesmanship that occurred at policy meetings," one staffer told me. Darman "had a talent for withholding 20 percent of the information necessary for a decision until the policy recommendation was ready to be sent to the President. He would thus have an advantage over others in offering policy suggestions. Sununu's mind was quick enough to adjust to and incorporate this late information, but most members of the Bush administration did not have this ability."[52]

Sununu's role as chief of staff departed markedly from the public rhetoric of the transition, and at times it could negatively affect the internal deliberations and dynamics of the Bush presidency. Yet at another level, some of its elements were needed, if not valued, by the president. As David B. Cohen notes, "George Bush enjoyed being the genial, likable leader. Sununu, on the other hand, not only didn't mind being the bad guy, he relished that role. Thus, by doing things Bush would or could not do, Sununu served a valuable proxy function for the president. This allowed Bush to remain the cheerful leader who rarely had to tell people what they did not want to hear. Rather that was Sununu's job."[53]

For his part, Sununu maintained at the time he left the White House staff that he was acting at George Bush's direction. As he acknowledged in 1998: "Contrary to legend, every decision that was arrived at in terms of who would and who wouldn't see the president, which way we would go on issues, it was not an evil chief of staff moving the system. It was a chief of staff that talked to the president constantly and found out from him what he wanted to do. . . . Some of those things that I had to do were not the easiest to do."[54]

What remains unanswered, however, is whether *how* he went about those tasks was at the president's direction or served the president's expectations and interests. And while that had not been a matter that had been settled during the transition, it was one that had certainly been raised by Sununu's critics then and brought to George Bush's attention.

Bush as Manager and Decisionmaker

Although Sununu can certainly be regarded as a strong chief of staff, it would be misleading to assume that Bush faced the kind of isolation experienced by Nixon under Haldeman. Nor is it fair to conclude that Sununu had created the kind of prime ministerial role that Don Regan had been thought to assume during the first part of Reagan's second term. The presence of a large number of former friends and associates both within the White House and throughout the cabinet and executive branch provided a range of informal networks that Bush liked to tap. Here, the transition's recruitment goals of placing Bush friends and associates in positions paid off and meshed with Bush's decisionmaking style and needs. As Bush himself framed it: "I really would find it very hard to visualize—not just the loneliness of it but the barrenness of it. . . . If you were making decisions in isolation, from reading briefing papers and selecting options a, b, or c, it just wouldn't be the same."[55]

Where Reagan might be content with the information presented to him, Bush did not hesitate to pick up the phone to call around about some policy matter. According to Frank Hodsoll, Jim Baker's former deputy who in February 1989 left the National Endowment for the Arts to take a position as associate director and chief financial officer at OMB, "Bush had antennae that stretched down into the bureaucracies to a greater degree than Reagan." Bush, in Hodsoll's view, was a "a little like Jack Kennedy." Periodically, Bush "would call up somebody he had worked with, say, in China or something like that. Bush also had all sorts of folks that weren't necessarily in the political system."[56]

Bush was not averse to immersing himself in the detail of policy or directly prodding his aides on a range of policy matters. According to Michael Duffy and Dan Goodgame, he had a kind of restless curiosity: "Senior officials' 'IN' boxes began to fill with paperwork churned out by Bush—reports they sent to him, returned with extensive editing, questions, additions in the margins and notes hanging out with more presidential scribbling." Ever attentive to the advice and information from his wide circle of friends, Bush would circulate any requests or queries to his staff asking "Is this legit?" or "Would you check this out?" Roger Porter reportedly set up a six-tiered system of in-boxes for Bush, with the first two devoted to Bush's notes, queries, and missives. Scowcroft "worked regularly until 10 P.M. to clear his desk," only to find the next morning a fresh, new pile of Bush queries, based on his evening reading of intelligence cables and press clippings."[57] According to another account, Bush "seemed to want to keep track of everything at once at the White House, poking his head in offices to see what was happening and writing little notes on stationery and ordinary notepaper signed 'GB' to check on various things." By one estimate, Bush averaged some two hundred notes per week, many of them typed on an electric typewriter he kept by his desk.[58]

In Jim Cicconi's view, Bush was in the habit of making "quite a few" marginal notations on the various memos and papers Cicconi would forward to him. "But it depended on what it was and when he read it. If it was during a busy week, odds are that he would go through it more quickly than if he was sipping his coffee on a Saturday morning at Camp David." Cicconi learned to adjust to Bush's schedule and work habits and would often wait until late Friday to send him the more lengthy policy papers: "I learned that he liked to get up at 7 A.M. and sit out on the porch and go through paper, without the phone ringing and without people running in on him. He would linger with these think-pieces and he would react to them in a much more thoughtful and lengthy way; so it was a lot better way to handle that particular type of document."[59]

In his capacity as staff secretary, Cicconi was in the critical position of monitoring the paper flow in and out of the Oval Office and, more important, making sure "that when the decision is presented to him that he has all the information and options; that he has a flavor for what might be behind it, as well as to protect him from bad information, special pleading, and the like." According to one administration official, Cicconi had the view that "he did a disservice to the president if he wasn't getting all the necessary views."[60]

Moreover, according to Cicconi, "Bush preferred more information." At the start of the administration, "One of the things we did early on was that I sat down and asked him how he wanted to handle the workload and how much he wanted to see, and I gave him some samples of exactly what the daily workload could be like." Bush told him, "'Look, let's start out with erring on the side of seeing most everything or at least a sample of most everything and then we'll gradually ratchet it back as I get a better understanding of what arrives on my desk and what is important and what isn't and you help me with that.' And that's what we did."[61]

Cicconi also tried to give Bush a better sense of what transpired in various deliberative processes of which Bush may not have been a part:

> He liked to get a flavor for discussions in meetings among his senior people. He used to like me to give him that. So there was a lot of things that I put cover notes on. If you go through the documents you will find on most of the decisions memos that, unless they were really cut-and-dried or routine, there was some sort of cover note that I would type up and put on it to give him this little extra flavor. Or [I would] explain the significance of what this document was or something of that nature.

As well, Cicconi "learned that he is clean-desk guy. If I sent him stuff, he did not leave that day without getting it all done."[62]

Interestingly, the shift from the vice presidency to the Oval Office was hard at times for Bush, especially in adjusting to the constraints on the president's time: "It was very hard to strike the right balance between what I wanted to know and what I needed to know or should know. Working out the procedure was painful." As vice president, Bush recalled, "I had loved the direct outreach and personal contact possible, but now Sununu understandably wanted to keep me from being inundated or too busy on the wrong things or overwhelmed with details. I missed reading all the materials that had come across my desk as DCI [Director of CIA] or even as vice president."[63]

In his account of Bush's decisionmaking, John Sununu especially cites the importance of Bush's daily 8:00 A.M. meeting with Sununu, Scowcroft, and (on many mornings when he was available) Vice President Quayle, a meeting in which, in Sununu's view, the president provided personal direction over the day-to-day activities of his administration. "It was up to us to raise all the issues we needed answers on at that meeting and I think we got very good at doing that," Sununu notes, but it was the president who "made it very clear what he wanted and didn't want done."[64] According to Sununu, this was not the end of his consultations with the president:

> This president was an extremely easy individual to work with. The practice was that twenty or thirty times a day I would go down from my office to his office and stick my head in and ask one or two questions to make sure that I understood every nuance he wanted on every issue we were trying to deal with. He was always willing to give an answer, an opinion, and to make a suggestion as to how things would move.[65]

Despite such openness to information and his attempts to create a more collegial atmosphere in the White House, Bush was inclined at times to be his own ultimate counsel, often acting with a degree of secrecy—a tendency that Marlin Fitzwater noted when he and the president-elect had discussions about Fitzwater's job back during the transition. According to one press report, "White House officials say Mr. Bush has emerged as a chief executive who plays his cards close to the vest, often surprising even his top aides with his decisions." In deciding policy, Mr. Bush "not only operates in secrecy, even from his own staff, but also with a measure of unpredictability. He frequently telephones lawmakers, friends or former associates before telling his staff what he's decided." In one case, during a European trip, Bush didn't inform his aides until the last minute about a proposed reduction in conventional arms as a way of deflating Gorbachev's growing popularity in that region.[66]

Even though Bush proved adept as an information gatherer and was attentive to the organizational needs of his presidency in a way that Carter and Reagan were not, other parts of his decisionmaking were more mixed. Most important, Bush's sense of loyalty to those around him was a critical part of the internal dynamics of his administration, something that had been manifest in the transition. But it was loyalty that could often emerge as a fault. As Andrew Card would later note, one of Bush's greatest qualities was his friendship, but "this loyalty that he displayed to friends became a flaw. . . . He allowed his loyalty to some of the people in his administration to last longer than it should have. As a result they were given many chances to make mistakes." Unlike Lyndon Johnson, "who would only give his aides half a chance," according to Card, "with President Bush, because no one lost their job even when visible mistakes were made, people thought they could not lose their jobs."[67] John Sununu offers a similar diagnosis:

> Frankly, quite often because he was such a decent, honest, straightforward guy, people—including sometimes his friends—took advantage

of him. It made the chief of staff's job a little bit tougher because sometimes when that was discovered, it was up to the chief of staff to try and straighten things out under the president's direction and it made some difficult times for me.[68]

As he had during the transition, Bush could be attentive to policy detail and willing to reach out beyond normal channels of communication. But personal ties to those around him—and they were considerable in this administration—required a sense of toughness and managerial grit that Bush did not wish to exercise. Problems in his policy process would be handled by others, Sununu most notably. But when the problems stemmed from Sununu or Darman themselves, that option would be foreclosed. Who guards the guardians?

Policy Outcomes

While Bush may have been a more active participant in the administration's inner circles than was publicly perceived, the perception began to develop among observers both within and outside the administration that Bush was having difficulty developing a coherent domestic policy agenda that would put his stamp on the presidency. Part of the problem no doubt stemmed from the budget constraints and a steadily worsening prognosis coming from Darman and the OMB, a situation that had been stressed as early as Bush's first meeting with his cabinet. Bush also was the first president elected since Herbert Hoover to have taken over from a predecessor of his own party. As Sununu told the press in the first week of the new administration, "Everyone is looking for some drastic change or redirection [but] this is a conservative Republican president taking over from a conservative Republican."[69] Still, part of Bush's problem stemmed from developments within the administration, several of them attributable to choices made and steps taken during the transition.

It is not wholly accurate to say the administration was bereft of domestic initiatives and that this was simply a presidency that focused on foreign affairs. As Bush himself emphasized in a luncheon meeting with reporters on March 31, he had proposed a budget agreement, as well as a plan for dealing with the savings-and-loan crisis, and was just about set to present to Congress legislation on drug policy, ethics in government, and education.[70] What was lacking was an attempt to translate campaign statements into concrete legislative proposals and then to bind these various proposals into some broader thematic formula—the "vision thing" that was so elusive, if not irritating, to Bush. Nor were there concerted efforts to create a sense of policy initiative that would capture public attention. Furthermore, in light of the deficit situation, few Bush proposals were—or perhaps even could be—backed up with significant fiscal commitments.

Media events were staged in the opening weeks of the administration to show Bush's commitment as the "education president," the "environment president," the "antidrug president," and so on, but these were not coupled with concrete proposals. Instead, legislation emerged piecemeal in subsequent months, with little thematic continuity and waning media attention. For example, on April 5, he sent up to Congress a merit- and magnet-schools proposal; April 12, ethics-in-government legislation; April 18, a proposal to expand Medicare coverage to children and pregnant women; May 9, a proposal for child-care legislation; May 15, legislation on violent crime; June 12, the Clean Air Act; June 21, a "youth in service to America" initiative, part of his thousand-points-of-light program; June 28, a proposed constitutional amendment on flag desecration; June 29, campaign finance reform; July 25, amendments to the job training partnership act; September 5, a report on a national drug control strategy; September 27–28, an educational summit at the University of Virginia. Bush also signed into law a whistleblower-protection act in April; vetoed an increase in the minimum wage in June (then signing compromise legislation with Congress in November); signed the savings-and-loan bailout bill in August; signed the ethics-reform legislation and worked out a final budget agreement in November; signed a steel trade liberalization act in December, as well as a North American wetlands act later that month.[71]

"We're getting a kaleidoscope," one former Reagan White House official noted; instead of focusing on "one big issue," they had ten little ones. "I think they're pissing away their honeymoon and getting nothing for it."[72] According to David Bates, secretary to the cabinet, "Some people on the staff were looking for a thematic approach or tried to build events around issues. What we got instead was an approach that was reflective of the president's own character: he moves in a lot of directions at once, content to keep his head down and make progress over time."[73]

Distracting Attention: The Tower Nomination

One problem that loomed over the early weeks of the Bush presidency and overshadowed his domestic initiatives stemmed from the earlier decision to continue to back John Tower's nomination for defense secretary, even as his chances for confirmation became more and more unlikely. As Card recalls, "It reminded us we were in a very partisan town. . . . It cost us a little bit of momentum. It also damaged some of the relations with members of the Senate, and it hurt the president personally because he had made a personal commitment to Tower."[74]

While the nomination may have been in deep trouble, there were indications that the staff system could have functioned better. No working group was created to oversee and troubleshoot what would become Bush's first political battle and test of wills with Congress. There were also slipups in the various groups charged with working on pieces of the nomination, coupled with a general lack of coordination. When a Bush aide called the Republican National Committee to ask about the talking points in support of the Tower nomination, the RNC official told him to go down the hall to the office of the public liaison. Fitzwater, in turn, was asked whether public liaison was issuing such materials in the fight; he replied that it wasn't. Bush's chief congressional lobbyist, Fred McClure, wasn't even informed that the White House and Tower had worked out a pledge that Tower would abstain from alcohol if confirmed, a deal that had been crafted by Sununu and Boyden Gray. He learned about the agreement several hours after it had been announced.

For their part, Bush and Sununu were on a scheduled Asian trip during the critical week when the nomination was before the Senate Armed Services Committee; Sununu reportedly had difficulty contacting McClure for reports and updates, relying instead on telephone calls to reporters in Washington. During the crucial weekend before the full Senate vote, Sununu was reported to have been back in New Hampshire attending a charity ski event.[75] According to one White House aide, "The supernova of John Tower whited out the rest of our agenda."[76]

Problems in Congressional Liaison

Problems with the organization and coordination of the administration's dealings with Congress were not just confined to the Tower nomination. According to some Republicans in Congress, "Mr. Bush's staff has sometimes sent mixed signals in the heat of legislative battle and . . . his congressional liaison is 'out of the loop' on decisions made by Mr. Bush, his chief of staff, John Sununu, and the budget director, Richard Darman." According to one senior Republican, McClure's staff was "inexperienced"; "[the] White House doesn't always tell his people what is going on."[77]

Putting the congressional affairs staff together had been one of the more difficult and delayed tasks of the transition. Unfortunately, a skilled congressional affairs staff was especially needed: Bush was the first elected president since Nixon whose party did not control at least one chamber of Congress, and in the House, Republicans controlled the smallest number of seats for any newly elected president in the twentieth century. Nor was there any sense of a Bush mandate coming out of the 1988 election; Bush's 54 percent victory was solid, but the Republicans lost seats in both the House and the Senate.[78]

Another part of the problem was a coordinated legislative strategy. Sununu did, at the start of the administration, begin to hold regular legislative strategy meetings as Baker had done under Ronald Reagan. But these became less frequent over time and were convened only ad hoc, as Sununu thought needed. Not only did they occur on an as-needed basis; they were often "without a lot of premeditation," Card recalls.[79] In some cases, Sununu and his colleagues proved adept in their legislative strategy. In the case of the Clean Air Act, they were able to fashion a compromise on several difficult and politically charged issues, especially in securing the support of Congressman John Dingell, a Michigan Democrat who was the powerful (and difficult to deal with) chairman of the House Energy and Commerce Committee. In other cases—the Tower nomination and the 1990 budget deal, for example—they were less successful.

In early August 1989, the House Republican leadership sent a letter to Sununu registering concerns over the White House's handling of several congressional matters. Although they did not explicitly target McClure's operation, they did convey a strong sense that "many of the day-to-day functions performed by the White House on behalf of their constituents are not being given enough priority by your offices." Among the problems cited were coordinating presidential trips with members of Congress, timely responses to requests for tickets for White House tours, and limits on the number of presidential photos. McClure's operation "seems to be functioning well in most respects and in transmitting these requests to appropriate offices. After requests are made, however, appropriate actions are not taken." While the members' concerns here were not momentous, the fact that they had to sign a joint letter to Sununu registering them indicates a lack of attention to the kind of political "massaging" of members that is par for the course for most presidencies.[80] Sununu forwarded the memo to McClure with the instruction, "Discuss with me, please."[81]

Yet Sununu's abrasive role may also have affected the administration's relationship with Congress, especially since Sununu was directly involved in negotiations with that body. No less an insider that Marlin Fitzwater recalls one instance in which a member of the House was at the White House making a presentation on environmental regulation of wetlands: "He was talking when Sununu arrived. John walked directly over to the congressman, reached down and grabbed the corner of his open [briefing] book, then slammed it closed with great flourish as his arm whipped around in exaggerated follow-through. The congressman was humiliated and would never forget it."[82]

What's more, the White House negotiating team (usually Sununu, Darman, and sometimes Porter and Brady) that made the final deals with Congress was not always skilled itself, whatever its broader reputation might have been. "Frequently Bush's negotiating team would go to the table with congressional leaders without understanding the end game," Card recalls. "The internal bottom line was seldom defined before the negotiating meetings, which meant that the administration's bottom line changed during the course of the negotiations. The President sometimes got into trouble as a result."[83]

Policy and Problems of Staffing and Organization

Some of the administration's difficulties with policy proposals can also be linked to organizational decisions made during the transition. The decision to place Lee Atwater as head of the RNC and to downgrade the political office within the White House may have especially limited the administration's ability to make timely political calculations and engage in the outreach efforts to build political support. So, too, the failed negotiations to bring Teeter on board full-time may have weakened Bush's hand (Teeter did agree to serve as a periodic consultant). According to one Republican political strategist, "Is there a missing political component at the White House? Yes, of course. Lee Atwater can't do it. Bob Teeter can't do it once a week." While Sununu did attempt to fill the breach and was "reaching out to the political community," he was "starting to find out what he can't do." "He needs at least one strong political person who is in the day-to-day loop on policy, and scheduling, and personnel."[84] Ed Rogers had even broached with Sununu the possibility of scheduling a regular weekly meeting with Atwater a few days into the new administration, but Sununu was reluctant to do it: "Do on need basis. No," he instructed his deputy.[85]

Yet the person who was in charge of the White House political office lacked the stature and rank to fill the breach. During the transition, a clear decision had been made to place Atwater at the RNC and to downgrade the political office. Jim Wray, who headed the office, did not even regularly attend Sununu's morning staff meeting. According to one report, "His role is aimed more at pleasing and servicing Bush loyalists and campaigners" rather than providing "political content to White House decisions on policy, scheduling, and the like."[86]

In 1990, the situation took a turn for the worse when Lee Atwater became terminally ill. By then, Sununu had taken over political strategy and delegated it to his own aides: Edward Rogers, who had been an advance man for the RNC, and David Carney, who had worked for Sununu in New Hampshire. "The White House has just been floating, without any strong ties to causes or issues or philosophy," observed Edward Mahe, a leading Republican consultant.[87]

Another problem was the absence of any process linking presidential activities and Bush's unfolding policy agenda. Even as early as March 1989, one former transition-team member was complaining that "there's no one whose job it is to keep hold of the agenda," think about long-term strategy, and decide how to spend the White House's political capital.[88] In the Reagan White House, presidential events, appearances, and important meetings were tentatively scheduled weeks and months into the future. But in the Bush White House, according to Andrew Card, "Scheduling was a major challenge because Sununu and the president were not interested in having 'long-range scheduling.' First, Sununu thought he could do a lot of that on his own and, second, the president didn't want anybody discussing the 'vision thing.'"[89]

During the transition, a decision had been made to place presidential scheduling—which had advanced to an art form under the direction of Mike Deaver during Reagan's first term—under the direction of Staff Secretary Cicconi. But unlike Deaver's efforts, it was not at the start connected to consideration of Bush's broader policy goals. In fact, lack of attention to scheduling had dissipated coverage of Bush's February 6 economic and budget speech to Congress. The next day, Bush traveled to Canada to meet with the prime minister rather than constructing events that might have bolstered his economic message; "in television terms, it's like ringing the doorbell and running away," observed one press report.[90] Bush did travel to South Carolina to deliver a follow-up speech on the budget when he returned from Canada, but none of the three major networks covered the speech on the evening newscasts. In an ABC News poll, only 50 percent of those surveyed said they had seen or even knew anything about Bush's budget speech. In one study of media coverage of the first sixty days in office for Carter, Reagan, and Bush, the Reagan administration had garnered 1,030 evening news stories, Carter 832, and Bush only 505. Of evening news stories focusing on the president alone, Carter had 520, Reagan 399, and Bush 265.[91]

Part of the problem was that Sununu thought he could do the job in concert with Cicconi and Joseph Hagin, Cicconi's deputy in charge of scheduling. But another part, which is indicated by documents at the Bush Library, is that Sununu would often refer some of these scheduling issues to the president himself. Not only did Sununu review the president's schedule with him personally, he often deferred to Bush's judgment about what events he wanted to attend. For example, on February 16, he raised such events as a lunch meeting with Agriculture Secretary Yeutter, a March 1 meeting with Governor Bill Clements of Texas, dinner appearances before the United Negro College Fund, the annual "Gridiron" event on April 1, the White House correspondents' association on April 29, a reception for the Republican "Eagles" on April 10, and an open invitation to meet with the Black Leadership Forum. For each of these events, Sununu provided a checklist for Bush— "accept," "regret," "hold"—plus space for additional comments.[92]

The White House staff began to recognize that better coordination and follow-through was needed. In March, Card began to hold ad hoc meetings, "and in the context of those meetings we would talk about how does this fit the overall objectives, without calling it the 'vision thing.'" Joining Card were Cicconi, McClure, Bates, Hagin, and Stephen Studdert.[93] Called the "Administration Action Committee" (AAC), its purpose was to

> centralize the White House staff approach to upcoming domestic agenda items. . . . Once the President has articulated his specific goals, it will be our responsibility to follow through. The AAC will develop an implementation strategy, set the day-to-day agenda, assign responsibilities, determine a timeline, monitor progress, and generally shepherd a given mission through to successful operation.[94]

Unlike Jim Baker's daily LSG meetings in Reagan's first term, the group was initially envisioned to meet only twice a week, with meetings lasting at least an hour. Although it was on paper a good plan designed for "establishing priorities and staying on the offensive," the group never developed as anticipated. According to Card, "We tried to make it a very inclusive group, and we would make recommendations up to Sununu. But it was hard to bring discipline to that process because there was no buy-in from the top."[95] Although Sununu was designated as chair of the group in the organizational memo, his daily schedules show no indication that he ever attended any of its meetings.[96]

A Problem of "Marketing and Selling"

Communicating and selling the Bush agenda—even those parts that had been defined—became a problem that dogged the Bush presidency, especially during the early months. One handicap was again organizational and a result of decisions made during the transition: the division of responsibilities between public events and the "thousand points of light" under Studdert, communications, intergovernmental relations, and "constituent groups" under Demarest, and day-to-day press contact under Fitzwater. In Demarest's view, the White House lacked an overarching "communications strategy group," in part because Sununu and Darman were concerned that no rival power centers develop.[97] Even information was tightly held. On February 21, 1989, a month into the new administration, Gregg Petersmeyer—in charge of the thousand-points-of-light effort—asked Sununu to be added to the list of people provided the president's daily and monthly schedules. Sununu's response: "No."[98]

In late April, Bush took a four-day trip to Virginia, Illinois, North Dakota, California, Texas, and Florida. The event garnered little media coverage. According to one report, on the flight back to Washington Fitzwater and Demarest took Sununu aside and told him the trip had not gone well and that the White House did not have an overall communications strategy. That Saturday, Sununu convened a meeting in the White House to review the trip, but according to one participant, it turned into a finger-pointing session of who was or was not doing their job effectively and who was talking to the press too much. According to one source in the White House, the administration lacked a central strategy for presenting Bush's domestic priorities; according to another source outside the White House, Sununu "thought he could do it himself, doesn't think it's that vital anyway, and now that it's not working out, is saying it is working, and if it isn't, it's not my fault."[99]

Part of the problem in not responding to communications needs may have been the false sense of security stemming from Bush's high public-approval ratings. In June, Bush's approval rating stood at 70 percent in a Gallup poll, higher than Reagan's 58 percent eight years before and second only to Kennedy's rating in 1961.

Another problem was execution in getting the message out. Bush had appointed Stephen Studdert, who had been an advance man under Deaver in the Reagan White House and later served as "events director" in the campaign, as assistant for "special activities and initiatives," a newly invented title. Studdert was the closest thing the Bush staff had to a presidential image maker. Yet Bush did not have in mind the kind of image making, political staging, and media handling that had characterized the Reagan presidency. Studdert told reporters, "This presidency doesn't have an image maker,"[100] and "I am not the Deaver" in this White House. Yet he was responsible for scheduling and orchestrating the sort of special events that Deaver had created to build support for Reagan and his programs.[101] In October 1989, Studdert left the White House.

In an ironic twist, Demarest's own communications operation suffered communications difficulties with the press. The issue concerned the mess privileges and other perks of the White House speechwriters. As noted earlier, during the transition Bush and his advisers tried to limit the title-creep of the Reagan years. When Demarest took over he followed suit, and he didn't want the new speechwriters to begin with the titles of their predecessors. "To the reporters that covered the White House, communication staff members were being downgraded, even though they were not the same people, and they wrote that the speech office was being downgraded." The fact that speechwriters did not have White House mess privileges was especially taken as a symbol of their lowly status. Yet as Demarest notes, no signal was intended; the new titles were not those of "commissioned" White House officials, which would have granted them mess privileges. The result, according to Demarest, was that "communications appears to be less important and Bush is painted as not caring about getting the message out. Hence communications problems could be used to explain why the country is in disarray. That flaw affected the first three months of Bush's presidency. Those first three months were not pleasant."[102]

But in the end, the problem was not mess privileges for speechwriters; the problem was George Bush's basic decisions about how communications would be handled in his presidency, a matter reflected in part in the organizational downgrading of some units during the transition. Moreover, unlike Reagan, he didn't want to be "managed," Andrew Card recalls. "He said that on day one. He didn't want the message of the day. He definitely was not looking for stage direction."[103] David Demarest also recalls that "President Bush did not like the message managed"; he did not even like to have "toe cards," which were index cards placed in position to indicate where the president was to stand during some appearance or ceremony.[104]

Yet Bush was certainly not isolated from the press, and he would hold more press conferences than any president in recent history, many of them relatively impromptu. In his first hundred days as president, Bush held eleven press conferences, about one per week, and had an additional nine question-and-answer sessions with the press. Yet even here, Card notes, Bush tried to downplay the effort: "He was the one who made the decision not to have press conferences in the style of Ronald Reagan. Where Reagan would use the East Room of the White House and the long march down the hallway, President Bush would only do that a couple of times." Most of Bush's press conferences were held in the briefing room. "So he was looking to be more informal, both in his presentation—his physical presentation—and also looking to be informal in how he discussed issues with the press."[105]

Bush did not get much credit for his performance and low-key style. In fact, Bush had good mastery of the material that might come up in a press conference, according to David Demarest, and he didn't have to issue many corrections following them. In the early days of the administration, Sununu, Darman, Fitzwater, Quayle, Scowcroft, Porter, and Demarest would convene for practice sessions. But Demarest soon realized after the third question that Bush knew his substance: "[The president] knew more than we did concerning what would be said to the press."[106]

Although in the end Card felt that Bush's policy formulation was "much better than the public knows . . . I think the marketing and selling was deficient because the management didn't live up to its expectations."[107] On March 7, six weeks into his presidency, Bush personally addressed the issue that his administration was adrift: "So I would simply resist the clamor that nothing seems to be bubbling around, nothing is happening. A lot is happening, not all of it good, but a lot is happening."[108] On March 16, again responding to criticism, Bush told reporters that "more is going on than meets the eye or makes headlines."[109] In late April, Bush's hundred-day mark passed with less notice and political fanfare than the Carter and Reagan presidencies.

Foreign Policy Decision Processes and Outcomes

Bush's Strong Suit: Foreign and National Security Policy

The organization, procedures, and interpersonal dynamics of foreign and national security policymaking in the Bush presidency differed from those in domestic matters, in marked contrast to recent presidencies. To some extent, Bush was more engaged and directly interested in foreign affairs than in domestic matters. He also provided more personal direction and attention than did his immediate predecessor, Ronald Reagan. He enjoyed the services of two competent and skilled chief advisers—Secretary of State Jim Baker and NSC Adviser Brent Scowcroft—who established a close working relationship with each other and with the president. The three were joined by two other knowledgeable and experienced figures: Secretary of Defense Richard Cheney and (later in 1989) General Colin Powell, the chairman of the Joint Chiefs of Staff. Together they would form a tight-knit decision-making group. Unlike the strong chief of staff setup on the domestic side, they established a more collegial model, albeit one that was at times restricted in its membership and often operated with a degree of secrecy.

Bush's selection of Scowcroft was a critical ingredient to the arrangement's smooth workings. Having served in the same position during the Ford administration, Scowcroft brought with him both policy and organizational expertise. Scowcroft's role as one of the three principal members of the Tower Commission's investigation of the Iran-contra affair reinforced his knowledge and instincts about what made for good and bad procedures and decisions.

Although he was the president's in-house counterpart to John Sununu, Scowcroft defined his role quite differently. He was less publicly visible and less proactive as a policy advocate, compared to both Sununu and many of his predecessors as NSC adviser, and he performed the neutral-broker role, as he had done under Ford. Yet Scowcroft was a trusted adviser to Bush, often at his side and often quietly offering advice. He filled what Kevin Mulcahy has called a "counselor" role for the NSC assistant: "actively guarding the president's interests in the policy-making process and advocating personal policy preferences, if convinced that a department proposal is inimicable to the president's interests." At the same time, Scowcroft did not presume to be the president's sole or even preeminent adviser, as had Kissinger and, to a lesser extent, Brzezinski. He was more a coequal partner with Baker and Cheney, careful not to usurp "their departmental prerogatives or presum[e] to be the sole instrument of the president's will."[110]

To smooth relations with his two principal counterparts, Scowcroft regularly convened Wednesday-morning breakfasts in his office. As Baker recalls, "He and Cheney and I compared notes to make sure we were all singing from the same hymnal." On occasion the three would read the talking points their respective staffs had developed and "discover in the process just how much the State, Pentagon, and NSC bureaucracies distrusted each other."[111]

Scowcroft especially attempted to make sure that decisions were not "slipped by" the president without the knowledge of his principal colleagues. He was no doubt mindful about the "process" problems that had been uncovered during the Iran-contra investigation, particularly any quick decisions made in meetings between the president and his NSC adviser or decisions by the NSC adviser without clear presidential approval. At his early-morning meetings with the president, Scowcroft had his deputy, Robert Gates,[112] attend in order to "take notes and serve as a check on the proper interpretation of communications which might have taken place, something I extended to formal NSC meetings as well."[113]

Scowcroft's role as neutral broker was central. According to Bush, "Brent always made sure the views of every 'player' were understood by him and me. If he could not resolve the impasse separately, then the principals would sort it out with me. . . . He took a lot of pressure off me by keeping an open, honest approach to the NSC job. He was one of the reasons why we had a really cohesive and sound policy-making process: key decisions were well vetted ahead of time. It was an imperfect system at times, but it worked."[114]

Together, Scowcroft and Gates thereby instilled a sense of teamwork among the NSC staff. "Although most had not worked together in the past, their bonds became tight at the beginning of the Administration . . . and a good-natured humor developed among us."[115]

No doubt stemming from insights he gathered as a member of the Tower Commission, Scowcroft sought to revitalize NSC processes and procedures. Although many of the reforms that Scowcroft had recommended in the Tower Commission's report had been implemented by his two predecessors, Frank Carlucci and Colin Powell, Scowcroft wanted to create a "principals" committee, essentially the NSC members without the president and vice president in attendance. The principals group superseded the numerous interagency committees of the Reagan years and, in Scowcroft's view, would "help clarify issues and positions among the principals before issues were taken to the president" and "save him considerable time."[116] Shortly after the inauguration, Scowcroft circulated a draft of the proposed change to Baker and Tower, who did not object. It was also a committee that Scowcroft himself would chair and Baker agreed to attend. The latter was a marked change from the Reagan years, when Secretary of State George Shultz would not attend any meeting at which the president was not present and presiding.

When the NSC did formally meet with the president in attendance, Scowcroft and Bush both recognized the need to keep the size of the meeting manageable, and Bush even restricted the number of nonstatutory members invited. This was necessary, in Scowcroft's view, "both to facilitate frank and open dialogue and to reduce the likelihood of leaks."[117] But Bush did grant exceptions to both John Sununu and Marlin Fitzwater, who generally attended NSC meetings.

Scowcroft also created two other tiers within the NSC structure. Directly below the NSC and the principals groups was the deputies committee, composed of second-level representatives of departments and NSC staff members, as well as representatives of other agencies as the situation demanded. This body essentially served to define policy alternatives for presentation to the NSC; it was chaired by Scowcroft deputy Robert Gates.

The group included Andrew Card, in his capacity as Sununu's deputy, who attended in order to better coordinate the domestic and national security "sides" of the White House. According to Card, "It was different from the Reagan White House and I think different from any White House. . . . I wasn't necessarily welcomed by the national security bureaucracy, but they did keep me on the invitation list."[118]

Below the deputies group were a variety of "policy coordination committees," essentially working groups comprising midlevel staffers and chaired by members of Scowcroft's staff. The aim of these groups (initially eight of them, far fewer than in the Reagan years) was to develop policy proposals for discussion by the deputies committee. Another change Scowcroft implemented as NSC adviser was to pay more attention to congressional relations, so he set up a small staff to handle those responsibilities. In Scowcroft's view, his proximity to the presidency gave him good leverage in dealing with Congress and "should not be wasted."[119]

Although the NSC system might have generated position papers and policy options that would wend their way to the president, by most accounts Bush's decisionmaking occurred within the small cadre of his core advisers. Bush confesses in his memoirs that "I relied heavily on Brent to sort out the flow of national security papers and who should see what," and Scowcroft's task was to "reduce the issues to the point where he and I, and perhaps Jim Baker or Dick Cheney, could sort out any remaining problems."[120]

Bush reinstated the practice of having the CIA brief him at his daily morning national security meeting. In the presence of Scowcroft, Gates, usually Sununu, and once or twice a week CIA Director William Webster,

Bush would read the CIA's report, and he would often ask the CIA briefer for more information or for Scowcroft to follow up on some item. In the second part of the meeting, Vice President Quayle (having already had his own CIA briefing) would arrive, and Scowcroft would then go over pertinent items where Bush's guidance was needed in addition to anything else requiring discussion. Bush (who by this time had scanned several newspapers and the White House daily news summary) "would frequently have questions or comments from his reading, and would raise issues of current concern or pursue other subjects that might be on his mind."[121]

Bush was mindful of what was needed to make his core group function smoothly. With respect to Scowcroft's role as a broker, "I was careful to make sure that he was informed and that he was not taken by surprise, especially on substantive, important decisions. Brent would generally be in the room if I was ever talking to Jim or Dick on a matter of significance." Although there may have been occasions when Baker or Cheney saw or telephoned Bush without Scowcroft present, "I never failed to inform Brent or share material with him." "Usually any request to get me on the phone regarding security or foreign policy would come through Brent anyway."[122]

Bush was especially aware of the potential rivalry between his NSC adviser and the secretary of state. He concedes in his memoirs that "Brent and Jim did get moderately crosswise, but very rarely." "Jim worried that he might be excluded from a decision that affected his department" and knew from his own experience as chief of staff how a "strong willed presidential advisor, if backed by the president, can easily isolate a cabinet member." For their part, Scowcroft and the NSC staff were "concerned what State might be up to." But "we tried very hard, and I think successfully, to keep all participants informed and eliminate any personality clashes which could undermine policy-making as well as effective diplomacy."[123]

In Jim Baker's view, "we often argued like crazy—and loudly." But "[our differences] never took the form of the backbiting of the Kissinger-Rogers era, or the slugfests of our national security teams during the Reagan years." Instead, we were "a group of experienced, collegial peers who had worked together in one capacity or another and who liked and respected one another. . . . We trusted one another."[124]

Baker particularly noted the lessons he and Bush had drawn from the "chaos and backbiting" and the "lack of organization and cooperation" during the Reagan years. "George Bush had seen it all unfold in eight years as Vice President, and as President he was determined that the system would work the way it was supposed to work. I think it did."[125]

Even in Foreign Policy, Some Difficulties

Yet at times the tight-knit system, though thoughtfully designed, was not without difficulties. On February 15, 1989, Bush announced that he would immediately undertake a "strategic review" of U.S. foreign policy in light of the changes taking place in the Soviet Union, China, and other places. But as Jim Baker concedes, it was "neither truly strategic nor a proper review." The slow process of Bush's friendly takeover meant that much of the review was run by Reagan administration holdovers, officials who, in Baker's eyes, "had a personal and psychological investment in the status quo." Second, the review was largely prepared by the bureaucracy itself. "This resulted in least-common-denominator thinking," with many interesting ideas "left out in the name of bureaucratic consensus." "In the end, what we received was mush."[126] In Scowcroft's opinion, the strategic review on the Soviet Union (National Security Review–3) was "disappointing," and it lacked "the kind of specific and imaginative initiatives needed." In light of these shortcomings, Scowcroft ordered an NSC team, led by Condoleeza Rice, to draft a new document.[127]

By the end of March, Scowcroft was also concerned that full-blown NSC meetings were not a productive forum for deliberations; discussion might be inhibited with staff present, and the risk of leaks was greater. In their place he proposed that the president meet only with a smaller, select group in the Oval Office. "This marked the beginning of a new pattern of top-level meetings. . . . An informal group became the rule rather the exception for practical decision-making."[128]

Although the good working relationship among Bush's inner circle and the president's hands-on interest in and management of foreign policy issues were a marked improvement over the Reagan years, the tight-knit, closely held process sometimes broke down or left the administration less than fully prepared to deal with a crisis. Most notable were intelligence and communications failures prior to the invasion of Kuwait by Saddam Hussein in August 1990. But even in 1989, there were signs of concern. The abortive October 3 coup in Panama against the government of Manuel Noriega caught Bush and his advisers unprepared. As Baker observes, "It's an understatement to say that administration decision making was less than crisp. . . . A prime opportunity to remove Noriega had been squandered."[129] The failed effort prompted the administration to tighten its crisis management, particularly by strengthening the role of the deputies committee's more effective planning activity; in George Bush's words, "Amateur hour is over."[130] However, in late December (when Bush finally decided to invade Panama), while the operation was deemed an overall success, it, too, was plagued by intelligence-gathering and communications failures, most notably the inability to locate the deposed strongman for several days following his overthrow.[131]

A Divergent Record

Noriega aside, the Bush-Baker-Scowcroft team faced, in the course of its four years, significant challenges that it by and large met successfully. As one White House staff member, albeit outside of the orbit of the NSC, states:

> I think the national security decision process was run as well as it has ever been run historically, and may never be run that well again. Bush and his associates successfully navigated through the demise of the Soviet Union, restarted the Middle East peace process, managed relations with China in a difficult period, orchestrated cutbacks in both conventional and nuclear forces, successfully crafted an allied coalition to fight the Persian Gulf War, and fostered the reunification on Germany. . . . Hell, any couple of those is [a] pretty good set of accomplishments for any president in a four-year term, and if you string them together, that is what he is going to be judged on.

Yet Bush's domestic agenda presents a divergent record. Although Bush's first year was not without some accomplishments, it was the proverbial pudding without a theme. And even if there was some subtle theme lingering there, it was not communicated convincingly to the public. That problem, in turn, can be traced back to the transition and Bush's own preference for a presidency that would not organize itself around getting the message out or developing the communications strategies and tactics of his predecessor, much less craft the "vision thing."

The difficulties of 1989 would intensify with the 1990 tax deal. That "broken pledge," in the words of David Demarest, "was central to the undoing of the Bush presidency." While the deal may or may not have been needed, the White House "did not act strategically," in his view; it was "a classic example of a disaster that could have been avoided if more people had been involved in the process." "None of the constituent groups had been warned," and the White House "political people didn't know the deal had been made. Neither those who were communicating to the media nor those people who were communicating with the business community knew how to respond to the criticism."[132]

In Jim Cicconi's view, following the budget deal there was a "circling of the wagons." And several media reports indicated that domestic initiatives had begun to suffer, that the much-vaunted team-player ethos of the first year was under severe strain, and that, at least in domestic policy, Bush had become too dependent on Sununu and Darman, who themselves were the subjects of increasing criticism.[133] Economic policy was not in much better shape; there Bush took the unusual step, in September 1991, of sending a memo to his top aides stressing that he wanted to see the EPC strengthened and to meet more frequently. The EPC, Bush wrote, "must work closely with the White House legislative staffs," and participants in the EPC must "develop a plan to make sure all departmental views are considered."[134] As 1991 wore on, Sununu's position as chief of staff became increasingly precarious, and he would finally resign in December. As the 1992 election neared, the administration would have trouble both dealing with a weakened economy and in crafting a strategy to sell George Bush once again to the American public.

* * *

Unlike his two immediate predecessors and his successor, whose preparations for the presidency were largely confined to their terms as governors, George Bush brought to the office an impressive résumé of legislative, political, and executive experiences, both foreign and domestic: business executive, member of Congress, Senate candidate, chairman of the Republican Party, UN ambassador, head of the U.S. liaison office in Beijing, director of CIA. His two terms as vice president offered him an inside view of the day-to-day operations of the Reagan White House and first-hand experience of its strengths and weaknesses. One would have expected, on the basis of his résumé alone, a successful transition to the presidency.

To some extent, that expectation was indeed borne out. Bush avoided many of the more egregious mistakes Carter made: inexperienced staff, lack of understanding how the White House and cabinet operate, and failure to comprehend the realities of dealing with Congress. Unlike Reagan, Bush was more directly involved in planning for his presidency and in its daily operations once in office. This was not a president averse to picking up the phone to ask others for advice or to more intimately involve himself in the details of his administration.

Yet on several dimensions—even though the transition was, for the most part, well organized and managed—some of its particulars would come back to haunt the Bush presidency. Decisions made would have consequences.

First was the matter of John Sununu. While several former members of the administration felt that Sununu was more effective as chief of staff than depicted in the media—and indeed may have been the *kind* of chief of staff Bush needed—Sununu's own conception of the job—coupled with his behavior on the job—led to advocacy that may have tilted deliberations through a propensity to give free vent to his own ego, ruffled feathers notwithstanding. Less noted at the time was a tendency to take on too much and to be overconfident in the areas of congressional negotiations and political strategy, coupled with disinterest in matters of scheduling and communications. A Sununu type may have been what George Bush wanted, but this was more than he bargained for.

Yet Sununu was only one part of the equation. Some of the organizational changes made during the transition also complicated things. In particular, units that would play a role in marketing and selling this presidency were the ones that tended to be downgraded—political affairs, public liaison, the speechwriting staff—or left out or otherwise absent—the kinds of operations Deaver and Gergen skillfully directed under Reagan.

What *wasn't* changed also may have mattered: Bush and his advisers early on decided to stick with the cabinet councils as they had operated in Reagan's second term. The tried and true, however, may not have served Bush well: they were directed by an organizationally weaker cabinet affairs office rather than the domestic policy staff and the chairs of those councils. Policy development in domestic and economic matters, moreover, was often worked out in more ad hoc ways. That is not unusual or necessarily a negative, but in an environment with some strong personalities at the top—Sununu and Darman especially—powerful chokepoints existed that may have stalled the kind of initiatives Bush needed. Bush's domestic policy, moreover, was hampered by the lack of much attention to its development during the transition, as well as the absence of an ability to tie the elements of it, which would emerge piecemeal over the first six months of the new administration, into a coherent policy agenda.

The contrast with Bush's foreign policy is especially notable in this context. Not only did it figure more centrally in Bush's policy calculus;

Bush's choices yielded also no surprises or misapprehensions. That is not to say that some missteps would not occur—they did. But Bush and his associates were more adept at learning from their mistakes, and they operated in an environment that played to Bush's interests and strengths. Unlike Sununu, Bush not only got a Scowcroft and a Baker— he knew what he got and got what he knew.

At one level, Bush's ability to enlist the services of those with some personal connection as well as practical experience would be one of the potential strengths of this presidency. But it could also yield problems. The Bush cabinet, while more collegial than in most recent presidencies, seemed to be unusually prone to policy freelancing and other actions that generated problems for the White House. Some of these were handled by Jim Cicconi in his job as staff secretary or by John Sununu; but others would yield a series of incidents that found their way into the press.

With staff members, familiarity led perhaps to some complacency in rectifying weaknesses; like Carter, it took far too long to replace staff members who were not up to the task. Indeed, through Bush's first year in office, few senior staff changes were made, save for Studdert's departure. Nor was there much in the way of an internal examination of ways of making the staff work more effectively.

As was the case in Carter's transition and early presidency, the figure of the sitting president looms large in this regard. Bush was directly involved in a range of personnel matters and was not averse to making the kinds of organizational decisions that Carter sometimes avoided. Yet while more actively and directly involved, Bush's end judgments sometimes were off. This is particularly the case for what is perhaps the blind spot of the Bush transition and presidency: a failure to recognize the need to better market and sell its policies. And it was a failure that can be linked to his own predilections and choices in these matters; he neither saw himself as possessing Reagan's communicative skills, nor did he want any Mike Deavers in his White House who would foster efforts in this direction. He was quite willing to bring aboard Bob Teeter, a capable political strategist, but when it became apparent that Teeter was unwilling to join the administration on the terms proposed, there was no further search for an alternative.

Thus, what is interesting is not only George Bush but also how his predilections and choices played out: first in the transition, where communications received organizational short shrift; then in the presidency itself, where it remained poorly organized. Bush's difficulties illuminate not only the impact of a transition on the ensuing presidency but

also the way transitions affect how organizational and personnel matters are decided and then get carried over into the new presidency.

Notes

1. Burke interview with David Bates, October 5, 1998. Andrew Card recalls that "Bush demanded that cabinet officials be able to have direct contact
with him. While there might have been a fear that the chief of staff . . . would
have too tight a control on the information flow to the Oval Office, the president basically guaranteed that the cabinet members would not be choked out of
their access to the president." Burke interview with Andrew Card Jr., September 17, 1998.

2. Edward J. Derwinski, "Organizing for Policy-Making," in Thompson,
ed., *The Bush Presidency I,* pp. 26–27. Bates, for example, recalls that "the
president would brief them on his summit meeting with Gorbachev, tell his
views on Tiananmen Square so they would know his views and everybody
would be singing from the same sheet. Jim Baker would come back and brief
the members on major foreign policy issues—meetings of his G7 counterparts.
Brady would brief them on the G7 finance ministers. Skinner would talk about
the cleanup from the *Exxon Valdez.*" Burke interview with David Bates, October 5, 1998.

3. Bates prepared a weekly report for the president on what each cabinet
member was doing and what was going on in their respective departments:
"We asked the cabinet departments to send a brief every close of business on
Thursday, which would talk about significant events in the department and
what the secretary had done each week, and what were the upcoming issues
for the next week—major speeches by the secretary, any major announcements, any major regulations that would be coming into place. My staff would
take those and do a summary report for the president, which he read very diligently every Saturday morning." Bates recalls that Bush looked forward to the
reports: "A couple of times when he didn't get it for some reason, I would get
a call at 8:00 A.M. on Saturday morning from him asking where his cabinet report was. So he stayed really in touch with what was going on in his cabinet
departments." Bates would also forward the same report to John Sununu.
Burke interview with David Bates, October 5, 1998. Bush was in the habit of
making marginal notes on the reports, according to Bates. Unfortunately, these
notations fall under the confidential advice and communications restrictions of
the Presidential Records Act. However, some of a more informational or in-
structional nature are open. For example, in the weekly report for July 29 to
August 4, 1990, Bush penned to Bates's successor as cabinet secretary: "Ede,
on p. 4 Lujan meets Mobil. I'd like a report on how that goes—what Mobil demands, etc. GB 7–29." Chief of Staff Files—Sununu, CF 000155, Box 17, BL.
Other examples of these reports can be found in the Chief of Staff Files—Sununu, OA 01806, Box 1, BL.

4. At least one cabinet member recalls being unhappy with the access he
was granted to the president. According to Derwinski: "One of the problems I

encountered was gaining access to the president. I didn't mind Mr. Sununu calling me and asking for the reason for my requested visit so that the president could be briefed and an appointment time could be scheduled. But when some 15th junior 'special assistant' to the president called, I would draw the line. As a cabinet officer, I had to cut through the maze, which I usually did by going directly to Mr. Sununu." But Derwinski did credit Sununu with running an efficient White House staff and with being knowledgeable and "decisive": "When Mr. Sununu left and Mr. Skinner came in, the White House bureaucracy collapsed." Edward J. Derwinski, "Organizing for Policy-Making," in Thompson, ed., *The Bush Presidency I*, p. 28.

5. Both Bates and Staff Secretary Cicconi also endeavored to keep track of any stray ideas, policy suggestions, and position papers that might have come informally to the president during his meetings with cabinet members and then feed them into the more formal policy machinery. According to Cicconi, "I covered John Sununu's rear so that others were not back-dooring him." "I used to copy him on everything after the fact that went in there." Burke interview with Jim Cicconi, April 29, 1998. "Nothing would go into the Oval Office or go out of it without Jim Cicconi . . . knowing about it," Card notes. "Were there violations? I am sure there were a handful of violations. I can't think of too many violations unless they came from a cabinet member himself—where the cabinet member would walk in and hand the president a briefing paper and then all of a sudden it would show up on Cicconi's desk after the fact." Burke interview with Andrew Card Jr., September 17, 1998.

6. Ann Devroy and Kathleen Day, "Deposit Fee Draws Wave of Protest," *Washington Post,* January 26, 1989.

7. Ann Devroy and Kathleen Day, "Deposit Fee Draws Wave of Protest," *Washington Post,* January 26, 1989.

8. "Interview with Gerald Boyd of the *New York Times* and Katherine Lewis of the *Houston Post*," January 25, 1989, *Public Papers of the President, 1989.*

9. Kathleen Day, "Treasury Offers S&L Tax Plan," *Washington Post,* January 25, 1989.

10. David Hoffman and Ann Devroy, "Bush's First Week: Plans and Pitfalls," *Washington Post,* January 29, 1989.

11. The incident, Maureen Dowd of the *New York Times* reported, "showed a lack of a central control mechanism in the White House. From the beginning the Reagan White House had such a mechanism." Maureen Dowd, "Review of Bush's Opening Week: A Few Ripples but No Bursting Bubbles," *New York Times,* January 29, 1989. In fact, in 1988 Brady had tried to get the Reagan administration to adopt the fee, but Reagan officials realized the proposal would be political dynamite.

12. HUD Secretary Kemp took immediate exception. At a press conference the next day, Bush was asked about the issue and replied, "I'd have to talk to him [Thornburgh] because I don't know. . . . We've got a good Cabinet system, and I encourage people to speak out. But the decisions on something of that nature will be made right here in that room, and they're not going to be made until I have all the facts." "Interview with Members of the White House Press Corps," April 20, 1989, *Public Papers of the President, 1989.*

13. In March, an impromptu decision by Bush and Bill Bennett, the drug czar, caused further consternation among the White House staff. In a telephone conversation with Bennett, Bush agreed to a ban on imports of semiautomatic assault rifles, which Bennett then publicly announced. Both the decision and the announcement surprised senior White House aides and left Roger Porter, according to one report, "fuming." Porter reportedly went to Sununu and told him, "We cannot have a situation in which key officials in the administration are not aware of policies being announced before it happens." Bernard Weinraub, "Unlikely Alliance Atop Bush's Staff," *New York Times,* June 19, 1989.

14. In May, it was now Sununu's turn to be incensed. He had learned that Veterans Affairs Secretary Derwinski had publicly announced, without consulting with the White House, that he was not going to challenge a court decision holding the government responsible for damage caused to Vietnam veterans by the U.S. military's use of the defoliant Agent Orange. Derwinski, in fact, had already determined that the affected veterans should receive a service-related disability classification. Although Derwinski's decision proved popular, the Justice Department and the White House were unhappy with Derwinski's unilateral action, since the solicitor general had wanted to appeal the decision. Edward J. Derwinski, "Organizing for Policy-Making," in Thompson, ed., *The Bush Presidency I,* p. 31.

15. In July, Defense Secretary Cheney objected to a decision, after it had been publicly announced, by Commerce Secretary Mosbacher to lift a ban on computer sales to Eastern European countries. Not only had Cheney not been made aware of the change; President Bush indicated that the policy change had not been brought to his attention until Cheney voiced his objections. In another case, involving a decision by EPA Administrator William Reilly to ban virtually all use of asbestos by 1997, the White House expressed surprise at the decision, then discovered that in fact Reilly had notified them in his weekly report and that the decision had gone through an extensive regulatory review. According to one White House official, "There was more of regulatory process than we realized." David Hoffman and Ann Devroy, "Cabinet Members Finding Many Roads Lead to Bush," *Washington Post,* July 30, 1989.

16. Bernard Weinraub, "White House," *New York Times,* May 19, 1989.

17. Burke interview with Jim Cicconi, April 29, 1998.

18. Peter Kilborn, "Player on Budget Team Enters Circle of Power," *New York Times,* March 2, 1989.

19. Burt Solomon, "When the Bush Cabinet Convenes It's a Gathering of Presidential Pals," *National Journal,* July 1, 1989, p. 1704.

20. Memorandum from David Bates to the President, "Domestic Policy Council Annual Report," February 27, 1990, Chief of Staff Files—Sununu, CF 00155, Box 18, BL. The archivists at the Bush Library were unable to locate any references to other annual reports for the DPC or annual reports for the EPC.

21. John Sununu attended many of the councils' meetings. He was kept updated on their deliberations since Bates reported through Sununu, forwarding him drafts of agendas for meetings of the cabinet as well as regular weekly

updates of the issues that were flowing through the two councils and their various working groups. Bates also prepared Sununu's "talking points" when he addressed the cabinet on particular items or issues. For example, in mid-June Bates forwarded a report to Sununu on the weekly activities of the councils. The DPC was working on adoption issues, budget reform, the Clean Air Act, disabilities legislation, drug control, education policy, and welfare reform, while the EPC was handling steel and high-definition television. Memorandum from David Bates to John Sununu, "Weekly Activities Report for the DPC and the EPC," June 16, 1989, Chief of Staff Files—Sununu, CF 11322, Box 30, BL. Other reports (as well as Sununu's talking points) can be found in Chief of Staff Files—Sununu, OA 01806, Box 1, BL.

22. DPC working groups or task forces dealt with children and family policy, Americans with disabilities, drug control, education policy, energy and natural resources, global environmental change, health policy, Hispanic education, immigration, infant mortality, low-income opportunity, budget reform, tort reform, and wetlands issues; the two proposed were for border control and federal facilities. Memorandum from David Bates to the President, "1989 Annual Report of the Domestic Policy Council," February 27, 1990, Chief of Staff Files—Sununu, CF 00155, Box 18, BL.

23. Burke interview with Jim Pinkerton, October 15, 1998; also see Pinkerton, *What Comes Next,* pp. 1–5.

24. Peter Kilborn, "Player on Budget Team Enters Circle of Power," *New York Times,* March 2, 1989.

25. Burke interview with Jim Cicconi, April 29, 1998.

26. Andrew Card, "The Bush White House and His Presidency," in Thompson, ed., *The Bush Presidency II,* p. 30. In one press account of the deliberations, contentious issues were also hammered out by a group that Sununu convened in his office; members included Sununu, EPA Administrator Reilly, Darman, and Energy Secretary Watkins. Michael Weisskopf, "Behind Clean-Air Bill: A Balancing of Interests," *Washington Post,* July 30, 1989.

27. Memorandum from David Bates to the President, "1989 Annual Report of the Domestic Policy Council," February 27, 1990, Chief of Staff Files—Sununu, CF 00155, BL.

28. These can be found in Sununu's "itinerary" files at Chief of Staff Files—Sununu, CF 00483, Boxes 47 and 48, BL.

29. Memorandum from Dan Quayle to George Bush, January 11, 1989, Chief of Staff Files—Sununu, CF 00498, Box 49, BL.

30. Porter's staff members chaired working groups on energy and natural resources, health policy, low-income opportunity, and wetlands issues. The other groups were chaired by a variety of departmental officials and others on the White House staff, such as science adviser Allen Bromley and drug czar Bill Bennett. Only one group—that on disabled Americans—was chaired by a member of the DPC staff. Memorandum from David Bates to the President, "1989 Annual Report of the Domestic Policy Council," Chief of Staff Files—Sununu, CF 00155, Box 18, BL.

31. Burke interview with Andrew Card Jr., September 17, 1998.

32. Burke interview with Andrew Card Jr., September 17, 1998.

33. As he told Cicconi in December: "Don't make it [deputy assistant] for policy development, make it for policy planning. In that way if the guy comes in and doesn't like me, it will be 'pretend I don't work for him.' That's actually the way it kind of worked." Pinkerton at times felt frustrated but didn't "bear Porter ill-will. He had his work. As Ulysses said of Telemachus, 'He's in charge of the kingdom.' Fine. I've got my work to do. We'll just get back in the boat and row around, 'til my fate meets the horizon.'" Burke interview with Jim Pinkerton, October 15, 1998.

34. James Pinkerton, "Life in Bush Hell," *New Republic,* December 14, 1992.

35. In fact, it was widely reported that Bush himself had to open a backdoor channel of sorts. As James Pfiffner points out, "This problem became public when both *Time* and *Newsweek* ran stories that senior Bush aides were so upset at being cut off by Sununu that the president was forced to open a post office box at his summer home in Kennebunkport, Maine as a backchannel so that his top advisers could contact him directly without Sununu's censorship." Pfiffner, "The President's Chief of Staff," p. 92.

36. Burke interview with Andrew Card Jr., September 17, 1998.

37. Burke interview with Jim Pinkerton, October 15, 1998. Pinkerton's "new paradigm" language did figure in at least one presidential speech. In 1990, addressing an audience of conservative activists, Bush said: "When old centralized bureaucracies are crumbling, the time has come for yet another paradigm." But the speech, Pinkerton notes, "was a throw-away talk that didn't even make it into the next day's *Washington Post*." James Pinkerton, "Life in Bush Hell," *New Republic*, December 14, 1992.

38. Burke interview with David Bates, October 5, 1998.

39. Burke interview with David Bates, October 5, 1998.

40. Colin Campbell, "The White House and Cabinet Under the 'Let's Deal' Presidency," in Campbell and Rockman, *The Bush Presidency,* p. 212.

41. The agreement with the Democrat-controlled Congress may or may not have been wise in theory, but the process was fraught with miscommunications and strategic and tactical errors that weakened the White House position. At the start of the negotiations in May, for example, Sununu's off-the-record (but easily attributable) comments to a reporter about Bush's pledge to enter into negotiations with the Democrats with "no preconditions" was interpreted by them as laying a political trap. ("It is their prerogative to put [taxes] on the table, and it's our prerogative to say no," Sununu said at the time.) As Colin Campbell explains: "Bush's credibility had suffered serious damage. With the administration's strategy revealed so baldly, Democrats simply refused during the rest of the negotiations to make a move unless the president stepped out in tandem." Campbell, "The White House and Cabinet Under the 'Let's Deal' Presidency," in Campbell and Rockman, *The Bush Presidency,* p. 215. Such a position, in turn, made Bush even more vulnerable to political criticism for violating the tax pledge. Sununu's missteps would be repeated in October 1990, at the height of Bush's battle with Congress over the budget and new taxes. Following a meeting with Republican senators and Bush over the

failed budget talks, Sununu told Fitzwater that the president had acquiesced in their demand that they opposed any tax increases for the wealthy. According to Maureen Dowd, "That may have been Mr. Sununu's way of steering Mr. Bush in the direction he felt was best. But when the President made it clear the next day that he had been merely listening to the senators, and that he still considered everything on the table, Mr. Bush looked confused and indecisive." Maureen Dowd, "Bush's Woes Stir GOP Grumbling Over Sununu," *New York Times,* October 29, 1990.

42. Burke interview with Andrew Card Jr., September 17, 1998, and Burke interview with Jim Cicconi, April 29, 1998; David Demarest, "The Bush Presidency and Communications," in Thompson, ed., *The Bush Presidency II,* p. 65.

43. Barbara Bush, *A Memoir,* p. 225. She also notes that Sununu "went through hell for George later on." "John is a hero of mine. He's such a bright man, such a funny man."

44. Burke interview with Jim Cicconi, April 29, 1998.

45. Burke interview with Jim Cicconi, April 29, 1998. One example worth noting is that Sununu kept his morning meeting of the senior staff to a manageable size. Unlike the situation in the Reagan years, when some two dozen staff members would attend the chief of staff's morning meeting, Sununu kept the membership typically at a dozen or so on any given day: Card, occasionally Ed Rogers, Cicconi, Scowcroft or Gates (sometimes both) from the NSC, Gray, Newman, Untermeyer, Fitzwater, Demarest, Porter, McClure, and usually someone from the advance office. The only regular attendees at the deputy level were Joe Hagin from scheduling and Susan Porter Rose from the First Lady's staff. Representatives from political affairs or public liaison did not regularly attend; their input would come from a member of Sununu's staff, usually Card or Rogers. As Newman recalls, "Sununu didn't mince words. If he didn't want you, you weren't going to be there. You didn't come uninvited. There was no way to wiggle your way into the room." Burke interview with J. Bonnie Newman, September 29, 1998.

46. Burke interview with Jim Cicconi, April 29, 1998.

47. Burke interview with Andrew Card Jr., September 17, 1989. Sununu himself served as a conduit for other streams of policy advice to the president. Shortly after Bush took office, Sununu developed a list of people outside the administration to whom he circulated policy proposals and speeches, asking for suggestions. Those contacted included the president's five children, Atwater, Fuller, Ailes, Richard Bond, Teeter, Fred Malek, Frank Fahrenkopf, Kenneth Duberstein, and Peter Teeley. Bernard Weinraub, "The Chief of Staff Has His Own Kitchen Cabinet," *New York Times,* June 30, 1989. Sununu was also unusually generous in the amount of time he spent with the press corps and members of Congress. For a chief of staff who was reputed to be so overly powerful and arrogant, his daily schedule lists a surprisingly large number of meetings with individual members (or small groups) of the press and of Congress, both Democrats and Republicans. These can be found in Chief of Staff Files—Sununu, CF 00483, Boxes 47 and 48, BL.

48. Burke interview with J. Bonnie Newman, September 29, 1998.

49. Burke interview with Jim Cicconi, April 29, 1998.

50. R. W. Apple, "Emotions in Check, Intellect Not, Sununu Wins Reluctant Respect in Capital," *New York Times,* September 13, 1989.

51. Phillip D. Brady, "Vice President and President Bush: His Chiefs of Staff and Staff Secretaries," in Thompson, ed., *The Bush Presidency II,* p. 45.

52. Andrew Card, "The Bush White House and His Presidency," in Thompson, ed., *The Bush Presidency II,* p. 32.

53. Cohen, "The Domestic Policy Vicar," pp. 16–17.

54. John Sununu, Miller Center of Public Affairs Forum, University of Virginia, November 13, 1998.

55. Maureen Dowd and Thomas Friedman, "The Fabulous Bush and Baker Boys," *New York Times Magazine,* May 6, 1990.

56. Burke interview with Frank Hodsoll, January 26, 1999.

57. Duffy and Goodgame, *Marching in Place,* p. 73.

58. Maureen Dowd, "White House," *New York Times,* July 27, 1989.

59. Burke interview with Jim Cicconi, April 29, 1998.

60. Burke interview with Frank Hodsoll, January 26, 1999.

61. The details in which Bush liked to submerge himself even included, according to Cicconi, "things he liked doing, as a personal courtesy, that used to get handled administratively." Most notable was that Bush enjoyed personally signing the presidential commissions given to top-level officials instead of having them done by autopen: "He knew most of these people he was appointing and as a gesture to them, he wanted it to be a personal signature on something they were hanging on their wall forever more. So I would save them and send them up to Patty Presock [Bush's personal secretary], and she would arrange them on the table in his private dining room. They were all layered, and he could literally go through and sign them all rather quickly but still personally. He would usually end up lingering and say, 'Here's Joe and there's John.' He liked doing that, and it was something he felt was a worthy thing to spend his time on." Burke interview with Jim Cicconi, April 29, 1998.

62. Burke interview with Jim Cicconi, April 29, 1998.

63. Bush and Scowcroft, *A World Transformed,* p. 32.

64. The meeting usually began with a fifteen-minute intelligence briefing by a CIA staffer, then a thirty-minute period during which Scowcroft (often accompanied by his deputy, Robert Gates) would review foreign and national security policy issues. Sununu would then have thirty minutes for domestic and economic policy issues, as well as other matters such as the president's schedule (Scowcroft generally did not attend this meeting, but Quayle did if he had been present earlier). Starting on June 27, 1991, the meeting was extended an additional half-hour for a "domestic update" by Sununu. Itineraries, Chief of Staff Files—Sununu, CF 00483, Boxes 47 and 48, BL; Sununu Daily Agendas, Chief of Staff Files—Sununu, CF 00500, Box 52, BL.

65. John Sununu, Miller Center of Public Affairs Forum, University of Virginia, November 13, 1998. Sununu's files at the Bush Library appear to

substantiate Sununu's account here. Ed Rogers, Sununu's deputy, would compile a daily list of "discussion items" for Sununu, many of which were issues to be brought to Bush's attention or for a decision in the course of the day. "Chief of Staff Discussion Items," Chief of Staff Files—Sununu, CF 00498, Boxes 49–51, BL.

66. Bernard Weinraub, "Unlikely Alliance Atop Bush's Staff," *New York Times,* June 19, 1998. In his February 6 address to Congress, Bush insisted on retaining a paragraph on a statehood referendum for Puerto Rico, which his aides argued ought to be discarded since it distracted from the economic and budgetary themes of the speech. In fact, Bush wrote out by hand a longer paragraph on Puerto Rico, and it was included in the speech. David Hoffman, "Bush's First Month: Many Modest Goals, No Overriding Mission," *Washington Post,* February 20, 1989.

67. Andrew Card, "The Bush White House and His Presidency," in Thompson, ed., *The Bush Presidency II,* p. 35.

68. John Sununu, Miller Center of Public Affairs Forum, University of Virginia, November 13, 1998.

69. Ann Devroy, "Bush Cabinet Given Austere Welcome," *Washington Post,* January 24, 1989.

70. "Remarks and a Question-and-Answer Session at a White House Luncheon for Journalists," March 31, 1989, *Public Papers of the President, 1989.*

71. In the 1989 budget deal with Congress, the White House was able to come to a basic agreement in April, and Bush was widely hailed as having presented one of the first budgets that wasn't "dead on arrival" in Congress in almost eight years. Yet the agreement not only did not address the deficit (as Darman had predicted, that would come in year two) but was far from the flexible freeze that Bush had proposed in the campaign. Darman agreed to allow nonentitlement discretionary spending authority for domestic programs to rise by $15 billion (from $142 billion to $157 billion, some 10 percent) in order to deter Democrats from reducing defense spending. The agreement met the $100 billion deficit-reduction target set by Gramm-Rudman-Hollings, but did so by accounting gimmicks, one-time savings, such as sales of federal assets, and increases in various user fees. Yet Bush did not technically violate his no-new-taxes pledge, and he developed what appeared to be a better working relationship with Congress compared to the annual budget battles of the Reagan years. The agreement, moreover, forestalled any big-ticket programs on the domestic side that the Democrats might pass and force Bush to veto. Implementing the budget resolution, in particular the revenue and appropriations bills, proved more difficult, and the degree of partisanship increased over the next six months. By the start of the new fiscal year in October, no reconciliation bill had been approved, and Bush was forced to order $16 billion in across-the-board cuts under the provisions of Gramm-Rudman-Hollings. Bush had continued to push for a cut in the capital-gains tax, but by November he agreed to set this aside until the next year. Finally, a budget bill was passed at the end of the session. As Paul Quirk notes, the final bill had only about half of the proposed reductions, "$14.7 billion—much of it by accounting gimmicks. . . .

Bush had managed to secure some outward manifestations of a cooperative budget process," but "the fight over capital gains had made most of the intermediate steps intensely conflictual. More important, the substance of a constructive agreement was largely lacking." Paul Quirk, "Domestic Policy: Divided Government and Cooperative Presidential Leadership," in Campbell and Rockman, eds., *The Bush Presidency*, p. 79. Yet it is interesting to speculate whether Bush might have avoided the political controversy he faced in 1990—when he agreed to raise taxes—by sticking instead to the flexible-freeze formula proposed in the campaign. A report on Bush's efforts during his first hundred days that listed the administration's initial policy efforts had been prepared by Roger Porter. Memorandum from Roger Porter to John Sununu, "Major Presidential Initiatives," May 4, 1989, Chief of Staff Files—Sununu, OA 01896, Box 2, BL.

72. Burt Solomon, "Bush's Disdain for Image Making May Come to Plague His Tenure," *National Journal*, March 11, 1989.

73. Duffy and Goodgame, *Marching in Place*, p. 60.

74. Burke interview with Andrew Card Jr., September 17, 1998.

75. David Hoffman and Ann Devroy, "Stumbling Mars Bush Team Debut," *Washington Post*, March 5, 1989.

76. Bernard Weinraub, "Bush Fights Perception That He Is Adrift," *New York Times*, March 13, 1989. Bush's continued commitment to Tower was also a commentary about George Bush. According to Chase Untermeyer, "George Bush was committed personally and intensely to the nomination of John Tower, and he felt John Tower had been getting a bum rap both in the press and especially in the Congress, and was not about to abandon him. It was a reflection of George Bush's soul rather than the polls. . . . In John Tower he had a person who had been his cohort in the Texas political wars . . . when there were not too many Texas Republicans around in the 1960s. Anybody who had gone through that experience would be in a 'band of brotherhood.'" See "The Reagan to Bush Transition: A Miller Center Panel and Colloquium," in Thompson, ed., *Presidential Transitions*, pp. 189–190.

77. Andrew Rosenthal, "Bush's Ties to Congress Show Strain," *New York Times*, October 16, 1989.

78. As Barbara Sinclair observes, "Republicans were not well positioned to shape legislation to Bush's liking. In the House, the Democrats' margin was large enough and their cohesion high enough that, when combined with the great advantages procedural control gave the majority party, Republicans were seldom able to build a winning coalition behind their preferred approach." In the Senate, the GOP "could seldom deliver legislation in the form Bush preferred. Nor did they always agree with the president and use their influence on his behalf." Barbara Sinclair, "Governing Unheroically (and Sometimes Unappetizingly): Bush and the 101st Congress," in Campbell and Rockman, eds., *The Bush Presidency*, p. 168.

79. Correspondence with Andrew Card Jr., December 11, 1998.

80. Letter to John Sununu, August 4, 1989, signed by Congressmen Bob Michel, Newt Gingrich, Jerry Lewis, Bill McCollum, Vin Weber, Dick Schulze,

Mickey Edwards, and Duncan Hunter. Chief of Staff Files—Sununu, OA 1806, Box 1, BL.

81. Memorandum from John Sununu to Fred McClure, August 7, 1989, Chief of Staff Files—Sununu, OA 1806, Box 1, BL.

82. Fitzwater, *Call the Briefing!*, p. 176.

83. Andrew Card, "The Bush White House and His Presidency," in Thompson, ed., *The Bush Presidency II*, p. 36.

84. Ann Devroy, "For the White House Political Operation, Focus Will Be Policy, Not Popularity," *Washington Post*, March 19, 1989.

85. "Discussion Items," January 25, 1989, Chief of Staff Files—Sununu, CF 00498, Box 49, BL.

86. Ann Devroy, "For the White House Political Operation, Focus Will Be Policy, Not Popularity," *Washington Post*, March 19, 1989.

87. Maureen Dowd, "Impasse on Budget Is Ended," *New York Times*, October 9, 1990.

88. Burt Solomon, "Bush's Disdain for Image Making May Come to Plague His Tenure," *National Journal*, March 11, 1989, p. 603.

89. Burke interview with Andrew Card Jr., September 17, 1998.

90. Lloyd Grove, "For Bush, a TV Tune-Out," *Washington Post*, February 17, 1989.

91. Ann Devroy, "For This President the Medium Is Not the Message," *Washington Post*, April 30, 1989. Data is from the Center for Media and Public Affairs.

92. "Discussion Items," February 16, 1989, Chief of Staff Files—Sununu, CF 00498, Box 49, BL. The March 29, 1989, discussion items included: "Ask [president] about Thurs. am meeting with bankers. Ask [president] about Friday am meeting with congressional leaders."

93. This list of participants comes from Card's later recollections. The memorandum establishing the group also listed Roger Porter, Dave Demarest, and Darman as members, with Sununu as chair, Jim Pinkerton as secretary, and others brought in as specific issues demanded. Burke interview with Andrew Card Jr., September 17, 1989.

94. Memorandum, "Administration Action Committee," and Memorandum, "A Plan for Establishing Priorities and Staying on the Offensive," March 1, 1989, Chief of Staff Files—Sununu, CF 00498, Box 49, BL.

95. Burke interview with Andrew Card Jr., September 17, 1989.

96. Itineraries, Chief of Staff Files—Sununu, CF 00483, Box 47, BL.

97. David F. Demarest, "The Bush Presidency and Communications," in Thompson, ed., *The Bush Presidency II*, p. 65.

98. Memorandum from C. Gregg Petersmeyer to John Sununu, "President's Schedule," February 21, 1989, Chief of Staff Files—Sununu, A 01806, Box 1, BL.

99. Ann Devroy and David Hoffman, "Sununu Rebukes Aides for Grousing to Media," *Washington Post*, May 2, 1989.

100. Burt Solomon, "Bush's Disdain for Image Making May Come to Plague His Tenure," *National Journal*, March 11, 1989, p. 602.

101. Studdert was not without his talents. "He was the classic advance person," according to Andrew Card. "Very good at the logistics necessary to meet the president's expectations on a trip, and he was good at focusing on . . . the '[big] picture'—grand external events. Most of his staff were kind of part-time volunteers, who would work in the field and get things ready for the president and his staff to go someplace. He was extremely good at detail. If something was supposed to be twelve inches tall, it was twelve inches tall and not twelve and a quarter inches tall." Burke interview with Andrew Card Jr., September 17, 1989. Yet Studdert's efforts were plagued with difficulties. In June, Bush appeared at the Family Motor Coach Association at the Virginia State Fairgrounds in Richmond. Bush followed a man juggling rubber chickens and came on stage and "gave a rambling speech about the environment. Many in the audience, coming from seminars entitled 'Let's Talk Diesel' and 'Hair Styles on the Road' seemed surprised to find the President in their midst," according to Maureen Dowd's report. "The episode was illustrative of travels with the President. Some of his trips have set off a spate of commentary about the scattershot way the White House presents the President and his message." Studdert also generated criticism following a Bush visit to a suburban Virginia high school to promote his educational initiatives. The school happened to be the one Studdert's son attended, and young Studdert was one of three students who met with the President and dined with him in the school's cafeteria. The event generated no evening news coverage, and White House officials were reported to be furious about the visit, which they thought should have taken place in an inner-city school. By October, Studdert had returned to his native Utah and was replaced by Sig Rogich, who had produced several controversial campaign commercials for Bush in partnership with Roger Ailes. Rogich was a wealthy Las Vegas advertising executive who included among his clients Donald Trump, Wayne Newton, and Frank Sinatra. Maureen Dowd, "An Image Polisher Leaves Nevada Neon to Sharpen a Beige White House," *New York Times,* October 3, 1989. According to Sununu, "This was one area where folks had suggested we needed a little bit of an extra dimension." Maureen Dowd, "The Man Who Puts Bush on the News, Maybe," *New York Times,* July 7, 1989.

102. David F. Demarest, "The Bush Presidency and Communications," in Thompson, ed., *The Bush Presidency II,* p. 61.

103. Burke interview with Andrew Card Jr., September 17, 1998.

104. David F. Demarest, "The Bush Presidency and Communications," in Thompson, ed., *The Bush Presidency II,* p. 60.

105. Burke interview with Andrew Card Jr., September 17, 1998.

106. David F. Demarest, "The Bush Presidency and Communications," in Thompson, ed., *The Bush Presidency II,* p. 63.

107. Burke interview with Andrew Card Jr., September 17, 1998.

108. Gerald Boyd, "Bush Tries to Dispel 'Drift' Image, Says Administration Is 'On Track,'" *New York Times,* March 8, 1989.

109. Bernard Weinraub, "Bush Says His Agenda Is Preparing for 21st Century," *New York Times,* March 17, 1989.

110. Mulcahy, "The Bush Administration and National Security Policy Making," p. 5.

111. Baker, *Politics of Diplomacy,* p. 25.

112. Gates had been an NSC staffer in the Ford and Carter administrations and had served as deputy director of the CIA. Unfairly caught up in the net of Iran-contra, Gates had asked President Reagan to withdraw his nomination as director of the CIA. Scowcroft felt that Gates would be "an alter ego," with substantive knowledge about foreign policy and how the NSC system operated. Moreover, like Scowcroft, Bush liked Gates and trusted him.

113. Bush and Scowcroft, *A World Transformed,* p. 31.

114. Bush and Scowcroft, *A World Transformed,* p. 35.

115. Bush and Scowcroft, *A World Transformed,* pp. 25–26.

116. Bush and Scowcroft, *A World Transformed,* p. 31.

117. Bush and Scowcroft, *A World Transformed,* p. 32.

118. Burke interview with Andrew Card Jr., September 17, 1998.

119. Bush and Scowcroft, *A World Transformed,* p. 31.

120. Bush and Scowcroft, *A World Transformed,* pp. 32, 25.

121. Bush and Scowcroft, *A World Transformed,* p. 30.

122. Bush and Scowcroft, *A World Transformed,* p, 35.

123. Bush and Scowcroft, *A World Transformed,* p. 36.

124. Baker, *Politics of Diplomacy,* pp. 21–22.

125. Baker, *Politics of Diplomacy,* p. 27.

126. Baker, *Politics of Diplomacy,* p. 68.

127. Bush and Scowcroft, *A World Transformed,* p. 40.

128. Bush and Scowcroft, *A World Transformed,* pp. 41–42.

129. Baker, *Politics of Diplomacy,* p. 186. For further discussion, see Haney, *Organizing for Foreign Policy Crises,* pp. 79–83, 104–106.

130. Woodward, *The Commanders,* pp. 100–101.

131. John Broder and Melissa Healy, "Panama Operation Hurt by Critical Intelligence Gaps," *Los Angeles Times,* December 24, 1989.

132. David Demarest, "The Bush Presidency and Communications," in Thompson, ed., *The Bush Presidency II,* pp. 60, 65.

133. See, for example, Maureen Dowd, "Bush's Woes Stir G.O.P. Grumbling Over Sununu," *New York Times,* October 29, 1990; Maureen Dowd, "The Sniping Begins and All Is Normal," *New York Times,* November 17, 1990.

134. Memorandum from George Bush to Nick Brady, Dick Darman, John Sununu, Mike Boskin, Roger Porter, and Ede Holiday, "Coordination of Economic Policy," September 7, 1991, Chief of Staff Files—Sununu, OA 11322, Box 1, BL.

7

Bill Clinton: Misplaced Efforts?

Recognizing the Task at Hand: Preelection Efforts

The Clinton administration provides a telling example of how a transition can affect—and in this case powerfully set back—the ability to take office smoothly, make decisions soundly, and govern effectively. It is in many respects a textbook case of how a transition can go awry and impede a presidency once in office. It is especially noteworthy given Clinton's attentiveness to policy matters and the desire of those around him to make a mark on the national political agenda. The campaign had made numerous promises, but the process that would translate them into policy proposals was largely lacking.

Although a host of difficulties would soon crop up, a failure to recognize the need to move early on transition matters was not one of them. Indeed, following what now had became a tradition among presidential candidates, Clinton began to think about his presidency well before election day. Shortly after the July 1992 Democratic National Convention, he tapped his campaign chairman, Mickey Kantor, to head up a small transition planning operation. Kantor was a prominent Los Angeles attorney, lobbyist, and Democratic Party activist (he had also run Walter Mondale's 1984 presidential bid), and he had come to know Hillary Clinton well, having served with her when both were on the board of directors of the National Legal Services Corporation. "You have to engage in transition planning now," Kantor told reporters in mid-September. "It would be irresponsible not to do so. On the other hand, it would be foolhardy to let it distract from the issue at hand, that's November 3."[1]

According to one participant, Governor Clinton had asked Kantor to begin a transition effort because he didn't want to wake up the day after the election wondering what to do next. But Clinton was also aware that planning for a presidency so soon might distract from his campaign. Clinton especially did not want someone who would create a high-profile operation.[2] Kantor apparently fit the bill in Clinton's mind, despite the fact that Kantor had much higher political visibility than Jack Watson, Pen James, or Chase Untermeyer.

Kantor set up shop several blocks away from the main campaign headquarters in Little Rock. It was a small operation—some ten to fifteen staff members were involved—and their efforts were at least nominally overseen by the five-person Clinton-Gore Pre-Transition Planning Foundation.[3] The group consisted of Warren Christopher, a prominent Los Angeles lawyer and deputy secretary of state in the Carter administration; Vernon Jordan, the former head of the Urban League and a well-connected Washington attorney; Madeleine Kunin, the former governor of Vermont; Henry Cisneros, the former mayor of San Antonio; and Kantor. Christopher, Jordan, and Kunin had all worked together during the summer assisting Clinton in selecting a vice presidential candidate. Christopher and Kantor were also longtime friends and had worked together on the independent commission investigating the Los Angeles police department in the aftermath of the Rodney King incident. Although all of them were prominent political players, none had any direct White House experience.[4] And unlike Meese's role in overseeing Pen James's operation in 1980, the only links to the ongoing campaign were through Kantor himself.

Kantor's efforts were not as ambitious as those Watson had undertaken in the last Democratic transition, but they went beyond Untermeyer's modest preparations four years earlier. A deliberate decision was made to take personnel issues off the table—at least before election day—so that there might be greater trust with the campaign staff. The Clinton transition was well aware of the problems that had developed with Watson's operation twelve years earlier. "Be low-key, honest brokers, and don't distract" were their mantras, according to one participant.[5]

But the group went well beyond simply laying out the requisites of a transition process should Clinton be elected. Some staff members, along with outside advisers, did in fact work on issue areas, such as the budget, economy, and foreign and national security policy. John Hart convened meetings with several groups and met with academic experts on presidential transitions as well as with some of those involved in the 1980 Reagan transition.[6] Meetings were held with representatives of the General Services Administration, which would handle the logistics of a possible Clinton transition. Washington lawyer James Hamilton began developing ethical codes of conduct for the transition staff. The Kantor group was preparing not only to present Clinton with information on how to organize the transition but also advice on how to send signals to the nation about his policy agenda and what kind of administration would unfold following his inauguration.[7]

The selection of Kantor to direct the preelection effort would soon prove problematic. Kantor, unlike Meese and Untermeyer, was not a longtime member of the candidate's inner circle, despite his prior association with Hillary Clinton. Notwithstanding his title as chairman, Kantor was not even involved in the day-to-day operations of the campaign.[8] That effort was undertaken by the much publicized and successful "war room," a tight-knit operation "marked by a powerful control over the release of information, a secretive, deliberate planning process, and a cohesion among staff members that minimized evidence of infighting."[9] The war room was on a potential collision course with any efforts on Kantor's part. In fact, according to one report, Kantor had "tangled" with such trusted Clinton aides as George Stephanopoulos and James Carville, and he had been given the transition job "in part to give him an area to direct separate from other campaign aides." Kantor, according to one campaign staffer, "went out of his way to alienate people."[10]

Regardless of the strengths Kantor brought to the job, there was no recognition that his stature and broad mandate might generate tensions with other parts of the Clinton camp. Although personnel may have been off the table, the broader lessons of the Watson-Jordan imbroglio had not been reckoned with, and there was little effort to still the concerns of the campaign war room; like Watson's situation, there was a problem in how much the campaign group needed to know about transition planning with the election outcome still uncertain. The formal transition board notwithstanding, there had not been the kind of daily oversight and troubleshooting (Meese in 1980) or periodic guidance (provided to Untermeyer in 1988 by Baker, Sununu, and George Bush himself). It was reportedly news to Clinton that there were problems afoot. The fact that Clinton did not realize Kantor was proving to be a controversial choice, and that he was perceived by the campaign war room to be the source of several problems, offers an early sign of Clinton's disinterest in organizational matters, particularly as they might impact the early planning for a possible presidency. However, those problems would soon become quite apparent.

Organizing a Transition: The Postelection Effort

Kantor's fate and how Clinton would respond to developing difficulties, as well as the pressing need to get this postelection transition up and running, provide an early example of his decisionmaking and some of its problematic consequences. Although Clinton was up until 4:00 A.M. after his election-night victory, he convened a meeting with the renamed Transition Planning Foundation that very day. One account of the meeting suggests that the planners presented Clinton with a thick briefing book, prepared by the Kantor group, recommending that Kantor be selected as transition director with Christopher serving as transition-board chairman. Clinton, not one to choose hurriedly or be delivered a fait accompli, deferred making a decision, telling them he was in no rush and was still weary from campaigning.[11]

Delay and Conflict

In the days following the election, latent conflicts and rifts had finally broken out openly among Clinton's advisers. In particular, concerns were raised over Kantor as director of the transition and, possibly, as Clinton's White House chief of staff. Kantor's critics charged that he had "alienated some by blocking access to Mr. Clinton and by sabotaging strategies he disagreed with." Long-dormant rivalries blossomed: "It's a bloody, ugly mess," one staff member was quoted as saying; another noted that "it's a very, very intense struggle."[12]

Kantor became the first casualty of the Clinton presidency. The disgruntled campaign team got to Clinton first. "They were hot," said one person who watched it unfold. "They chopped [Kantor's] legs off." Clinton was not aware that the campaign team had been kept in the dark about the transition planning Kantor had done, and he was surprised at the anger that had developed among his top aides; it was not a promising sign about Clinton's managerial abilities or his perceptiveness about staff matters.[13]

Instead of Kantor, Clinton turned to Vernon Jordan, who was selected as chairman of the transition with his base of operations in Washington, and to Warren Christopher, who would be transition director with headquarters located in Little Rock.[14] In tapping Jordan and Christopher, Clinton had picked not only two well-known political insiders but also two persons who had already been involved in his preelection transition efforts. Yet their selection also meant that Clinton would not have a strong voice in his inner circle who had practical experience in running the White House staff; at best Christopher could bring his experiences working in the State Department under Carter (and for a time as a trade negotiator in the Kennedy administration) and as a deputy attorney general under Lyndon Johnson. Christopher would later recount that aiding Clinton in selecting a cabinet was his chief priority. Clinton wanted him as transition director because he was "pleased with the process" during the vice presidential search, and "he wanted me to adapt it to the selection of his first cabinet." It was, according to Christopher an "offer I couldn't refuse."[15]

A President-elect Prone to Act on His Own

Yet Clinton did not delegate everything to Christopher and Jordan, and his own close involvement in some transition matters was an early sign of a president who was not restricted to organizational boxes and was prone to act on his own. Al From, the head of the moderate Democratic Leadership Council (DLC) and another Clinton associate of long standing, recalls meeting with Clinton the Thursday after the election: "We talked about the transition and that he ought to take time to figure out what to do. He told me at that point that I would have a role and he would let me know. The next Wednesday, he called me and asked me if I would be the head of domestic policy with Bruce Reed as my deputy."

On Thursday, From traveled to Little Rock. "[Clinton] said come on down, then go back over the weekend and get your stuff, and then come back." Were there clear lines of authority through Jordan or Christopher? "I don't think there were real clear lines. . . . I had some discussions with [Bruce] Lindsey, but mostly with Clinton. . . . I would not say we did not respond to Christopher and Vernon. The answer is that whenever Vernon called, whatever he wanted I did." But "my deal with Clinton was always a personal deal."[16]

Over the next few days, reports indicated that Clinton was proceeding slowly and at times secretly in his transition, in marked contrast to the quick, frenetic, and open style of the campaign itself. Here, too, there were signs of Clinton's decisionmaking style once in office. On November 11, the *New York Times* observed that the "skeletal transition board has only met twice and is still trying to work out a time-table to present to Mr. Clinton for his most important transition decisions."[17]

A Transition Finally Organized

On November 12, Clinton announced, at his first news conference since election day, that decisions had finally been made on the remainder of his transition team, and the names of some forty-eight appointees to the transition staff were released.[18] Among the more prominent were Alexis Herman and Mark Gearan, who were appointed deputy directors and placed in charge of transition operations in Washington, and Harold Ickes, who became one of Christopher's chief assistants. Dee Dee Myers continued on as press secretary, with Stephanopoulos serving as assistant director for communications.[19]

But their efforts were divided, with some of the staff operating out of Little Rock and others, such as Jordan, Gearan, and Herman, working at transition headquarters in Washington. The staff working on policy issues as well as the teams that would prepare reports and the briefing books on agencies and departments largely operated out of Washington, as did former South Carolina Governor Richard Riley (who was in charge of the personnel operation), the legal staff that vetted candidates for positions and prepared for the confirmation process, and a legislative strategy group headed up by Howard Paster. But cabinet selection, White House planning and appointments, and some of the more important pieces of Clinton's policy agenda, such as his economic program, were centered back in Arkansas.[20]

Organizational Problems Begin to Develop

It was, perhaps, a necessary division of labor since Clinton was still a sitting governor (although it might have been easily alleviated had he chosen to resign). But it did on occasion present problems. According to Al From, "Would I have spent more time with Clinton and maybe focused a little more on these issues earlier had we been together? The answer is yes."[21] Although Gearan recalled that the arrangement was viable, "In a perfect world you would have it all here in Washington [although Gearan did observe that it was basically workable]."[22] Another transition member, based in Washington, observed that

> the transition was overwhelmed by two things. One was this rush of bodies into the building, and the other was the oversight from Little Rock, which often created the situation where people who were appointed to run these clusters made decisions that then got overruled. It was totally chaotic. . . . They brought in people from outside to run some of these clusters—part of it was an effort to create diversity— and some of them had expectations that were not fulfilled.

Another part of the problem would develop in January. Some key members of Clinton's soon-to-be White House team, who had been based in Little Rock, would arrive in Washington only days before his inauguration. As a result, they had little time to familiarize themselves with their new positions or the political environment in which they would operate.

The delay in White House planning can also be directly linked to the management teams appointed to act as liaison with departments and agencies.[23] Initially, ten "clusters" were planned, but the one dealing with White House organization and other related White House matters was dropped. According to Gearan, "One of the biggest mistakes of our transition was that we did not do a briefing book on the White House . . . a fundamental error."[24] White House issues would be handled informally in Little Rock, a decision that would have repercussions later in the transition, if not through the first months of the new administration.

In fact, that decision was made at the very top. It was Clinton's view, according to one participant, that cabinet selection had to come first and was more important, drawing in part on his sense of the tensions that had developed between the cabinet and the White House staff in preceding administrations. His policy priorities, especially economic, also took first claim. As for the White House, Clinton had his own "sense of what kind of staff he wanted," and it would "come together" and "fall in place" on its own.[25] It would be one of the most important mistakes of the transition, it was Clinton who had made it, and it would be monumentally consequential in its impact.

Policy Teams

Of particular importance were the appointments Clinton announced for three major policy areas. Al From was named assistant director for domestic policy, Samuel "Sandy" Berger was picked for national security, with Robert Reich heading up the economic policy group. Reich, a fellow Rhodes scholar with Clinton at Oxford, was a faculty member at Harvard's Kennedy School; Berger had worked, along with Anthony Lake, on shaping Clinton's foreign policy positions during the campaign.[26]

Some of these choices bore significant policy consequences. Reich brought a particular perspective to bear on economic issues with his belief in investing in "human capital." From and his deputy, Bruce Reed, had strong DLC links; the DLC was a centrist Democratic Party group, which included Clinton as a member and hoped to move the party from its traditionally liberally moorings. It was expected that their role on the transition staff would lead to a significant "New Democrat" presence in the Clinton White House.[27] The Clinton transition and the ensuing administration, however, was not just a New Democrat operation; other ideological camps were represented. A challenge was thus posed about how—or even whether—Clinton would sort out these different political agendas.

Ethical Dilemmas

Clinton's pledge to have the most ethical transition and, following his inauguration, the most ethical administration in history created his first public-relations problem as president-elect. Clinton's rules for transition officials were more stringent than Bush's, which only required financial disclosure and a pledge not to use information for profit. Clinton went further and barred transition officials from lobbying agencies with which they had dealings for six months following the inauguration. He also prohibited their involvement in decisions that could affect their financial and business interests.

Perhaps as a foreshadowing of the ethics problems that would later develop in the Clinton White House, the rules did not uniformly apply and exceptions could be made, most prominently for Jordan, Christopher, and Thomas "Mack" McLarty, an Arkansas businessman, long-time Clinton friend, and his soon-to-be designated chief of staff.[28] In the view of one transition member based in Washington, despite the new rules and the presumption "that we are not going to have lobbyists and we are not going to do this or that, within two weeks of the opening of the building there were more lobbyists in that building than there were anything else. They created all kinds of high expectations and then didn't meet them." "There was this crazy overemphasis on ethics rules."[29] Tighter ethical rules made for good public relations at the time, but they may have set in motion unreasonable expectations that Clinton and the members of his administration, once in office, would not always easily meet.

Filling the Cabinet

Looking Like America

While the various transition operations labored on in Washington and Little Rock, the most important work was being done—at least as Clinton saw it—in his study in the governor's mansion. There Clinton and a small group of advisers spent enormous time and energy in deciding who would be appointed to his cabinet. Joining Clinton were Christopher,

Vice President–elect Al Gore, and wife Hillary. Only three other aides were invited to attend—Mack McLarty, Bruce Lindsey, and Gore deputy Roy Neel. It was by all accounts a cohesive group, and little of their deliberations would leak to the press.[30]

It was also a selection process that provides further signals about Clinton as a decisionmaker: long, discursive discussions, ideas floated at the last minute, and decisions based on Clinton's own comfort level and intuitive feel—all coupled with an unusually high degree of attention to how it would all play out with various political constituencies.

It was a laborious process with attention paid not just to the qualifications of various candidates but also to the programs and missions of particular departments and how they fit in with the Clinton political agenda. According to one account of the process, "Before talking about possible candidates for each agency, the group would conduct a seminar in American government—sometimes lasting an hour or more—on the role of that agency."[31] As the discussion meandered on, Warren Christopher would gently prod Clinton back to the matter of discussing candidates.[32] It was a pattern that would repeat itself time and again once he took office.

For each meeting, Christopher and his staff prepared a thick briefing book and a short list of potential nominees. But for several positions, names would be floated at the last minute, and as selections were made, losing candidates for one position would be shifted over to another. Such musical chairs is surely not unusual, but Clinton's efforts were complicated by his loose decisionmaking style, his propensity to delay a decision until the last minute, as well as the set of goals, often conflicting, that Clinton sought to achieve. He wanted a cabinet that he could comfortably work with and that would mesh with his own intentions to take the lead in several policy areas. He wanted a cabinet that would operate as a set of policy teams, not just a collection of diverse department heads with particular agendas. He wanted a cabinet that would be diverse in its ethnic, geographic, and gender composition, one that would "look like America," as he had pledged in one of the debates and reiterated at one of his press conferences following the election. And he wanted to finish picking the cabinet by Christmas Day.[33]

But the process took time, especially if Clinton didn't feel comfortable with an interview or if Christopher's short list was not to his liking. According to Elizabeth Drew, "He would ask for more names, saying the list didn't have enough people of stature or didn't contain the name of anyone who had helped him get elected. Sometimes he thought the vetting report on a candidate didn't make the case for choosing that person. . . . But sometimes Clinton's indecision stemmed from his own indecisiveness."[34] And while Clinton had vested an enormous amount of time and energy in getting a handle on departments, policies, and likely candidates, little attention was paid to how they might figure into the policy process of his administration or function either collectively or individually as part of a decisionmaking process, save for Clinton's desire for a "personal relationship."

Decisions Begin to Emerge

It was not until December 10 that Clinton announced his first appointments—the five members of his economic team: Senator Lloyd Bentsen, a Texas Democrat, as secretary of the treasury with New York investment banker Robert Altman as his deputy; Congressman Leon Panetta at OMB with Alice Rivlin as his deputy; and Robert Rubin as chairman of the soon-to-be-created National Economic Council (NEC). None was a surprise.[35] Over the next several weeks other appointments were announced: Robert Reich for Labor and Donna Shalala for Health and Human Services.[36] Clinton's commitment to diversity was in part signaled by the appointment of two African Americans—Ron Brown to Commerce and Jesse Brown to Veterans Affairs—as well as Henry Cisneros's appointment as HUD secretary.

As he had done with his economic team, Clinton presented his foreign policy team as a group. Warren Christopher, as secretary of state, would finally get the position for which he had been passed over during the Carter administration, and Anthony Lake would become NSC adviser.[37] The choice of defense secretary proved more difficult, but Clinton settled on Congressman Les Aspin, the chairman of the House Foreign Affairs Committee. The final member of the team was Madeleine Albright as UN ambassador, a position that would once again carry cabinet rank. Clinton also decided to give two other female appointees cabinet rank: Laura D'Andrea Tyson, a Berkeley economist who would chair the Council of Economic Advisers, and Carol Browner to head the Environmental Protection Agency, an agency that Clinton hoped to elevate to department status.[38]

A Difficult Final Round

With the exception of Richard Riley's appointment as secretary of education, the remaining cabinet positions proved more difficult for Clinton and his inner circle. They were especially pressed to make good on their commitment to diversity, satisfy several important political constituencies, and meet the Christmas deadline. Hazel O'Leary, an African American, surfaced at the last minute, and she was appointed secretary of energy.[39] Clinton especially worked hard to find more Hispanics (Bush had two, a record Clinton wanted to beat). Congressman Bill Richardson of New Mexico, who was Hispanic, was considered for Interior, but he was not viewed as reliable by environmental groups.[40] Clinton also faced a prickly political situation in choosing between two well-connected candidates to head up the Department of Transportation: James Blanchard, the former governor of Michigan, and William Daley, brother of Mayor Richard M. Daley of Chicago and son of *the* Mayor Daley. Clinton solved the impasse by selecting Federico Peña, the former mayor of Denver, for the position. With Peña on board, Clinton got another Hispanic. It also resolved the problem at Interior, since it now meant that Arizona Governor Bruce Babbitt, who was popular with environmentalists, could be moved over to that position.[41] Clinton also settled on Congressman Mike Espy of Mississippi, an African American, DLC member, and early Clinton supporter, for secretary of agriculture.[42]

Clinton's choice for attorney general proved especially difficult. On December 21, Vernon Jordan had been visited by a delegation from a variety of women's groups who demanded that one of the "big four" cabinet positions (State, Defense, Treasury, and Justice) be filled by a woman. Since Treasury had been filled and Clinton was set to name Aspin and Christopher the next day, that left the attorney general slot. Clinton lashed out at the "bean counters" at his press conference, but the Clinton inner circle was desperately searching for a woman to appoint.[43] Finally, just before Christmas eve, Zoe Baird's name was raised by Warren Christopher, and Clinton quickly agreed; she was general counsel for Aetna Life and Casualty and had once been a member of Christopher's law firm.[44]

Four Decisionmaking Problems

Clinton's cabinet-selection process would prove to generate four problems for his presidency. First, while attentive to the personal qualities of the candidates and his comfort level with them, Clinton undertook little consideration of how they would function as a group or otherwise provide a channel of information and advice separate from that of the White House staff. The emphasis was on people rather than process, which was par for the course with Clinton. The one exception was the effort to create the National Economic Council (discussed in more detail below).

Second, Baird's appointment as attorney general quickly ran into controversy. In 1990, Baird and her husband, Yale law professor Paul Gewirtz, had illegally hired an undocumented Peruvian woman to be their baby-sitter and the woman's husband as their driver (for a paltry $500 a week). Although their reputed income was over $500,000, they had also failed to pay social security taxes for the couple. Baird told the transition vetters that she and her husband had sought legal advice and were straightening out the situation. Christopher informed Clinton of the problem but thought it was being taken care of. Lawyers on the transition staff did not perceive it as a major issue.

But no one, the transition's legal adviser Bernard Nussbaum in particular, was worried that a prospective attorney general had broken the law (particularly immigration laws, which were under the jurisdiction of the Justice Department). They regarded it as being on the level of a "traffic ticket," and in the rush to wrap up the appointment of the cabinet by Christmas, no alarm bells sounded.[45] It was also a warning sign that appointees such as Nussbaum, while personally loyal and connected to the Clintons, might lack the sensitivity and expertise to detect trouble early on.

Third, Clinton had achieved the most diverse cabinet (using the baseline of gender and race) in history. Of the fourteen department heads, three were women, four were African American, and two were Hispanic. Among others given cabinet rank, three more were women: Albright, Tyson, and Browner.

But Clinton's commitment to diversity had its costs. There was pressure, often public, by women's, Hispanic, and environmental groups to appoint persons satisfying their demands. The notion that Clinton was responsive to such pressure created the perception that Clinton, as Elizabeth Drew put it, "could be rolled. . . . He appeared to be a willing hostage." His stance as a different kind of Democrat "was at jeopardy, at a very early moment." Clinton got diversity, "though too publicly, and this diminished some of the people who got the jobs."[46] Furthermore, as David Broder observed in mid-December, Clinton had "set up a situation where major constituencies of cabinet departments will be appealing decisions of 'their' secretaries to the White House and where . . . conflicts will likely have to go to the president for resolution" (or, one might add, to a presumably smoothly functioning and efficient White House staff).[47]

Fourth, the process of appointing subcabinet officials, under the direction of Richard Riley, proved more difficult. Clinton and his advisers sought something closer to the Republican model (closely controlling subcabinet appointments) rather than Carter's practice (letting cabinet members have a free hand). But Warren Christopher also emphasized that Riley's efforts would be a "cooperative process" between the transition and cabinet nominees.[48] However, progress was slow, and the hope of having two hundred subcabinet appointments named by inauguration day was scaled back in January to about one hundred.[49] The fact that Christopher and Riley had been appointed to cabinet positions in late December also slowed matters down, as their attention became increasingly focused on preparing for their confirmation hearings and taking over departments. Several reports indicated that Mack McLarty was filling in, although this was also the period when the White House staff was finally beginning to take shape. According to one transition staff member, "The personnel process was a complete disaster. They put Dick Riley in charge of it and then named him secretary of education. And he immediately moved out of it, and that deteriorated into a complete mess; it was just chaos . . . there were no real people with experience running it."

Crafting a Policy Agenda

Unlike Bush, whose policy offices during the transition consisted essentially only of the small effort Pinkerton directed, Clinton clearly sought to use the transition as a time for developing a policy agenda. Yet to some extent he went to the opposite extreme: a transition process that moved on too many policy fronts. In his victory speech on election night, Clinton used the occasion to recount the program and policies he had talked about during the campaign, and he told the crowd that these policies would be his highest priority during the transition. He especially singled out his commitment to reviving the economy (a plan would be in place by inauguration day), reforming health care (a plan would be before Congress during his first hundred days), overhauling welfare, putting in place his college-loan and community-service proposals, and developing tax incentives to encourage business investment. At his November 12 news conference announcing the transition staff, Clinton again sketched out the plans for his first months as president, including quick action on the economy, repeal of existing executive orders banning abortions at federally financed clinics, loosening of immigration bans on Haitian refugees, and development of tighter ethics rules. Clinton's agenda was beginning to resemble Jimmy Carter's laundry list.

Economic Policy Planning

But as Clinton had promised during the campaign and reiterated on several occasions following his election, doing something about the economy would be his most important priority during the transition. Shortly after the election, Clinton did take steps that seemed to presage a policy process in which economic decisionmaking would be given more order and prominence. On November 8, press secretary Dee Dee Myers announced that Clinton planned to create an "Economic Security Council" that would be modeled after the NSC and give high-level visibility and attention to economic issues. The council would be separate from the Council of Economic Advisers and would take over economic policy from the Domestic and Economic Policy Councils of the Bush and Reagan administrations. It was one of the few actions taken during the transition that related to Clinton's decisionmaking processes and the organization of his advisers that he would employ once he took office.[50] In fact, according to William Galston, who worked in the transition and later became one of Clinton's domestic policy advisers, the idea for the council must even have preceded the election: "There is no way they could have gotten the NEC idea as quickly as they did if it hadn't been discussed prior to the election."[51]

In December, the title of the new group was changed, to National Economic Council, which was perceived as less provocative in tone. At the December 10 press conference where he unveiled his economic team, Clinton took the opportunity to talk about the new NEC. He envisioned Rubin's role much like that of Brent Scowcroft under Bush: "His job will be to coordinate, to facilitate and to provide some direction to the deliberations of our economic council." But, he carefully added, Treasury Secretary Bentsen "will continue to be the principal economic spokesperson after the President."[52]

Yet the NEC was not up and running during the transition, and some of its key staff members hadn't even been asked yet whether they wanted to join the new administration. And although he would head the new NEC, Robert Rubin was not placed in charge of economic planning; that job was given instead to Robert Reich.

A decision about an economic plan could not wait: Clinton especially needed to decide which of his economic proposals would take priority. At the start of the transition, aides predicted that an initiative on job training, a public-works package of some $20 billion for roads, bridges, and other projects, and a plan to reduce capital-gains taxes directed at investments in new business would figure high on his list.[53]

Yet each had been fostered by a different set of economic advisers and represented different and often conflicting economic strategies: Reich favored investment in training and education; traditional Democrats pushed public works; and Wall Streeters in the Clinton camp favored tax breaks for business investments and action on the deficit. Moreover, Clinton's goals were compounded by a worsening deficit picture, the same situation George Bush had faced four years earlier, which again raised the question of whether any substantial budget commitments could realistically be made come January. And as we shall see in Chapter 8, delays in settling on his program would complicate his efforts with Congress.

A Slow Start

On December 14 and 15, Clinton convened the much touted economic summit. Some four hundred business executives, economists, and labor-union officials had been invited down to Little Rock to attend, along with Clinton's chief economic advisers. It was a long, twelve-hour meeting-discussion on economic issues. While the sessions produced less in the way of substance and direction, they were nationally televised and showed a president who cared about economic issues and was well versed in policy detail.

With the summit resembling more a public-relations gambit, it fell to Reich's economic policy group to begin to frame a specific set of economic proposals, a task that it was supposed to finish by mid-December. It got off to a slow start. According to one report, by mid-November Gene Sperling, Reich's deputy, could be found sitting in an entry hall of the transition headquarters pounding away at a computer. "If you find a computer that works, then just take it," he was reported as saying.

Meanwhile, Robert Reich was at work trying to sort out the president-elect's economic program, particularly the issue of whether it should be an economic-stimulus package or a more ambitious proposal aimed at increasing productivity, competitiveness, and job training. To assist him, Reich assembled an impressive array of economic talent.[54] Particularly noteworthy is how Reich brought this considerable talent to bear. According to one report, Reich followed a strategy of "counterstaffing" in assigning their respective tasks. Instead of playing to their strengths and expertise, he placed them in other areas (Ira Magaziner, most notably, was assigned long-term deficit reduction).[55] But by the end of January, while Reich and his associates had produced detailed briefing books, an economic plan was by no means complete. Richard Darman, the outgoing OMB director, would later write that he "expected the Clinton transition team to use OMB resources to get the quick start [on an economic plan] that candidate Clinton had promised. When they didn't, I guessed they were getting a surprise announcement ready. . . . To my surprise, there was no such surprise."[56]

On November 17, Clinton held a day-long meeting with the group. They were joined by Christopher Edley, a Harvard law professor and issues director during the 1988 Dukakis campaign; Harrison Wellford, who had been a transition adviser to Carter and had served in the OMB; Judith Feder, who was heading the health-care study team; and Michael Wessel, general counsel to House Majority Leader Richard Gephardt. But no major decisions were made.[57]

Despite Clinton's public-relations victory with the summit, behind the scenes the situation worsened. The Clinton economic team was now recommending that the budget be reduced by $145 billion for FY 1996 rather than the $90 billion that had been announced in the campaign. The change was based on a revised deficit estimate by the Congressional Budget Office, from $190 billion in 1996 to $290 billion.

An Opportunity Slips Away

As the budget picture worsened, the goal of presenting an economic plan before inauguration day (much less mid-December, as announced earlier) slipped away. Robert Reich had told reporters on November 24 that he hoped to meet that deadline so Congress could get to work on it right away. But the budget numbers and divisions within Reich's team about what to do made a quick solution impossible to achieve. Clinton also began to back off his promised middle-class tax cut due to the worsening budget situation.

The economic situation and the deficit problem came to a head at a January 7 meeting of Clinton with his top advisers. Panetta delivered the bad news about the deficit: initial projections were off, and a further $50–60 billion in shortfall was now projected by the OMB. The deficit could grow as high as $360 billion by FY 1997—which would begin in October 1996, shortly before the next presidential election.

Gene Sperling had more bad news. Clinton's promised stimulus plan, a central component of his "Putting People First" proposal, would cost almost $90 billion. Tyson indicated that recovery from the recession would be slow, and she projected growth at no more than 3 percent a year at best. Her deputy, Alan Blinder, cautioned that too much deficit reduction, while politically popular and welcome news to the financial markets, would further slow the rate of growth. Cutting the deficit by 1 percent of GDP—about $60 billion—would take money out of the economy and reduce growth by 1.5 percent. Clinton reacted with a question: "You mean to tell me that the success of the program and my reelection hinges on the Federal Reserve and a bunch of international bond traders?"

The meeting had begun at 9:00 A.M. and ended at 4:00 P.M. Clinton sought to square the circle by sticking to his earlier promise to cut the deficit but based on a figure of $290 billion rather than Panetta's $360 billion and thus projected a cut of $145 billion by 1997. Although Clinton had in practice violated his pledge to cut the deficit by half, if it all worked out, at least the deficit would be below $200 billion by 1997 (based on Panetta's higher projection).[58]

Health-Care Reform

In November, Clinton had announced that an assistant-director position for health policy was being created. It would be headed by Judith Feder, former staff director of the Rockefeller-Pepper congressional commission on health-care reform and codirector of Georgetown's Center for Health Policy Studies. Feder's appointment clearly signaled that health-care reform would figure significantly in Clinton's early legislative agenda. In fact, Clinton had made that decision quite early; according to Al From, "It was clear from day one when Clinton called me that he was going to have a separate person on health care."[59]

But Clinton's pledge to quickly present Congress a health care reform package encountered roadblocks. "The Clinton transition team worked feverishly to develop a health proposal, but its recommendations evidently disappointed the Clintons," one report noted. "We're stuck in the mud. Everybody is panicked. There is a very short window of time to get something done here," said one policy adviser.[60]

Yet the work of Judith Feder and her team had signaled that health-care reform would not be easy. Feder had especially avoided rosy scenarios in making cost projections. Her old boss, Senator Jay Rockefeller, a Democrat from West Virginia, counseled her to be honest with Clinton. "Of course, I was wrong. She got crushed. Clinton personally was furious at her, because he couldn't do what he wanted," Rockefeller would later recollect.[61]

Feder's projections indicated that health-care reform would either dramatically increase the deficit or, if phased in more incrementally, delay universal coverage until after the 1996 election. Neither prospect pleased Clinton. Yet instead of heeding a warning sign about the dangers in moving too boldly, too quickly, it was the messenger, Feder, who bore the blame. She felt "devastated, treated abominably," according to one account. For his part, Clinton "proceeded down a road that was even more hazardous."[62] Health-care reform would take more time and attention than Clinton had anticipated—but it might be saved through a major effort by Hillary Clinton.

Other Initiatives: A Mixed Picture

According to one transition-team member, the policy work undertaken from November through January "was not very helpful. A lot of it was wasted except in those instances where the people who did the policy work in the transition also ended up in the departments. . . . I didn't get the sense that much on the policy side was very real." Elaine Kamarck, who would be the staff member principally in charge of Al Gore's reinventing government project, recalls that she worked on welfare reform during the transition, but in 1993 "I ended up running reinventing government, but I did nothing on that during the transition."[63]

Yet others thought the policy development undertaken during this period had worked well. William Galston recalls that the two transition groups he worked with—on a national community-service program and a new student-loan program—were productive and "drew up the legislative specs that were translated into draft legislation early in the new administration and ultimately enacted into law." But Galston notes that he viewed his task not at creating pie-in-the-sky exercises or opportunities to put down on paper "what I thought best." Rather, they were "opportunities to take ideas that the president-elect had put into play during the 1992 campaign and translate them into specifications that had some chance of being enacted and were quite clearly translations of Clinton's own views."[64]

Bruce Reed, Al From's deputy, would later observe, "We had a team of fifteen or twenty people. We put together a book of actions that the president could take right out of the box. We also included a strategy for major domestic initiatives—crime, welfare, choice, reinventing government, and other major issues."[65]

In From's view, Clinton had a policy agenda, dating back to his earlier years with the DLC. "We had a [DLC] convention in 1991 before Clinton was a candidate that Clinton chaired, where we went through a lot of the big ideas that shaped his administration." From was also Clinton's personal representative on the platform committee at the 1992 Democratic convention. "There was a continuity of purpose that probably most people, and certainly most casual observers, would not have understood. Clinton was engaged in that whole effort, not just in the transition, but going back to 1989, 1990, and 1991." During the transition "we pulled all of this together."

Although From had originally planned to stay in Little Rock to work on the issues part of the transition (he and Bruce Reed had even rented a townhouse to share), he soon realized that most of the work being done in Little Rock was in the area of appointments. So he returned to Washington, where most of the issues staff was now located. "Most of what we did was try to put on paper," he would recall, "in a form that was useful to Clinton, early executive orders, policy planning, policy strategy, a sort of plan for how we would start all that. . . . We put together a notebook with both strategy memos that Bruce and I did and a lot of specifics on issues, plus a notebook on early executive orders."

In fact, From recalls, because the appointment process in Little Rock was taking such time, "once we put together our policy ideas, we were sort of waiting around for whoever was going to focus on it, to focus on it." Yet he states that "the work we did was terrifically important and had a lot of impact on the real accomplishments of the administration . . . from national service to welfare reform, from community policing to youth apprenticeships to reinventing government." And in From's view, "As it turned out, it all eventually happened. It took a little while to get it through the bureaucracy, but it happened."[66]

From also provided informal advice to the president-elect on how the White House staff needed to be organized to achieve his policy goals. From his perspective, the Democratic party was still in transition, so Clinton was never going to appoint just New Democrats. Still, Clinton needed to be attentive to their presence on the White House staff: "He needed a core group in the White House that would be the 'keeper of the flame' of his New Democrat approach." While Clinton did not fully heed From's advice, From "kept sending him [that memo] during the first six months of the new administration." "Slowly but surely that happened. But it took a while, and it wasn't always the easiest ride in the first two years."[67]

According to Bruce Reed, "We had a series of actions for him to take in early January," but a major part of the problem was Clinton's focus on the personnel process. "He didn't have as much chance to focus on those questions because he spent so much time on the cabinet and the staff." But the appointments process itself was not the only problem; the delay in naming the White House staff took its toll: "There wasn't a decisionmaking team in place to carry out the strategy, to act on it. The lines of authority weren't clear."[68]

Building Bridges

Clinton did use the transition period to begin building political support for his policy initiatives; his less than impressive 43 percent of the popular vote did not convey a political mandate. On November 16, Clinton met with congressional Democratic leaders in Little Rock, and he promised to end the "cold war" between the president and Congress. Speaker Tom Foley, Senate Majority Leader George Mitchell, and House Majority Leader Richard Gephardt came with their own message: the need to reduce the deficit and to follow Congress's agenda. Gephardt, in fact, used the occasion to lobby for Panetta's appointment as OMB director; in his view Panetta had both the knowledge and the political clout to get the job done as OMB director. Foley emphasized the need to cooperate with Congress, to see it as an ally, thereby avoiding the frosty relations that had plagued Jimmy Carter. Clinton, for his part, took a first step by telling them he was backing away from his support of a presidential line-item veto, something both he and Bush had promised in the campaign.[69] As well, Clinton backed off from a pledge to cut congressional staffs as a necessary match to his proposed cuts in White House staff. Following the Thanksgiving weekend, which he spent in Southern California at the beachside home of Hollywood friends Harry and Linda Thomason, Clinton returned to Washington and met with newly elected Democratic members of Congress.

But Clinton's relations with Congress, even then, weren't always rosy. As Bruce Reed would later comment, one thing that happened

> during the transition that was unfortunate was that the congressional leadership tried to impose its agenda in place of ours. . . . After a campaign in which Clinton had asserted his independence from Congress, the leadership was insisting that things go their way. It took the administration a couple of years to realize that the congressional agenda wasn't the same as the Clinton agenda. We made a lot of concessions in the name of unity that didn't turn out well.[70]

Distracting Attention from the Agenda

Just as John Tower's nomination presented problems in getting across George Bush's early policy message, Clinton, too, faced situations of his own making that proved distracting; the key problem was failing to heed early warning signals of political danger. One was the Zoe Baird nomination for attorney general and the persistence of Clinton insiders in regarding her hiring of an illegal alien as akin to a traffic ticket.

When news of the problem became public, the negative reaction was enormous, and "Nannygate" was born. Some in the Clinton inner circle persisted, however, in thinking that Baird could overcome the firestorm, despite the pleas of Democratic senators that the nomination was in trouble. Senator Joe Biden, the chairman of the Judiciary Committee, likened the issue more to a "freeway crash" than a traffic ticket. George Stephanopoulos came to this conclusion:

> No matter what we did, she wasn't going to be attorney general. The only questions were how this had happened, and how to get out. Her selection, the ensuing controversy, and the way we responded were emblematic of our early troubles. . . . We should never have let Baird's nomination get as far as it did, but our systems failed us at every crucial step.[71]

But Clinton would not pull the nomination, and relented only on January 21, the day after his inauguration, when Senate Democratic leaders told him the nomination was dead.[72] Defense Secretary Les Aspin later observed that the Baird episode had a "chilling effect" on the appointments process. "Things were moving along until that point and then they just ground to a halt."[73]

Don't Ask, Don't Tell: Didn't Work

The other issue deflecting attention away from Clinton's policy agenda was the decision to end the ban on gays in the military. It was perhaps more prominent in terms of public as well as inside-the-Beltway reaction. Like the Baird case, it indicates a failure to heed potential warning signs and a lack of sensitivity and attention to how to address or otherwise finesse a politically charged issue.[74]

The issue first arose in a speech Clinton made before a group of gay and lesbian supporters, but it did not figure much in the general election. It surfaced again during the transition. Shortly after election day, Andrea Mitchell of NBC asked whether Clinton intended to fulfill his campaign promise; Clinton replied that he did. In Clinton's view, while homosexual conduct in the military—as with all sexual conduct—should continue to be regulated, homosexual status should not.

Bruce Reed would later observe that the issue was a prime indicator of why "the transition did not provide a running start. Gays in the military flared up in the transition, and there were problems with it in the opening weeks of the administration, but it had gotten little attention in the campaign." Further, it "defined the administration early in a way the president didn't intend."[75]

No one in the Clinton inner circle had anticipated how controversial an executive order changing military policy would be (even some gay-rights advocates thought the effort misplaced, preferring instead that Clinton muster support for other civil-rights legislation). And although Clinton had transition staffer John Holum and others study the issue during the transition, no successful efforts were made to lessen any immediate political fallout. In Holum's opinion, Clinton had not been fully briefed on the complexity of the issue.[76] Nor did Clinton see the wisdom of Holum's suggestion in December that the issue be put off for six months of study by the administration, Congress, and the military, with a gradual phase-in of any changes in the ban. Holum had also found that the Joint Chiefs were willing to end the practice of asking recruits about their sexual orientation but were strongly opposed to a broader executive order entirely lifting the ban.[77]

According to Senator John McCain of Arizona, Clinton bungled the situation from the start: "A smarter scenario would have been to ask [the Joint Chiefs] down to Little Rock, during the transition, bring up the subject and say 'Look, I made this commitment, help me work my way through this.'" Instead, the Joint Chiefs "were just told to do this and do that."[78] (In fairness to Clinton he had added, in replying to Andrea Mitchell, "How to do it, the mechanics of doing it, I want to consult with military leaders about that. There will be time to do that." But the media, eager for a story, had played up the angle that Clinton wanted immediately to end the ban.)[79]

In the view of William Waybourn, director of the Victory Fund, the largest political action committee raising campaign funds for gay and lesbian political candidates, "The whole issue was very costly. Basically, it took a new administration and dropped it on its head for three months. . . . And what did we have? Nothing." In fact, according to Waybourn, it was a public-relations setback: "It was on the national news for months about gays in the showers. Horrible things, like when Senator Sam Nunn took the below-the-deck tour. . . . Every night on television we are getting this continual battering about what gays and lesbians do."[80]

Throughout the transition period, the controversy mounted, and it became clear that congressional opponents of lifting the ban might be able to pass legislation overriding any executive order. The Joint Chiefs of Staff remained opposed to the executive order, and on January 12 Colin Powell, chairman of the Joint Chiefs, told Naval Academy midshipmen that if they found the new plan morally unacceptable then resignation might be in order.[81] Clinton's proposal had now created a crisis in civilian-military relations, even generating difficulties in dealing with Sam Nunn and more conservative Democrats in the Senate.

At a meeting with his advisers on the Sunday before his inauguration, Clinton agreed to a plan that would refer the matter to his new defense secretary, Les Aspin, for a six-month study. That study led to a compromise agreement—"Don't Ask, Don't Tell"—that pleased neither gay groups nor the military.[82] Gay groups became particularly incensed when Clinton, at his first press conference, indicated that while gays might be permitted in the military, perhaps they should serve in segregated units (a compromise that offered an ironic twist to any supposed parallel to Truman's 1948 order desegregating the military).

The whole episode proved costly. It raised issues about Clinton's own political judgment, both in failing to appreciate the controversy it would entail as well as missing the opportunity to deal with the problem differently, as Holum, McCain, and others had advised. It had created, as Clinton political adviser Paul Begala would later realize, "opportunity costs" deflecting attention away from the public's more pressing concerns about the economy.[83] According to one set of White House polls, the issue caused a 20 percent decline in the president's favorability ratings in his first two weeks in office.[84] The new policy did not have any positive effect; quite the contrary, in fact. Later studies indicated that, in the first four years of Clinton's presidency, more gays and lesbians were discharged than had been the case under George Bush.[85]

Shaping the White House Staff

Although the Clinton transition sent signals the first week following the election that the White House staff would be an important priority over the coming weeks (Christopher and Jordan had both promised "structural changes" and a 25 percent reduction in the size of the staff),[86] the process of filling cabinet positions and other personnel decisions preoccupied Clinton and his top transition advisers. It was not until mid-December that Clinton finally settled on Mack McLarty as his chief of staff, and in the ten days leading up to his inauguration there was a rush to fill White House positions.

Matters relating to the staffing and organization of the White House had cropped up periodically during the transition, but no single set of transition officials consistently focused on them. Instead, there was a changing cast of characters: Jordan and Christopher, particularly at the start, then Richard Riley, then McLarty, and for a time Harold Ickes.

The appointments of Christopher and Riley to cabinet positions particularly set back the efforts; once selected, they began to focus on their respective departments and upcoming confirmation hearings. As Christopher recounts, following the announcement of his appointment, "I began to shift gears to preparing to assume leadership of the State Department."[87] The delay in naming McLarty also was a handicap. The Clinton effort departed notably from the pattern set during the Reagan and Bush transitions, where the early appointment of a chief of staff established clearly who would be in charge and gave that person (Baker, then Sununu) adequate time and authority to prepare for the new administration.

Shortly after the election, outgoing incumbent George Bush designated Andrew Card, then serving as secretary of transportation, to lead the outgoing administration's transition. Bush had thought about the transition, according to Card, and he wanted the Clinton team to "hit the ground running." "Let's pass them the baton so they don't drop it," Bush told Card. Bush "wanted to clear the decks. . . . He didn't want to have our people dragging their fingernails across the desk as their chair was pulled away."[88] Card contacted Vernon Jordan and Warren Christopher, meeting with the former on several occasions in Washington and talking to the latter, who was in Little Rock, over the phone.[89] Card would later meet on several occasions with Mark Gearan, who headed up Clinton's Washington office. According to Gearan, "The Bush administration was very generous with their time, extremely cordial, from the president to Card, in every session we had. It was highly professional, and they very much wanted to provide the best transition for the country."[90]

At the time, Gearan and Alexis Herman played a major role in serving as liaison between the White House and the Clinton transition. As Andrew Card recalls,

> I remember sitting down with Mark Gearan and telling him that it takes you nearly ten times as long to get somebody through the FBI clearance process than you think it will. It's probably more important that you get your White House people into the clearance process well before you're coming into the White House than it is to worry about

who you are going to have as secretary of the interior. Start the process early. Please respect the role the FBI and the secret service play in the clearance process.[91]

The timetable for appointing a staff, however, was out of Gearan's hands; decisions were to be made in Little Rock, and they came with much delay as Clinton and his advisers there focused on other matters.

To be fair to Clinton, it should be noted that the transition was not bereft of advice or counsel. In late November and through the first week of December, Vernon Jordan organized meetings of members of the transition staff with others who had been involved in prior transitions and administrations. On November 19, he convened a two-and-a-half-hour meeting of some fifteen senior officials of prior Democratic administrations. Among those attending were Theodore Sorensen, Joe Califano, and Richard Moe, Walter Mondale's former chief of staff. In early December, Jordan also held meetings with some of the Republicans who had served as chief of staff—Howard Baker, Ken Duberstein, Donald Rumsfeld, and Richard Cheney—as well as a separate meeting with John Sununu.[92] McLarty, too, once he had agreed to be chief of staff, met with some of his predecessors.

McLarty as Chief of Staff

One piece of advice that emerged from these deliberations was that Clinton needed an honest broker as chief of staff, "not a deputy president with his finger in every policy pie, not someone appearing on all the talk shows," as one participant put it.[93] On December 12, Clinton announced the appointment of someone who appeared to fit the bill: childhood friend Mack McLarty. McLarty was seen as someone who would be the opposite of John Sununu: "A man with no agenda but Bill's agenda," according to one transition staffer.[94]

Clinton had discussed the position with McLarty shortly after the election, but McLarty was not sure he wanted to join the administration. Clinton also may have delayed the appointment until a decision had been made about Christopher, who Clinton apparently considered appointing as chief of staff (according to Stephanopoulos, Bill Moyers had also been under consideration but was not interested).[95] Yet unlike his cabinet appointments, Clinton did not formally interview candidates for the position. And there were also reports that Clinton had toyed with the idea of not even appointing a chief of staff.[96]

McLarty appeared to fit the neutral-broker role that Clinton himself now envisioned for his chief of staff. "If you look at the chiefs of staff who have been successful," Clinton told reporters in announcing McLarty's appointment, "they have been people who have sought to be honest brokers." For his part, McLarty told reporters that he saw his role as a "facilitator," not a "spokesman on public positions."[97] Neither would he act as a gatekeeper for Clinton: "Bill Clinton is obviously a very engaged person. He is going to be deciding what gets to his desk." McLarty's business background indicated he would be able to delegate and that he was attentive to organizational issues. He also valued team-work: "That's become more and more apparent in business," he said in one interview. "You get everyone's ideas and you discuss them honestly and candidly and not in a confrontational or negative way. When you have an accurate picture, you move on, make a decision, build a consensus to support that decision, implement it and later follow up. If you find you have made a mistake, admit it and fix it."[98]

McLarty's vision of the role seemed suited—at least in theory—to the position he would hold. Yet he lacked the experience of how it might be successfully applied in the heated political environment of Washington, not a Little Rock corporate boardroom. His long friend-ship with Clinton would be a plus—he was more an equal than a Stephanopoulos or an Ickes—but he had never served with Clinton in any major administrative capacity and thus was not accustomed to Clinton's weaknesses and strengths as a decisionmaker. Clinton, for his part, did not think the Washington component was all that valuable. The problems that chiefs of staff encountered in prior administrations, he told reporters, had been caused by "other issues," not by any lack of familiarity with how Washington worked.[99]

The delay in appointing McLarty would have repercussions. It meant that the chief of staff–designate would have much less time in planning for the new White House staff. It also sent a certain message. As Andrew Card observes, by delaying "they sent the signal early on that they were going to have a weak chief of staff. And that, in turn, in-vited most of the senior White House staffers to believe that they had—and it turned out they did have—unfettered access and undisciplined access to the president. . . . It invited anarchy in the White House."[100] In the view of Anne Wexler, "I have no idea why they waited to pick him. It was a classic mistake; it's the first thing you have to do."[101]

Some Organizational Changes

Although McLarty's appointment was announced on December 12, it would be more than a month before other White House staff positions were finally in place. One cause of delay was fulfilling Clinton's pledge in his campaign book, entitled *Putting People First*, to cut the White House staff by 25 percent. Clinton had recognized that it would be better to make any cuts now rather than force some White House staffers out of their new positions once they had been hired. But like Carter and Reagan before him, Clinton and his advisers found the job of cutting positions easier in theory than in practice. In mid-December, Vernon Jordan had announced that the transition staff was considering transferring the 110-person Office of Drug Control Policy out of the White House to an appropriate department, possibly Justice or Health and Human Services.[102] Other units targeted were the Council on Environmental Quality (a perennial favorite for the ax) and Quayle's Council on Competitiveness; yet both were small fish in terms of employees and budgets. The Council on Competitiveness, for example, had only four permanent employees and relied on detailees from other agencies for most of its operations. Clinton also had considered shifting some of the political affairs slots to the DNC, not unlike the ill-fated arrangement of his Republican predecessor.[103]

By early January, the planned cuts in staff size had now emerged more as an eventual "goal" that might take months to achieve rather than an iron-clad commitment to cut by inauguration day, Stephanopoulos told reporters.[104] And again like Reagan and Carter before him, Clinton had not firmly set out what organizational baseline would be subject to the 25 percent figure. Would it be just the White House Office? If so, the cuts in the Office of Drug Control Policy wouldn't help, since the latter was part of the larger EOP. Would it indeed be the larger EOP? If so, then significant cuts would have to be made, especially in light of the OMB's and the Office of Trade Representative's significant piece of that large organizational pie (some 45 percent of the entire EOP). Or would it be some nebulous "White House staff," in which some units might be included but others (such as the OMB, the trade representative, or the Office of Administration) excluded from the calculation?[105]

Delays in Naming a White House Staff

Clinton's ability to put together the kind of White House staff he wanted, and to do so as soon as possible, was also complicated by several other factors, including Clinton's proclivity to involve himself in the process of selecting appointees. According to the *Washington Post*, both Clintons took an active and direct role in staff appointments, and

Clinton reportedly personally interviewed staff members, asking them how they envisioned their prospective jobs.[106] Earlier in the transition, according to Mark Gearan, "the president-elect wasn't ready to announce the White House staff," and there was "a sense that it would signal who was on the staff prematurely." Yet "it set us back coming into the White House."[107] Several staff members learned of their appointments only days before the start of the new administration.[108]

The commitment to diversity also may have contributed to the delay. According to one report, the perception that they needed more high-level appointees who were female may have especially led to delay in naming the domestic policy staff (Carol Rasco eventually got the job of director of the Domestic Policy Council; see Chapter 8).[109] Another delay was caused by a controversy surrounding Harold Ickes, under consideration as McLarty's deputy. Ickes had been serving as one of Christopher's assistants and had been centrally involved, for a time, in planning the organization of the Clinton White House. Ickes had done the office and organizational design in late December, had even worked out the salary structure, and was the point man in contacting possible candidates.[110] Given his work, it was anticipated he would become McLarty's deputy, according to Mark Gearan. But rumors about his possible appointment generated negative reports regarding his legal work for a hotel employees' union under investigation for mob links as well as questions involving financial dealings in the 1989 mayoral campaign of David Dinkins in New York City. Ickes would be cleared of the charges, but not in time to be named deputy chief of staff.

In the opinion of Mark Gearan, the fact that Ickes was not on board upset the schema for McLarty's own staff. McLarty had wanted two deputies—Ickes and Gearan—and a press person. Not only was Ickes unable to serve; the candidate for the press position decided to remain in Little Rock. Just days before the White House staff was to be announced in mid-January, Ickes bowed out, which left McLarty and Gearan scrambling to redefine McLarty's own staff, "so it changed very quickly toward the end," according to Gearan.[111]

Getting Jobs, Not Thinking About Positions,
Organization, and Process

Clinton's lag in filling top staff positions may also have resulted from what one member of the transition described as excessive "wrangling over who gets in and who does not."[112] According to transition veteran Harrison Wellford, who along with several others had prepared several reports on White House structure and organization during the preelection period and under Kantor's direction, "There was a tremendous amount of jockeying over who would consume the analysis that we prepared, who would interpret it for the president-elect. A lot of us felt that there was more concern about where some of these people were going to end up than there was a true interest in the analysis itself."[113]

According to one transition member, a concern for personnel—who would get positions—quickly eclipsed any real attention as to how those positions might be structured or organized. "It was an odd deal; they got so sucked into personnel stuff that they did not spend enough time as they should have looking at how decisions should be made, what structure they wanted to retain, and how to mold it to their own purposes. . . . Those of us who were cast with trying to make them think through all of this felt fairly frustrated by that process." Two members of the transition with whom this person worked "were regarded by many as the source of the problem. They were so anxious to preserve their access and to screen out others because they were hoping for significant positions for themselves, which they were successful in getting by the way. The price that was paid was a lot of other work wasn't getting done."

Yet in fact the problem went to the very top: "There was a fair amount of interest initially by the president-elect and by McLarty, but very little follow-up. They got so involved over who was going to serve in key positions that . . . the time spent in thinking about the system in which these people were going to work was relatively limited," one transition member observed. The organization of the transition itself may have affected the organization of the White House: "There was never a system set up around the president-elect or the chief of staff to really process the analysis or make sure that there was follow-through on issues that people in that inner circle couldn't possibly answer."

In Bruce Reed's view, the transition's "biggest failure was that it degenerated quickly into an agonizing effort to assemble a cabinet and a White House staff that took too much time. In the end, he was pleased with his team, but there were lots of problems in the choices that didn't pan out."[114]

Another piece of the problem was the absence of much effort to touch base with members of the outgoing administration, often an important source of practical hands-on advice. Wellford specifically recalls that there was no real attempt to interview outgoing members of the various units of the EOP, yet "all of those people . . . have a lot to say." This was in contrast to the Ford-Carter transition, where "we spent a lot of time trying to debrief the key Ford people before they left, and learned a great deal from that."

Nor was there any organized effort to establish transition teams for the EOP as had been done for agencies and departments: "There was almost no work done on the EOP units; as a result everything was delayed tremendously once January 20 came around, which was too bad because those early months are so precious and you don't want to lose time on silly things." In Mark Gearan's recollection, delay in naming the staff was a primary cause: "The lateness of the timing; by the time our folks were named, people had even moved out of the White House by that point."[115]

There were some exceptions. Bruce Reed would later recall meeting with Stu Eizenstat, who had held his position under Carter, as well as talking to David Gergen and Ede Holiday, whose cabinet affairs office coordinated the Domestic and Economic Policy Councils under Bush. One friend in the Bush White House even advised Reed "not to be overwhelmed" and to "make a list of things you want to get done, put it in your desk drawer, and take it out occasionally." Yet Reed also observed that "so few knew what they were going to do that it was hard to focus clearly on how to do it. If everyone had known six weeks earlier, we might have spent that time working together."[116]

All told, in Wellford's view, "I think on the whole there was less attention spent by the president-elect and his chief of staff on White House organizational issues than in any other—certainly than during the Carter and Reagan presidencies. . . . There was never a 'hands-on' strategic approach to getting on top of the office of the presidency." And as a result, he says, "there was a lot of unnecessary stress for the first six months."[117]

In Anne Wexler's view, delay in naming the staff "was a terrible mistake." Ironically, naming a staff early on was one piece of advice that Wexler and some of the other, more experienced hands from earlier administrations had urged months before when Kantor was heading up the transition effort before the election. According to Wexler, "The first two things that we have always recommended is: number one, pick your White House staff early; and number two, start your personnel process. Neither was done. . . . The White House is the pivot for everything else so that it is critically important to do that first, because everything radiates from there."[118]

A Staff Is Finally Unveiled

On January 14, six days before he was to take office, Clinton finally unveiled his White House staff. Save for the appointment of Mark Gearan as McLarty's deputy chief of staff, there were few surprises. A large number had worked on the campaign, including Stephanopoulos, who was tapped as communications director, Dee Dee Myers as press secretary, Bruce Reed as Rasco's deputy, Alexis Herman as director of public liaison, Rahm Emanuel as director of political affairs, Christine Varney as secretary to the cabinet, as well as Gearan. Some others had come from longtime Arkansas association with Clinton; these included Bruce Lindsey as personnel director and general-purpose adviser, David Watkins as director of management and administration, and Nancy Hernreich, Clinton's executive assistant during his time as governor, who was in charge of appointments and scheduling. Some had close associations with Hillary Clinton, including Bernard Nussbaum, the White House legal counsel, Vince Foster, Nussbaum's deputy and Mrs. Clinton's former law partner, and Maggie Williams, chief of staff to the First Lady. The only relative newcomer among those named was Howard Paster, who was placed in charge of the congressional liaison unit.

Unlike George Bush, who could draw on associates who had personal connection to him as well as White House experience, the twelve-year hiatus since the last Democratic president, plus Clinton's own "outsider" status, made the task of finding loyalists and those with some Washington experience more of a challenge. Clinton was able to bring in some who had associations with the DLC—such as Bruce Reed—or had served in various legislative staff positions—such as Stephanopoulos—or had experience as Washington lobbyists—such as John Podesta, the White House staff secretary. But for many, working in the White House was their first Washington experience. A few Carter-era figures did find their way into the administration, but mostly on the national security side: Anthony Lake at the NSC and Madeleine Albright at the UN.

Of the three top Arkansans in the administration, only Bruce Lindsey had some Washington experience, having served for a time as an aide to Senator David Pryor. The longest Washington résumé belonged to Howard Paster, who would become one of the earliest casualties of the new administration. As one Clinton associate put it the day after the staff appointments were announced, "It all doesn't add up to enough." According to Burt Solomon, "Clinton's staff is devoid of experienced Washington hands who might sense when he is about to do something he shouldn't. . . . Clinton's likely inner circle includes nobody much older than he is and—unless Vice President Al Gore Jr. is part of it—nobody who has more than a few years of Washington experience."[119] In Mark Gearan's view, while some members of the new staff had worked in the campaign or come to know each other in previous positions, "there wasn't the cohesion of a working staff. It was announced shortly before we started." "Because the Democrats were out of power for twelve years," he states, "no one had served in the White House prior to coming in."[120] This was a view that Bruce Reed shared as well: "We didn't have a deep bench; no wealth of experience. . . . A general problem of the Clinton transition was that the Democrats had been out of power for twelve years. Most of the people joining the White House staff didn't know how it was supposed to work."[121]

In organizational terms, Clinton appointed sixteen of his aides as assistant to the president—more than Bush had selected four years earlier. In so doing, he also returned to the pre-Bush practice of having the directors of public liaison, political affairs, and intergovernmental relations at that level. Clinton substantially expanded the White House communications operation. According to one report, where Marlin Fitzwater and his two deputies handled most press contacts and communications efforts in the Bush administration, "Clinton has what seems to be nine assistant press secretaries, some in the press operation, some in the communications operations. Their offices line both sides of half a floor in the Old Executive Office Building."[122] He also devised a new division of labor in his communications operation; while Stephanopoulos would be director of the office and Myers would serve as press secretary, Stephanopoulos would still be directly involved in daily press briefings. (In the first few months of the new administration, Myers would give the morning briefing, while Stephanopoulos presided in the afternoon.) But Clinton did initially follow Bush's practice of trying to rely more heavily on his party's national committee as a source of political advice. As Bush had placed Atwater at the RNC, Clinton put David Wilhelm in charge of the DNC. Within the Clinton White House, Rahm Emanuel presided over the political affairs office. A former ballet dancer, Emanuel had been chief fund-raiser for both the Clinton campaign and the DNC in 1992, and before that he had served as national campaign director for the Democratic Congressional Campaign Committee. According to one Clinton transition adviser who thought it a mistake for Wilhelm to go to DNC rather than the White House, "I have gone up and down the ladder on this with these guys."[123]

The Vice President and Mrs. Clinton

Clinton had, however, attended early on to one important matter: his relationship to the vice president. By all accounts, Gore and Clinton had developed a strong working relationship following Gore's nomination over the summer. In December, following McLarty's appointment as chief of staff, Clinton met with Gore to determine what role the latter would play in the new administration (McLarty and Roy Neel, Gore's deputy, also attended). Clinton and Gore would have a private lunch together once a week, a practice that Jimmy Carter had started with Walter Mondale. More substantively, Gore would take the lead on policy matters dealing with environmental and telecommunications issues. In foreign affairs, Gore would have responsibility in the area of arms control and serve as cochair of "commissions" dealing with the leaders of Russia, Ukraine, Egypt, and South Africa. In March, Gore was given the responsibility for the administration's reinventing government effort, a kind of consolation prize after Hillary Clinton was given the health-care portfolio and welfare reform was postponed until the second year of the new administration. It proved to be a much better and less controversial assignment.

Gore was also adept at integrating his own staff into White House operations. Gore's chief of staff, Roy Neel, would hold the title of assistant to the president and attend White House and cabinet meetings. Gore also arranged for his national security adviser, Leon Fuerth, to attend NSC and other cabinet-level foreign policy meetings.[124]

The final organizational matter that emerged before the inauguration concerned Hillary Clinton's role in the new administration. Following up on his early (but later downplayed) campaign rhetoric of a two-for-one presidency, Clinton had indicated in December that he wanted his wife to sit in on cabinet meetings and that she would continue to play a central role in developing policy and strategy as she had done during the campaign.[125] The designation of Hillary Clinton as domestic policy adviser had also been considered, then dropped.[126] But on one matter a change was made: on the day after the inauguration, it was announced that Hillary Clinton not only would have offices in the East Wing of the White House—the traditional locale for the First Lady and her staff—but also in the West Wing, which would be her "primary" office. The office-space issue had apparently been under discussion for some time and was reportedly opposed by Vernon Jordan and others involved in the transition.

Hillary Clinton initially sought the quarters on the first floor of the West Wing that the vice president had occupied in recent administrations. It looked like she would get what she wanted, especially since her friend Susan Thomases, according to one report, "had arrogated to herself the role of 'official office space designator' for the new administration."[127] But Al Gore successfully defended his turf. Hillary Clinton persisted and was assigned space on the second floor, as was her chief of staff, Maggie Williams.[128]

Asked why the first lady would be located there, Dee Dee Myers told reporters: "Because the President wanted her to be there to work. She'll be working on a variety of domestic issues. She'll be there with other domestic policy advisers."[129] Hillary Clinton's second-floor office in the West Wing was in direct sight of any domestic policy advisers heading downstairs to see the president. According to one former West Wing occupant, "If you do domestic policy, you have to pass her door on the way anywhere, and anyone on the way to her will pass you."[130]

But Bill Clinton had also made his mark on his White House staff. As one staff member would later put it: "I think it was always Clinton. Clinton was going to have a White House staff he was really comfortable with, so he tended to go with old friends, old associates. It was always Clinton."

* * *

In broad terms, the Clinton transition resembled that of its predecessors. There was a significant preelection effort. The basic organization of the transition once the election was over had policy groups, a personnel operation, and teams to dig into department and agency matters. There was due attention (and then some) to cabinet and subcabinet appointments. There were efforts to develop a policy agenda. And at least eventually, the White House staff fell into place.

Yet in other ways there was much missing. Despite pre- and postelection transition boards and the efforts of Kantor, then Jordan and Christopher (and, overshadowing all, Clinton himself), it was not managed well. The conflicts that had bedeviled Carter in 1976 between the transition and campaign staffs came back to haunt Clinton, despite some recognition of the problems that had emerged twelve years before. As a decisionmaking and management process, the transition lacked a certain organizational order and managerial competence. A changing cast of characters handled personnel and White House matters, conflicts festered, the work product of Kantor's efforts suffered with his fate, deliberations lumbered on without closure, and tasks that needed attention often went wanting while others took too much time and attention.

The development of a political agenda was delayed as it proved difficult to reconcile the different approaches to public policy within the Clinton coalition (particularly on economic matters) and as policies proved more complex and intractable than they had during the campaign—with Clinton all the while pledging to act by inauguration day or in the first hundred days. Early missteps also clouded the policy and political message: gays in the military, the failure to recognize the danger signals marking Zoe Baird's nomination, and the heeding of pressure from various constituency groups that undermined Clinton's commitment as a new kind of Democrat.

With respect to the White House, systematic analysis of its structure and operation dropped from sight, opportunities were lost in bringing appointees up to speed, and almost all of its personnel lacked much Washington and certainly prior White House or even executive-branch experience. Getting staff jobs took priority over thinking about what those jobs might entail as part of the policymaking process.

Most markedly, the transition is revealing about Clinton himself. It was he, in the end, who was lax about the need to manage this crucial process. It was he who had difficulty, ultimately, in reconciling policy priorities. It was he who thought the White House staff did not need much thought or analysis and would "fall in place," while other activities, such as filling the cabinet, were regarded as more important. At one level, it is indicative that people rather than processes mattered to him. At another, it offered a venue for his own deliberative style to powerfully come to the fore: endless meetings, delays, personal comfort, a need to try to satisfy all, and a president-to-be too much in the thick of things.

There were problems in recognizing the need to manage and to begin to put in place processes, not just people, for making decisions, surely a problem for the transition in its own right. But, more important, what was the impact once this administration and president were in office?

Notes

1. B. Drummond Ayres, "In Little Rock, a Group Plans for a Transition in Washington," *New York Times,* September 19, 1992.

2. Burke interview with John Hart, April 12, 1999.

3. Gerald Stern, a Los Angeles lawyer and friend of Kantor, directed day-to-day operations of the transition group, and he was assisted by John Hart, who had moved over from the campaign a few weeks after the convention.

4. As election day approached, Clinton added another member to the five-person board: Thomas "Mack" McLarty, the CEO of Arkla Gas and another Clinton friend, with an association that stretched back to their days as kindergarten mates in Hope, Arkansas. McLarty was appointed at Clinton's explicit direction: "I think he wanted someone who would be his voice at the table," one campaign official noted. "All the other folks have made contributions to the campaign but are sort of political acquaintances or people who are close to Mickey [Kantor]." Ruth Marcus and Edward Walsh, "A Call for a 'New Patriotism,'" *Washington Post*, November 4, 1992.

5. Burke interview with John Hart, April 12, 1999.

6. Burke interview with John Hart, April 12, 1999.

7. Barton Gellman and Dan Balz, "Clinton Transition Team Ready to Hit the Ground Running," *New York Times*, October 29, 1992; A. L. May, "Who Would Get Top Jobs If Clinton Wins Election?" *Atlanta Constitution*, October 25, 1992.

8. The campaign effort was directed by David Wilhelm, campaign manager; James Carville, chief campaign strategist and head of day-to-day operations; Mandy Grunwald, media consultant; Bruce Reed, issues director; George Stephanopoulos, communications directorl Dee Dee Myers, traveling press secretary,l Susan Thomases, chief schedulerl and Betsey Wright, research director and Clinton's former chief of staff.

9. Michael Kelly, "The Winners Shift Gears: What Now?" *New York Times*, November 5, 1992.

10. Ruth Marcus and Al Kamen, "Clinton Names Transition Chiefs," *Washington Post*, November 7, 1992.

11. Dan Balz, "Clinton Sidestepped Planners in Decision on Team Leaders," *Washington Post*, November 8, 1992. One decision that was made was to have two transition offices, one in Little Rock and one in Washington. The issue had been discussed by Kantor's group during the preelection period, and one piece of advice they received from their counterparts in the 1980 Reagan transition was to make sure that the president-elect's home base be formally and officially designated as part of the transition operation with the GSA. Burke interview with John Hart, April 12, 1999. Initially, Clinton planners had notified GSA that they would require space for six hundred staff members in Washington. But following the election, they told GSA they planned to keep seventy-five staff members in Little Rock and send "substantially less" than six hundred to Washington. The decision to have two transition operations was in part determined by Clinton's need to remain in Arkansas and wrap up affairs as sitting governor. Both transition staffs would be funded by $3.5 million allocated by Congress, the same amount that Bush received in 1988. Matt Marshall, "Musical Chairs in the Seat of Power," *Los Angeles Times*, November 10, 1992.

12. Gwen Ifill, "Clinton May Quickly Name Transition Chief in Effort to End Dispute Within Staff," *New York Times,* November 6, 1992. Kantor also faced ethical questions—stemming from meetings that his law partner, Charles Manatt, had held with corporate clients (one of which Kantor apparently had attended) in the months before the election. Concerns were raised, too, that he would bring a large number of fellow Californians on board the new administration. According to one Clinton supporter in California, "Kantor was pulling a big train loaded with people out of California and that hurt." James Barnes, "Changing of the Guard," *National Journal,* November 21, 1992, p. 2677.

13. Dan Balz, "Clinton Sidestepped Planners in Decision on Team Leaders," *Washington Post,* November 8, 1992. Several Clinton aides particularly "objected to Kantor's style and presumption. Clinton's mind was made up when Hillary agreed with him to deny Kantor the transition chairmanship and give him a mere seat on the transition board." Brummett, *Highwire,* p. 211. For his part, Kantor "felt betrayed" and was "devastated" by Clinton's decision, according to Webb Hubbell, one of Hillary Clinton's law partners who had befriended Kantor and who had housed the latter at his Little Rock home. "He felt these stories had been planted by people in the campaign. . . . He felt that George Stephanopoulos and his staff were behind it." In Hubbell's view, Kantor "was forced out in a palace coup." Hubbell, *Friends in High Places,* pp. 166–167.

14. Clinton considered asking McLarty to head the operation and then become White House chief of staff. But McLarty had not yet decided whether he would leave his lucrative position at Arkla and join Clinton in Washington. Brummett, *Highwire,* p. 211.

15. Christopher, *In the Stream of History,* p. 5.

16. Burke interview with Al From, March 10, 1999.

17. Thomas Friedman, "Change of Tone for Clinton: High Energy to Low Profile," *New York Times,* November 11, 1992.

18. Herman was deputy director of the Democratic National Committee, while Gearan had been deputy director of the Democratic Governors' Association. Harold Ickes, Maria Echeveste, Rodney Slater, and John Hart were appointed assistants to Christopher. Ickes, a prominent liberal activist and Jesse Jackson's 1988 campaign manager, had managed the Democratic convention, Echeveste had worked in the campaign's political department, Slater was deputy campaign manager, and Hart had been delegate director for the campaign. Hart was one of the few holdovers from Kantor's preelection operation. Two long-serving Clinton aides, Susan Thomases and Betsey Wright, were named to head, respectively, scheduling and public outreach. Two new members were added to the transition board: Anne Donnally, the director of the National Committee for the Prevention of Child Abuse, and Doris Matsui, an advocate for women's health issues and the wife of Congressman Robert Matsui, a Democrat from California.

19. Other top transition aides included Jan Piercy, a Chicago banker and classmate-friend of Hillary Clinton, placed in charge of personnel. David Wilhelm, the campaign's manager, was tapped to head the political affairs operation,

while Susan Brophy, who ran the Washington campaign office and was a former chief of staff to Senator Tim Wirth of Colorado, was given congressional relations.

20. Burke interview with Mark Gearan, March 3, 1999.

21. Burke interview with Al From, March 10, 1999.

22. Burke interview with Mark Gearan, March 3, 1999.

23. The teams that were created also faced delay. It was not until November 25—two weeks after Clinton's announcement about transition matters—that they were finally unveiled. Furthermore, with one exception, the "cluster coordinators" of the nine groups that were created were not the same people who would head the various issue teams (their appointments had been announced on November 12). The exception was Sandy Berger, who was placed in charge of the policy team for national security issues and the cluster working with the various foreign policy and national security departments and agencies. By late November, only the national security team was up and running.

24. Burke interview with Mark Gearan, March 3, 1999.

25. Burke interview with John Hart, April 12, 1999.

26. In appointing the three, Clinton passed over three aides who had directed policy in each of these areas during the campaign: Bruce Reed (domestic policy), Gene Sperling (economic policy), and Nancy Soderberg (foreign policy). Reed, Sperling, and Soderberg, however, were appointed as deputies to From, Reich, and Berger in their respective areas.

27. As it turned out, From remained at the DLC (a wish that he made known to Clinton at the start of the transition), while Reed, who had been issues director in the campaign, became deputy assistant for domestic policy under Carol Rasco, another Hillary Clinton associate. William Galston, a professor of political science at Maryland and a DLC academic favorite, was also placed on the domestic policy staff. Another key DLC representative was Elaine Kamarck, an expert on welfare reform, who joined Al Gore's staff and would head up his reinventing government task force. In Kamarck's view, it was not that the New Democrats were shunted aside but that "we realized—the DLC—with a sudden sort of gasp that we didn't have enough people as part of our movement to fill a lot of these jobs." The twelve-year hiatus in Democratic control of the White House was also a factor: "When you are out of power for so long, there are not a lot of people who have governmental experience. So a lot of these jobs ended up going to people who had governmental experience, but in fact who weren't necessarily New Democrats." When all was said and done, "We just didn't have the [DLC] horses." Burke interview with Elaine Kamarck, February 9, 1999. Yet while Al From would later agree that DLC staffers and policy specialists were in short supply at the White House, there was significant DLC presence in the cabinet—Bentsen at Treasury, Riley at Education, Espy at Agriculture, Babbitt at Interior, Panetta at the OMB, Dalton and Caldera (secretaries of the navy and army), and several others in sub-cabinet positions. According to From, just about every person from the DLC or the Progressive Policy Institute (the DLC's think-tank) who wanted to serve in the new administration did. Burke interview with Al From, March 10, 1999.

28. On November 13, George Stephanopoulos told reporters that the rules did not apply to Vernon Jordan, who served in several corporate directorships and whose law firm, Akin, Gump, and Strauss, handled important clients doing business with the federal government. Jordan was particularly under fire for his service on the board of tobacco giant RJR Nabisco, for which he was paid $50,000 per year; also, he reportedly held more than 30,000 shares of company stock. Asked whether Jordan would decline to participate in selecting a new U.S. surgeon general as several antismoking groups had publicly suggested, Stephanopoulos demurred and said Jordan had agreed not to attend any board meetings during the transition and that his role in such matters was merely advisory: "The governor's making the decisions," he told reporters. Within a week, Jordan announced that he was taking leaves of absence from his law firm and several corporate boards. At the same press conference, Stephanopoulos noted that Mack McLarty's role as chairman of Arkla would not necessarily bar him from involvement in selecting a new energy secretary. "It would depend on the level of discussion," according to Stephanopoulos. McLarty did eventually disqualify himself from savings-and-loan issues, since he had a financial interest in one such company involved in a dispute with regulators. But he didn't disqualify himself from energy-related areas. As for Christopher, would he be barred from discussing policies that may have bearing on clients of his law firm, which included Lockheed, United Airlines, Occidental Petroleum, and IBM? Not at all, Stephanopoulos replied; the connection was too tenuous, and Christopher was no longer involved in his firm's daily affairs. Another problem developed with the new regulations: they disadvantaged smaller labor unions and employers. Reports indicated that the six-month ban on lobbying by transition officials hit here especially hard because smaller entities often do not have separate legal and lobbying units. This problem surfaced in the transition group for transportation; several prospective members were officials of smaller, more specialized unions and whose members were exclusively airline employees, so they could not serve. Viveca Novak, "Changing of the Guard," *National Journal,* January 16, 1993, p. 141.

29. By early December, Clinton was still finding it difficult to formulate ethics rules for officials in the new administration. He had not yet decided what level of officials the rules would apply to, what time frame the restrictions would encompass, and what definition of "lobbying" would apply. It was not until December 9—the day before his first major round of appointments was announced—that Clinton finalized the new rules. They included a five-year ban on lobbying (up from one year), a lifetime ban on registration as a foreign agent (up from one year); and a five-year ban on involvement in trade negotiations for those in that area (essentially up from three years). The rules applied to some seven hundred officials requiring confirmation, as well as those with salaries of more that $104,000—some 1,100 people total.

30. There was, however, the usual media speculation about possible nominees. *New Republic* began a weekly feature called the "Hit List" naming those whom the editors thought unfit for positions. Included were Mickey Kantor, Congressman Lee Hamilton of Indiana, and Robert Reich. Johnetta Cole, who

headed one of the transition teams, came under particular attack from conservative groups, who argued she was an extremist and supported communist dictatorships in Cuba and Grenada. John Young, president of Hewlett Packard and a prospective commerce secretary, was criticized for the presence of his firm's technology at Iraqi military installations after the Gulf War.

31. Dan Balz, "Picking the Clinton Cabinet," *Washington Post Magazine,* May 9, 1993, p. 8.

32. Drew, *On the Edge,* p. 22.

33. Gwen Ifill, "Clinton's High-Stakes Shuffle to Get the Right Cabinet Mix," *New York Times,* December 21, 1992.

34. Drew, *On the Edge,* p. 28.

35. By most measures, it was a mainstream group drawn from Congress (Panetta and Bentsen were both committee chairs—House budget and Senate finance, respectively—while Rivlin had been director of the Congressional Budget Office) and Wall Street (Rubin was Goldman, Sachs cochairman, and Altman was a New York investment banker). It also had a decided policy cast to it: Panetta, Rivlin, and Altman were regarded as deficit hawks.

36. Shalala was the chancellor of the University of Wisconsin and a close associate of Hillary Clinton from their work at the Children's Defense Fund. Shalala's appointment was taken as a sign of Hillary Clinton's role and influence in the selection process, although transition officials denied Shalala's job had been hers to fill. When she was introduced, Shalala thanked both of the Clintons.

37. Although Clinton had considered others for State—including Colin Powell and Senator Sam Nunn—the choice of Christopher came as no surprise. Secretary of defense proved more difficult. Powell was again considered, as was Congressman David McCurdy of Oklahoma. Sam Nunn was again a leading candidate, but he told Clinton he already had enough involvement in defense matters and wanted to do other things.

38. Browner's name had been suggested by Al Gore (she had served on his Senate staff). Her selection was taken as a sign of Gore's influence within the Clinton inner circles as well as the influence he might have on environmental issues, a long-standing interest. Gore also prevailed in naming another member of his staff—Kathleen McGinty—to a top White House position dealing with environmental matters.

39. Colorado Senator Tim Wirth's name surfaced for two departments—Energy and Interior. Although Wirth, who was leaving the Senate, preferred Interior, he was widely touted—and himself expected—to be named energy secretary. Yet Wirth's possible appointment drew criticism from some of his Senate colleagues, Democrats as well as Republicans, and he was not popular with some energy-industry executives. Hazel O'Leary's name came up at the last minute (she was brought to Clinton's attention by a business acquaintance at a reception), and she was flown to Little Rock the next day. O'Leary, an African American, had both public- and private-sector experience; she had served in the Energy Department during the Carter administration and was the vice president of a Minnesota power company. "Hazel just fell out of the sky,"

one transition member said. "They didn't want Wirth to have it, and there was no one else outstanding. She was the closest thing to an affirmative action selection." Drew, *On the Edge,* p. 30.

40. Having lost Wirth for the Energy Department, they were not about to put up with someone they did not want at Interior.

41. Babbitt had been under consideration as U.S. trade representative. With that position freed up, Clinton could finally reward Mickey Kantor with that plum, which also carried cabinet rank.

42. Espy got along very well with Clinton and added to diversity; he beat out three other contenders, Congressman Dan Glickman of Kansas (who would eventually succeed him), George Sinner, the former governor of North Dakota and a Clinton friend, and Ruth Harkin, the wife of Senator Tom Harkin of Iowa. Clinton had even spent time interviewing Sinner as late as December 23, just the day before he announced Espy's appointment. Clinton later told Sinner, "George, I'm sorry. I can't make this work. I've got to go with Congressman Espy." Dan Balz, "Picking the Clinton Cabinet," *Washington Post Magazine,* May 9, 1993, p. 27.

43. Judge Patricia Wald, a federal appeals court judge, was an early favorite, but she turned the job down. Brooksley Born, a Washington lawyer active in women's legal issues, thought she had the job, but her prospective appointment drew criticism.

44. Baird had been under consideration for the White House counsel's office, and a preliminary vetting process had been undertaken. She also had the support of Lloyd Cutler, who worked with her in the legal counsel's office under Carter. Both Clintons knew Baird as well; she was a regular participant in the annual "Renaissance Weekend" held over New Year's at Hilton Head, South Carolina.

45. Drew, *On the Edge,* pp. 32–33.

46. Drew, *On the Edge,* pp. 24–25, 33.

47. David Broder, "Seeds of Cabinet Conflict," *Washington Post,* December 16, 1992.

48. Ruth Marcus, "Clinton Names Riley to Personnel Post," *Washington Post,* November 18, 1992.

49. Stephen Barr, "Transition Momentum Bogs Down at Sub-Cabinet Level," *Washington Post,* January 11, 1993.

50. Gwen Ifill, "Clinton to Summon Economic Leaders to Set Priorities," *New York Times,* November 9, 1992.

51. Burke interview with William Galston, February 22, 1999.

52. "Excerpts from Clinton's Announcement of Appointments to Economic Posts," *New York Times,* December 11, 1992.

53. Thomas Friedman, "Aides Say Clinton Will Swiftly Void GOP Initiatives," *New York Times,* November 6, 1992.

54. He brought in Lawrence Summers, a Harvard economics professor and chief economist of the World Bank, to work on tax policy, health-care costs, and the question of whether a fiscal stimulus package was needed. Laura D'Andrea Tyson, a professor of economics and business administration at

Berkeley, oversaw work on business investments and manufacturing productivity. Derek Shearer, a longtime friend of Clinton and a professor at Occidental College, headed a group working on education and job training. Ira Maraziner, a business entrepreneur and another Clinton friend, was charged with looking at long-term cuts in the budget. Others working with the group included Robert Shapiro, an economist at the Progressive Policy Institute (the DLC think-tank); Robert Rubin, cochairman of the investment banking firm Goldman, Sachs; and Robert Altman.

55. Jacob Weisberg, "Dies Ira," *New Republic,* January 24, 1994, p. 23.

56. Darman, *Who's in Control?,* p. 304.

57. On December 3, Clinton met with Federal Reserve Chairman Alan Greenspan in Little Rock, the first-ever serious conversation between the two. Scheduled for two hours, the conversation extended into the afternoon, with Greenspan stressing the importance of deficit reduction, market confidence, and a need to control inflation and bring down long-term interest rates. "We can do business," Clinton told Gore about his meeting with Greenspan, although Greenspan's message was not good news for Clinton's proposed stimulus package.

58. Woodward, *The Agenda,* pp. 82–92.

59. Burke interview with Al From, March 10, 1999.

60. Robert Pear, "First Lady Gets Office and Job in West Wing," *New York Times,* January 22, 1993.

61. Johnson and Broder, *The System,* p. 111.

62. Johnson and Broder, *The System,* pp. 110–111.

63. Burke interview with Elaine Kamarck, February 9, 1999.

64. Burke interview with William Galston, February 22, 1999.

65. Burke interview with Bruce Reed, June 4, 1999.

66. Burke interview with Al From, March 10, 1999.

67. Burke interview with Al From, March 10, 1999.

68. Burke interview with Bruce Reed, June 4, 1999.

69. Walker, *The President We Deserve,* pp. 165–166.

70. Burke interview with Bruce Reed, June 4, 1999.

71. Stephanopoulos, *All Too Human,* pp. 117–118.

72. Hearings before the Senate began on January 19. Both Baird and her husband wanted to tough it out, in part misled by signals that Clinton thought the nomination would succeed (Baird had told Paster that Clinton had told her—at the Renaissance Weekend over New Year's—that the nomination would be okay). On January 21, the day after Clinton's inauguration, Baird's position was deteriorating, and several key senators came out against her nomination (including Democrats Bennett Johnston and John Breaux of Louisiana and David Boren of Oklahoma and Republican Nancy Landon Kassebaum of Kansas). That evening, Senate Majority Leader George Mitchell and Senator Biden phoned Clinton and told him the nomination was dead ("Oh, God," was Clinton's reported response). A deal was then worked out with Baird. Baird might be given a job with the Clinton administration down the road (she eventually was appointed to the president's Foreign Intelligence Advisory Board),

and Aetna would hire her back. Letters of withdrawal and acceptance were faxed back and forth, and finally, at 12:42 A.M., wording was agreed upon and Baird withdrew her name. Clinton had suffered a major setback only two days into his presidency. Drew, *On the Edge*, p. 38.

73. Al Kamen, "Until the Nanny Flap, FBI Hadn't a Clue," *Washington Post*, April 20, 1993.

74. Clinton had, in fact, been told of the dangers involved. In August 1992, Senator Sam Nunn, an opponent of the proposal, met with Clinton to warn him of the opposition that was likely to develop and that, in Nunn's view, lifting the ban "was a real mistake." Robin Toner, "Respected but Sometimes Unpopular, Nunn Relishes Pivotal Advisory Role," *New York Times*, October 12, 1993.

75. Burke interview with Bruce Reed, June 4, 1999.

76. Tom Mathews, "Clinton's Growing Pains," *Newsweek*, May 3, 1993.

77. Indeed, there is some evidence that Holum never even met with Clinton to discuss his report. Brummett, *Highwire*, p. 61.

78. Michael Duffy, "Obstacle Course," *Time*, February 8, 1993.

79. Stephanopoulos, *All Too Human*, p. 125.

80. Yeager, *Trailblazers*, p. 205.

81. Powell was described as being particularly "emotional about this" and unpersuaded that an executive order lifting the ban on gays was in any way parallel to Truman's 1948 executive order ending racial segregation in the armed forces. Drew, *On the Edge*, p. 46.

82. Aspin's efforts were made difficult by a memo, written by two staff members, emphasizing that he should take a "no negotiation" position with the military. The memo had been left on a computer hard-drive system that was widely accessible in the Pentagon (and evidently even to Nunn's Senate Armed Services Committee), and it was leaked to the press. A reporter confronted Aspin with the memo on the Sunday-morning TV show *Face the Nation* following the inauguration. Aspin, who had been trying to establish a better dialogue with the Joint Chiefs over the issue, was blindsided, and it made his efforts look like a sham. According to *Newsweek*, "Powell and the chiefs felt betrayed. They were furious." Tom Mathews, "Clinton's Growing Pains," *Newsweek*, May 3, 1993. The leaked memo also infuriated Senator Nunn, who did not like its content or tone. Brummett, *Highwire*, p. 59.

83. Burt Solomon, "In Juggling the Tough Ones, Clinton Picks Pragmatism Over Principles," *National Journal*, July 24, 1993, p. 1884.

84. Drew, *On the Edge*, p. 48.

85. Steven Myers, "Gay Group's Study Finds Military Harassment Rising," *New York Times*, March 15, 1999. According to a Pentagon study, the military discharged 1,145 gays and lesbians in FY 1998, a 13 percent increase from the year before and "nearly double the number in 1993, the year before the policy took effect."

86. Gwen Ifill, "Clinton to Summon Economic Leaders to Set Priorities," *New York Times*, November 9, 1992.

87. Christopher, *In the Stream of History*, p. 7.

88. Burke interview with Andrew Card Jr., September 17, 1998.

89. On November 18, the same day that Clinton met with Bush for the now traditional meeting between the president and president-elect, Card, Untermeyer, and Robert Zoellick (of Jim Baker's staff) met with Jordan, Christopher, Gearan, and Herman at the White House. The Clinton people were particularly advised about the need to get some aides cleared quickly with the FBI so that FBI reports could be sent to them on potential nominees. The Bush team also talked about the structure of the White House, current ethics rules and regulations, and some of the difficulties they might encounter in the clearance process for potential appointees. According to one participant, members of the Clinton team "asked little." Ann Devroy, "Bush and Clinton Confer on the Transfer of Power," *Washington Post,* November 19, 1992.

90. Burke interview with Mark Gearan, March 3, 1999.

91. Burke interview with Andrew Card Jr., September 17, 1998.

92. Al Kamen, Ann Devroy, and David Broder, "Talking to Those Who Have Been There," *Washington Post,* December 17, 1992.

93. Al Kamen, Ann Devroy, and David Broder, "Talking to Those Who Have Been There," *Washington Post,* December 17, 1992.

94. Ann Devroy, "Clinton Picks Brown for Commerce Post," *Washington Post*, December 13, 1992.

95. Stephanopoulos, *All Too Human,* p. 147.

96. James Barnes, "Changing of the Guard," *National Journal,* December 19, 1992, p. 2900.

97. Burt Solomon, "Playing Majordomo in a Minor Key," *National Journal,* December 19, 1992, p. 2909.

98. Michael Kelly, "Clinton's Chief of Staff Ponders Undefined Post," *New York Times,* December 14, 1992.

99. Ann Devroy, "Clinton Picks Brown for Commerce Post," *Washington Post,* December 13, 1992.

100. Burke interview with Andrew Card Jr., September 17, 1998.

101. Burke interview with Anne Wexler, February 19, 1999.

102. Al Kamen, Bill McAllister, and Thomas Edsall, "Clinton May Relocate the Drug Czar," *Washington Post,* December 15, 1992.

103. Richard Berke, "Advisers Looking Askance at Pledge for 25% Staff Cut," *New York Times,* January 7, 1993.

104. Thomas Friedman, "Clinton Aide Demurs on White House Staff Cuts and Recovery Plan," *New York Times,* January 13, 1993.

105. As John Hart has ably detailed, the eventual cuts presented on February 9 were heavy on symbolism and based on a hefty dose of organizational juggling. The baseline for the cut was based on the figures for election day 1992, according to Hart, "an artificially inflated level because of the tendency to supplement the White House staff during the election campaign." Hart, "President Clinton and the Politics of Symbolism," p. 391. The units subject to the cut were neither simply the White House Office nor the larger EOP, but rather a proposed definition of staff that excluded the OMB and the Office of U.S. Trade Representative but included the White House Office and a variety

of other EOP units. Had the OMB and trade representative staffs been in-cluded, the cuts would have amounted to only 16 percent. Moreover, the White House Office was not deeply affected—it was slated for only a 9 percent cut. The "real cuts" came through the proposed elimination of the National Space Council, the Council on Environmental Quality, deep cuts in the Office of National Drug Control Policy, and significant cuts in the National Security Council and the Office of Administration. The Office of Policy Development, home to many of the president's domestic policy advisers, actually saw its proposed size increased by one employee. Hart, "President Clinton and the Politics of Symbolism: Cutting the White House Staff," pp. 385–403.

106. Ruth Marcus, "Campaign Veterans, Washington Hands," *Washington Post,* January 15, 1993.

107. Burke interview with Mark Gearan, March 3, 1999.

108. William Galston's experience in getting hired offers an interesting window through which to view the process. Galston had been working on two issue task forces and had finished work by late December. At that point, he was ready to return to the University of Maryland for the upcoming semester; books had already been ordered, students had signed up for his courses, and syllabi had been typed. Around January 10, he recalls that "the phone rang, it was Harold Ickes, whom I knew from previous presidential campaigns. I had usually met him on the field of presidential combat, usually on the other side." He told Galston to come down to Little Rock immediately. "I said, 'Can you tell me why?' He said, in effect, 'We will tell you when you get here.'" According to Galston, "He didn't have the sound of someone delivering some-one else's message; but he never does." Once in Little Rock, Galston met with Carol Rasco and was offered the position as her deputy. "It wasn't until the second week in January, just a few days before the Clinton gang broke camp in Little Rock and headed to Washington, and I was really stunned [by the offer]." Burke interview with William Galston, February 22, 1999. John Hart (who had been part of Kantor's preelection group, served as an assistant to Christopher after the election and then moved over to work with McLarty once he was designated as chief of staff) recalls that his job offer came only a day or so before the inauguration as he was flying from Little Rock to Washing-ton on McLarty's private plane. McLarty asked him what he wanted to do, and Hart, sensing the new administration's likely efforts to take state- and local-government initiatives seriously, replied that he was interested in intergovern-mental affairs. Hart was then hired as a special assistant in that White House unit. Burke interview with John Hart, April 12, 1999.

109. Rasco had served on Clinton's gubernatorial staff and had come to know Hillary Clinton through working in an advocacy group on children's and family issues that the latter had founded in Little Rock. Richard Berke, "Ad-visers Looking Askance at Pledge for 25% Staff Cut," *New York Times,* Janu-ary 7, 1993.

110. Burke interview with Mark Gearan, March 3, 1999; Burke interview with William Galston, February 22, 1999.

111. Burke interview with Mark Gearan, March 3, 1999.

112. Richard Berke, "Advisers Looking Askance at Pledge for 25% Staff Cut," *New York Times,* January 7, 1993.

113. Burke interview with Harrison Wellford, July 24, 1998.

114. Burke interview with Bruce Reed, June 4, 1999.

115. Burke interview with Mark Gearan, March 3, 1999.

116. Burke interview with Bruce Reed, June 4, 1999.

117. Burke interview with Harrison Wellford, July 24, 1998.

118. Burke interview with Anne Wexler, February 19, 1999.

119. Burt Solomon, "Sizing Up the Company Clinton Keeps," *National Journal,* January 23, 1993, p. 210.

120. Burke interview with Mark Gearan, March 3, 1999.

121. Burke interview with Bruce Reed, June 4, 1999.

122. Ann Devroy, "Where Proximity Prevails Over Perks," *Washington Post,* February 5, 1993.

123. James Barnes, "Don't Sweep Politics into a Corner," *National Journal,* January 2, 1993, p. 40.

124. The connection between the Gore loyalists and the Clinton White House would prove unusually strong. Not only would Neel become McLarty's deputy in May; others, such as Bruce Reed, Franklin Raines (who would become OMB director in Clinton's second term), Jack Quinn (who would succeed Neel as Gore's chief of staff, then move to the White House counsel position), and Thurgood Marshall Jr., had worked for Gore in the past or served on his vice presidential staff before moving on to White House positions. Erskine Bowles, who would serve as Leon Panetta's deputy before becoming chief of staff himself, was a supporter during Gore's ill-fated 1988 bid for the presidency and a Gore delegate from North Carolina at the Democratic National Convention that year. Zelnick, *Gore,* pp. 229–230.

125. Gwen Ifill, "Clinton Wants Wife at Cabinet Table," *New York Times,* December 19, 1992.

126. Drew, *On the Edge,* pp. 22–23.

127. Zelnick, *Gore,* p. 230.

128. Drew, *On the Edge,* p. 23.

129. Robert Pear, "First Lady Gets Office and Job in West Wing," *New York Times,* January 22, 1993.

130. Ann Devroy, "Where Proximity Prevails Over Perks," *Washington Post,* February 5, 1993.

8

Clinton in Office

Let us now turn to the relationship between the Clinton transition and the new administration's organization, decision processes, and policy outcomes. Clinton's late start in staffing his White House and the lack of much attention during the transition to its operations are perhaps the most obvious legacies of the transition. Clinton aides quickly realized that they were unprepared for the task ahead. Even the Clintons would come to recognize that the delay in attending to the White House staff during the transition was a major source of their ensuing problems. As Elizabeth Drew notes, "He and Mrs. Clinton had both said that choosing the staff six days before the first Inauguration, having spent most of the transition time on selecting the Cabinet, was their biggest mistake of the first term."[1]

Yet problems stemming from the delay in naming a White House staff may not have been the only matters affected by the transition. Would Mack McLarty's appointment as chief of staff, his business background, and his close association with Clinton bring the discipline and order needed to make the staff—and Clinton himself—operate effectively? Could McLarty compensate for his lack of Washington experience? Did his conception of the neutral-broker role fit the challenges he faced?

In terms of other parts of the decisionmaking process, at least one, more formal policy structure (the National Economic Council) had been crafted during that period. Did it bring, as might be expected, coherence and order to economic policymaking, especially compared to the Domestic Policy Council, which during the transition had not received similar attention?

One would also expect President Clinton, as he had during the transition, to play a personal and unusually large role in the policy deliberations of his administration given their fluidity and lack of much organizational definition. Did his own considerable political skills and propensity to enmesh himself in policy details overcome any weaknesses in the organization around him? Or, as during the transition, did they tend to exacerbate the problem?

Finally, with respect to policy outcomes, given the lack of attention to matters relating to decisionmaking particularly that might foster its effectiveness, do we find, as might be anticipated, an unusually high degree of problems in the decisions and policy outcomes issuing from these processes? Planning a policy agenda had proven more difficult than anticipated during the transition. Was there still time? Could programs be prioritized? Would the distractions of gays in the military and the Zoe Baird nomination pass? Could Clinton and his advisers finally fashion an economic program and devise a strategy that would gain congressional assent?

Decisionmaking Processes

Economic and Domestic Policy Organization: NEC and DPC

Given Clinton's aim during the transition of revitalizing economic policymaking, one would expect that the proposed National Economic Council would have significant impact on the new administration's policy processes. Indeed, at one level, that occurred: its creation by executive order on January 25 was one of Clinton's first orders of business. The NEC included eighteen members (eight of whom were departmental secretaries), as well as any others that the president might choose to designate as members. Despite the transition hype, however, its purpose was not all that different from the sundry economic policy councils that had existed under Bush, Reagan, and, even earlier, Ford. The one significant change was that its meetings (in the absence of the president) were to be chaired by the assistant to the president for economic policy, New York investment banker Robert Rubin, rather than by the secretary of the treasury, as had been the case under Reagan and then Bush.

Hopes for the NEC's success were high, and the choice of Rubin proved to be among the wisest appointments Clinton made. According to one White House staff member, "Rubin saw the NEC as a real forum for cabinet-level decisionmaking. It was not infrequent to have the cabinet officers at the table."[2] Yet Rubin quickly found the formal group sometimes unwieldy for some tasks and so often broke policy sessions up into smaller working groups and task forces. During the budget battle with Congress, Rubin created a "core" group to handle issues, while trade policy and negotiations with Congress over NAFTA were handled by working groups under the direction of two Rubin deputies, Bowman Cutter and Robert Kyle.[3]

Rubin was a strong voice for deficit reduction when economic policy was discussed at the highest levels of the administration, and his advocacy would prevail over the advice of those, such as Robert Reich and Laura D'Andrea Tyson, who were in favor of a "human investment" strategy. But within the NEC, Rubin was regarded as an honest broker during its deliberations. According to William Galston of the domestic policy staff, "I think he . . . created an arena within which individuals can speak their minds and make their points with a minimum of ego-jostling. I have never seen the least hint of intimidation."[4]

However, promise did not always match performance, and the NEC did not quite evolve into the policymaking body that had been initially touted. In a 1997 study, the Council for Excellence in Government noted that a fundamental issue surrounding the effectiveness of the NEC as Clinton began his second term was "whether the NEC is to come fully into its own as the central economic policy arena of the administration," or whether it continues to be "vulnerable to activity by strong administration players whose operations outside the NEC structure have often had the blessing or tacit consent of the president."[5] By June 1993, *National Journal* noted that "an early criticism of the NEC is that its operating style involves endless meetings with few conclusions."[6]

Although one might regard these observations as indicators of a transition idea that didn't fully pan out, they might also suggest the effects of the transition at another level: the fate of a more formal policymaking body caught within a decisionmaking process that was informal, ad hoc, and largely unplanned from the start. Endless meetings, for example, would prove to be something of a hallmark for the decisionmaking processes of this presidency. Vulnerability to displacement by the president and informal groups of advisers was also common. The fact that Rubin did as well as he did was no small matter.

The other organizational unit likely to be centrally involved in Clinton's policy development was the Domestic Policy Council. Like the NEC, its membership was large—twenty-three formally designated members, including twelve of fourteen cabinet departments; only State and Defense were formally excluded. And like the NEC, the assistant to the president for domestic policy was designated as the DPC chair in the absence of the president.

Yet unlike in the NEC, little attention was paid to the organization of domestic policy advice during the transition. In fact, it was not until August 17, 1993, that Clinton issued the executive order mandating the DPC's establishment. Asked about the delay in formally creating the council, one White House aide said that "it doesn't have any policy impact, so we weren't worrying about it."[7]

According to one DPC staff member, the "DPC had a prior existence [in other administrations], so it didn't need to be constituted in quite the same way, whereas the NEC would not have come into existence without an affirmative act." Yet that same staffer also recalled that

> it was clear to me from day one that NEC was hitting the ground running in ways in which the DPC was not. It was as though the NEC had been defined affirmatively, while the DPC had been defined negatively, as the residuum of what the NEC was not supposed to deal with. It may also have been an artifact of the shape of the agenda during that period, which was so strongly tilted toward macroeconomic policy.

Carol Rasco, the staff member charged with coordinating the DPC, was, like Rubin, widely regarded as an honest broker. Yet she brought to the table a different package of skills and experiences. She had worked on Clinton's gubernatorial staff and might have been more accustomed to his work habits, but she lacked Rubin's independent stature and visibility. Rasco more closely reflected the president's domestic agenda, one staff member would later reflect, particularly Clinton's "concern for children, empowerment, and letting the states innovate." Rasco's interest in devolving some policies down to the states "mirrored Clinton's own experience" and "was a useful barrier against the tendency of Washingtonians who like to centralize everything in the federal government."[8]

Not surprisingly, Rasco's operation differed markedly from Rubin's. "Cabinet-level meetings were much rarer," and "she saw herself more as staffing the president directly." Bruce Reed and William Galston, her deputies, were particularly influential participants, and there was more of a White House–centered and directed policy process than was the case with the NEC. Early on and at Rasco's direction, Reed and Galston—who had known each other through the Democratic Leadership Council—divided up the domestic policy agenda, with

Reed taking crime, welfare, and reinventing government, while Galston focused on education, job training, and family issues.[9] Neither, however, operated independently in setting the Clinton agenda; according to Galston, "Especially during the first two years, our agenda was almost entirely set by very high level presidential decisions and by the legislative calendar."[10]

Still another difference between the NEC and DPC was that the latter was more ad hoc in its procedures. One staff member later recalled little in the way of prior organizational planning, particularly any reports about the organization of the DPC that had been produced during the transition. One difficulty that William Galston remembered was the absence of a formal mechanism, early on, for adjudicating disputes among departments or between a department and the White House. But Galston cautions that much of their work focused on a particular department unlike the broader economic and budgetary concerns of the NEC that regularly crossed departmental boundaries, thus making any dispute-resolution mechanism less needed.

When disagreements did arise, Galston would create ad hoc groups: "But I invented those processes for myself." Reed and Galston also instituted, early on, a kind of early warning system on domestic matters by creating "a deputies meeting where the deputy secretaries would be invited to the White House twice a month; at least that was the formal schedule." Although at times it was a "show-and-tell operation," according to Galston, "on more than one occasion I became aware of complex jurisdictional questions that would have to be addressed through task forces that I would then construct on an ad hoc basis. We would work until there was some sort of consensus or until it was clear that one wasn't going to be reached."[11] The meetings might also alert the DPC staff members about problems with a particular department: "Sometimes we became aware of questions that would have to be resolved on a bilateral basis; that is, the DPC working with a particular department to coordinate the department's efforts with the president's objectives."[12]

Another difference between the NEC and the DPC was the intense focus on economic matters during the early months of the new administration. As Galston observes, "You have to understand that, during the first six months, most of that focused on the economic plan." Galston, who shared a West Wing office with Gene Sperling, Rubin's deputy at the NEC, recalls that "Gene spent endless hours with the president during that period. I didn't see [Clinton] very much because the issues that were consuming him were not for the most part the issues that the DPC was working on." "Things changed subsequently," Galston notes, but the period where reports of "endless meetings" appeared in the press "was also the period that economic issues dominated." Yet Galston did not feel cut off:

> I dealt with the president principally through memoranda. Early on, I gained a reputation as someone who could write good and balanced memoranda. I had virtually unimpeded access to the president via that route. That was plenty. It was better than "face time" because working hard at the memoranda I could lay out exactly what I wanted to say, very briefly, and present the issues cleanly to the president. As long as my relations with the staff secretary were good—and I took great care to ensure that they were—I knew that the memoranda would go to the president in a timely fashion and be returned from the president in a timely fashion. So I got everything I needed.

Galston would send his memos through Rasco, but "Carol trusted me in my areas of jurisdiction, so very rarely would she bounce one back."[13]

In terms of what it tells us about the effects of the transition, the operations of the DPC mesh with expectations about a policy body that had not been the focus of much prior attention. Unlike the NEC, it operated more as a traditional policy staff, less deliberative and more directly linked and responsive to the president (not unlike Eizenstat's experience under Carter). Moreover, its procedures and operations developed in a more ad hoc fashion.

What is noteworthy—and here we can perhaps see the effect of the persons chosen rather than processes designed and organized—was that Rasco, Galston, and Reed were able to work out a modus operandi. Reed and Galston, in particular, were able to divide up their policy areas and avoid the competitiveness that can sometimes exist in such an unstructured environment. Their ad hoc arrangements for adjudicating disputes and linking the DPC to agencies and departments also appeared to have worked. But while some of their initiatives would come to fruition—Americorps, a new student-loan program—others, such as welfare reform and a crime bill, would be put on hold. The impact of the DPC would turn on decisions made at higher levels in the Clinton administration.

The Cabinet

Was the cabinet one of those higher levels? Although Clinton had spent considerable effort picking his cabinet, there was no talk of cabinet government or any consideration of its use as a deliberative body—collective or otherwise. To his credit, Clinton avoided Carter's errors of twelve years before. Yet the opportunity was not taken to think about alternative ways of making use of a resource that Clinton had invested such time and effort into assembling.

During his first hundred days as president, Clinton convened his cabinet only three times—the first on January 22, on his second full day as president and largely as a ceremonial occasion, again on February 10, and not again until March 31; only four more meetings were held through 1993. On February 18, 1994, Labor Secretary Reich noted in a diary entry:

> The first cabinet meeting in months. We sit stiffly while [the president] talks about current events as if he were speaking to a group of visiting diplomats. I've been in many meetings with him, but few with the entire cabinet, and it suddenly strikes me that there's absolutely no reason for him . . . to meet with the entire cabinet. Cabinet officers have nothing in common except the first word in our titles. Maybe [the president] is going through the motions because he thinks that presidents are supposed to meet with their cabinets and the public would be disturbed to learn the truth.[14]

At best, cabinet members would make their influence and counsel felt through the NEC, DPC, NSC, or—more likely—through personal interactions with the president and his conception of their place in his decisionmaking. But as Shirley Anne Warshaw notes in her study of Clinton's cabinet, the process proved both time-consuming and self-defeating: "When the working groups failed to define objectives, cabinet officers developed their own objectives to meet departmental needs." Furthermore, collegiality suffered, and as "cabinet members often sought to frame the administration's policy," it generated "bitter disagreements within the cabinet." "Clinton's structure for dealing with his cabinet was as unstructured as every other facet of his leadership style," Warshaw concludes. "There was no regularity to cabinet meetings, no central theme to those meetings, no effort to forge a presidential team within the cabinet."[15]

Other Organizational Changes

Environmental policy also came under organizational scrutiny. In early February, the White House announced two changes. First, the campaign pledge to elevate the Environmental Protection Agency to department status was reiterated; it proved to be an elusive goal. Second, Clinton sought to emphasize the importance of environmental issues within the White House by creating the White House Office on Environmental Policy. The unit, headed by Kathleen McGinty, who had been an environmental adviser to Al Gore since 1990, was designed to replace the Council on Environmental Quality.

But there was less in the announcement than it might seem. Because the CEQ was created by statute, it could not be reorganized by presidential fiat, and it remained as a statutory part of the EOP. McGinty, moreover, was listed in the White House manual as director of environmental policy, but she was appointed at the deputy-assistant level rather than the higher rank of assistant to the president, the rank of most of her counterparts heading Executive Office and major White House units. Here early efforts proved more symbolic than real.

Symbolism and reality were to come together, however, in one of the earliest organizational changes made by the new administration. On January 21, his first working day as president, Clinton terminated the White House Council on Competitiveness, which had been chaired by Vice President Dan Quayle and had been useful to a variety of business interests in circumventing regulatory directives. Quayle's successor, Al Gore, issued a press statement on January 22 that took the council to task for providing "special interests" a "back-door to avoid the law" and serving "as an excuse for special favors for narrow interests and back-room decisions."[16]

White House Staff at Work?

The workings of the Clinton White House staff are an especially useful example for evaluating the effects of the transition. One would not expect an effectively functioning staff system if little thought or effort had gone into its organization and internal workings and if its members had little prior White House experience or even much time to acquaint themselves with its operation.

For George Stephanopoulos, it soon became apparent that "we have to work on our internal decision-making." "If he wants to talk to a lot of people, make sure the work has been done and then he does the deciding. All the backup work has to be done more quickly, more precisely, so that he can get on with decisions."[17] Yet it would be months, if not longer, until the White House staff would begin functioning with some semblance of efficiency and discipline.

Deputy Chief of Staff Mark Gearan likened the staff to a soccer game among ten-year-olds: "No one stuck to his part of the field during a game. The ball—any ball—would come on the field and everyone would go chasing it downfield."[18] Other reports indicated that "there's a campus culture afoot. They call the 18 acres that encompass the White House the 'campus,'" with aides talking about "dorm hours" and "all-nighters."[19]

The language was no surprise; by one account, sixty-three of the 450 staffers were under the age of twenty-four.[20] This did not come without costs: according to another report, Clinton's "youth brigades have turned the Old Executive Office Building into something resembling a college dorm. If they are fresh and idealistic, they can also be insufferably smug. And their tiffs with the national media do little to communicate a levelheaded image."[21]

The few senior aides with Washington experience were preoccupied with their own responsibilities. Anthony Lake, the only senior member who had served in a prior White House, was ensconced at the National Security Council, while Stephanopoulos (who had congressional staff experience) was preoccupied from January until June in heading up the communications operation. Bruce Lindsey, Clinton's closest and most trusted aide (and who had served a stint on a Senate staff), was immersed in personnel matters. According to one account, Lindsey's office was filled with résumés stacked on nearly every available surface. The stacks grew so high that they collapsed of their own weight, scattering paper across the room. "Bruce," according to one staffer, "is in a world of his own."[22]

More than a dozen aides had direct access to the Oval Office (compared to three or four under Bush). According to Bob Woodward, dozens of staffers had "all-access" passes, and "some would come in and sit down in the Roosevelt Room or the Cabinet Room meetings. No one would know who had invited them or whether they had been invited at all. Several became experts at attending any meeting that included the president or Hillary."[23] Since Clinton liked to sit "in the middle of a cacophony of voices and ideas," according to one cabinet member, it meant "that those who have the most time with him have the most influence, so there's a great deal of stampeding around him to have the most time with him."[24] Even as late as June 1994, when he took over as chief of staff from McLarty, Leon Panetta was dismayed to find that, as for access to the Oval Office, "as far as I know, anybody who walked down the hall, walked in." Panetta also recalled that when he asked to be shown an organizational diagram of the staff and its chain of command, none could be found detailing who did what in the Clinton White House: "No one had an organizational chart."[25]

The open-door, freewheeling style of the early Clinton White House was compounded by the numerous Friends of Bill, such as Hollywood producers Harry and Linda Thomason, or, in some cases Friends of Hillary, such as Susan Thomases. In Thomases's case, her photograph was even posted at the Secret Service booth at the northwest gate to the White House. The photo also had printed by it a note that she was to be given access to the second floor of the West Wing, where Hillary Clinton's office was located.[26]

Clinton was also a president who relied heavily on outside consultants to provide not only polling data but also ongoing political advice, and they were paid substantial amounts by the DNC for their White House service. James Carville and Paul Begala's firm received $300,000 a year, Stan Greenberg $25,000 a month (plus additional fees for polls), and Mandy Grunwald $15,000 a month. According to a number of reports, they were involved in a range of policy issues and other White House matters. Such involvement and access led to tensions with those "inside" the White House who thought the consultants were ignorant of governance and the need for political compromise.[27] The amount of money that was spent on polling alone is also revealing. While Bush spent $216,000 on polls in 1989 and 1990, Clinton spent $1,986,410 in 1993 alone.[28]

Relations with the press also began to deteriorate as the weeks wore on. During the transition, a decision was made to reduce press access. It came from the very top: acting under Hillary Clinton's direct orders, Stephanopoulos cut off press access to his office. It was quickly dubbed the "no-fly zone" and was a source of consternation to the White House press corps. In his memoirs, Stephanopoulos notes that the issue came up at his first press conference, and he thought to himself, "I'm not your problem; Hillary is. She and Susan Thomases cooked up this plan to move you to the Old Executive Office Building. . . . Closing the door was our fallback position."[29]

Even something as comparatively simple as the president's day-to-day schedule could not be predicted much in advance. Whereas other administrations planned meetings, speeches, and other appearances weeks and months in advance, it was not until October 22 that Dee Dee Myers could tell the press what Clinton's schedule was going to be a full week ahead of time. The communications staff was also perceived as having a low threshold of tolerance for media criticism and negative stories, as well as suffering from "overspin": "They don't know the difference between truth and lies," one reporter complained.[30]

Cutting the Staff by 25 Percent

Clinton's efforts to cut the size of the White House staff also had consequences on operations. As noted earlier, much of the proposed streamlining that Clinton announced in February involved cuts that were never likely to be achieved (such as the elimination of the CEQ, which required congressional approval) and a selective definition of what constituted the "White House staff" that would be subject to the reductions (both OMB and the trade representative's office were not included). But Clinton did increase the size of the White House intern program to make up for positions that were cut at lower levels of the staff, a move that would have repercussions later in his presidency.

The attempt to move most of the Office of National Drug Control Policy into a line department especially generated controversy. Although the White House contended that the office had become a political dumping ground under Bush, the proposed change generated much criticism and signaled that Clinton was not serious about the drug problem. William Bennett, who had headed the office under Bush, observed that "this obviously has no priority for them."[31] In May, perhaps in response to the criticism, Clinton's new drug czar—Lee Brown, the former police chief of New York City—was granted cabinet status.

Clinton and his advisers also sought to change the permanent White House staff. One move that garnered criticism was the decision to fire twenty career members of the White House correspondence unit, which deals with the millions of letters and telephone calls the White House receives. Many of these workers were older women who had worked for years—some as much as twenty—on the staff. Part of the so-called White House worker bees, these staffers served at the pleasure of the president but lacked any civil-service protection (in order to get their jobs, they sign agreements making them "exempted workers," unprotected by civil-service and other government rules). Unable to move automatically to other parts of the federal government, they were given only two weeks' severance pay and told to check federal job listings. "They never gave us a chance," one worker said. "We are career employees. We are the core of what keeps things moving. Our loyalty is to the presidency, to the institution, to the office and we are not highly paid or get many raises." Other career employees were "terrified that they are going to be next."[32] By June, the mail in the White House had begun to back up. Carts of unopened mail cluttered the Old Executive Office Building, and some were sent to the Navy Yard for storage. The White House had even looked into, but then dropped, the idea of shipping the mail out for mechanical processing.[33]

Despite the staff reductions, observers noted that the White House itself seemed to be more crowded than in the previous administration, with several aides occupying offices that had been assigned to only one person under Bush.[34] In late April, Patsy Thomasson, White House director of administration, was put on the hot seat in the Senate, trying to explain why, with the staff cut 25 percent, the White House was requesting a 7.6 percent increase in funding and a supplemental appropriation of $11.7 million for the current fiscal year. Thomasson was also reported to have difficulty in answering questions about how many "live bodies" actually worked in the White House and how many outside political consultants were employed by the president. "I'm having difficulty reconciling these proposals with press reports indicating that there are people sitting on top of each at the White House," Senator Christopher "Kit" Bond, a Missouri Republican, told her.[35]

McLarty as Chief of Staff

In early May, *Newsweek*'s "Conventional Wisdom" column offered a tongue-in-cheek appraisal of some of the key players in the Clinton White House.[36] Both Stephanopoulos and Myers were targeted: Stephanopoulos—"From wunderkind to Dukakis of the press room. Hint: Smile don't smirk"; Myers—"Token nonbrainiac, not telling us anything either." So, too, were the White House "youngsters"—"Government by all-nighters is getting tired. Go to sleep and get a life"; and Ira Magaziner—"Health-care propeller-head looking for liftoff. But is the prop attached?"

But what was particularly telling was the take on White House Chief of Staff McLarty: "So low-key you can't find him. Real job: 'You have a meeting, Mr. President.'" Although McLarty's corporate experience and professed honest-broker role promised much in December 1992, it quickly became apparent that he did not exercise much control or discipline over the staff system under his direction. Yet that was precisely what was needed. McLarty did not control who saw the president, and neither did he monitor meetings of aides with the president, as other chiefs of staff had done. Rasco and Rubin, for example, spent ten to fifteen minutes each day alone with Clinton to let him know what was developing in domestic and economic policy and get some guidance from him, yet McLarty did not attend.[37] According to Rasco deputy William Galston, "Especially during that early period . . . [McLarty] didn't insert himself on a regular basis between the assistants to the president and the president." Rasco, in fact, "reported directly to the president."[38]

McLarty's morning senior staff meetings devolved into show-and-tell, and sometimes McLarty did not even attend them, letting deputies run them instead.[39] McLarty's chief deputy, Mark Gearan, did not compensate for his boss's weaknesses. According to one account, Gearan was "the only man in the White House who might have been as cordial and courteous as [McLarty] is."[40]

The White House staff lacked "established procedures," as one staff member stated. "There were several instances when people would get together and settle on a policy," only to find it was changed later in the day by other staff members. "That was a really big problem and a fairly chronic problem." It had the effect of making the president and the administration "look confused and all over the place." According to Bruce Reed, "There are infinite appeals on decisions here in the White House. That's what makes life so difficult. You need to keep an eye on everyone to make sure they don't undo the deal you have just forged."[41] "You had to be your own lobbyist and persuade people," he would later recall. "Then you had to loop back and make sure nobody changed their minds."[42]

It would take Leon Panetta's appointment as chief of staff in 1994 to bring more order and discipline, especially among those who thought they could freelance on policy matters. According to one staff member, "People who were accustomed to almost unlimited access to the president found their feathers plucked to some extent." Panetta was also more inclined to have the president's top assistants report through him rather than directly to the president. As William Galston observes, "Leon was somewhat more aggressive in that regard, in part because he had more experience [in] dealing with policy matters."[43]

Although McLarty and Clinton had been boyhood friends and were personally close, McLarty lacked the ability to rein in a president prone to be disorganized in his decisionmaking. As one White House official observed at the time, McLarty is "smart, he's decent, he runs a nice meeting," but "beyond that he has no strategic or political sense. He can't seem to control Clinton—get him to make a decision, end meetings, not keep people waiting."[44] In Robert Reich's view, "Poor Mack [was] unable to impose discipline on a chronically undisciplined president and a chaotic White House staff."[45]

McLarty's initial lack of experience in the ways of Washington was a continuing source of difficulty. It especially affected his relationship with Howard Paster, the chief White House lobbyist with Congress. According to Jeffrey Birnbaum's profile of Paster in his book *Madhouse*, Paster felt that McLarty often let the simplest things go unaccomplished. For several months, Paster had been trying to find some patronage positions for Congressman Steny Hoyer, a powerful Maryland Democrat and Clinton supporter. But Paster's repeated calls and memos to McLarty went unanswered.[46] According to Bob Woodward, "Paster found working with McLarty maddening. McLarty was always cutting deals . . . behind Paster's back." "McLarty, a former CEO, was just not temperamentally suited to being a staff person."[47] In November, Paster resigned.[48]

During the transition, the selection of McLarty met the president's comfort needs. Yet McLarty's actions on the job failed to provide the discipline and organization needed not just for staff members but also for Bill Clinton. His conception of the neutral-broker role did not meet the needs of this particular White House, especially at this crucial point in its early history.

Clinton as Manager and Decisionmaker

The absence of much attention to organizational processes and structure during the transition, plus the particular roles played by the NEC and the DPC as the administration got under way, opened the way for Clinton's own proclivities as a decisionmaker to have an unusually large influence over policy processes and policy choice. While we expect a president to be the ultimate decisionmaker and, at least to some extent, for decisionmaking processes to reflect a president's workways and organizational preferences, in Clinton's case it was almost as if he had stepped into an organizational void in which processes and structures didn't really matter and his own loose style was give free rein. While this certainly suggests the importance of this president as a driving force in understanding the early days of his presidency, it also was a product of the transition itself: few structures or processes with practical effect existed because few had been planned or even contemplated as necessary. What's more, scant attention had been paid to the relationship of staffs and decision processes to the president's needs as a decisionmaker.

Although organizationally the Clinton White House resembled that of his predecessors (save for the addition of the newly created NEC),

Clinton was not a president who saw himself bound by any organizational boxes. Instead, he favored a more fluid, often ad hoc approach to policy issues, drawing on a wide and often changing cast of advisers both in and out of government. Formal titles often offered few clues about who was involved in the process or who held real influence. At the same time, it was a remarkably centralized process, with Clinton deeply and directly enmeshed in day-to-day deliberations and with an unprecedented number of aides having direct access to the president.

Clinton's preferred method was to convene meetings, often lasting for hours, that were freewheeling, open, but often inconclusive in outcome. In fact, this pattern began on day one. According to Stephanopoulos, Clinton and his advisers were up until 4:30 A.M. polishing his inaugural speech. "Our whole team slogged through another all-nighter. Adrenaline and anxiety were fueling Clinton, but the rest of us started to sag. . . . Every few seconds, Gore would jerk awake, then fall back asleep."[49]

In the weeks and months that followed, Clinton's usual reaction to a policy issue or a proposal brought to his attention was, "Let's have them all in and talk about it."[50] On key policy initiatives, advisers were summoned both from within and without the White House, yielding large group sessions that often lacked proper staffing beforehand and constructive discipline as they unfolded. According to Elizabeth Drew, "Harried presidential aides were typically scheduled to attend wall-to-wall meetings—with the President or otherwise—with little time to think." "When the President was in the White House, his top aides knew their schedules were meaningless."[51]

But such an approach fit Clinton's cognitive style. According to one aide, "Clinton is not sequential [in his decisionmaking]. When you put a list in front of some people—setting forth what is most important and what is least important—they go down the list. Clinton goes around the problem. He circles it and circles it." Yet it is not clear that while serving Clinton's cognitive needs, his policy goals were furthered. Even Mack McLarty came to realize that the process "tended at times to generate too much superfluous intellectual byplay and too many delayed decisions."[52] In the view of one cabinet member, "Clinton tended to toss off ideas that he hadn't fully considered. It was his long-standing method of trying out thoughts. But it could be confusing to the public and lead Clinton to put out half-baked ideas."[53]

Clinton had another take on the problem, however: those who surrounded him were at fault. In mid-April, Stephanopoulos was called into the Oval Office and jotted down his conversation with Clinton in

a note to himself: "He yelled at me for a few minutes, feeling he is losing control of his presidency. Feels we are making incremental, day-to-
day decisions because we don't have a core vision. Fears that many of
his appointees aren't committed to his goals. Also fears that his schedule and his government are not organized to achieve what he wants to
achieve."[54]

Yet while Clinton may have been right in some immediate sense,
part of the problem can also be traced back to his lack of concern about
organizational matters and his own expectations about the place of the
staff in his White House, especially McLarty's role and authority as
chief of staff. In 1993, Sidney Blumenthal, then writing for *New
Yorker*, noted that some close to Clinton "speculate that he put
McLarty in the slot in order to retain control himself." But the effect
"has been a self-defeating loss of control."[55] George Stephanopoulos
would later observe in his memoirs that "Clinton needed a stronger
chief of staff . . . [but] Clinton never gave him real authority."[56]

Policy Outcomes

Given the early disorganization of the Clinton White House and Clinton's own proclivities as a decisionmaker, it is not surprising to find the
early days and months of this administration replete with policy errors,
strategic missteps, and a range of miscalculations. Particularly noteworthy is that each can be linked to a variety of problems in the decisionmaking, staffing, and organization of the administration, as well as
the lingering effects of the transition. Several can be directly linked to
the transition—the delay in fashioning an economic program and the
failed Baird, Wood, and Guinier nominations. Others followed from
problems in the unfolding Clinton staff system—Travelgate, in particular. Still others—especially the effort to secure passage of Clinton's
economic program—resulted from a number of forces, presidential and
staff, at work.

Fashioning an Economic Program

The Clinton economic program of 1993, especially its emphasis on
deficit reduction and tax increases on the wealthy, is often taken as a
key contributor to the economic prosperity that would mark his tenure
in office. At some level that may be true, although untangling the
causal forces at work in the 1990s economy is no easy task. Yet as a

deliberative and policymaking process, the efforts of Clinton and his advisers were fraught with difficulties; they provide an early example of Clinton's decisionmaking in action and its attendant problems.

Again, the transition had some effect: Clinton had hoped to have an economic program ready by inauguration day. Yet by January 20, a program was nowhere close to being in place, despite the fact—as noted earlier—that an economic summit had been held in mid-December and Reich, Rubin, Kantor, and others had been working steadily since then. Reich and his economic team had prepared two fat briefing books, "Economic Transition #1" and "Economic Transition #2," but they "were full of undigestible tables, charts, forecasts, theories—with no overall theme to the pudding, no line of reasoning at all," according to one account.[57] Clinton's situation was also complicated by the fact that the Bush administration had decided not to present a detailed budget proposal to Congress, as other outgoing administrations had traditionally done. Instead, Bush and OMB Director Richard Darman submitted estimates of spending, taxes, and the deficit based on current policies, leaving the hard decisions to the new administration.[58]

It was not until January 29 that Clinton and his aides began to work in earnest on crafting a proposal for Congress by February 17, the administration's new self-imposed deadline. For the next two and a half weeks, meetings were held every day and often into the evening, including a marathon ten-hour session on Sunday, February 7. Clinton and Gore attended almost every one, as did a large group of advisers, including Bentsen and Altman from Treasury, Panetta and Rivlin from the OMB, Rubin and Cutter from the NEC, Tyson and Blinder from the CEA, Ron Brown and Reich from Commerce and Labor, and McLarty, Stephanopoulos, Sperling, and Paster from the White House staff. Some of Clinton's outside consultants, such as Paul Begala, were often present, as was a changing cast of other aides sitting around the sides of the room.

The meetings were crucial in thrashing out an economic plan that would try to fulfill a number of often conflicting proposals Clinton made during the campaign, particularly in attempting to reconcile Clinton's commitment to stimulate the economy, help the middle class, and establish new job-training and other programs aimed at raising worker productivity. Plus, Clinton wanted to reduce the budget deficit, which was now projected to be higher than the numbers used in the campaign and needed to be factored anew into Clinton's fiscal calculations.

What transpired is especially reflective of the absence of orderly procedures stemming from the transition and the free rein it gave Clinton's own decisionmaking style. The meetings operated on what now came to be dubbed "Clinton time": meetings set for two hours stretched into four, while others lasted into the night. Treasury Secretary Lloyd Bentsen called the marathon sessions "an incredible grind."[59] According to Elizabeth Drew's account of the process, "On a number of occasions when the president was going on and on, Rubin and Reich would glance at each other. The two men had private discussions about the absurdity of spending forty-five minutes of the President's time on a five or ten-million-dollar program—in an annual budget of $1.6 trillion."

Bob Woodward's account in *The Agenda* offers similar evidence. He describes one meeting as dragging on into the evening and "dissolving into virtual chaos." The participants were all tired, and "there was no clear direction, much less a consensus." Paul Begala, "seeing the situation was crazy and the meeting no longer productive for Clinton," approached McLarty and told him that he had to get Clinton out of there. So, too, did Stephanopoulos. But Clinton remained until he had to attend another event.[60] Clinton "found no detail too small for his attention."[61]

Others complained that "Clinton never stops thinking" and that "you couldn't really tell when he was making a decision and when he wasn't." For Clinton, the sessions, which often stretched late into the evening, were "fun." As the deadline of Clinton's February 17 speech approached, Gore intervened (at the urging of Panetta and Rubin), proposing a tight schedule: "On Monday we do this, Tuesday we do this." Clinton finally relented. "Until then," according to one participant, "we were having an intense seminar on government minutiae, led by Bill Clinton."[62]

But Clinton was still not finished, and work on his speech of February 17 before a joint session of Congress continued to the last minute. When Al Gore took his place on the dais of the House, he noticed that the teleprompter was scrolling back and forth with changes being made even as the president entered the House chamber. The teleprompter operator finally managed to scroll back to the beginning just as Clinton began to deliver his address.[63] In delivering his speech, Clinton ad-libbed about a third of the time ("He's riffing," Mandy Grunwald realized while watching the speech), and Clinton later sent a thank-you note to the teleprompter operator expressing his appreciation for keeping the machine on cue as he made extemporaneous changes.

Delay was not just endemic to the economic plan; it also beset the other major policy initiative intended to hallmark Clinton's first months as president—a comprehensive health-care proposal. The plan was originally to be completed in May, then changed to July, then to September. Part of the problem in fashioning a major health-care initiative was the sheer complexity of the issue. But its delay—as well as timely decisions on other policy initiatives—likewise stemmed from the fluidity of the process and a lack of closure and sense that decisions had been made. Jeff Eller, who served as a White House media adviser and whose principal task was to promote the first lady's health-care initiative, had a similar view: "It's hard to get a decision, and decisions don't stick. . . . This isn't the easiest place to work."[64]

Broader Effects: Prioritizing an Agenda

Even when decisions had been made, the White House was unable to rise above the particulars and set strategic priorities. As Bruce Lindsey observed at the time, the transition again set the stage for subsequent problems: "We had working groups during the transition—welfare, economic—but they hadn't put it all together. They each came up with plans and legislation in their area, but that's as far as it went. We had no time line before we came in. No one sat down and said, 'if you do A, B, C is your plate too full?'"[65]

Clinton himself, at least according to one account, did not have a sense that he needed to pare down his agenda. At the first informal dinner at the White House, Clinton told a group of his top aides that he was in charge of things and it was time to make good on his campaign promises. "He declared that he and his wife would flatly refuse to move slowly from one limited goal to the next. . . . Instead he would work on the 'hard things' all at once and right from the start."[66] Within three months, Clinton had either presented to the Congress or was in the process of presenting a stimulus and deficit-reduction proposal, comprehensive health-care reform, Gore's reinventing government effort, NAFTA, anticrime legislation, welfare reform, the Americorps national-service program, enterprise zones, community development banks, and a host of smaller initiatives.

All of these efforts, while perhaps meritorious in their own right, began to complicate Clinton's chief goal of securing congressional approval to his economic plan. Following his February 17 speech, Clinton went on to other things rather than focusing on his economic program. According to OMB Director Panetta, "After February 17, the message became confused. The president began to push health care and enterprise zones, community development banks, immunization. And foreign affairs—especially Bosnia—took more time than he expected."[67]

White House staff members began to refer to it all as the "great train wreck." One Clinton strategist grumbled that with so many initiatives in play, "We're worrying about Carterizing ourselves."[68] In late April, Panetta met with reporters and offered a gloomy assessment of the ability of the administration to gain support for its budget plan, economic stimulus package, as well as aid to Russia. He suggested that some programs—health care most notably—should be delayed until a later date. The interview became front-page news. The headline in the *Washington Post* ran "Panetta: President in Trouble on Hill," while the *Los Angeles Times* headlined its story with "Many Clinton Goals in Peril, Panetta Warns."

Clinton was described as being "unhappy and exasperated at first" but then was persuaded by McLarty that it was just a mistake by an overly tired and dispirited Panetta. Rather than a wake-up call, Panetta's comments were likened to David Stockman's conversations with *Atlantic Monthly* in 1981. "I don't want to take him to the woodshed," Clinton told reporters. "I need for him to get his spirits up."[69]

But problems with an overloaded agenda persisted. In May, Lloyd Bentsen warned Clinton in a private meeting, "You have too many issues out there, and the public is losing focus on what you're trying to do." Clinton replied that he made a lot of campaign promises. "Yes," Bentsen said, "but you have four years."[70]

By mid-May the problem had also begun to register with the public. In an article entitled "Close to Overload," *Newsweek* reported that poll results indicated that 59 percent of the public thought Clinton was trying to do too much and that his job-approval rating had dropped to 46 percent, the lowest score of any recent president at a similar point in his presidency.[71] By the end of May, Clinton's rating had sunk to 36 percent.

Yet Clinton had not gotten the message. In June, the White House presented Democratic leaders with new policy demands—that they take up action on enterprise zones, a crime bill, and a community banking measure. Clinton met with members of the House, and when a Democratic member asked Clinton to stop the "policy-a-day nonsense," other members in the room burst into applause.[72]

Problems in the Legal Counsel's Office

The White House's legal counsel office was a particular source of problems early in the Clinton presidency. First, it was staffed by personnel who may have been good lawyers but often lacked the broader experience needed for the job. It was headed by Bernard Nussbaum, a New

York corporate lawyer with no White House experience save for a stint on the House impeachment staff in 1974, along with (then) Hillary Rodham, who had been instrumental in his appointment. Nussbaum's deputy was Vincent Foster, a close friend of the Clintons and one of Hillary Clinton's law partners; another member of the Rose Law Firm, William Kennedy, also served in the office. Second, its internal difficulties were complicated by miscommunications with higher levels of the White House, most notably the president himself.

One vexing issue—and it had started back in December—that proved difficult was finding a suitable nominee for attorney general. The view that Zoe Baird's hiring of illegal immigrants would prove no more problematic than a traffic ticket proved illusory. Yet better political awareness was not forthcoming, nor had the administration fully learned its lessons from the Baird debacle.

Kimba Wood. One might assume that the legal counsel's office, in considering Baird's replacement for attorney general, would have proceeded more cautiously, especially in leaving no stone unturned in the vetting process before announcing a second nominee. Yet it didn't. By February 4, Hillary Clinton and Thomases had settled on Kimba Wood for the post; forty-nine years old, she was a federal district court judge. Wood was interviewed by Hillary Clinton, Nussbaum, and the president, and she apparently passed with flying colors. Later that day, the story of her appointment was leaked by the White House to several major newspapers. However, FBI background checks and a full investigation by Nussbaum's staff had not been completed, and later that evening Clinton was told that Wood, too, had hired illegal immigrants but, unlike Baird, had done so before it was a violation of federal law. (Apparently Wood had been asked if she had a "nanny problem" but interpreted the question in a legalistic way: since she had not broken the law—as did Baird—she had no problem.)

The next day, Clinton decided that he could not go forward with the appointment, and Wood—more accommodating than Baird—agreed to have her nomination withdrawn. Wood insisted, however, on releasing an immediate statement to the press about her decision. Unfortunately for the White House, that day was also the date set for the signing of the family-leave bill. Stephanopoulos and Nussbaum realized that the Wood announcement would eclipse reporting of the family-leave bill in the evening news, but they could not persuade Wood to delay an announcement (Wood's position was that news would leak anyway). Not only was there another episode of Nannygate and further stories of White House incompetence in vetting its nominees; the administration's efforts to publicize its first major piece of legislation and to move media coverage in a more positive direction had been damaged.

Lani Guinier. Clinton's inability to vet nominees properly and, in the event of problems or other embarrassing revelations, to act quickly to stem the damage was played out again several months later with the nomination of Lani Guinier, yet another friend of the Clintons, as head of the Civil Rights Division of the Justice Department. Again, the White House legal counsel's office played a major role and—as with the Baird and Wood nominations—Nussbaum again underestimated the political damage. Guinier, a professor at the University of Pennsylvania's law school, had written several academic articles that articulated potentially controversial positions on racial discrimination. Her writings, however, raised no alarm for Nussbaum and his associates; although alerted to them by another member of the counsel's office, Nussbaum felt that the Senate would not beat up on an African American nominee. Clinton was not even briefed on the articles' contents: Nussbaum merely told him they were "academic ruminations" and "not off the wall," advice Nussbaum had been given by others whom he had asked to read them.[73] As it turned out, one of the two Nussbaum had asked to review her work hadn't bothered to read her articles: he had assumed the nomination was a done deal. Clinton was told, however, that two leading constitutional law scholars had reviewed her work and found nothing particularly problematic.

But once Guinier's name was sent forward, an otherwise predictable controversy erupted (most notably in the pages of the *Wall Street Journal,* which dubbed her the "Quota Queen"). Nussbaum felt that the White House, even though the nomination was in trouble, should stick it out to the end. That advice proved costly to the president, who, after finally reading some of Guinier's articles, felt that he could no longer support her nomination. According to Senator Joe Biden, Clinton was "angry" about the advice he had been given on Guinier. "His tone was 'How did this happen again?'"[74]

For Senator Joseph Lieberman, a Democrat from Connecticut, the whole episode suggested yet another breakdown in the staff's work: "If they didn't know [about her writings], they did a bum job of review. If they did know and didn't stop the nomination, their judgment is off."[75] Nussbaum was especially singled out for criticism. According to one former Clinton staffer who had worked with him, he was "not fluent in all the issues he faced when he got here. He came into an environment very different from the one he came from and he was suddenly confronted with a whole set of different issues, which are not like the commercial or takeover litigation" that he did in private practice.[76]

Other troubles. In May, following the summary firing of seven members of the White House travel office, the legal counsel's office, plus a number of others in the administration, would come under harsh scrutiny. It was a case of a precipitous decision, and it provides stark evidence of the inexperience of those involved, further signs of disorganization and miscommunications, and a continued inability to heed political—and now legal—warning signs. The whole episode would eventually come under the purview of Kenneth Starr's investigation and two congressional committees, and it would involve a wide cast of characters in the Clinton White House, including the first lady.

Little consideration had been undertaken about the legal or political difficulties of firing these employees. As Elizabeth Drew notes, "That was it: no meeting, no aeration of the plan, no consideration of how it might go over in the press."[77] According to John Brummett, "No one asked the obvious: Shouldn't these employees be given a chance to defend themselves? Are we acting a bit recklessly? The White House was awash in lawyers, and yet none of them seemed to recall the need to build a case."[78] According to one senior member of Al Gore's staff, the vice president was "appalled by what he saw as stupidity and ineptitude. He complained there were too many people in the wrong jobs." Not only did Gore single out legal counsel Nussbaum for criticism: McLarty himself was at fault; they were "all in over their heads."[79]

Economic Program Redux

Following his February 17 address to Congress, Clinton and his advisers encountered more difficulties—many of their own making—in securing congressional assent to what they hoped would be the centerpiece of his first months in office. While part of Clinton's difficulties stemmed from congressional politics, others reflected problems internal to the administration's decisionmaking as it now sought to negotiate with Congress: the absence of an ongoing legislative strategy group, miscommunications between Paster and McLarty, McLarty's own disorganization, decisions made on the basis of questionable assumptions and hasty reactions, and a pattern of conflicting and confusing public statements by key players.

The program was ambitious in scope and contained three parts: a stimulus package, a deficit-reduction package, and a spending program for human capital (called an "investment" program to make it more politically palatable). It was one of the largest deficit-reduction packages, as well as one of the largest spending packages, ever presented to Congress.

Clinton had sought to craft a proposal that would appeal to Republicans and conservative Democrats, with its emphasis on controlling spending and reducing the deficit, as well as more liberal members of Congress, with its tax increases on higher incomes and fuel consumption coupled with new spending on job training and education. Clinton's plan called for tax increases and spending cuts that would total about $495 billion over four years. About two-thirds of that amount— some $325 billion—would be used to cut the deficit. The rest would go to new spending initiatives and tax breaks—the so-called investment program that would create new jobs, increase competitiveness, and address social needs. But it was not until April 8 that Clinton sent details of his budget proposal to Congress. And even then it was already out of date, since it did not reflect deals Clinton had made with Congress in the interim; it was also some $67 billion short (over five years) in what needed to be further reduced to meet the budget resolution that Congress had already adopted.

The stimulus element met a quick death. Although passed by the House, the package died in the Senate. While many in the Senate felt that economically it was no longer warranted, three mistakes had been made. The first was that Clinton and Paster relied on the advice and parliamentary leadership of Senator Robert Byrd, who devised a strategy for protecting the bill from any weakening amendments (the strategy had been worked out, moreover, at a meeting at the White House that the Senate Majority Leader did not attend). Byrd's tactics led to some resentment among his colleagues, and all forty-three Republicans in the Senate voted to sustain a filibuster of the bill. Second, Paster, accustomed to dealing with the House, had followed a fifty-one-vote, simple-majority strategy, far short of the sixty votes needed to block a filibuster. Third, the White House rejected a compromise offered by Democratic Senators John Breaux and David Boren, representing Louisiana and Oklahoma respectively.[80] According to Stephanopoulos, "The mistake we made is pretty clear." He would later recall that "the defeat of our economic stimulus [package] was the price we paid for legislative arrogance. Thinking we could roll right over the Republicans in the Senate, we rejected a moderate compromise by Senators Breaux and Boren, and lost everything."[81]

The fate of the investment package: forgetting Darman's 1990 caps. Clinton's so-called investment program fared little better. His five-year budget plan had called for $231 billion in new spending, largely in job training and education, with $30 billion proposed for the new fiscal year. The House, responding to the spending caps and trade-off requirements in the 1990 budget agreement, voted less than $1 billion—less than 3 percent—for the upcoming year and less than $6 billion for the next year.

Part of the problem was the concern among both Democrats and Republicans to reduce the deficit and hold the line on new spending. But part, too, was White House naïveté and miscommunication over legislative restraints on new spending; the administration's inexperience and disorder now came together. On April 7, Reich, Rubin, Sperling, and Stephanopoulos gathered in Clinton's office to deliver the bad news. Sperling explained that the 1990 budget agreement had set spending caps through 1994 and 1995 and that the House Democrats were unwilling to raise them. According to Reich's account of the meeting, Clinton "exploded": "Why didn't anyone tell me about spending caps? We spent week after week going over every little budget item, and no one had said a word about the caps." Turning "beet red" according to Reich, Clinton then added, "Why didn't *they* tell me?"—presumably referring to several in his inner circle who had extensive congressional and budget experience and who also happened to be the leading deficit hawks: Panetta—who had been House Budget Committee chairman; Rivlin—who had been director of the Congressional Budget Office; and Bentsen—who had been chairman of the Senate Finance Committee. "They wouldn't have intentionally sabotaged the President's budget," Reich pondered to himself, "would they?"

"I won't have a goddam Democratic budget until 1996!" Clinton continued to fume. "Education, job training—none of the things I campaigned for on. What'll I be able to tell the average working person I did for him?" At least, Clinton pondered, "I'll have health care to give them."[82]

Miscommunications, misstatements, and questionable compromises. As the separate budget package moved through the House and Senate, Clinton and his advisers made other tactical and strategic errors, several of which can be linked to internal disarray in the White House, particularly miscommunications among the principal players.

One ill-advised concession was in response to a group of Western senators concerned about White House proposals to raise grazing and mining fees and to reduce below-cost timber sales on federal lands.

Clinton, Gore, and McLarty decided to delete the proposed increases. However, it was a concession that they need not have made. House and Senate conferees had already decided to remove the grazing fees before the White House sent word that Clinton wanted them out. Senator Dale Bumpers of Arkansas, a proponent of the fees, had tried to reach McLarty for a day and a half to let him know the situation. By the time McLarty called him back, it was too late. Nor had Paster and his staff alerted the White House. Organizational disarray again raised its head.[83]

Major miscommunications resurfaced in June over the proposed energy-tax increase based on a broad-based BTU use calculation. The proposal was complex and politically unpalatable in energy-producing states. The White House felt, however, a broadly based energy tax made more environmental sense and had less direct effect on consumers than one based on one energy source such as gasoline; it was also projected to generate some $72 billion in revenues, a hefty contribution toward deficit reduction. There was considerable lobbying, and the House reluctantly went along with the proposal. Clinton had even personally met with the House Democratic Caucus and assured them he wouldn't leave them stranded by abandoning a BTU tax once the budget bill got to the Senate.[84]

The Senate was a different matter, and key senators whose votes were needed—particularly Boren and Breaux, who had been spurned earlier—were adamantly opposed to the BTU proposal. As with the grazing fees, Congress would have likely worked out its own compromise. But before it could do so, the administration again sent signals it was backing off, and the White House was once again caught in an embarrassing position.[85]

On Saturday, July 3, the issue of devising a strategy to pass the president's program and achieve better coordination finally reached a head at a meeting Hillary Clinton asked McLarty to convene. Both Clintons, Gore, the outside consultants, and a dozen top aides attended what became a pointed and at times emotionally charged debate. Toward the end, Hillary demanded that a "war room" be created that would coordinate the effort. Her anger ignited Clinton's ire, and he yelled at his associates that he wanted a coordinated strategy developed. "I'm leaving and I'm going to Tokyo [to attend a G-7 summit meeting]. . . . Mack and Al, you two, I want it solved, I want it done before I get home."

On July 8, McLarty approved a memo that contained within it four steps that ought to have been taken back in February: (1) the establishment of a "boiler room" that would bring together the key players in the budget battle; (2) the assignment of a senior person from each department to the room for the duration; (3) creation of a daily morning meeting of the key advisers involved; and (4) an order that all of this should be up and running by the time the president returned from Tokyo.[86]

In early August, Congress finally—and by the narrowest of margins—approved the budget program; the vote was 218–216 in the House and 50–50 in the Senate, with Vice President Gore's vote breaking the tie. Although it represented a major legislative victory for Clinton, the final bill was a mixed blessing. The stimulus package was long gone, and the investment program was smaller than had been proposed.[87] The main thrust had been to reduce the deficit by an estimated $500 billion over five years (roughly half would now come through new taxes, the other half through spending cuts).[88]

In the view of Senator Joe Lieberman, "He really tried to have an investment program but now it's essentially all gone."[89] "I want to celebrate tonight. I want to feel the thrill of victory," Robert Reich mused to himself the night of the vote, "but I don't feel celebratory. I look down the road and much of what I hope for seems imperiled."[90]

Changes, May and June 1993

Of the four recent presidencies we have examined—Carter, Reagan, Bush, and Clinton—it was Clinton who made the fastest course correction in response to early shortcomings. One might argue that the administration did so because a need for change had become obvious and problems were severe. Whatever the reasoning behind them, did such changes solve the problems at hand?

Clinton's first hundred days were barely behind him when the first of several changes in the White House staff were undertaken. On May 6, Clinton's 107th day as president, Roy Neel was appointed as a second deputy chief of staff to McLarty. Neel had been Al Gore's chief of staff and had worked for the vice president since 1977. During the campaign, Neel developed a close relation to Mark Gearan, the other deputy chief of staff who had also headed up the Gore campaign. In effect, Neel's new job was to be chief of staff to the chief of staff. He was charged with making the staff operate more smoothly and relieving McLarty of some of his management burdens; this freed McLarty to focus on the economic program and act as liaison to moderate Democrats in Congress. Gearan, in turn, would concentrate on longer-range strategy. As he recalls,

With Roy doing the day-to-day piece, my task was to look in a more strategic planning context: the blend of the president's communications, press, scheduling, and legislative agenda. . . . [We needed] to get a bit ahead of the curve, or that was the intent. There was a tremendous sense in the opening days—it really went on all that year—that so much is on the plate day-to-day that no one was getting a prospective look . . . a long-term strategic look.[91]

On May 4, Clinton had himself told reporters, "There needs to be a little tighter coordination, to make sure that we've got our priorities straight and those priorities are communicated all the way down."[92]

Neel's appointment and Clinton's call for tighter coordination did not end Clinton's staff problems. In the days following, the White House faced two major problems. The first was an embarrassing fracas over a $200 haircut the president received while Air Force One idled on the tarmac of Los Angeles International Airport, reportedly delaying flights. The second was the firing of the White House travel staff. Both incidents pointed, in part, to continued problems with the White House staff, and they led McLarty to think about other staff changes. On May 28, McLarty told reporters that the current team was "a bit frail" and that he had "a little sharper understanding now than he did then [in December]" about what was needed in the White House's "basic organizational structure and framework."[93] McLarty was careful to suggest that the changes had been in the works for some time and were not related to events over the previous days, such as Travelgate and the haircut by Christophe.

The most important change was the hiring of David Gergen as a kind of all-purpose adviser on media and communications. For some time, McLarty had been pondering what to do about Stephanopoulos, who was increasingly unpopular with the White House press corps yet a valuable political adviser. Among the options discussed was having Stephanopoulos forgo daily briefings of the press and concentrate instead on strategic planning and coordination.[94] McLarty had also been having informal discussions with Gergen about Clinton's problems with the media and the difficulty of getting his message out. In one of these conversations, McLarty found Gergen receptive to the idea of joining the White House staff. (According to Stephanopoulos, McLarty had also sounded out Bill Moyers, who professed disinterest, just as he had when Clinton had invited him to Little Rock during the transition to discuss the possibility of serving as chief of staff.)[95]

Clinton concurred—Gergen would provide not only communications expertise but also some partisan balance—and so he was hired. Gergen, however, was careful to negotiate a position as counselor to the president; the White House communications office would technically be under the direction of Mark Gearan, who was moved into Stephanopoulos's old role.

Gergen provided what the White House lacked: political savvy, experience in dealing with the media, and a keen sense of how Washington worked. His one liability was that his expertise stemmed from his service to three Republican presidents. There was also some irony to the appointment: Gergen had been one of the authors of Reagan's hundred-day plan and the media strategy that had been important in building support for Reaganomics, which Clinton's proposals sought to undo.[96]

With Gergen in charge of communications, McLarty attempted to solve another problem by moving Stephanopoulos to a newly defined position as a general adviser to the president. Not only would it better tap Stephanopoulos's skills; it would provide a ready outlet and sounding board for the president. Before the change, according to *Newsweek,* "Clinton was dangerously left to free-associate with cabinet officers and lawmakers who promptly babbled to the press. Clinton looked indecisive as his naturally curious mind circled a problem. Now Clinton does most of his plotting in private with Stephanopoulos."[97] But in the view of one staff member, it still left Stephanopoulos as a free agent within the staff system, unfettered from its strictures and discipline, an arrangement that would change only after Panetta replaced McLarty as chief of staff.[98]

For his part, McLarty became more assertive as a manager. In late May, according to one official, McLarty was "taking more personal charge of the meetings, he's demanding more things." As the economic program moved through Congress, he began to hold thrice-weekly meetings in the Roosevelt Room to keep track of the horse-trading. "Mack intervened to force a decision on how we were going to handle the reconciliation effort," one White House staff member noted at the time. "We had too many internal debates, too many occasions where the president staffs himself in making decisions. Mack simply intervened and shut that process down and brought some order to it."[99]

In late June, McLarty cut down the roster attending the senior staff meeting each morning, from nearly three dozen to two dozen, and specifically disinvited some of the deputies whose principals attended. That month, McLarty told reporters, the White House staff was "beginning to function effectively." According to one White House official, "We're catching things earlier." According to another, who was more cautious, "Is everything great? Hell no." But "you don't want to just go jump off a bridge somewhere." The troika of Gergen, Stephanopoulos, and McLarty "calmed down the process . . . started making it rational and consistent."[100]

Even with all of the changes, there still remained a lingering sense, even as late as December 1993, that the White House staff system was not operating effectively. That month, McLarty made yet another round of changes when Neel resigned and Philip Lader (another old friend of the Clintons who had been serving under Panetta in the OMB) was brought on board (Harold Ickes would later be added as well).[101] According to one aide, "I think Roy [Neel] deep down inside is leaving because of McLarty. McLarty empowers and vests and then pulls it back."[102] Late November also saw Howard Paster's resignation as head of the congressional liaison operation. What's more, Gergen's appointment was not going well. According to Elizabeth Drew, "The early talk of a troika of McLarty, Stephanopoulos, and Gergen had long since ceased, and relations between Gergen and Stephanopoulos had reached a point of open warfare."[103]

By the end of the year, Clinton had named four deputy chiefs of staff, two directors of congressional liaison, two communications directors, two scheduling directors, two directors of intergovernmental relations, and two political directors.[104] According to the *Washington Post,* Clinton's problems with his staff were reminiscent of similar problems in the campaign: "For months there were no clear lines of authority, and campaign advisers were driven to distraction by Clinton's style of reaching beyond his inner circle of friends outside the campaign for strategy and advice." Just as it had taken McLarty months to work out staff and personnel problems, "it took almost nine months for Clinton's campaign to get organized. The vaunted war room in Little Rock really did not take shape until after the convention, and only then did Clinton agree to put consultant James Carville in charge of day-to-day operations of the campaign."[105]

Unfortunately, the comparison was not quite accurate. While for Carville the election still loomed ahead, by the time McLarty and then Panetta had begun to get Clinton's house in order, valuable time had been lost and opportunities squandered.

Foreign Policy Decision Processes and Outcomes

Clinton hoped that foreign policy issues would not preoccupy his presidency as they had George Bush. Domestic and economic issues would take center stage in his presidency. As he put it, "Foreign policy will come into play as it affects the economy." On the day after his election victory, his aides did not even disturb him when early-morning, congratulatory phone calls from Russia's Boris Yeltsin, Britain's John Major, and

Germany's Helmut Kohl came through. "No, let him sleep," aides were instructed by Bruce Lindsey.[106]

Yet in a post–Cold War era, Clinton could not escape the press of world affairs, his own agenda notwithstanding. Even during the transition, Clinton encountered a series of vexing foreign policy problems in Bosnia, Haiti, Somalia, North Korea, Iraq, and Russia. Clinton's problems were compounded by his own lack of foreign policy experience and that his party had been out of power for twelve years, a period in which the world scene had radically been transformed.

Haiti, Somalia, and Iraq especially posed early challenges, ones that Clinton would have to grapple with even before he became president. During the campaign, Clinton had criticized the Bush policy of repatriating Haiti's so-called boat people rather than allow them asylum in the United States. But during the transition, he was forced to reverse his position following reports that many Haitians were preparing rafts and other makeshift crafts to leave the island pending Clinton's change in policy.

Iraq continued to loom as a problem. On January 14, at a press conference that was called to announce his choices for White House staff positions, Clinton angrily insisted that he had been misunderstood in an interview he had given to the *New York Times*. The newspaper suggested that he might be open to normalizing relations with Iraq if Saddam Hussein complied with UN resolutions. It was his first taste not only of the consequences of offhand remarks but also of a foreign policy problem that would linger throughout his presidency.

Clinton also faced the consequences of Bush's decision to send ground troops to Somalia to protect humanitarian-aid workers in the war-torn country. While Bush and Clinton had discussed the mounting problem in Somalia, and Clinton's transition team was aware that intervention was being considered, Clinton and his aides were not told of the decision to send troops before word leaked to the press. Bush and his advisers had hoped to wrap up the Somalia problem by inauguration day (in mid-January the Pentagon even announced the removal of the first Marine battalions), but it was unresolved as Clinton took office and would later flare into a major policy dilemma. The humanitarian mission soon evolved into direct U.S. involvement.

Comparably Better Organization

Unlike the situation with his White House staff, Clinton was better organized to face the nation's foreign policy dilemmas. Sandy Berger, who headed both the foreign policy transition team and the foreign policy task forces, had begun his work earlier and in a more concerted way than had Reich and the others who were working on economic and other domestic issues in the weeks leading up to inauguration day.

On January 21, his first full day as president, Clinton signed a policy directive setting up his national security system. It essentially replicated the tripartite structure that Brent Scowcroft had developed four years before: (1) a principals' committee of the main NSC members to address issues before they came to the NSC; (2) a deputies' committee headed by Berger that included the deputies of key agencies; and (3) working groups to handle medium-range issues and composed of representatives from departments and agencies involved.[107]

But Clinton, unlike Bush, signaled his intentions that economic concerns would have a place at the foreign policy table. Unlike the Bush-Scowcroft practice of restricting NSC membership, Clinton sought to expand nonstatutory membership by including his chief economic advisers. Treasury Secretary Bentsen and NEC leader Robert Rubin were designated members of the NSC (as was UN Ambassador Albright). NEC deputies were also designated to join the deputies' committees when issues of economic import arose.

In the days following the inauguration, the NSC ordered up twenty-nine studies of foreign policy issues, including four tackling the most pressing problems in Haiti, Somalia, Iraq, and the Balkans. Reports indicated that the administration hoped to avoid the hasty decisions often taken by new presidents and to give Clinton a set of broad strategies to overcome foreign problems rather than pursue piecemeal, tactical responses that might lead to policy fiascoes.[108] Such hope would prove elusive.

Informal Deliberations Prevail Nonetheless

Like Bush, Clinton did not view the formal structure of NSC meetings as the chief arena to deliberate foreign policy issues. Clinton chaired only eight NSC meetings from January through October. The meetings were usually convened after a crisis developed or, in the words of one administration insider, "when the needle has pushed him over into the red alert zone." And they tended to focus on public presentation of the administration's response "rather than fundamental elements of the crisis itself."[109] Clinton, in fact, did not hold an NSC meeting on one of his more successful efforts: Russia. Instead, he met in informal consultation with a few top advisers.

Clinton had hoped to create a foreign policy team that functioned smoothly. Warren Christopher and Anthony Lake had served in prior administrations, as had UN Ambassador Albright. Les Aspin, although not Clinton's first choice to head the Pentagon, likewise brought considerable expertise from his service in Congress, particularly as chairman of the House Armed Services Committee. The members also got along reasonably well, and there were few reports of turf battles and personality conflicts, at least in the first six months, that often plagued presidents before.[110] Lake, Christopher, and Aspin met for lunch every Wednesday in Lake's West Wing office. Lake established a close relationship with Stephanopoulos and kept him informed of foreign policy developments; they talked every morning before McLarty's senior staff meeting, which Lake attended.

Lake met with Clinton every morning for his daily intelligence briefing by the CIA, and Gore, Berger, and Leon Fuerth (Gore's representative on the NSC staff) often attended. The meeting usually lasted fifteen minutes, followed by a discussion of items Lake wanted to bring to the president's attention. Like others in the first year, Lake had direct access to the president and often popped into his office several times a day as the situation merited.

Although the NSC structure and Lake's role as a close adviser continued in some ways the process that had been present under Bush and Scowcroft, there was one crucial difference: the level of interest and participation in foreign policymaking by the president himself. As Elizabeth Drew points out, although Clinton was briefed regularly by Lake, "unlike every President since Truman, Clinton had no regularly scheduled meetings with his foreign policy team."[111] The president was informed of the principals' deliberations, but only when necessary, according to one report: "We don't want to take up his time," one senior aide explained.[112] Some participants complained of their access to the president. According to one report, CIA Director James Woolsey "had such trouble getting on Clinton's schedule that he called upon retired Admiral William Crowe [a Clinton supporter and former chairman of the Joint Chiefs] to bring something up with the President."[113] According to Fred Barnes, "Face time with Clinton became a rare occurrence for [Defense Secretary] Aspin."[114]

Policy was largely threshed out below the presidential level in the principals' committee (Christopher, Aspin, Lake, Woolsey, Albright, and Colin Powell); Berger and Fuerth also attended. The presence of a vice presidential representative in this context was a new twist. When Clinton attended a meeting, which did not occur regularly, McLarty and Gore also came along. Lake presided over the meetings of the principals. According to Christopher, "Almost all major foreign policy issues were taken up" by the group, and "the usual formal product of a meeting was a set of recommendations to the president."[115]

Several principals did have the advantage of having worked to-gether before, yet they operated in a system where Clinton stood at the center as key decisionmaker. His disinterest in foreign policy notwith-standing, Clinton had personally approved every top-level appointee at Defense and State. Yet when his advisers met with Clinton, "the meet-ings sometimes meandered as [he] was bombarded with conflicting ad-vice and took time to make up his mind. The division within the for-eign policy group contributed to a division in the mind of a President who had few strong instincts on foreign policy questions."[116] Even as late as May, when it was clear that foreign policy required more atten-tion than anticipated, Clinton still voiced concerns that it was taking too much time: "I felt really badly because I don't want to spend any more time on [Bosnia] than is absolutely necessary, because what I got elected to do was to let America look at our own problems."[117]

Moreover, none of the principals was prepared to enter the breach and offer a broader vision that Clinton might embrace. Both Lake and Christopher were suited to serving a president who was prepared to take the lead. Yet as Leslie Gelb noted during the transition, while Lake, Christopher, and Aspin were highly experienced problem-solvers, "none of the trio seeks limelight, and all will fit comfortably with Mr. Clinton's plan to make policy in the White House." Christo-pher, in particular, "is not a policy maker and has no known policy agenda." "He thinks case by case. But he can take any policy paper and find its flaws and make it viable."[118] Christopher's skills were as a ne-gotiator, not as a foreign policy architect. According to one subordi-nate, "He's a good fielder, but a lousy hitter."[119] Aspin was viewed as an indifferent, disorganized manager and not very skilled as a bureau-cratic infighter. Even Clinton once described Aspin as a man with "1,000 brilliant questions" but few answers.[120] According to David Broder, "All three of them seem to indulge, if not encourage, Clinton's penchant for talking issues to death." The result, according to Demo-cratic Congressman Lee Hamilton, a leading foreign policy expert in Congress, was that "our policy has not been as well-defined, well-ar-ticulated, and well-formulated as it should be."[121]

Bosnia

The administration's response to the deepening crisis in Bosnia illumi-nates the major problems that stemmed from the administration's in-ternal deliberative processes and decisionmaking. Bosnia was one of the few foreign policy issues upon which Clinton took a stand during the campaign, criticizing the Bush administration's alleged inaction and pledging to do something about Serbian ethnic cleansing. Yet it was not clear what course the administration would take once Clinton was in office. Clinton's three chief advisers held somewhat different views. Aspin was for doing as little as possible, Lake pushed for strong action, while Christopher took several different positions.

Following several lengthy meetings in February, agreement was reached to stiffen economic sanctions against Serbia, call for the United Nations to authorize a no-fly zone over Bosnia, and drop food supplies by parachute to Bosnian Muslims. There was some debate about how to drop the supplies and what kind should be provided, with the administration settling on meals-ready-to-eat left over from the Gulf War. But the decision "was made rather casually and, given its importance, received little public notice."[122]

Apparently, it was not clear to all the principals precisely what U.S. policy entailed. In early March, Aspin remarked while visiting Capitol Hill that the food drops had been suspended because convoy trucks were now allowed to pass through Bosnian Serb checkpoints. His comments contradicted not only press reports—which indicated that the situation had not changed—but also administration policy. Both Clinton and Gore publicly corrected him and said the airdrops would continue.

Although Clinton and Christopher both thought the administration should take a more hawkish stance toward the Serbians, the principals found it difficult to formulate a policy. In late March and through April, the situation in Bosnia worsened, especially with the attack on Srebrenica. A series of meetings were convened and a number of options were discussed, but Clinton and his advisers could not reach a decision.

The protracted agonizing, said one high official, was a "bad sign." He added, "It wasn't policy-making. It was group therapy—an existential debate over what is the role of America, etc."[123] A month after Lake had begun a new round of meetings to find a new policy, no decisions had been made. According to Defense Secretary Aspin, "People are all over the lot. . . . I have never seen a government problem before with totally no good options."[124] At the same time, returning to the Bush administration policy of doing nothing had essentially been foreclosed. As Elizabeth Drew has observed, "By saying so often that something must be done to stop the ethnic cleansing, Clinton got himself in a corner. Whatever his misgivings, doing nothing wasn't an option."[125]

By late April, following a series of meetings among the principals with the Joint Chiefs and congressional leaders, a decision was reached,

dubbed "lift and strike." Essentially, it was a proposal to lift the existing arms embargo—thus providing the Bosnian Muslims with arms to
give them more of a level playing field with the Serbs—coupled with
air strikes against the Serbs if they took advantage of the situation before the arms reached the Muslims. It also included, for the first time,
U.S. participation in a peacekeeping force should a cease-fire be
achieved and the parties agree to the UN cease-fire plan (the so-called
Vance-Owens agreement) then under consideration.[126]

Christopher was then dispatched to sell the proposal to the NATO
allies, who were firmly against lifting the arms embargo. Their view,
especially those nations with troops among the UN peacekeeping
forces, was that lifting the embargo would enflame the situation and
endanger their forces. According to one account, "There was no real
reason for the President and Christopher to believe the trip would succeed. They had set themselves up for an embarrassing failure."[127] Despite the fact that the British and the French made it clear they would
not support lifting the embargo, Clinton felt that Christopher could
somehow sell the proposal to them. He couldn't. Christopher also was
hampered when, on the day of his arrival in Europe, the Bosnian Serbs
agreed to sign on to the Vance-Owens proposal. That seeming agreement further weakened any European resolve to get tough, and it placed
Christopher in the position of selling two plans—lift and strike plus a
possible new peacekeeping force to enforce Vance-Owens. (The Bosnian Serb assembly later rejected the plan, so the latter became moot.)

There is also some evidence that Clinton himself had second thoughts
while Christopher was off in Europe selling the plan. At one point, following a meeting with the president, Aspin called Lake and told him that
Clinton was "going South on this policy. His heart isn't in it. We have a
problem here. We're out there pushing a policy that the President's not
comfortable with. He's not on board."[128] As Christopher would later state,
when he returned to Washington, "It became evident that there had been
a sea change in attitudes during the week I had been away. No one else
argued in support of pursuing the lift and strike options with our allies.
. . . The President reportedly had been reading books on Balkan history
that presented a grim picture of prospects for reconciliation."[129]

Clinton's problems were also complicated by his frequent rhetoric
that the United States needed to do more in Bosnia. Both Christopher
and Vernon Jordan cautioned him about this as well as about talking in
advance about meetings, thus raising expectations. "He was advised to
simply announce a policy when it had been decided upon."[130] In May,
a strategy of containment was adopted, with three hundred U.S. troops

sent to Macedonia as part of a UN force, thus indicating that the United States was prepared to do something, even if it was unwilling to further intervene in Bosnia. According to one Clinton adviser, "It's face-saving. It's a way to look like we're doing something so maybe our incompetent Bosnia policy won't be noticed."[131]

On May 18, Christopher told a congressional committee that this was a "problem from hell" and "at heart this is a European problem." Finally, in late May, in part to head off a Russian-led solution to the crisis, the United States took the lead in crafting an allied policy of protecting Bosnian Muslim "safe areas" by force if necessary. The United States, however, would not provide ground troops if needed, but would be in charge of any air strikes or support. The plan did little about Serbian aggression and contained the possibility of parceling up the Muslims in six permanent garrison-like areas.

According to one participant in the meetings that led to Christopher's mission, "Isn't there anyone outside the government with some bright ideas? Someone who could help us?"[132] Another insider described the whole decision process as "rudderless." By August 1993, four State Department officials would resign over the administration's lack of a firm policy in Bosnia. One of them, in his resignation letter to Christopher, said policy had become "misguided, vacillating, and dangerous." Christopher even met privately with several dozen midlevel officials in his department to head off further controversy and, possibly, even more resignations.[133]

While Christopher thought the situation workable, Lake did not think the Bosnia problem would go away. It will be back, he warned.[134] Later in the year, similar problems in decisionmaking and strategy would emerge in the administration's handling of crises in Somalia and Haiti.[135] In testimony before the Senate Foreign Relations Committee in November 1993, Warren Christopher conceded that Bosnia, Haiti, and Somalia were "difficult situations" where "things have not gone exactly as we planned."[136]

Mixed Record

Although Clinton had a rocky road on many of his major initiatives, his first year was not without its accomplishments. By the end of the year, he had managed to have Congress pass family-leave legislation (which Bush had previously vetoed), a "motor voter" registration bill, a national-service program for younger Americans, a new student-loan program, and the long-stalled Brady Bill, which established a waiting period for handgun purchases. Although opposed by a majority of the Democrats in both the House and Senate, with Republican support, NAFTA was passed. Through executive order, Clinton had curtailed some of the restrictions placed on fetal-tissue research and the availability of abortion services that had been imposed by his two Republican predecessors. Health-care and welfare reform, however, were postponed until 1994.

Yet the problems with Clinton's staff and his decisionmaking in general would persist. In his diary, Labor Secretary Reich would note in entries dating from April through July 1994, fully eighteen months into Clinton's term, that White House organization and orderly procedures continued to suffer:

> Nothing gets done in this wildly disorganized White House unless [the president] orders it done (and even then there's no guarantee).
> *—April 29, 1994*
> Federico Peña, the secretary of transportation, phones me to ask me how I discover what's going on at the White House. I have no clear answer for him. The place is so disorganized that information is hard to come by. The decision making "loop" depends on physical proximity to B.—who's whispering into his ear most regularly, whose office is closest to the Oval, who's standing or sitting next to him when a key issue arises. . . . In this administration you're either in the loop or you're out of the loop, but more likely you don't know where the loop is, or you don't even know there is a loop.
> *—June 6, 1994*
> I'm losing confidence that my memos are getting to B. And even when they are, a fair number leak to the press.
> *—July 15, 1994*[137]

On Hillary Clinton's advice, Reich developed his own loop: "Send them to me," she told him. "I'll make sure they get to him. Use blank sheets of paper without any letterhead or other identifying characteristics. Just the date and your initials." "Now I have my own loop," Reich noted. It had taken a year and a half.

* * *

In the first months, if not the first year, of the Clinton presidency as Clinton's record indicates, much of the predicted effects of the transition were borne out. Clinton's late start in staffing his White House and the lack of much attention during the transition to its operations would plague the start of his presidency. The chief of staff's operation, the communications apparatus, the legal counsel's office, intergovernmental affairs, the political office, and Paster's congressional affairs office all encountered difficulties in operation. The lack of attention to how all the pieces would come together in a coherent process generated its own set of problems: meetings open to all comers, lack of staff discipline and lack of clarity about responsibilities, memos and phone calls unanswered, decisions made and then unmade as the day wore on, and a premium placed on "face time" with the president. Even the more formally structured operations such as the NEC, DPC, and NSC were often bypassed by more ad hoc and changing venues for making policy in this administration. Organizational design, even when undertaken, was not necessarily met with organizational commitment.

There were some bright spots. The roles and relationships that were worked out informally by Galston and Reed in domestic policymaking or Rubin's efforts to be a neutral broker within the NEC seemed to have been beneficial. McLarty made some changes: attempts at tighter coordination, changes in his own staff, smaller senior staff meetings, and more assertiveness as a manager (although McLarty may have run up against the limited authority that Clinton had vested in him, as well as the limited authority he was willing to vest in subordinates such as Roy Neel). The foreign policy principals got along reasonably well, although here the positive effects on policy are much less clear—Bosnia, Haiti, and Somalia were hardly decisionmaking success stories.

As during the transition, once in office Clinton was largely inattentive to the role of organization and process as assets for his own decisionmaking. While not above blaming the staff for shortcomings—often with great anger—he persisted in the view that the staff would fall into place on its own, and he was overconfident in his own ability to pull it all together and make correct policy choices. Organizational disarray and fluid decision processes, however, were recipes for policy disaster. Unchecked, the worse of Clinton's proclivities as a decisionmaker could come to the fore: endless and meandering meetings, poor staff work, and delayed decisions.

Most important, all of this contributed to a mounting pattern of strategic and tactical errors and policy mistakes, and it can be in good measure traced back to the transition—delays in crafting and prioritizing a policy agenda and early missteps such as the gays-in-the-military proposal and Baird-Wood-Guinier nominations. Once Clinton was in office, problems in staff organization and Clinton's own decisionmaking set in motion further misjudgments: Travelgate, the various strategic errors and miscommunications during the battle over Clinton's economic program, Bosnia, Somalia, Haiti. As Bruce Reed, one of Clinton's domestic policy advisers, would later observe, "The transition was just the first evidence that this was not going well."[138]

Notes

1. Drew, *Whatever It Takes*, p. 257.
2. Burke interview with William Galston, February 22, 1999.
3. John B. Judis, "Old Master," *New Republic*, December 13, 1993, p. 25.
4. John B. Judis, "Old Master," *New Republic*, December 13, 1993, p. 21. Yet reports indicated that his chief deputy, Gene Sperling, was something of a "keeper of the flame," often reminding participants of the president's campaign pledges. According to one of them, "If you're in a policy discussion and you come to a decision point, and you decide that Option A is not such a good policy, Gene will say 'Let's rethink that. After all, the president did make a strong commitment.'" Paul Starobin, "Brokering Advice," *National Journal*, June 19, 1993, p. 1477.
5. Council for Excellence in Government, *1997 Prune Book*. The Council for Excellence in Government is a nonprofit organization of former government officials, now working in the private sector, who seek to improve public-sector performance. A study of the NEC by the Brookings Institution came to similar conclusions. Although it felt the NEC exposed "the president to all sides of controversial issues, minimizing turf competition, and ultimately retaining support for the president's decisions among those whose advice he did not follow," it worked less well in creating "a consistently effective decision management structure below the deputy level." The NEC's "informal, ad hoc operational style" created a "collegial environment." But it also had drawbacks: "long and sometimes unfocused meetings with unclear outcomes, an absence of predictable or consistent procedures (except for the recent weekly meetings among deputies), and a failure of the NEC to establish strategic priorities on a systematic basis." Juster and Lazarus, *Making Economic Policy*, pp. xviii–xix.
6. Paul Starobin, "Brokering Advice," *National Journal*, June 19, 1993, p. 1477.
7. Ruth Marcus, "Belatedly, White House Forms Domestic Policy Unit," *Washington Post*, August 19, 1993.
8. Burke interview with Elaine Kamarck, February 9, 1999.
9. Burke interview with Bruce Reed, June 4, 1999; Burke interview with William Galston, February 22, 1999.
10. Burke interview with William Galston, February 22, 1999.
11. Burke interview with William Galston, February 22, 1999.
12. Burke interview with William Galston, February 22, 1999.
13. Burke interview with William Galston, February 22, 1999.
14. Reich, *Locked in the Cabinet*, p. 150.

15. Warshaw, *Powersharing,* pp. 218, 221.

16. White House Press Release, Office of the Vice President, "Statement of Vice President Al Gore," January 22, 1993, *Public Papers of the President, 1993.*

17. Drew, *On the Edge,* p. 56.

18. Evan Thomas, "This Thing Is a Turkey," *Newsweek,* June 13, 1994.

19. Dan Balz, "The Young and the Rest-Less," *Washington Post,* April 14, 1993.

20. Thomas Rosensteil, "POTUS and the POSTIES," *Los Angeles Times Magazine,* May 16, 1993.

21. Tom Mathews, "Clinton's Growing Pains," *Newsweek,* May 3, 1993.

22. Michael Duffy, "That Sinking Feeling," *Time,* June 7, 1993. By early April, Clinton had about the same number of appointments named as Bush: 184 versus Bush's 183. Clinton, however, had only formally nominated and sent to the Senate eighty nominations with fifty confirmed, while Bush had sent 102 with only thirty-seven confirmed. By contrast, Reagan had 123 nominated by this point. Al Kamen, "Clinton, Bush Neck and Neck on Vacancies," *Washington Post,* April 14, 1993. By mid-July, Clinton had about 60 percent of his top positions filled, with 403 nominated, 150 confirmed, 193 pending confirmation, and 236 announced. According to one report, the pace was faster than under Bush but slower than under Reagan or Carter. Al Kamen, "About 60% of Top Posts in Government Are Filled," *Washington Post,* July 21, 1993.

23. Woodward, *The Agenda,* p. 244. In June, this was finally changed when key political meetings were moved to the upstairs solarium, where access could be better controlled.

24. Drew, *On the Edge,* p. 99.

25. John F. Harris, "The Man Who Squared the Oval Office," *Washington Post National Weekly Edition,* January 13, 1997.

26. Al Kamen, "The New Regime," *Washington Post,* February 19, 1993.

27. Drew, *On the Edge,* p. 124.

28. George C. Edwards III, "Frustration and Folly: Bill Clinton and the Public Presidency," in Campbell and Rockman, eds., *The Clinton Presidency,* p. 234.

29. Stephanopoulos, *All Too Human,* p. 112.

30. Mickey Kaus, "Tribal Hatred," *New Republic,* June 21, 1993.

31. Michael Isikoff, "Under Clinton, Drug Policy Office's Hot Streak Melts Down," *Washington Post,* February 10, 1993.

32. Ann Devroy, "Clinton Fires White House 'Worker Bees,'" *Washington Post,* February 7, 1993.

33. Ann Devroy and Ruth Marcus, "Bags and Bags and Bags of Mail," *Washington Post,* June 14, 1993.

34. Ann Devroy, "Clinton's Vow to Cut Staff Is Half Fulfilled," *Washington Post,* March 5, 1993.

35. Meanwhile, a House committee was investigating reports of backdated pay increases and appointments for White House staff members, some going back three months to inauguration day. White House officials stated that the

backdating was a result of having to process so much paperwork at the start of the administration. It was the first of a number of concerns raised about questionable White House practices. Kevin Merida, "Senate Panel Questions Cuts and Accounting at White House," *Washington Post,* April 28, 1993.

36. "Conventional Wisdom," *Newsweek,* May 3, 1993.

37. Burt Solomon, "A One-Man Band," *National Journal,* April 24, 1993, p. 971.

38. Burke interview with William Galston, February 22, 1999.

39. Drew, *On the Edge,* p. 130.

40. Brummett, *Highwire,* p. 87.

41. Birnbaum, *Madhouse,* p. 126.

42. Burke interview with Bruce Reed, June 4, 1999.

43. Burke interview with William Galston, February 22, 1999.

44. Joe Klein, "What's Wrong?" *Newsweek,* June 7, 1993.

45. Reich, *Locked in the Cabinet,* p. 180.

46. Birnbaum, *Madhouse,* p. 47.

47. Woodward, *The Agenda,* p. 232.

48. Paster also felt that McLarty was obsessed with press coverage. When Paster told him that *Newsweek* had contacted him for remarks on a feature story on the chief of staff, McLarty had Paster call the reporter back immediately so that McLarty could listen in on Paster's end of the conversation. When Paster resigned in November, he met with Clinton to convey the news, but since McLarty was also there, Paster could not tell the president that the real reason he was leaving was that he could not work with McLarty. According to Woodward, "Paster believed that McLarty had failed to manage the White House. Its staff, the administration, the outside consultants were not coordinated. Everyone and anyone free-lanced." Woodward, *The Agenda,* p. 319.

49. Stephanopoulos, *All Too Human,* p. 115.

50. Drew, *On the Edge,* p. 98.

51. Drew, *On the Edge,* p. 98.

52. Brummett, *Highwire,* p. 27.

53. Drew, *On the Edge,* pp. 67, 56.

54. Stephanopoulos, *All Too Human,* p. 140.

55. Sidney Blumenthal, "Dave," *New Yorker,* June 28, 1993, p. 37.

56. Stephanopoulos, *All Too Human,* p. 284.

57. Woodward, *The Agenda,* p. 77.

58. Tomkin, *Inside OMB,* p. 224.

59. Tom Mathews, "Clinton's Growing Pains," *Newsweek,* May 3, 1993.

60. Woodward, *The Agenda,* p. 131.

61. Woodward, *The Agenda,* p. 127.

62. Drew, *On the Edge,* pp. 67–68.

63. Woodward, *The Agenda,* p. 137.

64. Birnbaum, *Madhouse,* p. 74.

65. Drew, *On the Edge,* p. 36.

66. Birnbaum, *Madhouse,* p. 13.

67. Drew, *On the Edge,* p. 82.

68. Tom Mathews, "Clinton's Growing Pains," *Newsweek,* May 3, 1993.

69. Ann Devroy, "President Discounts Panetta's Doubts," *Washington Post,* April 28, 1993.

70. Drew, *On the Edge,* p. 166.

71. Tom Morganthau, "Close to Overload," *Newsweek,* May 10, 1993. Kennedy had 83 percent approval, Carter 63 percent, Reagan 68 percent, and Bush 55 percent.

72. Michael Duffy, "That Sinking Feeling," *Time,* June 7, 1993.

73. Drew, *On the Edge,* p. 199.

74. Drew, *On the Edge,* p. 206. As in the Baird episode a few months earlier, Guinier chose not to go quietly, despite attempts by Solicitor General Drew Days and legislative aide Howard Paster to convince her otherwise. Finally, Clinton met with Guinier for more than an hour. Guinier interpreted Clinton's concerns as a political problem that had gotten out of control; Clinton staffers felt that he had broached her views and his reservations about them in a substantive way. Whatever was said, Clinton did not tell her directly that he could not go forward. He telephoned her later in the evening and told her a decision had been made. According to McLarty, "Nothing has taken a toll like that night." Brummett, *Highwire,* pp. 144–145.

75. Bob Cohn, "So Long, Lani," *Newsweek,* June 14, 1993.

76. W. John Moore, "West Wing Novice," *National Journal,* June 5, 1993, p. 1339. For her part, Guinier felt embittered by the experience. Except for one letter Paster had sent to Senate Majority Leader Mitchell, she would later write in her memoirs that "the White House hadn't lifted a finger in support of me." In her view, the manner in which Clinton "would treat a friend" revealed an "insight into his character as a human being"; it also "would become an unexpected peek into his character as a leader." Guinier, *Lift Every Voice,* pp. 112, 113.

77. Drew, *On the Edge,* p. 179.

78. Brummett, *Highwire,* pp. 125–127.

79. Zelnick, *Gore,* p. 232.

80. The intransigence of Clinton, Paster, and Byrd not only doomed the stimulus bill but also poisoned the atmosphere for securing passage of other parts of the president's plan. The loss of Boren's support was especially crucial: the Senate Finance Committee, which would handle the economic program on the Senate side and on which Boren sat, was closely divided: eleven Democrats and nine Republicans.

81. Stephanopoulos, *All Too Human,* p. 143. According to Elizabeth Drew, the Breaux-Boren plan "might have saved the stimulus bill in the Senate." Drew, *On the Edge,* p. 117.

82. Reich, *Locked in the Cabinet,* pp. 104–105. According to another account, Clinton had been informed about the caps, but "Panetta had presumed that the House would be willing to accept the administration's proposal to raise the caps to make funds available for the investment package as presented in the economic plan. The error had not been in neglecting to explain budget law to the president, but in failing to gauge the increased interest in deficit reduction in the new Congress." Tomkin, *Inside OMB,* p. 230.

83. The needless concession also damaged Clinton's bargaining position with Congress, and it raised the specter of a president too prone to compromise and quick to cave in—a bad omen given the more difficult negotiations that lay ahead. Nor had the White House extracted any support from Western senators over the deal, support that could be useful in the future. Even Senator Max Baucus of Montana, a Democrat who had led the effort, later thought that "this is a problem. They are going too far." Drew, *On the Edge,* p. 100. It signaled that this president could be "rolled"; "a group of senators had asked only for a dialogue, [and] a few days later they were handed a convincing victory that would cost them nothing." Brummett, *Highwire,* p. 105. Clinton and his advisers had now miscalculated twice: an effort to compromise had been missed with the stimulus package, and a needless compromise had now been made over the grazing fees.

84. Drew, *On the Edge,* p. 167. On May 27, the House passed the reconciliation bill 219–213. Thirty-eight Democrats voted against it, while no Republican voted for it.

85. There were several culprits this time around. One was Chief of Staff McLarty, who had discussed the tax with Breaux (whom McLarty knew well from his time as head of Arkla); McLarty indicated that while he couldn't be specific about what could be done in the Senate, the BTU tax would be changed. (McLarty had a similar discussion with Congressman David Mc-Curdy of Oklahoma—another friend from his Arkla days—on the eve of the House vote on the budget.) Another was Howard Paster, who told Roger Altman, the deputy secretary at Treasury, that he realized a BTU tax wouldn't pass the Senate but that "we have to call it BTU for the House, so we should try to get a blend" (i.e., with some broad-based tax that was neither BTU nor just based on gasoline). Drew, *On the Edge,* p. 171. The seeming shift in the administration's position came into the open when Dee Dee Myers told the press that Clinton sought a "broad-based energy tax" (perhaps picking up on the change in phraseology in the Clinton inner circles), which was taken as a signal that Clinton was prepared to abandon the BTU tax. Clinton added to the problem, in replying to a press question at a photo-op whether the BTU tax was dead, that he "didn't want to get into the name game." Treasury Secretary Bentsen confounded the problem that night on PBS's *MacNeil/Lehrer Newshour,* commenting, "As [for] a BTU tax, I don't think you're going to see that." Watching the broadcast, Gore thought Bentsen had simply made a mistake. However, as Woodward observes, Bentsen had not made a mistake: his senatorial instincts had told him that the BTU tax *was* dead. "That was the way it was. He hadn't felt a need to consult with anyone, even the president, so he had gone ahead on his own. It was not only a matter of his authority, it was a matter of his responsibility." Woodward, *The Agenda,* pp. 221–222.

86. Woodward, *The Agenda,* pp. 259–260.

87. The plan increased taxes on social security earnings for some retirees, raised income-tax rates for those with the highest taxable incomes (affecting about 1 percent of taxpayers), raised gasoline taxes rather than the broad-based BTU proposal Clinton and the House had earlier favored, and raised the

corporate-tax rate. On the spending side, it sharply decreased defense spending and placed restraints on the growth of some Medicare and Medicaid programs. Clinton had managed, however, to make the tax code more equitable: the earned income tax credit had been expanded, taxes on about 10 million lower-income taxpayers had been reduced a bit, and tax rates on higher-income earners had been increased. Yet even here, the earned income tax credit was less than proposed, and funds for empowerment zones were deleted.

88. At the January 7, 1993, meeting between President-elect Clinton and his economic advisers in Little Rock, Panetta had forecasted a FY 1997 budget deficit of $305 billion (potentially as high as $360 billion if a further projected shortfall of $50-55 billion was included). The actual FY 1997 deficit was only $22 billion, to be followed the next year by a budget surplus. And Clinton's tax increases had not produced an economic downturn, as many Republicans had predicted back in 1993. Wall Street and the Federal Reserve, in fact, responded favorably to Clinton's deficit-reduction efforts, and long-term bond rates—and, hence, interest rates—began to decline (they were almost at 7.75 percent in 1993). As Alan Blinder, a member of Clinton's Council of Economic Advisers and a participant in the January 1993 meeting, observed in 1996: "I never thought we'd get the bond rate down to 5.8 percent [by January 1994]. If you polled economists back then and said we're going to drive the long-term interest rate below six percent, I don't think one in a thousand would have believed you." John Cassidy, "Ace in the Hole," *New Yorker,* June 10, 1996, p. 40. Other observers, it should be noted, attributed the economic boom of the Clinton years and the reduction in deficits to the persistent efforts of Alan Greenspan and the Federal Reserve to control inflation. See, e.g., Richard Stevenson, "The Battle of the Decades: Reaganomics vs. Clintonomics Is a Central Issue in 2000," *New York Times,* February 8, 2000.

89. Helen Dewar and Eric Pianin, "Clinton Finds Success, but at Cost to Goals," *Washington Post,* June 20, 1993.

90. Reich, *Locked in the Cabinet,* p. 119.

91. Burke interview with Mark Gearan, March 3, 1999.

92. Burt Solomon, "Clinton Tinkers with His Staff to Counter His Own Failings," *National Journal,* May 15, 1993, p. 1192. In mid-May, the White House also released the results of a time-management study Clinton had ordered to see how much time he spent on various issues. Clinton later told reporters that it showed he had spent little time on the gays-in-the-military issue (a total of two and a half hours), contrary to popular impressions. He had spent 25 percent of his time on foreign policy, 40 percent on health-care and economic issues. Ann Devroy, "Clinton's Time Management," *Washington Post,* May 14, 1993.

93. David Van Drehle and Ann Devroy, "White House Plans Broad Staff Shifts," *Washington Post,* May 29, 1993.

94. Ann Devroy and Ruth Marcus, "White House Needs 'Tighter Coordination' Clinton Concedes," *Washington Post,* May 5, 1993.

95. Stephanopoulos, *All Too Human,* p. 147.

96. Yet someone of Gergen's expertise—though perhaps not his political background or affiliation—was needed: one poll put Clinton's approval rating

at 36 percent, another at 42 percent. Clinton's rating (36 percent) compared unfavorably to his predecessors at this point in their presidencies: Ford at 42 percent, Reagan at 59 percent, Bush at 62 percent, Nixon at 62 percent, Carter at 64 percent, Kennedy at 74 percent, Eisenhower at 74 percent, Johnson at 78 percent, and Truman at 92 percent.

97. Eleanor Clift and Bill Cohn, "Seven Days," *Newsweek,* July 12, 1993.

98. In June, McLarty directed his attention to White House political operations, and he replaced Rahm Emanuel with Joan Baggett, who had been his deputy. Emanuel was shifted over to the communications office as deputy director. In August, Marcia Hale, who had been in charge of scheduling, replaced Regina Montoya as director of intergovernmental affairs. Criticism of Montoya had appeared in the press as early as May. Montoya was regarded as ill-prepared for the job and was "seen as an ineffective advocate." The appointment of Baggett and Hale also promised better working relationships between each of their respective offices and with the public liaison operation headed by Alexis Herman. According to one report, the intergovernmental, political, and public liaison operations did not mesh well during the early months of the administration. "People are much less turf-conscious now," one White House aide noted. Susan Page, "Clinton Draws Criticism for Hands-On Management Style," *Burlington Free Press,* May 6, 1993; and James Barnes, "A Staff Reshuffle That Could Pay Off," *National Journal,* August 21, 1993, p. 2095.

99. Ruth Marcus, "Vote Victory Was Vital Boost for Clinton's Beleaguered Chief," *Washington Post,* May 29, 1993.

100. Dan Balz and Ann Devroy, "White House Staff Starting to Shift into Drive," *Washington Post,* June 27, 1993.

101. Yet Lader's appointment was not without controversy. Like McLarty, Lader had a corporate rather than political background, and according to one staff member, they were "two peas out of the same corporate pod." Ann Devroy, "Latest White House Reorganization Plan Leaves Some Insiders Skeptical," *Washington Post,* December 12, 1993. Lader also carried baggage as yet another Friend of Bill: he was the chief organizer of the New Year's Renaissance Weekend that the Clintons regularly attended in South Carolina. As Elizabeth Drew points out, "Once again the Clintons had indulged in selecting a friend for the staff. But some other friends of theirs were bothered by the choice, feeling they had selected someone much like McLarty." Drew, *On the Edge,* p. 347.

102. Drew, *On The Edge,* p. 347.

103. Drew, *On the Edge,* p. 349.

104. Dan Balz, "Changing the Capital, but More So the Man," *Washington Post,* January 17, 1994.

105. Dan Balz, "For the Candidate and the President, Then and Now Are the Same," *Washington Post,* May 16, 1993.

106. Walker, *The President We Deserve,* p. 161.

107. Don Oberdorfer, "New NSC Framework Established," *Washington Post,* January 22, 1993.

108. Dan Oberdorfer, "Balkans, Haiti, Iraq, and Somalia Head NSC Policy Study List," *Washington Post,* January 31, 1993.

109. Jim Hoagland, "Flaws and Fissures in Foreign Policy," *Washington Post,* October 31, 1993.

110. By September 1994, reports emerged of conflict between Lake and Christopher, particularly over policy in Haiti. Reports also indicated that Clinton had openly criticized Christopher and had failed to come to his defense when he was under attack. Elaine Sciolino, "2 Key Advisers in a Bitter Duel on U.S. Foreign Policy," *New York Times,* September 24, 1994.

111. Drew, *On the Edge,* p. 144.

112. Doyle McManus, "Clinton Defers to Aides on Foreign Policy," *Los Angeles Times,* February 14, 1993.

113. Drew, *On the Edge,* p. 153.

114. Fred Barnes, "You're Fired," *New Republic,* January 10, 1994.

115. Christopher, *In the Stream of History,* pp. 129–130.

116. Drew, *On the Edge,* p. 145.

117. J. F. McAllister, "Secretary of Shhhh," *Time,* June 7, 1993.

118. Leslie Gelb, "Clinton's Security Trio," *New York Times,* December 20, 1992.

119. J. F. McAllister, "Secretary of Shhhh," *Time,* June 7, 1993.

120. Fred Barnes, "You're Fired," *New Republic,* January 10, 1994.

121. David Broder, "Wobbling Dangerously," *Washington Post,* October 13, 1993.

122. Drew, *On the Edge,* p. 146.

123. Drew, *On the Edge,* p. 150.

124. Daniel Williams, "No Good Options on Balkans," *Washington Post,* April 20, 1993.

125. Drew, *On the Edge,* p. 153.

126. The fact that the administration did not seek an alternative to the Vance-Owens plan is also noteworthy. Some in the Clinton inner circle felt that the plan rewarded Serbian aggression by moving Bosnian Muslims into enclaves and dividing the nation into autonomous provinces. Yet an alternative to the plan was not forthcoming. According to Democratic Congressman David McCurdy of Oklahoma, it also raised the specter of the administration's ties to the Carter era (Vance had been Carter's secretary of state and Christopher's former boss); an alternative to Vance-Owens, in his view, offered "a clear opportunity to shed the perception that this administration has a heavy Carter legacy." Dick Kirschten, "Muscled Up?" *National Journal,* February 20, 1993, p. 455.

127. Drew, *On the Edge,* p. 155.

128. Drew, *On the Edge,* p. 157.

129. Christopher, *In the Stream of History,* p. 347.

130. Drew, *On the Edge,* p. 160.

131. Michael Kramer, "Drawing a Line in the Quicksand," *Time,* May 24, 1993.

132. Bruce Nelan, "Reluctant Warrior," *Time,* May 17, 1993.

133. Norman Kempster, "4th State Department Officer Quits Over Bosnia," *Los Angeles Times,* August 24, 1993.

134. Drew, *On the Edge,* p. 163.

135. In October 1993, the administration faced two challenges in Somalia and Haiti that were, by most accounts, policy fiascoes. In Somalia, Bush's humanitarian mission had shifted to a military one. On October 3 and 4, in an attempt to capture Mohammed Aideed, one of the Somalian warlords, eighteen U.S. soldiers were killed and their bodies dragged through the streets of Mogadishu. The grisly event was captured by TV cameras and led to public and congressional calls for the United States to withdraw its forces, a policy that Clinton announced on October 7. Unlike Bosnia, Somalia had not even been on the administration's front burner of pressing issues. Policy had been handled by the second-level deputies' committee, and reports indicated that Clinton and his top aides had not convened to discuss Somalia until after the events of October 3. In Haiti, Clinton thought he had worked out an accord with the nation's junta to restore to power the democratically elected Aristide government by October 31. But on October 11, just days after the Somalia disaster, a U.S. Navy vessel carrying two hundred military advisers and engineers sailed into Port-au-Prince harbor, only to be met by a rag-tag mob of demonstrators. Instead of docking, the ship turned back. It was a major embarrassment to the administration. The episode painfully demonstrated that the Haitian military was not prepared to live up to its agreement to restore Aristide. But more troubling were reports indicating that the administration was aware of the deteriorating situation but saw no danger signs in sending in the lightly armed military team. According to one senior official, Clinton and his advisers "saw very early this thing was headed for a train wreck." But, as Meena Bose points out, "intelligence reports either did not reach the most influential officials, or failed to have an effect." Bose, "Priorities and Policy Making," p. 5.

136. Elaine Sciolino, "Christopher Spells Out New Priorities," *New York Times,* November 5, 1993.

137. Reich, *Locked in the Cabinet,* pp. 171, 179, 180.

138. Burke interview with Bruce Reed, June 4, 1999.

9

Lessons

Six General Propositions

A General Proposition: Decisions About Decisionmaking

This concluding chapter begins with a general proposition that underlies this study of presidential transitions. Transitions matter for presidencies for a range of reasons, but at their core they matter because they are decisionmaking processes in and of themselves—that is, they affect the organization and management of presidential decisionmaking that follows. And as we saw for each of these presidencies, how decisionmaking took place and the policy choices that were made, once a president is in office, can be linked in a variety of ways to what was done as well as to what was not done during the transition in preparation for the task ahead. This is not to deny that other factors have consequence; as I note in the Introduction, a range of causal forces can have an impact. But it is to suggest two realities of presidential administrations in the United States: that the decisionmaking underlying policy choices has great effect; and that the way in which transitions craft, or do not craft, those processes has consequences, sometimes severe.

At a general level, it is striking how the four presidents-elect studied here—Carter, Reagan, Bush, and Clinton—followed the same path leading up to their presidencies: preelection planning, organizing a postelection transition, creating policy teams, starting a policy agenda, sending groups into departments and agencies, making cabinet and subcabinet appointments, tending to other personnel matters, and shaping a White House staff. At the same time, there is much variation in how they went about these tasks, which were deemed more significant than others, and what they respectively accomplished.

The most significant element, however, is not merely the particular pieces but the differences in how they fit them into a larger whole: the decisionmaking processes of their presidency and their own roles as decisionmakers. Each of these four presidents, in fact, reflected different levels of recognition about that larger task.

For Clinton, some of these pieces received short shrift, the delay in naming his White House staff most notably. But there was also a failure to recognize how these pieces of the transition needed to come together as a resource for his presidency. Not only was there a lack of effort; the planned task force on the White House simply dropped away, to be handled informally (and ultimately not very well) by Clinton and his Little Rock advisers. It was a major error that even those in the Clinton inner circle came to realize. Attention was clearly paid to "people" but not to the process in which they would operate. Clinton was at times skilled in projecting a public face for his transition. Yet to some extent, that public face was itself disfigured by his own decision failures during the transition: gays in the military, a failure to anticipate problems with nominees, and a caving-in at times to constituency groups and other sources of pressure. Once he was in office, the absence of an orderly and organized decision process allowed Clinton's own predilections as a decisionmaker to come to the fore, and both process and decisionmaker merged to produce policy decisions that marred his early performance as president.

Carter clearly saw the tasks ahead, perhaps more clearly than did his predecessors. He also had a general idea of how he wanted to operate: a broad conception of cabinet government coupled with a collegial White House staff. Yet during his transition, there was no planning for either. At best, this amounted to a concern about the size of the White House staff and an effort to avoid a Nixonesque imperial presidency. As a result, he ended up with a decision process that was compartmentalized rather than collegial and a cabinet that didn't play the role he anticipated; he quickly became a president overburdened in policy detail with little ability to manage White House staff.

For Reagan (or, more correctly, his advisers) there was a clear recognition of organizational needs and larger processes. A division of labor was worked out at the top of the staff early on, and that early start enabled key actors, especially James Baker, to use the transition to get up to speed. Reagan's desire to use his cabinet members more centrally in his decisionmaking was recognized; moreover, unlike Carter's, the

Reagan transition provided an opportunity to devise the process and structure that would eventuate in the cabinet-council system Meese announced in early February. Yet while the transition provided a decision process that served Reagan's needs, its design could prove problematic. It placed Reagan in a highly dependent position: a process that left him uninvolved in the early stages of policy formulation, one that required close coordination among his principal aides, particularly in their ability to integrate the policy, politics, and management tasks that divided their labor, as well as a general and continuing need for trust and competence among all to whom much had been delegated.

Compared to Reagan, Bush showed more personal involvement, both during the transition and after, as decisionmaker and manager. But some choices would prove problematic: during the transition, downgrading some of the staff units that market, sell, and otherwise communicate the president's program; as well as combining the White House's economic and domestic policy operations under the direction of a skilled coordinator but whose substantive expertise was largely in economic affairs. Bush's choices for chief lieutenants accounted for his own strengths and weaknesses—but with a fuzzier definition of their roles; one (Scowcroft) would work out, while the other (Sununu) would prove difficult.

For each of these presidents, moreover, the impact on their policies and broader agendas could be considerable. Where recognition was least—Clinton and Carter—failure was greatest. But even Bush and Reagan do not offer clear success stories, merely less egregious patterns of error.

A subproposition: the limits of strategic choice and rationality. Presidents-elect seem at times to bumble through the transition, often with limited recognition of the consequences of their choices—even, in some cases, that choices need to be made. This provides strong evidence against the tendency to overdetermine activity and behavior as a product of *strategic* choice and rationality. For example, in their analysis of presidential governance, Charles Walcott and Karen Hult proceed "from the premise that staff structures emerge primarily from strategic responses by presidents to environmental demands."[1] Yet as these transitions demonstrate, such responses are often not strategic (in the sense of being part of some broader plan); they are not just presidential (other actors are often powerfully at work: whether a Meese, Baker, Sununu, or Watson); nor are they merely linked to demands coming from the broader environment (internal dynamics are clearly important when rival groups emerge, as are the president-elect's own deliberative and interpersonal style and proclivities).

The assumption that presidents act rationally and strategically during transitions is especially troubling for "rational actor" models of the presidency. That approach may have some utility in understanding other aspects of the presidency, but when applied to transitions and the early days of new administrations its value is suspect.[2] First, the assumption of rationality seems wide of the mark, especially in light of what participants fail to recognize and do during the transition.[3] Second, even when recognition is present and actions are taken, it is the variety of ways that presidents-elect respond to the challenge of transition that is interesting: they pull us to "an understanding of why individual presidents make the specific decisions they do," which some rational-choice advocates, such as Terry Moe, explicitly reject.[4]

In some strands of rational-actor theory, institutions are key in understanding the context of choices made as well as the resulting strategic actions. This might seem promising, especially since transitions are in some measure process-, structure-, and institution-building activities. Yet as Moe notes, this "new institutionalism" regards institutions as fundamental and behavior derivative; "the crucial thing is that they are impersonal."[5] As I discuss below, an institutional perspective can be useful in understanding transitions, but it is a very different understanding of how the institutional presidency operates. The rational-actor concept of institutions, by contrast, would posit the importance of institutional constraints on the transition itself, especially the impact of institutionally set rules, norms, and "games" within which participants operate and which structure their choices and behavior. Yet what is the relevant institution here: the transition planning organization? Or is it the institutional presidency–to–be, which in some measure is the outcome of such choice? The latter clearly presents conceptual difficulties, since the outcome of choice simultaneously would operate as the constraint on choice.[6]

Another assumption of some rational-actor theories is that presidents will centralize power in the White House as part of a rational strategy for control. While such centralization of power occurred to a degree (I have argued elsewhere that it is a prime effect of the institutional presidency),[7] it is not clear that it operates as strongly as posited by the rational-actor approach or in the way it posits. Reagan is interesting in this regard, since his transition arguably was the most successful of the four; but the Reagan transition centralized *less* (i.e., in its attempt to use the cabinet more productively in decisionmaking rather than use the conventional strategy—a process directed and centered in the White House staff). For Clinton, centralization would quickly emerge, but this was less the result of strategic choice, since little in the way of White House planning was undertaken. The Carter case is even more problematic under the rational-choice model: again we see centralization, but the initial goal was the diametric opposite—some form of cabinet government.[8]

Indeed, if there is a single methodological lesson to be learned from this study, it is this: the presidency needs to be studied in detail, especially regarding the complexity and variation in how presidents and their associates conduct themselves in office or, in this case, prepare to take office. It may come at some expense to parsimony and theoretical elegance,[9] but it offers a firmer foundation to understand how presidencies develop, particularly what they fail or succeed in doing at this critical point.[10] Moreover, examining what those involved in transitions actually intended and did, rather than assuming rationality, also has predictive value (a chief claim that the rational-actor approach appropriates for itself): as we have seen, what transpires or fails to transpire during a transition can be linked to what happens or doesn't happen once an administration is under way. Finally, this type of study has a measure of practical value. It may not meet the goal of some scholars for elaborate theory-building, but it can establish an empirical record that is vastly more useful for the practical lessons that can be drawn for those confronting that task in the future.

A Second General Proposition: Factoring Strengths and Weaknesses of Presidents as Decisionmakers

Each of these transitions points to a second proposition: even if decisionmaking processes are attended to during the transition, how they relate to the president-as-decisionmaker is important in understanding performance early in the term. Whatever the decisionmaking structures or systems that exist, they will matter only to the extent and in the ways the president chooses to make them matter. Carter's propensity to micromanage and, at times, to show his mastery of policy detail undermined his own desire to devolve policymaking to agencies and departments. Bill Clinton's attention to policy detail and a propensity to hear a range of policy views contributed directly to the endless meetings and the general disorder and disorganization of his early presidency. Ronald Reagan seemed to lack a curiosity about what was produced for him and rarely reached out for other views (although he was guided by a larger agenda and had the ability to be decisive). George Bush could step out of organizational channels and contact a broad network of friends and associates, but at least in domestic policy he had trouble finding that broader set of policy commitments that had so well served his predecessor.

Conventional wisdom suggests that staff systems and modes of processing information and making decisions ought to fit a president like a suit of clothes. This is partly true: one would not be wise to impose upon a president a decisionmaking environment or processes that could prove uncomfortable or nonproductive. A process that emphasized meetings, with adversaries pounding away at one another, might have been a delight for Franklin Roosevelt, but it clearly would not have served Nixon well.

But the evidence also suggests that more attention needs to be given to how that suit of clothes might be tailored. What presidential weaknesses need to be compensated for? What strengths need to be accentuated?

Simply adopting past practices from one's service as a governor, senator, or even vice president might not prove workable in the new setting of the White House. In Reagan's case, Meese and others recognized that the department-based process used in Sacramento required adaptation at the federal level. For Bush, there was recognition that he needed a different kind of chief of staff—"someone who had been sheriff"—than had been the case during his vice presidency. For Clinton and Carter, there was the absence of attention to decisionmaking; their past practices as decisionmakers were largely transferred, leaving them to fend as best they could.

In Carter's case, he thought policy papers provided enough information and analysis to make a decision; only later did he become convinced that meetings were necessary to understand the nuances underlying the written words. Moreover, with Carter there was even the absence of recognition as to how he was acting as a decisionmaker. He felt that he was good at delegating, for example, yet clearly those around him had a different view. Nor did he appreciate how his close monitoring of Stu Eizenstat's policy operations could thwart his goal of devolving policymaking down to the departmental level; although he would caution Eizenstat about his workload, week by week it increased, often at Carter's instigation, and a powerful domestic policy shop reemerged in the Carter presidency.

Even for Bush and Reagan, while some change and adaptation to the realities of the White House occurred, there was less attention paid to strengths and weaknesses, particularly cognitive, analytic, deliberative, and interpersonal styles. Bush worked with his staff secretary, Jim Cicconi, to determine how much policy detail needed to cross his desk, and Sununu adjusted to Bush's propensity to reach outside the chain of command or to consult more informally with his cabinet members and others. But the White House staff structure marketing and selling his programs and policies was more reactive than proactive to Bush's predilections in making him a better communicator. The existence of back channels for policy advice (most notably the post office box in Kennebunkport that Bush opened so that aides could reach him directly without going through Sununu) signal that his staff system was not fully serving his needs. Even in foreign policy, where Bush was on more comfortable and successful ground, his close and smooth working relationship with Scowcroft and Baker could sometimes tilt toward a like-mindedness not sensitive to new intelligence information or developing crises.

For Reagan, the attempt to mold a comfortable system compensated for his failure to immerse himself in policy detail. But it could leave the president unprepared when the process produced not consensus but disagreement, and it was up to him alone to make decisions (as in some of the budget disputes that made their way to him) or where the process had not functioned well in providing the full implication of the choices before him (the political costs of social security reform).

Presidents obviously cannot be wholly remade in their decisionmaking capabilities; their prior career experiences especially affect how well they are able to meet the challenges ahead. As Charles O. Jones notes, "Presidents-elect arrive in Washington with a background and operating style that help to explain their behavior and approach during the transition."[11] Yet just as those decisionmaking patterns developed over time, so, too, will they continue to develop in this new context. Aspects of decisionmaking that are not so deeply rooted in personality may especially be subject to modification or serve as areas of attention for possible organizational compensation. Staff systems and other parts of the decisionmaking environment especially can be organized so that weaknesses can be reckoned with and strengths taken advantage of.

Transitions are times for crafting a new administration. But they are also times for presidents themselves to undergo a transition: to closely examine their own qualities as a decisionmaker and to understand and factor in their strengths and weaknesses in preparing for decisionmaking responsibilities to come.

A Third General Proposition: Assessing the Strengths
and Weaknesses of Those Around the President

If presidents have strengths and weaknesses as decisionmakers, so do those who advise and serve. And as the personal capabilities of presidential decisionmakers require further attention, the capabilities of those around them need to be factored in as roles are defined, responsibilities assigned, and offices established. Furthermore, while presidents-elect (and then presidents) are important in understanding transitions and early administrations, I do not mean to suggest that only they count: clearly we have seen, both during the transition and after, that the chief executive's team also has an impact on what transpires.

Conventional wisdom suggests that presidents-elect need to be wary of bringing too many former associates on board. At one level, this seems to be the case. The comfort level and sense of loyalty and trust presidents have with top aides are not to be ignored, but where those immediately around the president are drawn from prepresidential associates, particularly if that association develops outside Washington, it is a recipe for disappointment if not disaster. Carter's reliance on fellow Georgians provided a sense of loyalty and trust but not necessarily competence. Clinton, in his first months in office, might have avoided some errors—and scandals—if there had been fewer Bernie Nussbaums, William Kennedys, Craig Livingstones, and Dave Watkinses and more Lloyd Cutlers who could detect trouble fast. So, too, with the temptation to use the White House as a reward for service in the campaign. The twenty-somethings in the early Clinton White House created a kind of campus culture, which was widely but not appreciatively noted. Management and policy skills, not just loyal service or working hard during the campaign, are needed.

But conventional wisdom also suggests that too many Washington insiders, while bringing expertise and experience, will follow their own career concerns and policy agendas rather than the president's. The Califanos, Haigs, Kemps, and Darmans brought considerable expertise and experience to their positions, but they were no less problematic than the Jordans and McLartys.

Personal loyalty and Washington expertise are likely to mesh if the president-elect's own career path is Washington-based and his associates are drawn from that experience. Of the four cases here, only Bush fit that mold. In fact, Bush not only benefited from close personal association but also had many who acquired some White House experience in the Reagan years (a clear benefit to a successor presidency, especially if the vice president is adept at placing his own people at the start of the new administration). This served many of them well during the transition, since they could not only draw upon their own experience but also tap into the advice and expertise of Reagan counterparts as they took over positions. It may also have facilitated a degree of teamwork; while Bush did not score a perfect record by any means, many Bush aides noted the collegial and cooperative relationships among the Bush staff.

The Reagan presidency is especially interesting, a seeming "outsider" who blended loyalty with expertise and experience. Not everyone fit this pattern, Al Haig most notably. But even during the transition, Reagan was able to draw upon personal supporters who also had a degree of Washington experience: Weinberger, Shultz, Casey, Allen, Anderson, and Pen James. Jim Baker's hiring patterns are also notable: the consummate insider reaching outside. While he did bring two longtime associates on board as deputies, other White House units were headed by Lyn Nofziger, Elizabeth Dole, and Rich Williamson, a protégé of Senator Paul Laxalt. Baker also developed a close working relationship with Mike Deaver.

Reagan's personal warmth and interpersonal style may also have been a factor in generating loyalty. In addition, teamwork figured importantly in Ed Meese's operational code; during the transition, part of the aim of his morning meetings as well as other events was to bring the staff together, to make sure, in Meese's words, that "there weren't any mysteries or little antagonisms." Once in office, Meese attempted the same with cabinet members, periodically calling them together for breakfast meetings without Reagan present in order to resolve any disagreements, problems of communication, and the like.

Of course, Reagan benefited from the short interval since the last Republican administration, which increased chances for blending loyalty and Washington experience. Neither Carter nor Clinton had that benefit. And in Clinton's case, following a twelve-year Democratic hiatus, there was also a desire to avoid unnecessary associations with Carter's late-1970s failures.

But Reagan also suffered from the fact that the initial setup could not be sustained in the long run. Meese's and Baker's efforts to keep peace, especially among subordinates, would fray as Baker's power was perceived to grow. As time went on and initial appointees moved elsewhere, replacements would not always share their degree of commitment.

Sometimes it may just be knowing enough about the White House to place a particular person in the right position. Jimmy Carter needed a Bert Lance—a more senior figure, more of an equal, someone with good political instincts—in his White House; yet Lance might have been a better fit in the position of counselor to the president rather than at OMB. Stephanopoulos might have been better suited as a general adviser to Clinton at the start, rather than facing a half-year of difficulties with the media.

The Clinton and Carter cases also have an interesting parallel. In both, an associate who served as a general policy adviser and, especially, political adviser—Hamilton Jordan for Carter, Bruce Lindsey for Clinton—was initially placed in charge of personnel operations. At one level this may have maximized presidential control, but at another both became quickly enmeshed in the appointments process to the detriment of their advisory roles at the worst possible time.

How particular roles are defined also bears attention. Bush did realize he needed a stronger chief of staff to compensate—or perhaps act as a lightning rod—for his more easygoing style. Yet there seems to have been little fine-tuning or even attention to how that role was defined in practice once Sununu was in office and as problems began to develop. Once Teeter was out, there was no realization that perhaps too much now fell to Sununu, who thought he could oversee all aspects of White House operations. Some tried to fill the gaps, particularly Andrew Card's attempts to put together a group to examine long-run scheduling and agenda planning. But as Card notes, "There was no buy-in from the top." Sununu, moreover, was at best half-heartedly committed to having a Baker-like legislative strategy group, yet something of the sort was sorely needed on a regular basis. Legislative strategy and negotiations proved to be particular weaknesses in this administration.[12]

The conventional wisdom about chiefs of staff and NSC advisers serving as "neutral brokers" also needs more scrutiny and definition. Today, practically all pay lip service to that concept (even Sununu did). Yet what does that mean in practice? How does it mesh with a president's decisionmaking needs? With the kind of staff system that is envisioned? To take one example, Mack McLarty had little in the way of a personal policy agenda, hence fulfilling the broker role in that way, but he was less successful in curbing the president's propensity to immerse himself in too much detail, hold endless meetings, and delay decisions. Clinton needed a broker who not only alerted him to the information coming to the Oval Office; he needed one who could manage—and at times ride herd on—the president himself.

Brent Scowcroft's role as NSC adviser under two presidents, Ford and Bush, also might be noted. Under Ford, Scowcroft was more the traditional broker, concerned with the quality of the information and advice the president received and the processes in which policy was considered. Under Bush, he continued some of this, but he also successfully blended it with a pattern of providing more of his own advice to the president than had been the case before. Nor did it appear to lead to the same kind of tensions that his predecessors more prone to advocacy—Kissinger and Brzezinski—generated. Bush's role in Scowcroft's appointment is also important: as we saw, while he considered him for other positions, he decided that putting him again in the NSC slot would signal the importance of the NSC system to his foreign policy decisionmaking as well as putting in place the kind of senior counselor he wanted.

At what point the neutral-broker role should be introduced within the staff structure also merits analysis. Roger Porter, by all accounts, was well suited to the role. Yet would Bush have been better served by a more proactive policy advocate in that position, particularly one that might have been adept at countering the advocacy of Darman and Sununu?

The willingness of a president to invest actual authority in key staff members is another issue that emerges in some of these cases. Again there is something of a parallel in the Clinton and Carter experiences. Clinton made McLarty chief of staff, but there was a pervasive sense that he was unwilling to grant him the real authority to carry out the job and was too willing to tolerate (and may even have valued) policy freelancing by other top aides. Hamilton Jordan later recalled that he might have been willing to serve as a more forceful coordinator in the early days of the Carter presidency, but he feared that Carter would not back him up, especially with cabinet members. Moreover, the absence of someone with authority was a problem not only for Hamilton Jordan; it spilled over into the staff system. As Watson notes, it wasted time and energy and generated conflict. The authority problem, moreover, proved endemic in the Carter presidency: in 1978, Carter appointed Jordan staff coordinator but not chief of staff, and Jordan brought in management expert Al McDonald, whose attempts at reform were thwarted, in part, because he lacked sufficient authority to carry them out.

More careful consideration of those who serve principals and their relations to others in the administration is yet another part of the equation. McLarty wasn't able to put together the kind of personal staff he wanted during the transition: the plan to appoint Harold Ickes as his deputy had to be aborted, and he could not enlist the services of the press officer he wanted. McLarty's difficulties would persist, moreover. Even when Roy Neel came on board as de facto chief of staff to the chief of staff, Mark Gearan, who had been slated to take over long-range planning, was moved over to the communications operation a month later. The arrangement with Neel did not work out, particularly in light of McLarty's own unwillingness to invest him with the author-ity to do his job. By contrast, Jim Baker enlisted highly skilled deputies, Dick Darman and David Gergen most notably.

How the pieces are put together and coordinated is also important. The division of labor between Meese and Baker was a necessary re-sponse to the internal dynamics of the Reagan inner circle, but it also brought with it the challenge of integrating policy, on the one hand, and politics and management, on the other, requiring close communi-cation between them. When that broke down, the consequences for pol-icy could be severe. In foreign policy matters, the fact that NSC Ad-viser Allen reported through Meese was particularly consequential. Not only did Meese prove to be a bottleneck at times; it put Haig in a much stronger position. Allen could not coordinate policy, much less provide a policymaking counterweight.

Baker's morning staff meetings provide an example of how internal coordination could work, at least as far as the areas under his jurisdic-tion. They were designed to look not only at the day ahead but also to the "month or months to come"; they also sought to engage in the "out-reach stuff" and "consensus building and constituency work." The Carter senior staff meetings, by contrast, were more haphazard, agenda-less affairs; key players like Jordan and Frank Moore often did not at-tend. Carter's foreign policy process offers a different twist. Here the Thursday meeting of Vance, Brown, and Brzezinski proved to be an im-portant occasion for discussion, consensus, and agenda formation, par-ticularly as it was directed at their luncheon meeting with Carter the next day. Yet Carter, while thinking the lunches were productive, was not aware of how much had gone on the day before, particularly if a consensus on some issue had already been reached.

For Clinton, broader integration and coordination proved especially problematic. Rubin's NEC was one bright spot; it was also one of the few clearly thought out efforts. But even here its organization and work could prove vulnerable to "administration players," and it was subject to the "endless meeting syndrome" that was pervasive in the Clinton presidency. Clinton's domestic policy operation is also instructive. Its internal operations had received little attention, but it does offer an in-teresting case where its principals—Rasco, Galston, and Reed—were informally able to make their operations work. It offers an example of how the staff itself may need to fill an otherwise empty organizational void.

A Fourth General Proposition: The Need for Presidents as Managers

While presidents are the recipients of information and advice and at some point become decisionmakers, they are also managers of those processes. It is true that others in the administration, most important the chief of staff and the NSC adviser, are often concerned with the quality of information and advice the president is receiving, how well processes are functioning, the kind of organizational culture present, and so on. But so, too, can presidents share in this task; indeed, they are particularly important in setting the general tone of the organizations that operate beneath them.[13] Although they fall outside the parameters of our study, both Eisenhower's and Kennedy's attention to organizational matters, particularly as they had impact on their own decisionmaking, were important forces at work in their presidencies. Likewise, Johnson and Nixon provide examples of presidents who failed to measure up to these tasks.[14]

Particularly striking in each of these four cases is the rather limited attention to management as an object of ongoing presidential attention and a recognition of its effects on performance in office and, ultimately, successful governance. For Reagan and Bush, there may have been some sense that this was a task properly vested in their chief lieutenants. Yet it was also a matter that at times required presidential attention *that those around them in fact recognized.* In Ed Harper's view, with Reagan there was a "lack of willingness to direct the White House staff" and "too many games being played beneath him."[15] For Helene von Damm, he had strengths, but "management wasn't one of them. . . . Never in his whole life did he understand how to manage a staff or appreciate the importance of staff work."[16] According to Brzezinski, Jimmy Carter "didn't use people well at times, and certainly didn't know how to discipline them."[17] Bush, too, was highly tolerant of his subordinates' behavior. According to Andrew Card, too many "were given many chances to make mistakes . . . people thought they could not lose their jobs."[18] With Bill Clinton, there was little awareness that organization mattered, much less that it needed to be managed. In fact, Clinton sometimes made matters worse. Although his anger would often flare with subordinates, his operating style evoked a sense of agreement, understanding, and empathy that was not always conducive to securing improved performance or getting at the root of policy differences.

Another common thread (at least among three of the four) is the essential trust placed in those working for them—but it was trust that could be misplaced. Especially for Carter, Reagan, and Bush, there was little sense that aides might not be wholly committed to the president's agenda or up to the tasks at hand. In Lyn Nofziger's view, Reagan "was too trusting" and had "a terrible time firing people."[19] Carter, according to one of his aides, "assumed that everybody would be a team player and be responsive to him."[20] Because Bush "was such a decent, honest, straightforward guy," John Sununu would later observe, "people—including sometimes his friends—took advantage of him."[21]

But loyalty on the president's part did have some positive effects. In Carter's case, if an adviser lost out on a particular argument, that did not mean their influence as a whole evaporated. Bill Brock recalls that Reagan also did not make a loser feel that he was out of favor; he was "gracious, yet firm."

There are other facets of management that are important as well. To what degree is the president willing to tolerate infighting and bureaucratic competition among his staff? At one level, this is a matter that will in some measure be determined by the kind of persons the president initially chooses to hire. In Carter's case, the various participants who had been at odds with each other during the transition were then carried over into the new administration. But it also may require presidential attention once in office, especially if the cleavages run all the way to the top. For Reagan, while Meese and Baker tried to make their arrangement work, competition between the "ideologues" and "pragmatists" emerged at lower levels, as it almost surely would. Yet Reagan, in the view of some who served him, was oblivious to infighting and intramural tensions. By contrast, Bush had a clearer notion of the kind of aides he wanted—no "cowboys," as one member of the administration put it—although his two closest aides, Sununu and Darman, had quite different operating styles, to put it mildly, than other members of the Bush team. For Clinton, personal comfort and loyalty were key, not the team effort required to make things work.

A Fifth General Proposition:
Coming to Terms with the Institutional Presidency

As I note in the Introduction, analyzing transitions may shed light on the effects of the institutional presidency that are important in understanding the operations of the modern presidency, especially the internal challenges faced in making that office work effectively. This facet of presidency scholarship emphasizes the growth in the White House staff over the last sixty years and the impact that a large-scale staff system—in essence a large bureaucracy—can have on the office.

For some scholars, the presence of an institutionalized presidency suggests that organizational direction and management by presidents are less important in understanding the office. In one of the few quantitative analyses of the institutionalization of the presidency, Ragsdale and Theis observe that the presidency has, since the late 1970s, exhibited a high degree of institutionalization as measured by its autonomy, adaptability, complexity, and coherence. But they also conclude that national-government activity is the most important driving force of institutionalization, with presidential activities and their management efforts having at best a modest impact: "The very political independence of the office rests less on innovations of presidents than on changing environmental conditions." Even with respect to the duration of EOP units, although "presidents are indeed the ones announcing decisions to open and close EOP units, factors outside their administrations determine the nature of those decisions and the resulting effects on duration."[22]

At one level, Ragsdale and Theis are right to assert that by the 1970s "presidents' staff management had less to do with the shape of the presidency as an institution than it had earlier."[23] With the exception of Carter's Office of Administration and the Reagan-Bush Office of National Drug Control Policy (which itself had earlier incarnations under Carter and Ford), no major units have been added to the EOP. Yet their analysis of presidential effects on organization and management *at the level of EOP units* misses important dynamics that this study of transitions and other approaches to the linkage of organization and management, on the one hand, and institution, on the other, suggest.

First, even at the level of the EOP itself, how presidents use these units—particularly as a part of their policy deliberations—varies a great deal.[24] A formalized domestic policy operation has existed as part of the EOP since 1970, but its organization and use has varied greatly under Nixon, Carter, Reagan, Bush, and Clinton. For Carter, the domestic policy staff was initially envisioned as a coordinating body for what was hoped would be a cabinet-dominated policy process; it soon became more a White House–centered operation and its own source of policy initiative. Under Reagan, the Office of Policy Development was part of a more elaborate council system that sought to facilitate cabinet input as well as serve as a way for the OPD staff and White House to direct and control policy initiatives. Further variance also occurred in

the Bush and Clinton domestic policy staffs.[25] In national security matters, the impact of the NSC adviser and NSC staff have also differed:
one need only compare Brzezinski and Kissinger to Richard Allen, or,
more recently, Brent Scowcroft to Anthony Lake.

Second, when we look more deeply into how policy processes develop, the interesting dynamics occur within the EOP units, particularly the White House Office. It is here that presidents focus more of
their attention during the transition. They may not do it well, but how
roles are defined, subunits organized, and day-to-day deliberations set
up are subject to direct efforts on the president's part and exhibit a high
degree of variance. Although Shirley Anne Warshaw concludes that the
White House domestic policy operation has become institutionalized,
her extensive and thorough analysis of its organizational changes from
administration to administration *and* within particular administrations
points to the impact of organizational choice and management direction as vital to understanding the presidency even if one buys the notion that the EOP as a whole has become institutionalized.[26]

Similar variation also exists within other White House units. All of
these presidents have had a legislative liaison operation, but compare
Carter's staff to that of Reagan (and add in Baker's legislative strategy
group). All have had some communications operation, but compare that
of Gergen and Deaver to Demarest under Bush or Stephanopoulos
under Clinton. As with the EOP units, one can trace somewhat similar
functional groupings within the White House Office, yet their internal
organization, operations, and significance as part of the policy process
can vary greatly. That is why, as I suggest in the Introduction, a more
detailed and comprehensive analysis of each of these transitions and
subsequent presidencies is needed; the devil is indeed sometimes (and
I think quite often) in the details.[27] And in the details, moreover, we
can discover what matters.

Let me be clear that I don't disagree with the notion of taking the institutional presidency seriously. In my own work, *The Institutional Presidency,* I have noted a series of institutional effects that seems to persist
from administration to administration: centralization of control over the
policymaking process by the White House staff, centralization of power
within the staff by one or two key aides, and the emergence of behavior
and routines that are typical of bureaucratic organizations. But in addition to this, I have also emphasized how institutional forces interact with
and can be affected by the managerial and organizational abilities and
skills that presidents and those closely around them, for better and
worse, bring to the task of defining and furthering policy deliberations.

In one sense, transitions are in great measure about crafting the organizational resources that assist presidents in that task in a variety of ways. The various components of an institutional presidency, which persist from administration to administration, moreover, are obviously part of those organizational resources. The three initial propositions discussed above—decisions about decisionmaking, presidents as decisionmakers, and assessing the strengths and weaknesses of those around them—have already provided some evidence about how presidents-elect and their transitions have recognized this organizational and managerial challenge, and part of that discussion is obviously relevant to the impact of the institutional presidency and whether its resources are used or not.

But my approach to the institutional presidency—a staff system that can take on the characteristics of a bureaucratic organization—also prompts a particularly important question about its relationship to presidential transitions: While the impact of the forces at work in the institutional presidency may well play out throughout a presidency, what impact did these transitions have at the start? This is important because transitions and the early days of the new administration are a time when presidents are, at least in theory if not in practice, in the best position to make their own impact on the presumed institution greatest felt; the day-to-day pull of the institution has yet to set in and the possibility of organizational change and management direction is most favorable.

In Jimmy Carter's case, the failure to devise a way of making his cabinet work effectively led to a White House staff that, even in the first year of the new administration, began to centralize policy control in its hands.[28] With respect to centralization of power within the White House, while Carter initially wanted to avoid a powerful White House chief of staff, instead a compartmentalized staff system resulted. In foreign affairs, Brzezinski quickly became a powerful NSC adviser. Bureaucratic infighting also quickly emerged, and problems of loyalty and morale developed. Carter, however, was averse to dealing with these issues, just as he had been averse to stilling the conflicts that had erupted during the transition. Carter's propensity to let his top staff members work out problems among themselves also exacerbated the problem; his decision during the transition to address organizational matters through an elaborate, and ultimately time-consuming, reorganization project delayed any process of corrective remedy.

For Reagan, the experiment with the cabinet councils was a useful attempt to bring non–White House channels of information and advice into the administration's deliberations. Its success, however, varied by council, and over time—especially by the end of Reagan's first term—policymaking became increasingly White House–centered. The division of labor between Meese and Baker initially promised a more balanced distribution of power within the White House, but here, too—and largely as a result of its design—Baker became a dominant force and Meese's influence began to wane. Within the staff, the working relationship that Baker and Meese developed at the top was not replicated; in Deaver's view, the mood in the White House became, over time, "a period of self-rampant paranoia."[29] The efforts of Reagan and his associates during the transition and in the early months of his presidency offer an important example of an attempt to make use of the institutional resources of the presidency but to deflect some of its negative effects. But those efforts also indicate how much attention must continue to be given to management and organization issues as time goes on. Where Paul Light might see a "cycle of increasing effectiveness," there also may be a cycle of institutional detriment at work as well.[30]

George Bush's proclivity to reach out to a range of sources for policy advice, plus the fact that his cabinet was well stocked with friends and associates, deflected to some extent the centralization of policymaking in the White House staff. Bush's deliberate efforts to create a collegial White House staff, plus the fact that most had ties to Bush personally and often to each other, may also have deflected some of the patterns of bureaucratic behavior that developed in other administrations. The relationship among his foreign policy team was also unusually cooperative, although Baker and Scowcroft were well aware of and had personally experienced the tensions that can develop between the NSC operation and the State Department. Bush was less successful, however, in dealing with the emergence of a powerful chief of staff in John Sununu and a powerful OMB director in Dick Darman.

In Clinton's case, policymaking was largely concentrated in the White House, particularly in the NEC and DPC staffs. Cabinet members often felt shut out, witness Reich's and Peña's concerns about being "out of the loop." McLarty's relatively weak role as chief of staff did not initially centralize power internally in his office, but it did have the effect of making Clinton himself a powerful (although not necessarily effective) de facto chief of staff. With Panetta's appointment, the chief of staff again became a central figure, like Baker and Sununu. Clinton's staff often exhibited a degree of policy freelancing during the first year and was the source of an unusually high degree of gaffes, missteps, even embarrassing scandals. The organizational culture that developed in the Clinton White House would culminate in tolerance for

Clinton's misbehavior as the Lewinsky scandal unfolded. As Michael Isikoff, the *Newsweek* reporter who first broke the scandal, would later recount: "The lies were told at first by Mr. Clinton and then spread and magnified by everybody around him—his top aides, his lawyers, his spin doctors. . . . A culture of concealment had sprung up around Bill Clinton and, I came to believe that summer, it had infected his entire presidency."[31]

With Clinton, we see not only institutional forces at work but also the problems that arise when presidential management and thoughtful organization are neglected or otherwise missing.

A Sixth General Proposition:
Compensating for the Absence of Institutional Memory

A common problem for new presidents is the absence of institutional memory about these matters—knowledgeable personnel or a record of information that gets carried over from one administration to another. Unlike a new chief executive of a private corporation, presidents do not enter office with an organization largely intact, with an ongoing level of activity, or with easily accessible data about past activities and performance; the needed management changes cannot be made slowly, at will, and in a more deliberate fashion. Rather, every new president encounters a "corporate headquarters" in which the top positions are vacant and most offices empty. Basic information no longer exists or has been carted away to await the opening of the predecessor's presidential library.[32]

While institutional memory is not available, surrogates can be found to fill the breach. In each of the four transitions, either in the transition planning process or through individual efforts of new staff members, some efforts were made to contact those who had served in similar capacities in the past. Jim Baker, John Sununu, and Mack McLarty, for example, all had contact with some of their opposite numbers from prior administrations. Even in Jimmy Carter's case, while there was no chief of staff, the reorganization project that Harrison Wellford directed undertook interviews with Ford staff members. As Baker's notes from his meetings in 1980 suggest, the information and advice provided can be a candid and valuable source in giving a new chief of staff a leg up on the job, even if all details are not applicable or always followed. I was particularly struck, in looking at some of the archival material and in some of the comments made in interviews, by how cooperative former officeholders can be with their successors, even when there are wide ideological and partisan differences.

When power passes to the president of the same party, a particularly important opportunity surfaces. Chase Untermeyer's work with Robert Tuttle of the Reagan personnel office provided him information and permitted contacts before election day that would not have occurred had it been a Democratic administration. As well, the White House prepared extensive briefing books for Untermeyer, which he and his associates would find extremely useful once Bush was elected. C. Boyden Gray, working with Reagan's office of legal counsel, also quickly developed materials and a plan of action for dealing with the clearance process once the appointment process was under way. Early work here seems especially beneficial since prospective candidates need to be aware of the legal constraints on their appointment, especially financial-disclosure requirements.

A number of new Bush staff members could also contact their counterparts in the Reagan administration with relative ease, not just at the highest staff levels but also lower down. But as noted earlier, all of these opportunities become more tenuous if decisions about the White House staff are late in coming. Little can be gained if there is no time left to contact outgoing staff from the previous administration.

The efforts of those who plan the transition before election day are another avenue for bringing past experience and knowledge to bear. In his preelection work for Carter in 1976, Jack Watson met with former White House staff members, and he and his staff tapped policy experts within and outside of government. Limited to personnel planning, not much similar occurred in the preelection efforts undertaken by Pen James in 1980 and Chase Untermeyer in 1988. But both the Reagan and Bush experiences offer another twist on possible avenues of early and informed preparation: the decisions to have Baker take charge of White House planning during the transition and then to become chief of staff and, in 1988, the early decision by Bush to place Untermeyer and Boyden Gray in the White House positions they were working on during the transition.

Another source of institutional memory is the transition veterans themselves. Harrison Wellford has been a participant in every Democratic effort since 1976; Anne Wexler is another. Untermeyer and Card are their opposites on the Republican side. The problem here is whether their efforts are utilized. In 1992, the materials Wellford and others compiled on the White House and other matters were part of Kantor's preelection operation, but they apparently fell by the wayside after he lost out in the postelection struggle and as the proposed team on White House planning was dropped. The fact that institutional memory of a sort can be gleaned is no guarantee that it will have an impact.

Finally, there is also a kind of memory that is drawn from knowledge about prior transitions. Carter's lack of control over subcabinet appointees was well known in the Reagan transition. The Bush transition thought the Reagan effort overorganized and overstaffed. Clinton and his advisers wanted to make better use of the transition as a publicity effort for a policy agenda. Some perceptions made sense. But the danger arises of fighting the last war or drawing the wrong lessons of history. At the very least, they may cloud or otherwise obscure tasks that they must uniquely focus on.

Other Lessons

Beyond these broader propositions, the four transitions and their outcomes offer other lessons. These especially involve the transitions themselves and how they might operate more smoothly and effectively.

The Dangers of Preelection Transition Planning: Conventional Wisdom Versus Reality

In *Passages to the Presidency,* Charles O. Jones notes the conventional wisdom that "preelection transition planning must be done as though it were unnecessary, even dangerous." Jones regards this as an unsound fear and cites the benefits for presidents-elect in paying attention to preelection planning.[33] Both propositions, in one sense, are correct, and they are not necessarily contradictory: one could have a secretive operation that is nonetheless subject to greater attention by the candidate. Bush's transition, in fact, fits this pattern. In Chase Untermeyer's appointment to lead the 1988 preelection effort, Bush explicitly recognized the need for a more limited operation, one that wouldn't become an "alternative center" attracting "the energetic and ambitious." But Bush continually oversaw Untermeyer's operation, something Carter and Clinton failed to do.

The analysis suggests a more complex picture. The four recent transitions engaged in some preelection effort and sought to keep that effort under wraps. The two transitions that ran into more difficulty—those under Carter and Clinton—saw more publicity (a point for conventional wisdom). But both were also led by individuals who particularly lacked the trust of campaign members—Jack Watson and Mickey

Kantor; the Reagan and Bush operations, in contrast, relied on more low-key figures—Pen James and Chase Untermeyer.

There were also differences in the scope of their mandates. James was charged with setting up a personnel operation, while Untermeyer was even more restricted to planning for a personnel operation plus producing a memo on the steps Bush would need to take should he be elected. By contrast, Watson's mandate was largely unbounded. So, too, was Kantor's, although personnel matters were supposedly off the table. While prospective jobs may have been a cause of the tensions that emerged in the Carter and Clinton camps, the person in charge and the scope of the mandate may have been equally, if not more, irritating— witness the concerns raised by some of Hamilton Jordan's associates in 1976. Perhaps there is something of a paradox: in order to accomplish more during the postelection transition, "less is more" in regard to the preelection effort, especially anything that generates publicity. That is not to say, however, that more informal efforts by the candidate and others should not be undertaken. Both Reagan and Bush, despite limits on James's and Untermeyer's mandates, began to make decisions before election day that fostered a more effective postelection effort.

Preelection Transition Planning and the Campaign Effort:
Oversight Rather Than Integration?

Jones offers an important insight when he notes the benefits of "integrating the two organizations [preelection transition and campaign] through campaign leadership." At one level, the lack of integration in Watson's and Kantor's efforts was another cause of difficulties; in Watson's case, Jordan was irritated by not only what Watson was doing but also the lack of control over and information about his efforts. On the positive side, the Reagan preelection effort in 1980 was better, but again it presents a more complex picture. Meese provided oversight, but James's efforts remained organizationally and physically separate from the campaign. Also, James benefited from the presence of Reagan loyalists such as Helene von Damm on his staff, which may have been an important asset in stilling fears among Reagan loyalists in being passed over for jobs. In the Bush case, Untermeyer's efforts were also organizationally separate from the campaign, although here, too, oversight was provided by Bush, Sununu, and Baker. "Integration" may thus be less important than the presence of oversight by a respected figure like Meese or the enlistment of longtime associates of the candidate who, while not part of the campaign, still informally signal that the concerns of those involved in the campaign will not be ignored. Kantor's situation is especially interesting in this regard; he was the campaign's chairman and its preelection transition head (perfect integration in some sense) yet remained distrusted and soon paid a significant price.

Watson's and Kantor's situations following the election also had repercussions as to how much of their preelection work was utilized and, more generally, whether they leveraged the preelection period for subsequent postelection activities. Especially for Kantor, there are indications that his work product was linked to his own fate and that as his star fell so, too, did his work product. For Watson, the link is more difficult to establish; his thoughtful, albeit lengthy, memos to Carter might have set in motion better organizational analysis and perhaps led to more effective decisionmaking processes than in fact took place. The merits of the work product, unfortunately, can be hitched to the fates of the principal actors.

Transition Planning: Formal Versus Informal Efforts

The Bush and Reagan cases suggest that not all relevant planning needs to be undertaken by those formally assigned to the transition operation. Those within the more informal circle of advisers have a role to play as well. In Reagan's case, Meese, Deaver, Stu Spencer, and others had given some thought as to what a Reagan administration, particularly a Reagan White House, would look like. The fact that Ed Meese did not become chief of staff was in the works for some time. In Bush's case, he had clearly thought about appointments, noted especially by his preelection conversation with Jim Baker, when he offered him the secretary of state's position. As well, Bush may have begun to think about what his White House staff was going to look like (he at least had John Sununu's appointment as chief of staff in mind). So, too, with his early decisions on Boyden Gray as White House legal counsel and Chase Untermeyer as director of White House personnel.

Postelection Changes: The Imperative of Presidential Action

The Reagan and Bush preelection operations also differed from those of Carter and Clinton in that the expertise of the two principals, James and Untermeyer, was largely in the area of personnel. Once election day was over, more central figures took over the transition—Meese for Reagan and Craig Fuller and Bob Teeter for Bush. Both sets of decisions were made quickly and without controversy (another difference), and the persons involved had both campaign connections (Teeter and Meese) and long career associations (Fuller and Meese). Watson and Kantor, by contrast, might have been candidates to lead their respective post-election transitions, but by election day both had become the object of considerable controversy.

Another difference is in how quickly the four recent transitions were up and running. For Carter and Clinton, concerns about the preelection transition operation led to delay in deciding who would head the post-election effort. In Carter's case, it was particularly acute and generated a period of heightened conflict and tension between the Watson and Jordan camps. Carter was unwilling to settle the matter himself, preferring his aides work it out. Internal problems as well as external effects were generated: rifts were widely reported in the media, and Carter's own managerial competence was called into question. While a modus operandi of sorts did emerge, responsibilities were often conflicting and particular duties often shifted. This was especially apparent in the personnel process, with a number of groups charged with making recommendations and sorting out appointments. Clinton more directly intervened in quelling the controversy raised by Kantor's possible emergence as his transition director. But here, too, a legacy was left. While Warren Christopher and Vernon Jordan brought a certain political and symbolic cachet to the job, neither had a working knowledge of the Clinton governorship—familiarity with his day-to-day workways, his decisionmaking style—or with the operation of the White House staff; at best, Christopher could bring a departmental-based perspective from his prior service as a Carter undersecretary of state. For that matter, Richard Riley, Harold Ickes, Bruce Lindsey, Mark Gearan, Al From, and even Mickey Kantor did not have any prior White House experience.

In 1992, Clinton's preoccupation with appointing his cabinet was apparently one factor in selecting Christopher to direct the transition. As Christopher himself would later acknowledge, Clinton was impressed with how he had handled the vice presidential selection process over the summer and thought he could apply the same skills and methods to the cabinet. While perhaps an asset at that task, Christopher was less skilled at other parts of the transition. Moreover, Christopher himself became distracted with preparing for his responsibilities in the new administration once his own cabinet position had been secured.

Key Appointments: Early Action Solves Management Problems

In 1980 Jim Baker was in a position to plan not only for the White House staff but also for a staff he was to head. This emphasizes the importance of making decisions about the White House staff, especially key players, early in the process. In 1988, Bush moved quickly—nine days after the election—in formally naming Sununu as chief of staff (although that decision had been in the works for some time). Although there was some politicking in the interim about a resurrection of the troika, Sununu was in the position to plan for White House operations early in the transition, and he actively did so. Bush very early firmed up Untermeyer's appointment as his personnel chief, a matter that had been decided before the election, as well as Boyden Gray's job as White House legal counsel; both were announced at Bush's first post-election press conference.

But even in Bush's case, valuable time was lost in setting up a domestic policy shop and bringing on board someone with experience in overall strategy in the attempt to find a place for Robert Teeter. The matter was not settled until early January, and when Teeter decided not to join the new administration on a full-time basis, Roger Porter was quickly shifted over from the trade representative's office to head the domestic and economic policy staffs. Domestic policymaking was a bit rudderless in the interim.

The advantages of moving early on top appointments are several. First, it begins to quell the controversies and uncertainties of those in the transition eager for jobs. The earlier the top layers are decided, the quicker second- and third-level staff positions can be filled. It also extends the period in which the official-designate—whether chief of staff, legal counsel, or OMB director—can begin to get a handle on the new position, both in gathering pertinent information and understanding how the job operates. This allows someone like Baker more time to contact his opposite numbers in other administrations and factor in, where appropriate, their thoughts and experiences. And the sooner staff positions are filled, the sooner the officials designated for those positions can contact their opposite numbers in the outgoing administration. In 1992, by contrast, the week or so (in some cases even less) most incoming Clinton staffers had between their selection and inauguration day allowed little time for contact with the Bush White House staff; in some instances, their Bush counterparts had already vacated their positions.

Defining an Agenda and Establishing Priorities: Complex Tasks

Conventional wisdom suggests that presidents-elect must begin to define agendas and establish priorities during the transition. This is not to suggest that the only agenda that counts is the president's own. As many have argued, in a constitutionally separated system of powers, Congress and other political actors powerfully affect how that agenda is ultimately defined and what proposals achieve legislative success.[34] Yet even in a more competitive and, at times, disadvantaged position, presidents will pursue policy goals and seek to define some political agenda, no more so than in the early days of their presidency. As Bond and Fleisher concede, "a president's greatest influence over policy comes from the agenda he pursues and the way it is packaged."[35] Moreover, presidents are especially likely to be effective early in the administrations; as Edwards notes, "being ready to send legislation to the Hill early in the first year" exploits the honeymoon period and "is related to the setting of priorities." First-year proposals, moreover, "have a considerably better chance of passing Congress than do those sent to the Hill later in an administration."[36]

Agenda-building and prioritization: organizational and management tasks. The Bush and Clinton transitions illustrate the importance of agenda-related activities; both had acute problems in domestic policy. But they point not to the need to parse out whether Congress or the president had the upper hand (although that is not an unimportant question at some level). Rather, they direct attention to what went on—or didn't go on—in-house, especially how their transitions were organized and managed to handle their early political agendas. Policy agendas are outcomes, but they issue from processes that have bearing on how presidents— and, in our case, especially presidents-elect—will define or otherwise decide on them.

Bush's domestic policy transition planning, for example, was a hollow operation. The two initiatives that did take shape in the transition—savings-and-loan reform and Latin American debt restructuring—were important and needed, but they were hardly the stuff to capture the political imagination or build Bush's reputation as a policy activist. In Clinton's case, while policy issues had begun to percolate during the transition, he resisted prioritizing his policy agenda well into his presidency. Moreover, not only was prioritizing a problem; as Bruce Reed would later observe, "There wasn't a decisionmaking team in place to carry out the strategy, to act on it. The lines of authority weren't clear." For Carter, the issue was making use of the advice at hand. Watson's preelection planning had established a time line and a prioritizing schema, but there was no action-forcing mechanism or other way of making Carter take heed of it.

Reagan's 1980 transition was an obvious contrast. Reagan benefited from the plethora of policy groups organized in the preelection period, the Wirthlin-Gergen initial-actions task force, Meese's daily senior staff meetings, and Darrell Trent's operation, which sought to educate cabinet members and others in the new administration about the Reagan agenda. Reagan also got some mileage in selling his program to Congress by bringing some of its members, Laxalt from the Senate and Evans from the House, directly into its operations.

But even in 1980, further effort was sometimes needed: the policy task forces, Shultz's economic coordinating group, and the initial-actions report were often short on specifics. On budget matters, this placed Stockman in the difficult position of translating broader policy objectives into concrete budget proposals in a short frame of time. In welfare reform, by contrast, Robert Carleson's gubernatorial experience with Reagan plus his own leadership of the HHS task force and then his appointment in the Office of Policy Development allowed him to move quickly on that policy front, gaining Reagan's agreement to a key initiative even before inauguration day.

Agenda issues are also linked to how other channels of information and advice are organized and structured. To take one example: how the cabinet and its departments are linked to the White House staff may have repercussions on agenda matters. Issues and policies that are largely department-centered might be useful matters for the new White House to co-opt, orchestrate, or otherwise take credit for. Even some anniversary or occasion—say, the fiftieth anniversary of social security or the twenty-fifth anniversary of EPA—might be an occasion for a presidential rather than a departmental event. Other matters might usefully lead to a White House heads-up (or, for that matter, a heads-down). The numerous slipups among George Bush's cabinet members particularly illustrate the importance of attention here, especially better coordination with the White House.

Agenda-building does not stand alone. Crafting a policy agenda during the transition is not a discrete task. Problems in other parts of the transition also can bear on agenda matters. Delays in appointing the cabinet can put transition staff members in the position of writing "option papers for God knows who," a problem that was especially noted by Carter and Clinton staffers. Transitions that use departmental teams but stock them with campaign workers and other political supporters lacking substantive expertise also hinder efforts to provide the kind of policy information and institutional history that might be needed. Questionable nominations—Tower by Bush, Baird by Clinton—can absorb attention, as can offhand comments about gays in the military or a new policy toward Iraq (in Clinton's case). For George Bush, the decision to cut down on the number of top-level White House aides combined domestic and economic policy together; this, coupled with Roger Porter's late arrival on the scene, made the emergence of a bolder domestic agenda more difficult.

Early warning signs also appear during transitions. Judith Feder's sober assessment of the costs of health-care reform might have caused Clinton to pause in his assessment of how easy it might be and how soon it could take place. The concerns over Frank Moore's role as Carter's liaison to Congress surfaced during the transition, as did criticism of Carter's charge to Jim Schlesinger to formulate a comprehensive energy plan in secret.

Charles O. Jones is correct when he states that a president-elect who emerges from the election with a mandate will be in a more advantageous position: "Presidents-elect who win convincingly with a clear message and collateral support in Congress have an advantage in effecting the conventional transition."[37] Yet the Reagan mandate of 1980—the only recent transition that arguably enjoyed such status— still suggests the wisdom of further planning, organization, and management. The public may have bought into the need for domestic budget cuts, defense increases, and tax reductions in its electoral verdict, but squaring them into concrete proposals and policy initiatives still awaited Reagan and his associates after election day. Presidents-elect in less auspicious positions, moreover, face an even more difficult challenge: crafting a sellable agenda is especially needed when electoral victories are more fragile and mandates unclear.

Paul Light offers a different take on the difficulties presidents face. In his view, domestic policy is becoming "less responsive to presidential intent" even though presidents still need to craft an agenda: "Ideas appear to be growing more polarized, opportunities for action more constrained, problems more intractable, assumptions more politicized, research more ideological, solutions more varied."[38] Thus the agenda task for presidents-elect will remain, but within a context requiring even more thought, organization, and effort.

The task will be more difficult for future presidents-elect (at least in the short run) for another reason. Three of the four presidents studied here faced budget constraints and deficit problems that, in part, deflected some pressure from offering other, more ambitious policy initiatives. Should current surpluses continue, successors will likely face greater agenda expectations, especially in addressing the big-ticket issues: social security, Medicare, and health-care reform.

The Link Between Campaigning and Governing: Internal Organization and Planning

"Campaigning for policy" may now be in the process of replacing conventional notions of presidential transitions, as Charles O. Jones argues. Even so, the communications efforts underlying it still require thought, organization, and decisions. In Bush's case, Bob Teeter's appointment might have brought on board the communications and public-relations skills that would soon prove sorely needed in his presidency, but an organizational arrangement could not be worked out. Absent Teeter, his potential contributions were not fully replicated elsewhere.

Clinton's presidency may have redefined the way in which presidents seize policy advantages and then campaign for their adoption. But Clinton's transition does not offer a positive set of experiences for what, arguably, developed much later. At times he erred in setting up his communications operation. Despite favorable coverage during the campaign, Clinton's relationship with the media was not good to begin with; both Clintons were defensive about media criticism and negative reporting in general. The failure to adjust to the White House media— as opposed to those covering the campaign—further soured the atmosphere. And Hillary Clinton's decision to cut off media access to Stephanopoulos's office, plus the dual arrangement of Dee Dee Myers and Stephanopoulos as well as their own operating styles, led to confusion and further distrust.

Appointing a Cabinet: A True Management Task

At one level conventional wisdom is right: the process of appointing a cabinet is one of the most important activities of a president-elect during the transition, but it can take up too much time and attention. It is also the most visible and publicized activity during this period, and it can engage the president-elect in an exercise of symbolic politics that can bring benefits as well as costs. Clinton's goal of selecting a cabinet that "looks like America" initially scored a public-relations plus, but it also heightened pressure from constituent groups and led to a sense that Clinton could be "rolled" under such pressure.

Transitions shed light on some of the management and organizational tasks associated with the process. First, the transition's legal office needs especially skilled and attuned personnel to detect problems early. Clinton's nominations of Zoe Baird and then Kimba Wood were regrettable and costly lapses in the vetting process, and they can be linked in part to weakness in the transition's efforts in this area. Each of these cases not only made filling the positions difficult; each carried over into the postinaugural period, deflecting attention from more important parts of the president's early policy agenda and raising issues about competence, political and otherwise.

Second, there is a need for continuity in the transition's personnel operation, particularly for lower-level appointments. Bush's early appointment of Untermeyer provides one positive example, especially since Untermeyer was unlikely to be a candidate for other staff and cabinet positions. By contrast, when Richard Riley, who was designated to oversee this area for the Clinton transition, was nominated to a cabinet position, his attention began to focus on his own confirmation. As one Clinton transition member put it, "The personnel process was a complete mess" with Riley gone; "it was just chaos . . . there were no real people with experience running it." A similar pattern also occurred when Clinton's transition director, Warren Christopher, was tapped to become secretary of state. While all recent transitions have recognized the importance of cabinet and subcabinet appointments, they must be overseen with diligence and care by a figure who clearly has both expertise and the confidence of the president. Perhaps the worst danger is the one Clinton faced: a personnel operation and transition whose principals end up with cabinet positions to the detriment of the personnel process.

Today, presidents-elect must also recognize that appointing and then securing confirmation of cabinet and subcabinet personnel is likely to be a long process. Where nominations are delayed, planning must be undertaken early, particularly where that department's or agency's policy area figures importantly in the president's early legislative initiatives. Indeed, some backward planning might be needed: a focus first on those appointments that are most central to the upcoming agenda. Pendleton James did this in 1980, for example, concentrating first on economic-related positions that were central to the Reagan agenda.

Even in other cases, steps must be taken, particularly if a confirmation process is delayed or otherwise in trouble. A newly elected president might find, for example, that a lower-ranking member of the previous administration is now the acting head of a department, at least for a time. Even in the easy cases, the process of finding the right appointee and then moving from nomination to confirmation has lengthened considerably. This lag can be especially problematic if an inter-party transition of power occurs, as was the case in 1993 when the Justice Department was headed, for a time, by a Bush administration holdover. Webb Hubbell, a Clinton friend and Hillary's former law partner, was slated for a top position at Justice, but even his confirmation had not yet gone through. Hubbell showed up for work anyway and served as Clinton's de facto representative, although Stuart Gerson, the head of the department's civil division under Bush, was acting attorney general. According to Hubbell, while the "job was getting done," "the effect of this situation was twofold. The administration couldn't get its program under way because it still had a Republican attorney general. And the media began focusing on what they called a leadership vacuum at Justice."[39]

In 1980, by contrast, Pen James recalls that there was a clear recognition that at least one Reagan appointee, at some level, be in place by inauguration day so that the work of the department would be directed by a member of the new administration. In 1992, Fuller and Teeter sent a memo to all department heads informing them that incumbent officials "are free to remain at their posts until their successors arrive for duty." In their view, such a policy "assures continuity of leadership and an effective transition of authority." But, they added, the policy "will in no way impede the flexibility of newly appointed agency heads, upon confirmation, to accept the resignations of subordinate incumbents immediately."[40] In this case, the order applied not only to top personnel but also to all presidential appointees, including noncareer senior executive service and Schedule-C officials.

Transitions, the Cabinet, and Decisionmaking

The role of cabinet members in the president's decisionmaking processes is important in its own right and will impact both how they view themselves and the advice they give. Conventional wisdom—that cabinet government is illusory—is correct, but that is not to say that cabinet officers have no place in the administration's policy deliberations. They clearly do, especially since a range of policy initiatives are departmentally centered and, at a minimum, call for White House oversight and participation (witness the Bush cabinet's numerous slipups). Other initiatives often involve a range of departments and agencies, which in turn requires some mechanism or structure for integration and coordination.

Even in cases where policymaking is centralized in the White House, departmental input and some measure of powersharing is required for defensive purposes. In its absence, as Shirley Anne Warshaw notes, "the White House staff will seek to dominate the policy process, and cabinet officers will retreat to their own departments and seek to implement their own policy agenda."[41] The latter is now especially problematic; as Paul Light has observed, the institutionalization of the presidency tracks with the "thickening" within departments: "the steady thickening of the White House staff with added layers of deputies and associates of one kind or another can actually be viewed as a stimulus for parallel thickening in federal agencies."[42]

Transition steps for determining how the cabinet will function are not only desirable but feasible. During the 1980 transition, for example, much discussion occurred within the Reagan team about how the cabinet would be organized, particularly in light of Reagan's experience as governor and a sense of Carter's difficulties over the previous four years. The supercabinet idea, the concept of a cabinet executive committee, and even assigning them offices in the White House proper were all raised during the transition, in part as a way of linking them to Reagan's deliberations, in part as an attempt to tailor a large cabinet to a group of more workable size. But beyond size, there was also the explicit recognition that they needed better coordination and a closer working relationship with the White House staff. In the view of William French Smith, some of these ideas would be useful in order to "defuse" departmental advocacy. While not identical to what emerged with the cabinet-council system in February, these discussions were useful in working through various models and approaches early on.

Some analysis of the role of the cabinet in the administration's policy deliberations is also desirable, given that various forms of domestic and economic policy councils have emerged in the presidencies since Reagan. At a minimum, the transition is a time for deciding how such councils will be organized and how they will be integrated and coordinated with White House–based policy operations. Unlike the NSC, there is no statutory guidance here, and a president-elect has a larger degree of organizational and administrative discretion. Will the councils be chaired by a cabinet member, as they were under Bush and Reagan, or will they be led by a White House operative, as under Clinton? How will the staffwork of the councils be undertaken? Will coordination be principally provided by the White House's cabinet affairs office, as was the case for Bush and in Reagan's second term, or will the larger domestic policy staff take the lead role, as occurred in Reagan's first term and under Clinton?

Transitions are also a time when presidents-elect can undertake the more informal tasks of making the cabinet work effectively, whatever more formal structures are created. Most important, transitions are occasions when the creation of a sense of teamwork, a commitment to the administration's broader agenda, and an effort to wean cabinet members away from the more parochial pressures of their respective departments can begin take place. The most notable example of this occurred outside the historical period we have examined, in 1952, during President-elect Eisenhower's December trip to Korea. In this case, several cabinet members–designate joined him on various parts of the trip; business was done, but so, too, was the process of letting them get to know each other and beginning to function as a team. Team-building also figured into the rhetoric Eisenhower used on the voyage and in the two cabinet meetings he convened before inauguration; in the latter, Ike especially emphasized that cabinet members were there to advise him and to candidly express their views, not serve as the representatives of their departments.[43] Both Reagan and Bush made similar, although somewhat less successful, efforts in the meetings they convened with their cabinet members before they took office.

A Final Proposition:
The Need for Early Adaptation and Learning Behavior

Even if new administrations fail to hit the ground running—and each of these four presidencies did, albeit to different degrees and in a number of different ways—the possibility for change, adaptation, or some general form of learning behavior is not foreclosed. Yet it is notable how little of this occurred early on or, when it did, how limited were its parameters.

Paul Light is correct to assert that there is a "cycle of increasing effectiveness" as presidencies mature over time.[44] But the cases suggest that while that may have occurred at the individual level as members of the administration become more skilled and adept at their particular tasks, efforts at a broader organizational "stock-taking" during the early months are less apparent. This is not surprising in some sense, of course: where attention to organization and management is lacking in the first place, not much by way of corrective remedy is likely.

Furthermore, even when problems arise and a need for change does register, corrective steps are often quite limited. In Clinton's case, where competence and expertise were especially problematic and changes were made in May and June 1993, the solution was essentially limited to moving problem cases into new positions rather than addressing the deeper problems in the organization and workways of this presidency. Early on in Carter's presidency, his reorganization project undertook an extensive critique of his decisionmaking and its effects on policy outcomes, and its analysis pulled no punches in its criticisms. In his memos to Carter, Hamilton Jordan was not averse to making similar points. But remedies were minimal, and change would come only as Carter's reelection prospects began to dim. The facts that George Bush had to open a post-office box in Kennebunkport so that views could reach him without going through Sununu and, under Clinton, that Robert Reich and Federico Peña would muse about how to crack into the presidential "loop" and the CIA director would go through a former chairman of the Joint Chiefs to get on the president's schedule should have been warning signs that something was amiss and that channels of communication were not operating well.

The kind of learning behavior that John Kennedy exhibited after the Bay of Pigs fiasco is often regarded as the textbook case in how presidents ought to respond to early organizational difficulties and policy errors. But what is really telling is how so few of Kennedy's successors have followed suit. Changes, of course, do eventually come. Cabinets are shaken up, problematic chiefs of staff resign, party losses in midterm elections may shift the direction of policy initiatives. But by that time it may be too late. As Jack Watson was to lament, by the time of his own appointment as chief of staff in 1980 a mandate for change in the Carter White House had finally come. But it was not to be: "The system had just been in place so long, and the grooves so deeply etched. . . . We were accustomed to our grooves." The fact that they had become accustomed to grooves so "deeply etched" was one part of the problem; that they were "our grooves" is equally telling.

In his memoirs, Eisenhower cautioned that "organization cannot make a genius out of an incompetent," nor "can it make the decisions which are required to trigger the necessary action." But he also noted that disorganization can scarcely fail to result in inefficiency and can easily lead to disaster. Organization makes more efficient the gathering and analysis of facts, and the arranging of the findings of experts in logical fashion. Therefore organization helps the responsible individual make the necessary decision, and helps assure that it is satisfactorily carried out.[45]

That task, as Ike himself recognized, is ongoing and continuing. As the travails of his successors illustrate, it is one that begins when the presidency itself may be only an elusive glimmer.

Notes

1. Walcott and Hult, *Governing the White House*, p. 5.
2. For a general critique of the rational-actor approach, see Green and Shapiro, *Pathologies of Rational Choice Theory*, and Zey, *Rational Choice Theory and Organizational Theory*. On its merits see, e.g., the essay by Terry Moe in Edwards et al., eds., *Researching the Presidency*, as well as Terry Sullivan, "Soon They Will Walk Among Us." Weko's *The Politicizing Presidency* offers an especially interesting account of the strengths and weaknesses of the rational-actor account in his examination of the institutional development of the White House personnel office.
3. Neither is it the result of individuals making decisions under conditions of uncertainty, as the rational-actor approach might see it.
4. Moe, "Presidents, Institutions, and Theory," in Edwards et al., eds., *Researching the Presidency*, p. 343.
5. Moe, "Presidents, Institutions, and Theory," in Edwards et al., eds., *Researching the Presidency*, p. 353.
6. To be fair to Moe, he does point out that "individuals create institutions, but institutions condition individual choice." But if the latter has yet to exist and the former operates during transitions, the "new institutionalism" would seem to have little light to shed here. We are, in effect, back to the conventional wisdom, which holds that the style and individual proclivities of presidents (presidents-elect here) really do matter. Moe, "The Politicized Presidency," in Chubb and Peterson, eds., *The New Direction in American Politics*, p. 238. Elsewhere, Moe makes a similar point when he acknowledges that the institutional context is "endogenous" and "a dynamic product" of presidential behavior: "This means that presidents can alter their own power through the politics of structural choice and that leadership is not simply about the exercise of power, per se, but about developing the structural capacity for its exercise. It is about institution building." Moe, "Presidents, Institutions, and Theory," in Edwards et al., eds., *Researching the Presidency*, p. 378.
7. See Burke, *The Institutional Presidency*, pp. 35–40.
8. A second part of the problem is the emphasis on presidential *control.*

While control—what Moe terms "responsive competence"—is important, it by no means defines the universe of presidential needs. Presidents also have information-gathering needs, a desire for personal reinforcement and other emotional needs, and even needs for "neutral competence." For further discussion, see Burke, *The Institutional Presidency,* pp. 209–216.

9. In Moe's view, presidency scholars need to "move toward a methodology that values simplicity and parsimony rather than complexity and comprehensiveness." Moe, "Presidents, Institutions, and Theory," in Edwards et al., eds., *Researching the Presidency,* p. 338.

10. By contrast, in Moe's view, scholars "are more likely to be successful if they concentrate their theoretical resources on the institutional side—essentially omitting personal factors from their theories." Moe, "Presidents, Institutions, and Theory," in Edwards et al., eds., *Researching the Presidency,* p. 338.

11. Jones, *Passages to the Presidency,* p. 184.

12. On Bush's difficulty in congressional negotiations, see Pious, "The Limits of Rational Choice."

13. This sense of presidential management is thus not restricted to one of management control but rather a broader concern for the quality of information and advice and the character of their decisionmaking and deliberative processes. As Walcott and Hult point out, "A focus principally on control is incomplete, for it threatens to underplay the substance of what presidents do." Walcott and Hult, *Governing the White House,* p. 4.

14. For further discussion of the importance of a president as organizational manager and the differences among these presidencies, see Burke, *The Institutional Presidency,* pp. 53–116.

15. Harper, "The Reagan White House: The Approach, the Agenda, and the Debt," in Thompson, ed., *Leadership in the Reagan Presidency II,* p. 137.

16. Von Damm, *At Reagan's Side,* p. 184.

17. Brzezinski, Miller Center Oral History, p. 91, CL.

18. Burke interview with Andrew Card Jr., September 17, 1998.

19. Lyn Nofziger, "Reagan: The Person and the Political Leader," in Thompson, ed., *Leadership in the Reagan Presidency I,* p. 84.

20. Moe, Miller Center Oral History, p. 74, CL.

21. Sununu, Miller Center of Public Affairs Forum, University of Virginia, November 13, 1998.

22. Ragsdale and Theis, "The Institutionalization of the American Presidency," p. 1311.

23. Ragsdale and Theis, "The Institutionalization of the American Presidency," p. 1315.

24. Indeed, from Carter through Bush, all the units that Ragsdale and Theis list as new additions to the EOP (with the possible exception of the National Critical Materials Council, which never had more than a very small staff) were the result of presidential initiatives: the Office of Administration (a result of Carter's 1977 reorganization project); the Office of Drug Abuse Policy (the Carter unit Peter Bourne headed), which in turn became the Office of National Drug Control Policy at the end of the Reagan presidency; the Office

of Private Sector Initiatives (part of the deregulation effort that Vice President Bush headed); the Points of Light Foundation and the Office of National Service (another set of Bush initiatives); and the National Space Council (created as part of Vice President Quayle's responsibilities). Only the Office of Administration and the Office of National Drug Control (and that just barely) would survive the first months of the Clinton presidency. Clinton also sought to make more use of the CEQ, placing it under the direction of White House aide Kathleen McGinty.

25. Roger Porter's operation under Bush differed from Martin Anderson's operation under Reagan and certainly from the informal Rasco-Reed-Galston arrangement that was worked out under Clinton.

26. Warshaw, *The Domestic Presidency*. A similar point might be made about the variations in the relationships between the White House and the cabinet that Warshaw discusses in her book *Powersharing*. On variations in particular units, such as congressional liaison, see Collier, *Between the Branches;* on communications operation, see Maltese, *Spin Control*.

27. One area that is especially worth pondering is economic policymaking. It is surely one of the "big three" along with domestic and national security policy, but its institutionalization is more questionable: the Ford-era Economic Policy Board, the more informal economic policy group under Carter, the Cabinet Council of Economic Affairs under Reagan, the Economic Policy Council under Bush, and now the National Economic Council under Clinton. Each differed significantly in organization, coordination, and linkage to the White House, as well as in impact on the economic policymaking of the respective administrations.

28. The reorganization project's eight case studies of decisionmaking early in the Carter presidency noted particularly the failure of cabinet-led initiatives to work; especially noted was the policy advocacy coming from the White House staff in these policy initiatives. President's Reorganization Project, "Decision Analysis Report," June 28, 1977, Jordan Files, Box 37, CL.

29. Deaver, *Behind the Scenes,* p. 170.

30. Light, *The President's Agenda,* p. 37.

31. Isikoff, *Uncovering Clinton,* p. 168.

32. Sometimes the lack of institutional memory is less than conventional wisdom suggests. In 1988, Ken Duberstein, Reagan's last chief of staff, sent a memo to all Reagan appointees outlining the steps to be taken for the Bush transition. The bulk of the memo was taken verbatim from a similar memo that (then) Chief of Staff Jack Watson had sent out to the Carter administration in 1980.

33. Jones, *Passages to the Presidency,* p. 185.

34. Edwards, *At the Margins;* Jones, *The Presidency in a Separated System,* esp. pp. 147–181; Bond and Fleisher, *The President in the Legislative Arena*.

35. Bond and Fleisher, *The President in the Legislative Arena,* p. 230.

36. Edwards, *At the Margins,* p. 205.

37. Jones, *Passages to the Presidency,* p. 185.

38. Light, "Domestic Policy Making," p. 3.

39. Hubbell, *Friends in High Places*, p. 185.

40. Memorandum from Craig Fuller and Robert Teeter to Cabinet Agency Heads, "Memorandum for All Cabinet Agency Heads," January 6, 1989, Chief of Staff Files—Sununu, OA 1806, Box 1, BL.

41. Warshaw, *Powersharing*, p. 232.

42. Light, "Domestic Policy Making," p. 9; see also Light, *Thickening Government*.

43. Attorney General Herbert Brownell later recalled that the trip to Korea "provided the setting for the president to bring us together in preparing his inaugural address and in taking stock of our views on the political agenda he might pursue in the early days of his administration. The trip enabled me to get to know the other cabinet members better especially since I hadn't worked with any of them before except John Foster Dulles." Brownell with Burke, *Advising Ike*, p. 295; see also pp. 137–140.

44. Light, *The President's Agenda*, p. 37.

45. Eisenhower, *Mandate for Change*, p. 114.

Bibliography

Primary Sources

This study draws on archival materials from the following sources:
Carter Presidential Library, Atlanta, Georgia.
Reagan Presidential Library, Simi Valley, California.
Bush Presidential Library, Texas A&M University, College Station, Texas.
Papers of James A. Baker III, Fondren Library, Rice University, Houston, Texas.
Personal papers of Richard Wirthlin and Alonzo McDonald provided to the author.
A number of those involved in the transitions and subsequent administration provided interviews for this project: David Q. Bates, Ralph Bledsoe, John Block, Danny J. Boggs, Herbert Brownell, Andrew Card Jr., Robert Carleson, James Cicconi, Al From, William Galston, Mark Gearan, John Hart, Frank Hodsoll, Elaine Kamarck, John McClaughry, Alonzo McDonald, Edwin Meese, J. Bonnie Newman, James Pinkerton, Roger Porter, Bruce Reed, Richard Schweiker, Leslie Thornton, Chase Untermeyer (correspondence), Harrison Wellford, Anne Wexler, and Richard Wirthlin.
Additional interview material was drawn from the oral histories undertaken by the University of Virginia's Miller Center Oral History Collection, copies of which are available at the Carter Presidential Library. Oral histories consulted include those of Madeleine Albright, Robert Bergland, Zbigniew Brzezinski, Landon Butler, Bert Carp, Jimmy Carter, Stuart Eizenstat, Hamilton Jordan, Charles Kirbo, Bruce Kirschenbaum, Bert Lance, Al McDonald, Richard Moe, Frank Moore, Jody Powell, Gerald Rafshoon, David Rubenstein, James Schlesinger, Charles Schultze, Jack Watson, and Anne Wexler. The White House exit interviews of David Aaron, Zbigniew Brzezinski, Jim Gammill, Greg Schneiders, Jack Watson, and Anne Wexler were also consulted; these exit interviews are also available at the Carter Library. Although the Reagan Library does not

have many oral histories covering the presidential years, it does have a collection of White House exit interviews. Those I found helpful included the exit interviews of Martin Anderson, Ralph Bledsoe, Kenneth Duberstein, Becky Norton Dunlop, Edwin L. Harper, E. Pendleton James, Alfred Kingon, John Rogers, and Jack Svahn. The Reagan Library also has a set of audio cassettes documenting the three-day presidential conference on Ronald Reagan, held at Hofstra University in April 1993, which contain a number of presentations and commentaries by former Reagan administration officials that I found useful.

Secondary Sources

Adams, Bruce, and Kathryn Kavanagh-Baran. 1979. *Promise and Performance: Carter Builds a New Administration.* Lexington: Lexington Books.

Anderson, Martin. 1990. *Revolution: The Reagan Legacy.* Stanford: Hoover Institution.

Anderson, Patrick. 1994. *Electing Jimmy Carter.* Baton Rouge: Louisiana State University Press.

Baker, James A. III. 1995. *The Politics of Diplomacy.* New York: G. P. Putnam's Sons.

Barilleaux, Ryan J., and Mary Stuckey, eds. 1992. *Leadership and the Bush Presidency: Prudence or Drift in an Era of Change.* Westport, Conn.: Praeger.

Barilleaux, Ryan J., and Nolan Argyle. 1986. "Past Failures and Future Prescriptions for Presidential Management Reform," *Presidential Studies Quarterly,* 16: 716–733.

Barrett, Laurence I. 1983. *Gambling with History: Reagan in the White House.* New York: Doubleday.

Bell, Griffin B., and Ronald J. Ostrow. 1982. *Taking Care of the Law.* New York: Wm. Morrow.

Bell, Terrel. 1988. *The Thirteenth Man: A Reagan Cabinet Memoir.* New York: Free Press.

Birnbaum, Jeffrey H. 1996. *Madhouse: The Private Turmoil of Working for the President.* New York: Times Books.

Bond, Jon R., and Richard Fleisher. 1990. *The President in the Legislative Arena.* Chicago: University of Chicago Press.

Bose, Meena. 1999. "Priorities and Policy Making: The Use of Force in the Carter Administration, 1993–1998," *PRG Report,* 21: 4–6.

Bourne, Peter G. 1997. *Jimmy Carter.* New York: Scribners.

Brauer, Carl M. 1986. *Presidential Transitions: Eisenhower Through Reagan.* New York: Oxford University Press.

Brownell, Herbert, with John P. Burke. 1993. *Advising Ike: The Memoirs of Attorney General Herbert Brownell.* Lawrence: University Press of Kansas.

Brummett, John. 1994. *Highwire.* New York: Hyperion.

Brzezinski, Zbigniew. 1983. *Power and Principle.* New York: Farrar, Straus, and Giroux.

Burke, John P. 2000. *The Institutional Presidency: Organization and Management from FDR to Clinton.* Baltimore: Johns Hopkins University Press.

Bush, Barbara. 1994. *Barbara Bush: A Memoir.* New York: Scribner.

Bush, George. 1999. *All the Best: My Life in Letters and Other Writings.* New York: Scribners.

Bush, George, and Brent Scowcroft. 1998. *A World Transformed.* New York: Knopf.

Campbell, Colin. 1986. *Managing the Presidency: Carter, Reagan, and the Search for Executive Harmony.* Pittsburgh: University of Pittsburgh Press.

Campbell, Colin, and Bert A. Rockman, eds. 1991. *The Bush Presidency: First Appraisals.* Chatham, N.J.: Chatham House.

———. 1996. *The Clinton Presidency: First Appraisals.* Chatham, N.J.: Chatham House.

Cannon, Lou. 1991. *President Reagan: The Role of a Lifetime.* New York: Simon and Schuster.

Carter, Jimmy. 1982. *Keeping Faith: Memoirs of a President.* New York: Bantam Books.

Christopher, Warren. 1998. *In the Stream of History: Shaping Foreign Policy for a New Era.* Stanford: Stanford University Press.

Chubb, John E., and Paul Peterson, eds. 1985. *The New Direction in American Politics.* Washington, D.C.: Brookings Institution.

Clifford, Clark, with Richard Holbrooke. 1991. *Counsel to the President.* New York: Doubleday.

Clinton, W. David, and Daniel G. Lang. 1993. *What Makes a Successful Transition?* Lanham, Md.: University Press of America.

Cohen, David B. 1997. "The Domestic Policy Vicar: John Sununu as White House Chief of Staff," paper prepared for delivery at the Conference on the Bush Presidency, Hofstra University, April.

Collier, Kenneth E. 1997. *Between the Branches: The White House Office of Legislative Affairs.* Pittsburgh: University of Pittsburgh Press.

Council for Excellence in Government. 1997. *1997 Prune Book: Making the Right Appointments to Manage Washington's Toughest Jobs.* Washington, D.C.: Council for Excellence in Government.

Darman, Richard. 1996. *Who's in Control?* New York: Simon and Schuster.

David, Paul T., and David Everson, eds. 1983. *The Presidential Election and Transition, 1980–1981.* Carbondale: Southern Illinois University Press.

Davis, Eric. 1979. "Legislative Liaison in the Carter Administration," *Political Science Quarterly,* 95: 287–302.

Deaver, Michael. 1987. *Behind the Scenes.* New York: Wm. Morrow.

Drew, Elizabeth. 1994. *On the Edge: The Clinton Presidency.* New York: Simon and Schuster.

———. 1997. *Whatever It Takes.* New York: Viking Books.

Duffy, Michael, and Dan Goodgame. 1992. *Marching in Place: The Status Quo Presidency of George Bush.* New York: Simon and Schuster.

Edwards, George C. III. 1989. *At the Margins: Presidential Leadership of Congress.* New Haven: Yale University Press.

Edwards, George C. III, John Kessel, and Bert A. Rockman, eds. 1993. *Researching the Presidency: Vital Questions, New Approaches.* Pittsburgh: University of Pittsburgh Press.

Eisenhower, Dwight D. 1963. *Mandate for Change, 1953–1956.* Garden City, N.Y.: Doubleday.

Evans, Rowland. 1981. *The Reagan Revolution.* New York: E. P. Dutton.

Evans, Rowland, and Robert D. Novak. 1972. *Nixon in the White House: The Frustraton of Power.* New York: Vintage Books.

Fink, Garry, and Hugh Davis Graham. 1998. *The Carter Presidency: Policy Choices in the Post New Deal Era.* Lawrence: University Press of Kansas.

Fitzwater, Marlin. 1995. *Call the Briefing!* Holbrook, Mass.: Adams Media.

Green, Ronald, and Ian Shapiro. 1994. *Pathologies of Rational Choice Theory: A Critique of Applications in Political Science.* New Haven: Yale University Press.

Greenstein, Fred I. 1982. *The Hidden-Hand Presidency: Eisenhower as Leader.* New York: Basic Books.

Guinier, Lani. 1998. *Lift Every Voice.* New York: Simon and Schuster.

Haig, Alexander M. Jr. 1984. *Caveat: Realism, Reagan, and Foreign Policy.* New York: Macmillan.

Haldeman, H. R. 1994. *The Haldeman Diaries: Inside the Nixon White House.* New York: G. P. Putnam's Sons.

Haney, Patrick J. 1997. *Organizing for Foreign Policy Crises: Presidents, Advisers, and the Management of Decision Making.* Ann Arbor: University of Michigan Press.

Hargrove, Erwin C. 1988. *Jimmy Carter as President: Leadership and the Politics of the Public Good.* Baton Rouge: Louisiana State University Press.

Hart, John. 1995. *The Presidential Branch.* 2nd ed. Chatham, N.J.: Chatham House.

———. 1995. "President Clinton and the Politics of Symbolism: Cutting the White House Staff," *Political Science Quarterly,* 110: 385–403.

Henry, Lauren L. 1960. *Presidential Transitions.* Washington, D.C.: Brookings Institution.

Hess, Stephen. 1988. *Organizing the Presidency.* Washington, D.C.: Brookings Institution.

Hill, Dilys, and Phil Williams, eds. 1990. *The Reagan Presidency: An Incomplete Revolution?* New York: St. Martin's.

———. 1994. *The Bush Presidency: Triumphs and Adversity.* New York: St. Martin's.

Hubbell, Webb. 1997. *Friends in High Places.* New York: Wm. Morrow.

Isikoff, Michael. 1999. *Uncovering Clinton.* New York: Crown.

Johnson, Haynes, and David S. Broder. 1996. *The System: The American Way of Politics at the Breaking Point.* Boston: Little, Brown.

Jones, Charles O. 1994. *The Presidency in a Separated System.* Washington, D.C.: Brookings Institution.

———. 1995. *Separate but Equal Branches: Congress and the Presidency.* Chatham, N.J.: Chatham House.

———. 1998. *Passages to the Presidency: From Campaigning to Governing.* Washington, D.C.: Brookings Institution.

Juster, Kenneth I., and Simon Lazarus. 1997. *Making Economic Policy: An Assessment of the National Economic Council.* Washington, D.C.: Brookings Institution.

Kaufman, Burton I. 1993. *The Presidency of James Earl Carter.* Lawrence: University Press of Kansas.

Kessel, John. 1983. "The Structures of the Carter White House," *American Journal of Political Science,* 27: 431–463.

———. 1984. "The Structures of the Reagan White House," *American Journal of Political Science,* 28: 231–258.

Kissinger, Henry. 1979. *The White House Years.* Boston: Little, Brown.

———. 1999. *Years of Renewal.* New York: Simon and Schuster.

Kolb, Charles. 1994. *White House Daze: The Unmaking of Domestic Policy in the Bush Years.* New York: Free Press.

Kurtz, Howard. 1998. *Spin Cycle: Inside the Clinton Propaganda Machine.* New York: Free Press.

Lance, Bert. 1991. *The Truth of the Matter: My Life In and Out of Politics.* New York: Summit Books.

Light, Paul C. 1995. *Thickening Government: Federal Hierarchy and the Diffusion of Accountability.* Washington, D.C.: Brookings Institution.

———. 1999. *The President's Agenda: Domestic Policy Choice from Kennedy to Clinton.* Baltimore: Johns Hopkins University Press.

———. 1999. "Domestic Policy Making," paper prepared for delivery at the Conference on Reinventing the Presidency, Center for Presidential Studies, Texas A & M University, October 1–2.

Mackenzie, G. Calvin, and Robert Shogan, eds. 1997. *Obstacle Course.* New York: Twentieth Century Fund.

Maltese, John Anthony. 1992. *Spin Control: The White House Office of Communications and the Management of Presidential News.* Chapel Hill: University of North Carolina Press.

Meese, Edwin. 1983. "The Institutional Presidency: A View from the White House," *Presidential Studies Quarterly,* 13: 191–197.

———. 1992. *With Reagan: The Inside Story.* Washington, D.C.: Regnery Publishers.

Mervin, David. 1996. *George Bush and the Guardianship Presidency.* New York: St. Martin's.

Moens, Alexander. 1990. *Foreign Policy Under Carter: Testing Multiple Advocacy Decision Making.* Boulder: Westview.

Morris, Dick. 1997. *Behind the Oval Office.* New York: Random House.

Mosher, Frederick C., W. David Clinton, and Daniel G. Lang. 1987. *Presidential Transitions and Foreign Affairs.* Baton Rouge: Louisiana State University Press.

Mulcahy, Kevin V. 1990. "The Bush Administration and National Security Policy Making: A Preliminary Assessment," paper prepared for delivery at the annual meeting of the American Political Science Association, San Francisco. August 31–September 2.

Newland, Chester A. 1983. "A Mid-term Appraisal—the Reagan Presidency: Limited Government and Political Administration," *Public Administration Review,* 43: 1–22.

Niskanen, William A. 1988. *Reaganomics: An Insider's Account of the Policies and the People.* New York: Oxford University Press.

O'Neill, Tip. 1987. *Man of the House.* New York: St. Martin's.

Persico, Joseph E. 1990. *Casey: From the OSS to the CIA.* New York: Viking Books.

Pfiffner, James P. 1993. "The President's Chief of Staff: Lessons Learned," *Presidential Studies Quarterly,* 23: 77–102.

———. 1996. *The Strategic Presidency: Hitting the Ground Running.* Lawrence: University Press of Kansas.

Pfiffner, James P., and R. Gordon Hoxie, eds. 1989. *The Presidency in Transition.* New York: Center for the Study of the Presidency.

Pinkerton, James P. 1995. *What Comes Next?* New York: Hyperion.

Pious, Richard M. 1999. "The Limits of Rational Choice: Bush and Clinton Budget Summitry," *Presidential Studies Quarterly,* 29: 617–637.

Podhoretz, John. 1993. *Hell of a Ride: Backstage at the White House Follies, 1989–1993.* New York: Simon and Schuster.

Powell, Jody. 1984. *The Other Side of the Story.* New York: Wm. Morrow.

Public Papers of the President. 1989. Washington, D.C.: Government Printing Office.

Public Papers of the President. 1993. Washington, D.C.: Government Printing Office.

Ragsdale, Lynn, and John J. Theis. 1997. "The Institutionalization of the American Presidency, 1924–1992," *American Political Science Review,* 41: 1280–1318.

Reich, Robert B. 1997. *Locked in the Cabinet.* New York: Knopf.

Schieffer, Bob, and Garry Paul Gates. 1989. *The Acting President.* New York: Dutton.

Shogan, Robert. 1977. *Promises to Keep: Carter's First Hundred Days.* New York: Thomas Y. Crowell.

Smith, Hedrick. 1988. *The Power Game: How Washington Works.* New York: Random House.

Stephanopoulos, George. 1999. *All Too Human: A Political Education.* Boston: Little, Brown.

Stockman, David. 1986. *The Triumph of Politics: How the Reagan Revolution Failed.* New York: Harper and Row.

Strober, Deborah, and Gerald S. Strober. 1998. *Reagan: The Man and His Presidency.* Boston: Houghton Mifflin.

Sullivan, Terry. 1998. "Soon They Will Walk Among Us: A Beginner's Guide to Understanding Formal Theory," *PRG Report,* 21: 15–21.

Thompson, Kenneth W., ed. 1992. *Leadership in the Reagan Presidency I: Seven Intimate Perspectives.* Lanham, Md.: University Press of America.

———. 1993. *Leadership in the Reagan Presidency II: Eleven Intimate Perspectives.* Lanham, Md.: University Press of America.

————. 1993. *Presidential Transitions: The Reagan to Bush Experience.* Lanham, Md.: University Press of America.

————. 1993. *Foreign Policy in the Reagan Presidency.* Lanham, Md.: University Press of America.

————. 1994. *Reagan and the Economy: Nine Intimate Perspectives.* Lanham, Md.: University Press of America.

————. 1997. *The Reagan Presidency: Ten Intimate Perspectives of Ronald Reagan.* Lanham, Md.: University Press of America.

————. 1997. *The Bush Presidency: Ten Intimate Perspectives of George Bush I.* Lanham, Md.: University Press of America.

————. 1998. *The Bush Presidency: Ten Intimate Perspectives of George Bush II.* Lanham, Md.: University Press of America.

Tomkin, Shelley Lynne. 1998. *Inside OMB: Politics and Process in the President's Budget Office.* Armonk, N.Y.: M. E. Sharpe.

Tower, John G. 1991. *Consequences: A Personal and Political Memoir.* Boston: Little, Brown.

Vance, Cyrus. 1983. *Hard Choices: Critical Years in America's Foreign Policy.* New York: Simon and Schuster.

Von Damm, Helene. 1989. *At Reagan's Side.* New York: Doubleday.

Walcott, Charles E., and Karen M. Hult. 1995. *Governing the White House: From Hoover Through LBJ.* Lawrence: University Press of Kansas.

Walker, Martin. 1996. *The President We Deserve: Bill Clinton, His Rise, His Falls, His Comebacks.* New York: Crown.

Walker, Wallace E., and Michael R. Reopel. 1986. "Strategies for Governance: Transition and Domestic Policymaking in the Reagan Administration," *Presidential Studies Quarterly,* 16: 734–760.

Warshaw, Shirley Anne. 1996. *Powersharing: White House–Cabinet Relations in the Modern Presidency.* Albany: State University of New York Press.

————. 1997. *The Domestic Presidency: Policy Making in the White House.* Boston: Allyn and Bacon.

Weinberger, Caspar W. 1990. *Fighting for Peace: Seven Critical Years in the Pentagon.* New York: Warner Books.

Weko, Thomas J. 1995. *The Politicizing Presidency: The White House Personnel Office, 1948–1994.* Lawrence: University Press of Kansas.

Williams, Walter. 1993. "George Bush and Executive Branch Domestic Policymaking Competence," *Policy Studies Journal,* 21: 700–717.

Woodward, Bob. 1991. *The Commanders.* New York: Pocket Books.

————. 1994. *The Agenda: Inside the Clinton White House.* New York: Simon and Schuster.

————. 1999. *Shadow: Five Presidents and the Legacy of Watergate.* New York: Simon and Schuster.

Yeager, Ken. 1999. *Trailblazers: Profiles of America's Gay and Lesbian Elected Officials.* New York: Haworth.

Zelnick, Bob. 1999. *Gore: A Political Life.* Washington, D.C.: Regnery.

Zey, Mary. 1998. *Rational Choice Theory and Organizational Theory: A Critique.* Thousand Oaks, Calif.: Sage.

Index

382–383; press visibility, 397; and
tensions in, 6. *See also* Bush
transition; Carter transition; Clinton
transition; Ethics issues; Media and
transitions; Reagan transition
President's Council on Physical
Fitness, 209
Press and transitions. *See* Media and
transitions
Pryor, David, 313

Quayle, Dan, 199, 208, 210, 218, 241,
249, 260, 264, 336

Rafshoon, Gerald, 80
Ragsdale, Lynn, 9, 391
Raines, Howell, 152
Rasco, Carol, 310, 332, 334, 340, 388
Rational actor theory, 7, 379–381
Reagan, Ronald, 3, 5, 14n.5, 33, 76,
95–131, 143–189, 191, 195, 206,
214, 236, 247, 258, 260–261, 309,
300, 377–411; cabinet, selection of,
100–104; cabinet, use of, 98,
105–108, 124, 128–130, 143–151,
163–165, 167, 177, 236, 378, 409;
and chief of staff, 116–128,
143–144, 147, 151–156, 164, 168,
171, 176–178; and conflict
management, 106, 147, 161, 175;
and Congress, 97, 111, 138n.78,
158–159, 167, 170; decisionmaking
of, 105, 108, 113, 118–120,
130–131, 149, 156–161, 164–165,
170, 175, 179, 379, 381, 383; and
foreign policy, 110, 171–176; and
media communication, 112, 159; in
meetings, 113, 117–119, 152,
157–160; and NSC adviser, 83–85,
117, 120, 171–173, 175–176, 178,
216, 388; and staff management,
130–131, 161–162, 189n.117, 385,
389–390; and White House staff,
concept of, 119–120, 156, 161–162,
391. *See also* Reagan administration;
Reagan transition
Reagan, Nancy, 111, 118, 127, 152
Reagan administration, 143–189,
192–195, 204–205, 209–211, 215,
221–222, 235–236, 239, 262,
263–265; and cabinet use of,

143–151, 154, 160, 163–165, 167,
168, 174, 177; and communications
strategy of, 111–112, 172; conflicts
within, 127–128, 152–153, 156,
173–178, 394; and Congress, 153,
158, 163–164, 166, 179; economic
program, 114, 116, 151, 166–171;
legislative strategy group, 153, 158,
165–166, 170, and personnel
operation, 152, 195; and policy
agenda, 110, 150, 157, 166; and staff
changes, 176; and staff meetings,
152, 164, 170, 173; and White House
organization, 145–146, 151–156,
171–173, 175–176, 178. *See also*
Reagan, Ronald; Reagan transition
Reagan transition, 95–131, 151, 167,
198, 202, 306, 380, 398–402; and
appointments, 95, 100–105, 122,
124, 126–127; conflicts within, 96,
100, 107–108, 129, 225; and
Congress, 97, 107, 109–112, 116,
128, 130, 138n.78; and contact with
outgoing administration, 99–100,
111, 121, 125–126, 130, 395;
financing of, 132n.4, 134n.23;
organization of, 96–99, 109, 115;
and outside experts, 101–103,
122–123, 132n.9, 137n.67; and press
visibility, 96–98, 129, 136n.39; and
policy agenda, 96–98, 108–109,
111–116, 130, 132n.9, 165; and
scheduling, 112, 123; and vice-
president-elect, 125–126; and White
House organization, 97–98, 107, 111,
116–128, 130. *See also* Reagan,
Ronald; Reagan administration
Reed, Bruce: and Clinton
administration, 332–334, 341, 367,
388; and 1992 transition, 287, 289,
300–303, 311–312, 314, 318n.8, 402
Regan, Donald, 103, 115, 145, 150,
160, 168, 179, 181n.7, 236, 247
Reich, Robert: and Clinton
administration, 331, 335, 341, 346,
353, 355, 366, 394, 410; and 1992
transition, 289, 292, 296–297, 345,
360
Reilly, William, 241, 272n.15
Reinventing government, 300–301,
315, 333

About the Book

Burke's detailed and comprehensive account of the four presidential transitions from Jimmy Carter to Bill Clinton explores how each president-elect prepared to take office and carefully links those preparations to the performance and effectiveness of the new administration. Enriched by interviews with the key participants, this sobering tale of the difficulties that new presidents have encountered demonstrates the importance of well-organized and well-managed transitions to successful terms in office.

John P. Burke is professor of political science at the University of Vermont. His publications include *The Institutional Presidency* and, with Fred Greenstein and others, *How Presidents Test Reality* (recipient of the 1990 APSA Richard Neustadt Book Award).